delinquents

and

Debutantes

delinquents

and

Debutantes

Twentieth-Century American
Girls' Cultures

edited by

Sherrie A. Inness

New York University Press

New York and London

NEW YORK UNIVERSITY PRESS
New York and London

© 1998 by New York University

Library of Congress Cataloging-in-Publication Data
Delinquents and debutantes : twentieth-century American girls'
cultures / edited by Sherrie A. Inness.
p. cm.
Includes index.
ISBN 0-8147-3764-1 (clothbound : acid-free paper)
ISBN 0-8147-3765-X (pbk. : acid-free paper)
1. Girls—United States—History—20th century.   2. Girls—United
States—Social conditions.   3. Girls in popular culture—United States—
History—20th century.   I. Inness, Sherrie A.
HQ777. D39 1998
305.23—ddc21   98-9047
                        CIP

New York University Press books are printed on acid-free paper,
and their binding materials are chosen for strength and durability.

Manufactured in the United States of America

10 9 8 7 6 5 4 3 2

For

Cathy Ebelke

Contents

Acknowledgments

First on my list of people to thank would have to be all those who contributed to this collection. Their unstinting efforts have made this anthology possible. I could not have asked for a more thoughtful group of scholars with whom to work. They have made editing this collection a pleasure. I would also like to thank those who have read drafts of essays included in this collection, including Kathryn M. Burton, Ruth Ebelke, Faye Parker Flavin, Julie Inness, Michele Lloyd, and Diana Royer. Their criticism helped to tighten up the entire collection.

I would like to thank my friends, among them Alice Adams, Martina Barash, Carolyn Butler Palmer, Kate Johnson, Eric Palmer, Cindy Reuther, Judith Russo, Kathryn Shevelow, and Wendy W. Walters. They provided support throughout this anthology's production. I would also like to thank my colleagues at Miami University for their friendship. They help to make the school a rich intellectual environment that furthers all my scholarship. Finally, Jennifer Hammer and her colleagues at New York University Press were a pleasure to work with. Their expertise did much to help improve this collection.

My research has benefited from a number of scholars in children's literature and girls' culture, including Kathleen Chamberlain, Miriam Formanek-Brunell, Jerry Griswold, Peter Hunt, Deidre Johnson, Sally Mitchell, Claudia Nelson, and Lynne Vallone. These are a few of the many who make the study of girls' literature and culture a particularly vibrant area today.

Thanks must be reserved for my mother, father, and sister, who provided a much needed support network throughout the process of the editing of this collection. Their encouragement sustained me as I dealt with a broken kneecap and a car accident while working on this anthology. Cathy Ebelke deserves special appreciation as the greatest cousin anyone is likely to ever have. I dedicate this book to her in gratitute for her being a friend and role model to me.

For permission to include revised versions of previously published work, I wish to acknowledge the following journal and books: Rachel Devlin, "Female Juvenile Delinquency and the Problem of Sexual Authority in America." *Yale Journal of Law and the Humanities* 9.1 (1997): 147–82; Jennifer Scanlon, "Boys-R-Us: Board Games and the Socialization of Young Adolescent Girls." *Images of the Child*. Ed. Harry Eiss. Bowling Green: Bowling Green State University Popular Press, 1994. 103–14; Vicki L. Ruiz, "The Flapper and the Chaperone." *Out of the Shadows: A History of Mexican American Women in the United States, 1900–1990*. New York: Oxford University Press, 1997.

Introduction

In many ways, girls are inconsequential. Due to their youth and gender, girls are granted less social status than men and boys. They are relegated to an inferior place in American society because of the strength of the cultural stereotype that girls and their culture are insipid and insignificant, unworthy of close attention. Even in Toyland, who gets to deal with serious issues, G.I. Joe or Barbie? G.I. Joe confronts his enemies with a hand grenade; Barbie, presumably, whips out her blow dryer. G.I. Joe is concerned with life and death and war, while Barbie's main interest is what color bikini to wear to the beach.

American society's disparaging attitude toward girls' culture is also apparent in higher education. Although girls' culture is receiving increased attention, an English major can graduate without ever having read a book written for an audience of girls. A history major can graduate without knowing anything about the culture of girls in the United States over the past centuries. A sociology or anthropology major can get a degree without considering the place of girls in a culture. In graduate school, the situation is little different. The new Ph.D. in American Studies probably took no classes that considered girls' culture. The holder of a doctorate in English probably did not write a dissertation on the place of girls' reading in girls' culture. The belief that girls' culture is no culture at all proves to be remarkably tenacious, as does the belief that studying girls' culture lacks the importance and significance of studying a "weightier" issue, such as the development of the American political system or the reasons women continue to be economically disadvantaged in our society.

An anthology such as this one is especially needed because scholarly work on girls' culture has been insufficient. For much of this century and earlier ones, children's and girls' culture have been regarded by the general society as undeserving of serious criticism. The components of children's culture (including books, television shows, and attire) have appeared intrinsically less important to adults than their adult counterparts. In the past three decades, children's literature classes have become a standard part of the curriculum of many colleges and universities, and the study of children's culture more generally has gained a significant toehold in academe. A number of recent scholarly works have focused on children's and youth culture, but none of these focuses exclusively on girls.[1]

This situation is beginning to change. In the late 1980s and 1990s, a number of scholars, many influenced by feminism and its tenets, have introduced gender into their work and acknowledged the importance of studying the previously trivialized culture of girls. Over the last decade, interest in girls' culture has grown, resulting in a number of new works that address girls' culture in insightful ways.[2] These books are reconceptualizing girls' culture and acknowledging its true importance in helping to constitute not only children's gender roles but also those of adults.[3] What these works do is bring the same careful and rigorous scholarship to girls' culture that earlier scholars interested in gender issues brought to women's culture. The essays in this anthology will broaden the dialogue about girls' culture further, making a new group of readers recognize the importance of considering girls as well as women when trying to understand the construction of U.S. culture.

The aim of the essays in this collection is to demonstrate how American girls' culture in its many forms has played and continues to play a vital role in shaping our culture's girls into women; far from being a marginal topic, studying girls' culture is essential to understanding how gender works in our society. In particular, this is a collection of essays about the different ways that cultural discourse shapes both the young girl and the teenager. These essays are concerned with the myriad ways that discourse in a wide variety of formats, including juvenile novels, popular girls' magazines, and advertisements helps to form a girl's experience of what it means to be a girl and, later, a woman. I hope that after reading the essays, readers will be persuaded that girls' culture, far from being worthy of only fleeting attention, demands careful critical analysis because it plays a central role in shaping our society.

This collection stems from my long-standing interest in girls' culture. My earlier scholarship explores how popular literature plays a central role in defining young women's roles.[4] In this present study, I have brought together essays that move beyond solely studying literature in order to understand how a wide variety of factors influence girls, helping to socialize them into women.

But before we can turn to the essays, we must first determine what girls' culture actually is, at least as I shall use it in this book. This is a vexing term to describe because its boundaries are ill-defined. What makes up a "girl" in the first place is not something that people agree upon. Some refer only to prepubescent females when they mention "girls." Others use the term more generally to refer to both young girls and teenagers. Yet other individuals use the term generically to refer to *all* women, whether they are six or sixty. For this collection, my definition of girls has fallen between the two extremes. We need to recognize that young girls share a culturally distinct position from that of older "girls" of forty of fifty; thus, I believe it is important to use "girls" to refer specifically to the younger females in our culture. Yet, I also believe it is equally important to avoid narrowing the term too greatly. Narrowing "girls" to refer only to preteenage girls, I believe, establishes an artificial distinction between teenage girls and younger girls since both share many similar traits that mark them as "girls" in our culture. They have relatively little social power; they cannot vote; they are typically dependent on their parents; they form a culture where certain rules about what is acceptable behavior for girls are reinforced whether a girl is seven or seventeen. Because of the importance of recognizing that girls' culture encompasses a wide range of age groups, I have tried to include essays that discuss both younger girls and teenagers. Such a range is necessary in order to show the lasting influence of girls' culture over a girl, whether she is five or eighteen.

Girls' culture is no easier to define when one considers the second word of the term: "culture." This is also a troublesome word as it can be interpreted in many different fashions. Girls' culture can refer to the culture that girls themselves make, such as the girl-created zines and other items manufactured by girls and targeted at an audience of girls. Girls' culture can also refer to the countless mass-marketed commodities (books, television shows, magazines, dolls, toys, and other items) that are manufactured by adults and sold to an audience of girl consumers, both for profit and to culturally indoctrinate them into the behavior that society expects. When studying girls and their cultures, we need to acknowledge both of these aspects of girls' culture and how they help to

shape girls' lives. It is important to consider the culture that girls themselves create as active producers and shapers of their realities as well as
the culture that is created and shaped by adults and then marketed to
girls, who, in their turn, shape market-place commodities in ways that
might or might not have been intended by their adult creators. The essays
here explore both types of cultures.

Clearly, "girls' culture" is a tricky term to define and one that resists
the imposition of narrow boundaries. One could argue for a broad definition, claiming that girls' culture has existed as long as there have been
young females, but that is perhaps too encompassing a generalization
since scholars recognize that girlhood has had very different cultural
meanings and has not always been perceived as a period separate from
adulthood. What we can say is that a distinct girls' culture has existed at
least throughout the eighteenth and nineteenth centuries and has flourished in the twentieth century. In their edited collection *The Girl's Own:
Cultural Histories of the Anglo-American Girl, 1830–1915* (1994), Lynne
Vallone and Claudia Nelson describe girls' culture as already entrenched
throughout the nineteenth century. Sally Mitchell pinpoints the beginnings of a distinct girls' culture at a later date. She argues that "between
1880 and 1915 [in England] both working-class and middle-class girls
increasingly occupied a separate culture" (3). Whether one agrees with
Nelson and Vallone or Mitchell as to the beginning date of girls' culture,
what is evident is that girls' culture has long been an important element
of Anglo culture (as well as of many other cultures) and has long served
to socialize girls in specifically gendered ways. Thus, it is impossible to
understand Anglo culture without understanding the role of girls' culture,
which, rather than being marginal, is central to the understanding of
American and world cultures. As Lynne Vallone writes in *Disciplines of
Virtue*, "the study of girls' culture and girls' reading is crucial to our
understanding of femininity, women's history and literature, and ideologies of domesticity, conduct, and class" (4). Elaborating on Vallone's idea,
I go even further in claiming the centrality of girls' culture, arguing that
understanding it is essential to understanding how our *entire* society has
been structured on gendered lines and the important role played by girls'
culture in instilling the notion that the division between girls and boys is
"natural" and "right," a perspective that remains remarkably strong
today.

Perhaps no epoch is more important to study when considering the
influence of girls' culture than the twentieth, a century in which the

commodities of girls' culture have had the ability to travel further and be utilized by a greater number of girls than ever before. Whether a Cabbage Patch doll, a Nancy Drew novel, a recent edition of *Seventeen* magazine, or a television show featuring super-saccharine Strawberry Shortcake, the commodities of girls' culture now have the power to reach millions of consumers. Our society is saturated with girls' culture, and it reaches virtually every girl in the United States (and many girls beyond American borders). This type of cultural saturation has never been seen before in the history of humanity and is only achievable because of a wide variety of twentieth-century technologies that have made a mass-market girls' culture both possible and profitable. The essays in this collection will untangle a small portion of the intricate web that constitutes twentieth-century girls' culture and show how girls' culture socializes its subjects and also serves as a venue for social protest by girls themselves.

Because of the diversity of girls' culture in America, this anthology can only provide an introduction to it. Many important aspects of girls' culture and its divisions have had to be left out due to space and time limitations. For example, I have not included essays that focus on the importance of sports or music in girls' lives, both important subjects that deserve complete books of their own. This collection cannot address in depth such important issues as ethnicity, race, socioeconomic background, sexual orientation, and age, that influence how girls develop distinct cultures, although many of these issues are touched on. I hope, however, that other scholars will take up some of the issues related to girls' culture that this present study has not been able to address fully.

Despite space limitations, the essays in this collection do cover a broad number of subjects and reveal many issues that have gone into defining and creating twentieth-century girls' culture. All the essays seek to broaden the parameters of girls' culture, showing that it is far more complex and diverse than once commonly perceived. Whether it is Rachel Devlin discussing the role of the female delinquent in U.S. society or Melinda L. de Jesús demonstrating how the Nancy Drew books helped perpetuate colonialism in the Philippines, these essays all show the multiplicity of attributes that compose girls' cultures in the United States. Readers should feel encouraged to further explore the rich culture of girls in America and the rest of the world.

The essays in the first part of the book explore the many ways that institutional forces shape and mold girls, socializing them as "correctly" gendered young women. The focus of the chapters in this section is on the societal discourses that help establish desirable and undesirable behavior for girls. A wide variety of different texts are intimately involved in establishing the parameters of girls' behavior. Advice books, marriage and family textbooks, legal treatises, and a large number of other texts help to establish what is considered to be acceptable behavior for girls and young women. The section's essays explore how these discourses operate and in what ways they serve to reaffirm traditional gender roles for women. The essays, however, do not only look at girls as malleable beings, helpless in the face of larger social forces. Instead, the essays show how girls are shaped by institutional forces but also how they rebel against them.

The book begins with Laureen Tedesco's study of Girl Scout manuals from the early twentieth century. She argues that these seldom studied texts provide an important way to investigate changing gender mores of this period. By examining the changes made when Boy Scout manuals were altered to produce Girl Scout manuals, this chapter explores how these manuals instilled socially acceptable gendered behavior in young men and women and different societal expectations about how girls and boys should behave.

The next chapter is also concerned with how twentieth-century popular texts have inculcated girls with our society's ideology. Mary C. McComb inspects the mass-marketed advice manuals and marriage textbooks produced for a juvenile audience during the Depression years. She argues that these works played an important role in establishing societal norms of behavior for young people, especially in relationship to the etiquette associated with dating and romance. This chapter suggests that these Depression era texts helped to "normalize" youth at a time when normalcy was touted as highly socially desirable. In addition, at a time when masculinity was perceived as endangered because of the lack of jobs, McComb points out that advice manuals and their ilk reestablished "normal" gender relationship based on the superiority of the male. Thus, these texts reassured their audience that, despite the economic chaos of the era, gender relationships were not seriously threatened by the Depression.

Miriam Formanek-Brunell takes a different approach from previous scholars in her chapter on 1950s girls' culture, arguing that teenage girls in this period were not nearly as docile as earlier scholars have indicated. By exploring the discourses surrounding babysitters and their culture after World War II, this chapter suggests that teenage girls were far from passive. Instead, they were often outspoken in demanding their rights, even forming babysitters' unions in three communities. Formanek-Brunell's essay, like others in the anthology, seeks to reshape our perception of girls and their lives and to shed light on a little researched area.

Rachel Devlin's essay is also concerned with girls' culture after the war. It analyzes delinquent girls and explores how female delinquency became a major social issue. Devlin argues that delinquency in girls changed from being primarily a private matter before the war to being a public problem about which all members of society were expected to be concerned. Devlin discusses how the theories of psychoanalysis, particularly those related to the Oedipus complex, came to be directed at the wayward girl. The supposed rift between father and daughter became a favorite theme in popular culture, including films and popular psychology treatises, and was one sign of a society that was increasingly concerned about the seeming lack of paternal authority after the war. She points out that the growing split between father and daughter was an early sign of the mass teenage unrest of the 1960s. This chapter reveals how unruly, disruptive girls have been contained in the twentieth century through a discourse that emphasizes their psychological illness. The author shows that demonizing the "bad girl" is one method society has used to contain the danger of girls who seemed increasingly uncontrollable.

While the essays in the first section share a common concern about the institutional forces shaping girls, those in the second focus on the girl as consumer. These essays explore a few of the ways that girls are taught to be consumers; by analyzing the relationship between girls and consumption, they reveal how we can gain a better understanding of the relationship between grown women and consumption, too. Moreover, the essays suggest the ways that consumption has long been used to indoctrinate girls into what society assumes are their "normal" gender roles.

Rhona Justice-Malloy studies the role of girls' clothing in the early years of the twentieth century. She focuses on the Sears catalogue, arguing that an analysis of this popular catalogue suggests a great deal about the changing gender roles of girls and women in this period. This chapter points out that fashion and how it is defined is indicative of the changing roles of girls in our culture. This essay is one of a number in the collection that stress the importance of studying a wide range of formerly neglected texts, such as store catalogues, in order to understand girls and their socialization.

Like Justice-Malloy's chapter, Kelly Schrum is also concerned with girls and consumer culture. She explores the connections between the development of a distinct teenage culture after World War II and *Seventeen* magazine. The chapter argues that *Seventeen* played an important role in establishing the teenage girl as a consumer, whose thoughts and desires had to be taken seriously by companies trying to target the newly emerging teenage market. By studying the editorial content of *Seventeen* and its promotional materials, Schrum shows the ways that the magazine not only described the teenage girl consumer but also helped to create her through the use of a cagey campaign carefully designed to strengthen the power and influence of the teenage girl marketplace. Moving beyond merely selling commodities, *Seventeen* also helped to tailor an ideal image of who the teenage girl should strive to be. Schrum suggests that the popular magazine encouraged its readers to be good citizens, which often entailed purchasing commodities, and to take an interest in both national and international politics. She shows the ways that *Seventeen* and similar magazines help to constitute culture for both girls and women. Rather than being merely a magazine that sold the teenage girl her shampoo and nail polish, *Seventeen* is revealed to be a magazine that suggested a whole lifestyle for its teenage readers and that encouraged the growth of the teenage culture that was to become even more dominant in the 1960s.

Sherrie A. Inness's chapter focuses on the American Girls, a collection of historical dolls and novels that have been highly successful in the 1990s, as well as in the late 1980s. Relying on Robert D. Sutherland's theories about the nature of political ideologies in children's literature, the chapter points out how the American Girls are inevitably intertwined in our culture's ideologies in ways that are both harmful and beneficial. By exploring what Sutherland categorizes as the politics of advocacy, attack, and assent and showing the role they play in the American Girls collection, this chapter stresses the importance of recognizing that girls' reading and culture are never as ideologically naive as parents and educators often might like to believe. It is easy to assume that just because a book or toy is part of girls' culture these items convey no meaning other than what they appear to portray on the surface: *Anne of Green Gables* is only a delightful story about a spunky red-haired girl; Strawberry Shortcake is only an overly sweet doll popular with small girls. But whether Anne of Green Gables, Strawberry Shortcake, or the American Girls, the characters who inhabit girls' culture and the world in which they dwell is as ideologically complex and dense as the world of adulthood.

Jennifer Scanlon reveals some of the ideological complexity of girls' culture in the last essay in this section. She argues that girls' board games and girls' play in general have been disregarded by the critical establishment, resulting in a lack of understanding of the material culture that shapes girls' lives. Scanlon focuses on board games directed at an audience of girls and discusses the messages of such games, arguing that even in the "liberated" nineties, girls' games offer them a traditional and stereotypical perspective of their future roles and present a world in which finding a "hot" date is more important than curing cancer. Scanlon's essay demonstrates that in order to understand girls' culture and how social values are passed down to girls, scholars need to study the multiplicity of objects that compose girls' culture and recognize the different messages that different material artifacts might convey to their users.

The essays in the final section of the anthology all seek to question, explore, and critique traditional notions of American girlhood. In particular, the authors seek to demonstrate that the white middle-class American girl is far from the only model for girlhood in the United States. In addition, the writers suggest the importance of hearing from actual girls when studying girlhood, rather than having adults discuss girls and their cultures without reference to the actual girls themselves.

Beginning this section, Vicki L. Ruiz examines the lives of Mexican American adolescent girls. Relying on numerous oral history sources, Ruiz reflects on what the American experience meant for these girls, exploring how they were influenced by U.S. culture but also how they resisted the influence and were guided by the mores of Mexican and Mexican American cultures. Ruiz's essay makes clear the importance of recognizing that the American girl has never been solely white or middle class, and there is a need to study all the myriad varieties of experiences that different girls from varied cultural backgrounds experience.

In her chapter, Melinda L. de Jesús provides a new reading of the famous girl detective, Nancy Drew. Using her own life experiences as a young Filipina girl who adored Nancy Drew, de Jesús explores what it meant for her to identify with the Anglo girl detective. The author reflects on how the race of the reader complicates the interpretation of children's literature and suggests that readers from different racial backgrounds might carry away very different messages from such classics as Carolyn Keene's Nancy Drew books. This chapter argues that the Nancy Drew series presents a fictional world in which being a blonde middle-class white girl living in America is highly desirable, and so formed one aspect of the cultural imperialism of the United States in the Philippines. De

Jesús suggests that maintaining the hegemony of this All-American Girl helps to make the majority of girls from different cultures, races, and socioeconomic backgrounds disgruntled and unhappy as they yearn for a life that they can never mimic perfectly.

Like de Jesús, Julia D. Gardner in the following chapter discusses girls' series and how they have been perceived in radically different ways by different audiences, by analyzing the Nancy Clue novels of Mabel Maney. These 1990s novels satirize the Nancy Drew mysteries and Cherry Ames nursing stories of earlier years and bring the novels' submerged lesbian and gay undertones to the surface. Gardner explores how Maney manages to rewrite the earlier novels in a distinctly queer fashion, thereby sexualizing the world of girls' series. Gardner also points out the ways that Maney critiques the dominant whiteness of girls' literature. Maney's work shows some of the cultural, racial, and sexual differences that are often elided in traditional girls' fiction. Like de Jesús, Gardner contends that contemporary scholars need to re-examine girls' literature and study more closely how it helps to construct cultural norms that work to perpetuate the dominance of middle-class whites. Both of these essays reveal the role that children's literature plays in teaching young girls about how they should strive to look and act.

By using reader response theory and interviews with girl readers, Angela E. Hubler demonstrates that girls are more astute critics and readers of both canonical and noncanonical fiction than has generally been assumed by scholars. Studying the responses of girls to a variety of texts from *Caddie Woodlawn* to the Sweet Valley High series books, Hubler shows that the girls she interviewed are not naive readers who accept the ideologies that a book promotes. Instead, they are active critics who subscribe to certain aspects of a book, while disregarding others. In this fashion, girl readers understand a book very differently from adults, employing reading strategies that show that girls are willing to either accept or reject the notions of womanhood that a book suggests are desirable.

In the final chapter, Mary Celeste Kearney critiques what she views as the prevalent bias in girls' cultural studies that depict girls as only consumers, not producers. Kearney argues that for scholars to understand contemporary girlhood it is essential to study how girls are becoming producers in ever greater numbers by relying on modern technology such as computers, copy machines, and the internet. Examining modern "zines" produced by girls, this chapter shows that girls are taking the tools of production into their own hands. Thus, they create a very different vision of girlhood from that provided in more traditional venues, like the girls' magazines *Seventeen* and *Sassy*, which Kearney also discusses. Like Hubler's essay, Kearney's suggests that the voices of girls of all ages must be heard to create a field of girls' cultural studies that is truly sensitive and aware of the subject position of those it studies.

Whether Devlin's essay on the discourse surrounding the delinquent girl after World War II, Schrum's on the development of teen magazines, Ruiz's on Mexican American girlhood, or one of the others in this collection, each essay will, I believe, give readers a better understanding of the multiplicity of girls' culture in twentieth-century America. One of the lessons conveyed by these works, representing a wide range of perspectives, is that the boundaries of girls' culture are flexible and encompass a vast variety of concerns, subjects, and commodities. It is vital to recognize that girls' culture springs from a number of different sources and can come both from adults who seek to target a market of girls and girls themselves. Only by understanding the intricate relationship between *all* the different elements that compose girls' culture can we fathom how the many aspects of American girls' culture work to shape American girlhood in all its different forms.

Along with showing the complexity of girls' culture, the essays provide their readers with a better understanding of the different forms and genres of written discourse that shape girls and their lives. The Nancy Drew books discussed by de Jesús, the advice manuals McComb describes, the Girl Scout manuals Tedesco studies—all suggest that it is insufficient to understand girls' culture as constituted only through girls' reading of literature. A host of other genres also need to be explored to more fully understand how different texts shape girls' experiences. These often ephemeral texts sometimes fall through the cracks in the study of girls' culture. I hope this collection might inspire some of its readers to regard with new seriousness the texts of girls' culture over the last century and recognize that only by studying such texts will scholars be able to understand how girlhood and womanhood have been constituted.

Finally, the anthology should convince its audience of the centrality of the study of girls' culture to anyone interested in understanding how women are shaped into gendered beings. Too often girls' culture is shunted aside by scholars as less significant or less important than the study of adult women's issues, but girls' culture is what helps to create not just an individual woman but *all* women in our society. As the essays in this anthology show, a thorough understanding of girls and their culture is crucial to understanding our society and the place women have in it. We remain woefully uninformed about girls, as Penny Tinkler points out: "we still know very little about the configurations of gender, class, age and race for the conditions of girlhood and its cultural construction" (2). These essays make clear the centrality of girls' culture when it comes to understanding gender divisions in the United States (and the world) in the past, present, and future.

NOTES

1. See Elliott West and Paula Petrik's edited collection *Small Worlds: Children and Adolescents in America, 1850–1950*, which discuss children's culture in general. Harry Eiss's anthology *Images of the Child* also discusses children's culture, although few of the essays are concerned specifically with girls. Carmen Luke addresses children's culture in *Constructing the Child Viewer: A History of the American Discourse on Television and Children, 1950–1980*. Marsha Kinder discusses both girls and boys' reactions to the popular media in *Playing with Power in Movies, Television, and Video Games: From Muppet Babies to Teenage Mutant Ninja Turtles*. Also, see Joe Austin and Michael Willard, eds., *Generations of Youth: Youth Cultures and History in Twentieth Century America*; Kathryn Castle, *Britannia's Children: Reading Colonialism through Children's Books and Magazines*; Dan Fleming, *Powerplay: Toys as Popular Culture*; Johan Fornäs and Göran Bolin, eds., *Youth Culture in Late Modernity*; Christine Griffin, *Representations of Youth: The Study of Youth and Adolescence in Britain and America*; Stephen Kline, *Out of the Garden: Toys, TV, and Children's Culture in the Age of Marketing*; Kathleen McDonnell, *Kid Culture: Children and Adults and Popular Culture*; Grace Palladino, *Teenagers: An American History*; Murray Pomerance and John Sakeris, eds., *Pictures of a Generation on Hold: Selected Papers*; Douglas Rushkoff, *Playing the Future: How Kids' Culture Can Teach Us to Thrive in an Age of Chaos*; and Ellen Seiter, *Sold Separately: Children and Parents in Consumer Culture*.

2. See Miriam Formanek-Brunell, *Made to Play House: Dolls and the Commercialization of American Girlhood, 1830–1930*; Bonnie J. Ross Leadbeater and Niobe Way, eds., *Urban Girls: Resisting Stereotypes, Creating Identities*; Sally Mitchell, *The New Girl: Girls' Culture in England, 1880–1915*; Lynne Vallone and Claudia Nelson, eds., *The Girls' Own: Cultural Histories of the Anglo-American Girl, 1830–1915*; Judith Rowbotham, *Good Girls Make Good Wives: Guidance for Girls in Victorian Fiction*; Penny Tinkler, *Constructing Girlhood: Popular Magazines for Girls Growing Up in England, 1920–1950*; and Lynne Vallone, *Disciplines of Virtue: Girls' Culture in the Eighteenth and Nineteenth Centuries*.

3. Other studies of girls' culture include Tom Engelhardt's essay "The Short-cake Strategy" that discusses girls' television extensively although not exclusively. Susan Willis addresses the gendered nature of toys for both boys and girls in a chapter, "Gender as Commodity," from her book *A Primer for Daily Life*. Kerry Carrington and Anna Bennett's essay " 'Girls' Mags' and the Pedagogical Formation of the Girl" discusses popular girls' magazines. Lesley Johnson describes life for girls growing up in Australia in, *The Modern Girl: Girlhood and Growing Up*. In *Feminism and Youth Culture: From "Jackie" to "Just Seventeen,"* Angela Mc-Robbie explores the connections between girl readers and popular magazines in Great Britain. Shirley Foster and Judy Simons discuss girls' popular reading in *What Katy Read: Feminist Re-Readings of "Classic" Stories for Girls*, as does Kimberley Reynolds in *Girls Only? Gender and Popular Children's Fiction in Britain, 1880–1910*.

4. See "The Feminine En-gendering of Film Consumption and Film Technology in Popular Girls' Serial Novels, 1914–1931"; "Girl Scouts, Camp Fire Girls, and Woodcraft Girls: The Ideology of Girls' Scouting Novels, 1910–1935"; *Intimate Communities: Representation and Social Transformation in Women's College Fiction, 1895–1910*; " 'It Is Pluck, But Is It Sense?': Athletic Student Culture in Progressive Era Girls' College Fiction"; and *Nancy Drew and Company: Culture, Gender, and Girls' Series*.

WORKS CITED

Austin, Joe, and Michael Willard, eds. *Generations of Youth: Youth Cultures and History in Twentieth Century America*. New York: New York UP, 1997.

Carrington, Kerry, and Anna Bennett. " 'Girls' Mags' and the Pedagogical Formation of the Girl." *Feminisms and Pedagogies of Everyday Life*. Ed. Carmen Luke. Albany: State U of New York P, 1996. 147–66.

Castle, Kathryn. *Britannia's Children: Reading Colonialism through Children's Books and Magazines*. New York: St. Martin's P, 1996.

Eiss, Harry, ed. *Images of the Child*. Bowling Green: Bowling Green State U Popular P, 1994.

Engelhardt, Tom. "The Shortcake Strategy." *Watching Television: A Pantheon Guide to Popular Culture*. Ed. Todd Gitlin. New York: Pantheon Books, 1986. 68–110.

Fleming, Dan. *Powerplay: Toys as Popular Culture*. New York: Manchester UP, 1996.

Formanek-Brunell, Miriam. *Made to Play House: Dolls and the Commercialization of American Girlhood, 1830–1930*. New Haven: Yale UP, 1993.

Fornäs, Johan, and Göran Bolin, eds. *Youth Culture in Late Modernity*. Thousand Oaks: Sage Publications, 1995.

Foster, Shirley, and Judy Simons. *What Katy Read: Feminist Re-Readings of "Classic" Stories for Girls.* Iowa City: U of Iowa P, 1995.

Griffin, Christine. *Representations of Youth: The Study of Youth and Adolescence in Britain and America.* Cambridge: Polity P, 1993.

Inness, Sherrie A. "The Feminine En-gendering of Film Consumption and Film Technology in Popular Girls' Serial Novels, 1914–1931." *Journal of Popular Culture* 29.3 (1995): 169–82.

———. *Intimate Communities: Representation and Social Transformation in Women's College Fiction, 1895–1910.* Bowling Green: Bowling Green State U Popular P, 1995.

———. " 'It Is Pluck, But Is It Sense?': Athletic Student Culture in Progressive Era Girls' College Fiction." Lynne Vallone and Claudia Nelson 216–42.

———. "Girl Scouts, Camp Fire Girls, and Woodcraft Girls: The Ideology of Girls' Scouting Novels, 1910–1935." *Continuities in Popular Culture.* Ed. Ronald J. Ambrosetti and Ray B. Browne. Bowling Green: Bowling Green State U Popular P, 1993. 229–40.

———, ed. *Nancy Drew and Company: Culture, Gender, and Girls' Series.* Bowling Green: Bowling Green State U Popular P, 1997.

Johnson, Lesley. *The Modern Girl: Girlhood and Growing Up.* Philadelphia: Open UP, 1993.

Kinder, Marsha. *Playing with Power in Movies, Television, and Video Games: From Muppet Babies to Teenage Mutant Ninja Turtles.* Berkeley: U of California P, 1991.

Kline, Stephen. *Out of the Garden: Toys, TV, and Children's Culture in the Age of Marketing.* London: Verso, 1993.

Leadbeater, Bonnie J. Ross, and Niobe Way, eds. *Urban Girls: Resisting Stereotypes, Creating Identities.* New York: New York UP, 1996.

Luke, Carmen. *Constructing the Child Viewer: A History of the American Discourse on Television and Children, 1950–1980.* New York: Praeger, 1990.

McDonnell, Kathleen. *Kid Culture: Children and Adults and Popular Culture.* Toronto: Second Story P, 1994.

McRobbie, Angela. *Feminism and Youth Culture: From "Jackie" to "Just Seventeen."* Boston: Unwin Hyman, 1991.

Mitchell, Sally. *The New Girl: Girls' Culture in England, 1880–1915.* New York: Columbia UP, 1995.

Palladino, Grace. *Teenagers: An American History.* New York: Basic Books, 1996.

Pomerance, Murray, and John Sakeris, eds. *Pictures of a Generation on Hold: Selected Papers.* Toronto: Media Studies Working Group, 1996.

Reynolds, Kimberley. *Girls Only? Gender and Popular Children's Fiction in Britain, 1880–1910.* Philadelphia: Temple UP, 1990.

Rowbotham, Judith. *Good Girls Make Good Wives: Guidance for Girls in Victorian Fiction.* Oxford: Basil Blackwell, 1989.

Rushkoff, Douglas. *Playing the Future: How Kids' Culture Can Teach Us to Thrive in an Age of Chaos*. New York: HarperCollins, 1996.

Seiter, Ellen. *Sold Separately: Children and Parents in Consumer Culture*. New Brunswick: Rutgers UP, 1993.

Tinkler, Penny. *Constructing Girlhood: Popular Magazines for Girls Growing Up in England, 1920–1950*. London: Taylor and Francis, 1995.

Vallone, Lynne. *Disciplines of Virtue: Girls' Culture in the Eighteenth and Nineteenth Centuries*. New Haven: Yale UP, 1995.

Vallone, Lynne, and Claudia Nelson, eds. *The Girl's Own: Cultural Histories of the Anglo-American Girl, 1830–1915*. Athens: U of Georgia P, 1994.

West, Elliott, and Paula Petrik, eds. *Small World: Children and Adolescents in America, 1850–1950*. Lawrence: UP of Kansas, 1992.

Willis, Susan. "Gender as Commodity." *A Primer for Daily Life*. New York: Routledge, 1991. 23–40.

Part I

Law, Discipline, and Socialization

1

Making a Girl into a Scout

Americanizing Scouting for Girls

Laureen Tedesco

The history of American Girl Scouting is a narrative of resistance: Boy Scout founder Robert Baden-Powell resisted admitting girls into his organization,[1] the Boy Scouts of America resisted the rivalry of the Girl Scouts in America, and early Girl Scout "volunteers" resisted being commandeered by founder Juliette Low, who used her deafness as an excuse for ignoring protests (Kerr, "Juliette Low" 87). Additionally, authorized Girl Scout accounts note Low's abandoning the Baden-Powell name for the girls' group, Girl Guides, in favor of the "more American" Girl Scouts. The histories of the movement in the biographies of Low and the Girl Scout manuals replay again and again Low's and the girls' tenacity in forging an adventurous program for American girls despite opposition or disinterest.[2] These histories build an ethos of Girl Scouting as a program of girl advocacy: Girls and their adult leaders wrested the program from the unwilling and triumphed.[3]

Girl Scouting seems to have had a stake in emphasizing the struggle, fighting for the right to play what were once boys' games. The organization's self-portrait may help to explain the enduring popularity of Girl Scouting, which has absorbed or outlasted most of the other all-girl outdoor clubs of the early twentieth century. Girl Scout literature from the 1910s and 1920s—roughly the first twenty years of the American movement—promotes the organization as comparable to the boys' group but self-sufficient and distinctly American, using rhetorical strategies that simultaneously imply links between Boy Scouting and Girl Scouting and establish a separate sphere for the girls. That "separate sphere" is delineated in the homemaking, nursing, and mothering skills taught in Girl Scouting and Guiding. Both the boys' and girls' programs present themselves to potential recruits as extending a (male) tradition of chivalry and scouting that transcends cultural boundaries, but the girls' program incorporates a domestic regime that the boys' program does not.

The Girl Scout movement's blend of outdoor activity, self-improvement, and homemaking pursuits addressed the concerns of a number of American groups, mainstream and otherwise, at the dawn of the century: Youth workers and social reformers, progressivists, nature education enthusiasts, physical education specialists, eugenicists, and advocates of domestic science training as well as suffragists all had an interest in training the girl physically, emotionally, and morally, if not spiritually. Spiritual training, in fact, was available in abundance through myriad Christian Endeavor Societies, YWCA work, sectarian girls' societies, junior Women's Aid Societies, and other church-based groups. The Girl Scouts and the Camp Fire Girls, like boys' groups such as the Woodcraft Indians and the Sons of Daniel Boone, touted their new programs as nonsectarian, transmitting an "American" ideal that transcended denominational and cultural barriers.

The attempt to provide a culturally unifying ideal, an American model for girlhood, appears in the first Girl Scout handbooks, which taught Girl Scouts to perceive themselves as nearly equal to American boys and more independent than their mothers and the British Girl Guides. The Girl Scout texts combined traditional blueprints for feminine conduct with a newer behavioral model combining robust activity, emergency preparedness, and social agency. Sherrie A. Inness and Sally Mitchell have demonstrated the ways the manuals and fiction for Girl Scouts and Girl Guides reinforced gender stereotypes, teaching girls to aspire to making the home their natural field of activity. In this essay I will expand upon a comment Inness makes in passing, that "scouting in fiction and reality might offer girls a fleeting feeling of agency" (234). Inness analyzes the scouting movement's complicity in reproducing "suitably socialized bourgeois women" (234). I would like to look at the sense of agency, however fleeting, that the manuals transmitted even while reinforcing traditional domestic constructs.

This essay will analyze the ways the Girl Scout manuals of 1913 and

1916 sought to shape girl readers' conception of themselves as Scouts: members of a cross-gendered, cross-generational fraternity dedicated to righting wrong and preventing disaster. The manuals told girls that they could inherit a male tradition of chivalry and frontier scouting by strengthening their minds and bodies, practicing rescue skills, and adhering to the Scout law.

The manuals offered girls real-life opportunities to participate in this male tradition. Girls could already imaginatively identify with male heroes of the past in the boys' fiction they read.[4] Girl Scout manuals provided the novelty of syntactically linking girls to their boy contemporaries and giving them a syllabus for excelling at boy-dominated activities such as shooting, independent camping and tracking, detective work, and electronics. The manuals supplied technical instructions and references to expert sources (rather than juvenile how-to books), and they suggested that time and practice were all girls needed to acquire life-saving skills and the inner resources to meet any disaster. The books also established a peer group, the Girl Scout organization that sold and studied the books, in which girls could learn and practice the skills necessary for scouting.

Most of the previous work on Girl Scouts and Guides and their manuals explores either their militarism or their domesticity. For example, historians Anne Summers, Allen Warren, and John Springhall have examined the correspondence and executive decisions of the British Boy Scout and Girl Guide programs to determine their commitment to militarism before and during World War I. Richard A. Voeltz has chronicled the expansion of the Girl Guides during World War I, linking the organization's improved social status to its members' war work, which gave Guides a reputation for curing girls of flapperdom and of "act[ing] in unrestrained, even bold and brazen ways" ("Antidote" 627).

Examinations of Scouting's domesticity include an earlier Voeltz essay, which suggests that Guide manuals hold out motherhood and wifedom as the last hope for the British Empire ("Adam's Rib" 91). Sally Mitchell demonstrates that the first Girl Guide manual (published in 1912) gained a girl audience for instruction in traditional feminine pursuits such as childcare, self-improvement, and cooking by exploiting girls' yearning for boyish activities and arranging "the more adventurous activities" first in the manual (125). Consequently, the sections on tracking, woodcraft, first-aid, self-defense, and camping precede those on home life, health, and patriotism. Carol Dyhouse also traces a Girl Guide agenda of providing domestic training for girls, but she does not refer to the manuals. Inness brings a brief discussion of Girl Scout manuals into a larger consideration of the socializing agenda of juvenile fiction about Girl Scouts, Camp Fire Girls, and Woodcraft Girls.

My argument mediates between the militaristic and domestic focuses of early work on Girl Scouting and its predecessor Girl Guiding. I contend that Girl Scouting's military overtones enabled the program to attract a girl audience that might have rejected yet another cooking and sewing club. The first Girl Scout manuals, published in 1913 and 1916, demonstrate the organization's attempts to address the perceived needs of future wives and mothers while at the same time interesting girls and volunteers eager to participate in "male" pursuits. The Girl Scout manuals do this by inviting girls into Scouting, an undertaking seemingly analogous to the "scouting" presented to readers of Baden-Powell's *Scouting for Boys*.

Scouting for Boys calls boys into scouting, lowercased, establishing a universal brotherhood with scouts of all ages and religious creeds since the beginning of mankind. Although the Girl Scout manuals make a similar appeal to universality, their preference for the capitalized term Scouting implies a contemporary, institutionally linked group that includes both boys and girls. The Boy Scouts of America and the Girl Scouts were in reality unconnected; Boy Scout officials, in fact, periodically campaigned to stop the girls' group from imitating the Boy Scouts (D. Macleod 183). Even so, the girls' manuals sustained an impression of sympathy between the two programs by using the term "Scouts" at least as frequently as "Girl Scouts," tracing the Girl Scouts' origin to Baden-Powell's British Boy Scouts and Girl Guides, and retaining many of the badges and much of the language of *Scouting for Boys*. The American girls' manuals, aided by the American use of the name Girl Scout rather than the British Girl Guide, advance an unspoken argument for similarity to the boys' program at the same time that they assert the program's suitability for girls and incorporate domestic badges and training.

The Girl Scouts in the United States developed as a direct offshoot of the Girl Guides in Great Britain: Baden-Powell recruited the American-born Low as a Girl Guide leader in England, where she lived after her marriage and subsequent widowhood. She started Girl Guide patrols in her hometown of Savannah, Georgia, on a visit to the United States in 1912. Low left the new patrols in charge of friends and family to return to England, and about a year later she revisited the United States to establish the Girl Scouts, a name she then favored, nationally. Low and Savannah naturalist W. J. Hoxie rewrote the Girl Guides' manual, which Savannah troops had used till then, to reflect American concerns, and Low sold the Americanized book, badges, and uniforms from Girl Scout headquarters in Washington (Johnston 109–11).

Low adopted the name "Girl Scouts" for her American Guide troops when negotiating with the Camp Fire Girls to unite all the girls' organizations in the United States under one name and organization: the Girl Scouts (Shultz and Lawrence 323). The Camp Fire Girls held out, refusing to accept the Scout Law, which Low insisted upon as fundamental to a character-training program. Low adapted the British Boy Scout Law to develop a code of conduct for Girl Scouts, ten tenets the girls would memorize and promise on their honor to try to obey. In the 1913 manual, the Girl Scout Laws stated:

1. A Girl Scout's Honor Is to be Trusted.
2. A Girl Scout Is Loyal.
3. A Girl Scout's Duty Is to be Useful and to Help Others.
4. A Girl Scout Is a Friend to All, and a Sister to every Other Girl Scout no Matter to what Social Class she May Belong.
5. A Girl Scout Is Courteous.
6. A Girl Scout Keeps herself Pure.
7. A Girl Scout Is a Friend to Animals.
8. A Girl Scout Obeys Orders.
9. A Girl Scout Is Cheerful.
10. A Girl Scout Is Thrifty. (Hoxie 4–6)

Except for some changes in capitalization, the laws remained the same in the 1916 manual. Low insisted upon retaining the Girl Scout Laws because she considered them "very clear and practical, and besides they followed the Boy Scout laws closely" (Schultz and Lawrence 323).[5]

Although the Camp Fire Girls refused to accept the Scout Laws and the Girl Scout name, Low was able to unite other girls' outdoor groups under the Girl Scouts banner, including the Girl Pioneers of America, the Bee Hive Girls, the Girl Guides of America, and the separately organized Girl Scouts of America, all started between 1910 and 1915 (Hinding 746). Low incorporated her group as the Girl Scouts Inc. in 1915; the group retained that name until it dropped the "Inc." in 1943, subsequently becoming the "Girl Scouts of the United States of America" (Girl Scouts of the U.S.A., *Highlights* 6, 16, 18). Low successfully established a national Girl Scout organization, in contrast with previous efforts to create a nationwide girls' character-training program. Other people's attempts to unite isolated troops calling themselves Girl Scouts failed, probably for lack of a strong central organization and public sympathy. Low was able to supply both, employing the political networking and media saturation strategies Baden-Powell had used to establish the British Boy Scouts.

The daughter of a prominent Southern family with highly placed relatives in Chicago and Washington, Low drew upon her family's vast political, social, and military connections—her father had been a general in the Spanish-American War and her mother had established a convalescent hospital for American soldiers in Florida—to garner support and draft volunteers for the Girl Scouts. According to her biographers, Low's status as a member of an influential Southern family gave sanction to the tomboyish activities Low and her handbook promoted (Shultz and Lawrence 321). Low's and her mother Nellie Gordon's ability to make friends and engage in witty repartee also contributed to the success of the Scouts, as did Low's persuasive tactic of offering a friend a job and then catching a train without acknowledging the refusal. Knowing whom to ask also helped. One coup of Low's included interesting First Lady Ellen Axson Wilson in becoming honorary president of the organization in 1917 (Girl Scouts of the U.S.A., *Seventy-Five Years* 10). The White House endorsement, still in effect today, helped the organization gain national prestige.

Low's program drew opposition, however, from officials in the Boy Scouts of America who feared the encroachment of girls on the boys' program (D. Macleod 183). These officials envisioned the Boy Scouts of America as reestablishing a standard of manliness, an antidote to the increasing feminization of American schooling and American society (Baden-Powell had similar concerns in England). While delineating a masculine sphere and fitting boys to fill it, national Boy Scout leaders kept a jealous eye on the boys' preserve: "Lee F. Hanmer of the BSA executive board was adamant that Scouting must be different for boys than for girls" (D. Macleod 46). Hanmer believed boys should be raised to be fighters and girls to be homemakers.

The Girl Scout program, which David I. Macleod recognizes as endorsing the domestic values of other girls' organizations, nonetheless aroused the ire of some BSA officials as too close to Boy Scouting. In 1911, in fact, three national Boy Scout officials helped establish the Camp Fire movement, which made no attempts to compete with the Boy Scouts (50). Camp Fire Girls founder Luther Gulick, "anxious to maintain sex difference," considered it " 'fundamentally evil' to copy Boy Scouting" (qtd. in D. Macleod 50). The Camp Fire Girls initially outnumbered the Girl Scouts, but war work during World War I benefited the latter's public image (183). Girl Scouts plunged into a round of patriotic activities including "working in hospitals, staffing railroad station canteens for trains supporting servicemen, growing vegetables, selling bonds, and collecting peach pits for use in gas mask filters" (Girl Scouts of the U.S.A., *Highlights* 6). Girl Scouts sold more than $9 million in war bonds, which the U. S. Treasury Department rewarded by minting a Girl Scout Liberty Medal. Membership growth during this period was substantial. The Girl Scout publication *Highlights in Girl Scouting, 1912–1996* charts prewar membership at roughly 5,000 in 1915, without distinguishing between girl and adult members, and then records nearly double that number in January 1918, with 9,714 members, 8,400 of them girls and 1,314 of them adults (6–7). By November 1918, *Highlights* reports, the Girl Scouts experienced "[a] membership increase of nearly 20,700" (7). The publication does not say whether the increase dated from January or from the previous year, but by December 1919, the membership count was at 36,846, so that "the total number of Girl Scouts has doubled in a year" (7).

Noting the war-era boom in Girl Scouting, Boy Scouts of America officials again promoted the Camp Fire Girls (D. Macleod 184). Scout Executive James West tried to get the Girl Scouts to change their program or name, and some BSA officials tried to persuade the Girl Scouts to become Camp Fire Girls. However, the khaki-clad Girl Scouts, selling war bonds and marching in parades "just as the boys did" (D. Macleod 184), attracted media attention and public approval; the group's membership reached 50,000 in 1920, finally outnumbering the Camp Fire Girls in 1930 (184).

Baden-Powell maintained "uneasy neutrality" on the dispute between the Boy Scouts of America and the Girl Scouts (D. Macleod 184), although his own organization discouraged the public identification of Girl Guides and Boys Scouts; as Low had once told her parents in a letter, Girl Guides were not allowed to talk to Boy Scouts in uniform (Shultz and Lawrence 299). Local American Boy Scout troops often cooperated with nearby Girl Scout troops and seemed to view the movements' aims as similar, but the dispute at the national level centered on differences that proponents of the Boy Scouts of America wanted to increase: the groups' names, activities, and separate functions (D. Macleod 184).

The name "Girl Scouts" was precisely what the girls' organization was unwilling to give up. It was perhaps the most powerful argument for Girl Scouting's newness. Girl Scout narratives usually explain the name change from Guides to Scouts in ways that argue for the group's Americanness and girl-advocacy. The explanation usually follows the story that Baden-Powell did not want girls in his movement but was forced to accept them due to their perseverance. The American group not only outfaced Baden-Powell's objections but appropriated a name he had rejected as well.

This triumph at Baden-Powell's expense adds to a self-history that insists that Girl Scouts are determined and resist the odds. According to Baden-Powell biographer Tim Jeal, however, Baden-Powell officially welcomed girls to the movement in several articles in the Scouting leadership magazine and initially recommended Scouting for girls in one of the first pamphlets promoting the Boy Scouts in 1907 (469). Jeal refutes the notion of Baden-Powell's "early revulsion against the very idea of girls using the sacred word 'Scout' in their collective name" (469), citing Baden-Powell's signed 1908 articles in the *Scout* that said, "I think girls can get just as much healthy fun and as much value out of scouting as boys can" (R. Baden-Powell, "Can Girls" 94) and "I am always glad to hear of girls' patrols being formed . . ." (qtd. in Jeal 469). Although "Can Girls Be Scouts?" alleges that girls *can* be scouts, Baden-Powell maintains his separatist emphasis and never offers the girls training from headquarters. And even while arguing for girls' scouting potential, the Chief Scout speaks condescendingly of girls' and women's ability to become "as brave as men"; they can, he promises, if, "like scouts, they prepare themselves for it beforehand and make up their minds that they will see the danger through and not lose their heads and squeal, or faint" (94).

Baden-Powell claimed to have sought a way to include girls all along and to have chosen a name (Girl Guides) that the girls themselves preferred to the name "Girl Scouts" (Low 7). While the first claim is substantiated to some degree by the periodical articles Jeal mentions, the second statement has the appearance of a clever marketing claim; the girls who appeared at the 1909 Crystal Palace Rally for Boy Scouts had named themselves "Girl Scouts." Jeal cites Baden-Powell family correspondence that indicates that Baden-Powell wanted the girls trained just like the boys until his Victorian mother talked him out of it (470), but the written record shows a change in Baden-Powell's official memory, just as it shows a change in the Girl Scouts' own view of their development. In the Girl Scout manuals and histories, the name "Girl Scout" and the very activity of Scouting become privileges wrested from an unwilling Baden-Powell and brought to an eager, modern America, where the movement could find equal status with the boys' movement. Scouting was to furnish the girl's whole identity and occupy all her time, just as acquiring scouting skills was expected to consume the energy of Baden-Powell's Boy Scouts.[6]

The strategic use of the word "Scout" alone, rather than "Girl Scout," in the 1913 and 1916 manuals implies a sameness not only between the boys' program and the girls' but also between the boys and the girls. Perhaps the identification with the boys made the manuals' domestic hints and moral advice more palatable to girls, whose routine reading abounded with similar hints and advice. Whether the writers intended it or not—and the evidence suggests that some of the implied freedoms occurred as unexpected byproducts of the way the manuals for girls were produced—the 1913 and 1916 Girl Scout manuals offered girls new self-constructs that challenged the manuals' own assumptions about the girl's role as nurturer and inspiration of men.

The manuals descend linearly from *Scouting for Boys*. For the first full-length American manual, *How Girls Can Help Their Country* (1913), Low adapted *How Girls Can Help to Build Up the Empire* (1912), which Baden-Powell and his sister Agnes had developed from *Scouting for Boys* as a Girl Guide manual (Kerr, *Story* 19–20).[7] Low initially provided a seventeen-page version of the Guide manual (*How Girls Can Help* [1913]), appending a history of the American flag and the words to the Star-Spangled banner. She revised the full-length *How Girls Can Help Their Country* slightly for a 1916 edition by the same name, adding some badges from the boys' program that had previously been omitted. The 1913 and 1916 manuals retain much of the wording and many of the badge requirements of the Girl Guide manual and, consequently, *Scouting for Boys*. The girls' manuals also reproduce many of Baden-Powell's instructional drawings for rescue operations, although these drawings depict boys performing the rescues. The Girl Scout organization produced its 1920 manual independently of Low and without reworking the Baden-Powells' books, modifying the basic program concepts and introducing the title *Scouting for Girls*, which was reflexive of Baden-Powell's founding text.[8]

The seventeen-page booklet, *How Girls Can Help* (1913), demonstrates the Guides' initial reliance on the boys' material and the resulting effect on the reader's imaginative identity. In her haste to get the American Guide groups going, Low seems to have simply published what was available to her, the skeletal draft of *How Girls Can Help to Build Up the Empire*. In doing so, she missed what the Baden-Powells overlooked in the handbook: The frequent references to a male reader and a male code of honor. For example, the initial, short handbook explains that Guides salute because the salute is "a sign between men of standing" (*How Girls Can Help* 17) and communicates friendly intention when an armed man meets "a defenceless person or a lady" (10). Girls can never be "men of standing," but they can be ladies, which by juxtaposition in the sentence implies that they are also "defenceless" persons.

The potentially frustrating contradictions, however, are blunted by a broadened outlook that Baden-Powell probably never intended. Reading that a salute was a sign between men of standing elevated and empowered the girl reader at the same time that it excluded her; by saluting, she entered into a military world of male privilege that was previously denied her, and, at least in her imagination, she left the world of the "defenceless."

If the initial girls' manuals had been written independently of *Scouting for Boys*, they would probably have been more similar to contemporary conduct manuals for girls, with a tendency to overprotect or dictate to their readers. Instead, they retained Baden-Powell's habit of addressing his readers as peers, giving them detailed instructions for fairly sophisticated tasks and, as Robert H. MacDonald notes, referring them to expert, adult sources on matters of skill (127). The transfer of long passages from *Scouting for Boys* to the girls' manuals gives the 1913 and 1916 manuals a military tone, a tendency to address juvenile readers as peers of an experienced author, and an emphasis on independence, a privilege not often granted girls of the World War I era.

The difference between the girls' and boys' versions of these first manuals lay primarily in the degree of imaginary danger the reader was allowed. Both the boys' and girls' manuals emphasized sleuthing, tracking, and emergency skills, but the boys' manual presented those skills through games of pursuing and killing enemies or preventing murder. The girls' manuals dropped the assumption that readers would one day become real frontier or war scouts and eliminated most of the war games and murder references. The girls' observation skills could lead to the return of lost or stolen articles but never to the apprehension of dangerous criminals.

The text of *Scouting for Boys* argues repeatedly that boys must prepare while young if they hope to possess the survival skills and stamina they will need to endure life in the British colonies as either colonizers or soldiers. Hardy specimens of British manhood have become increasingly rare, Baden-Powell informs his readers, and only by learning scouting can

British men prevent foreign attack, the dissolution of the British Empire, or self-annihilation (19). The book presents itself as a textbook, arranged as a series of Camp Fire Yarns and scouting skill competitions, to help the boy reader develop his own skills as a future scout. The Camp Fire Yarns and instructions on outdoor living frequently employ stories of heroism in war or of survival in the British colonies of Africa and India, and the games and the narrative insist that scouting skills will help the boy triumph over enemies or apprehend life-threatening criminals. The text always assumes that the boy really will become a scout, either as a civilian or on the frontier.

The girls' book is half the length partly because the game structure disappears; girls are training as Scouts, members of an organization, rather than as apprentice scouts. *How Girls Can Help to Build Up the Empire* retains competition in camping skills, games that hone powers of observation, and races that require the girls to find their way in unfamiliar terrain or reach a certain destination unseen. The adapters interpolate new material on woman's role as Angel of the House, the person chiefly responsible for the moral virtue of an entire society. This material on womanly influence blends poorly with the manual's exhortations to pursue outdoor knowledge, athletic prowess, and emergency skills.

The passages on womanliness appeal to the reader as a right-minded comrade who will recognize her own sentiments in the text. The reader of *How Girls Can Help Their Country* learns that natural law has determined woman's role as moral exemplar:

> One of the most fundamental laws of life is that, in the natural course of things, the influence of women over men is vastly greater than that of men over one another.
>
> This is what gives to girls and women a peculiar power and responsibility, for no Girl Scout or other honorable woman—whether old or young—could use her influence as a woman excepting to strengthen the characters and to support the honor of the men and boys with whom she comes in contact. . . . (Low 9–10)

The role of Angel gains new force here by its association with Scouthood and the power it offers the girl reader, who suddenly acquires status as a woman (the book is addressed to girls ages ten to seventeen). Passages like this one, giving the girl a power of influence rather than independent action, temper the revolutionary character of Girl Scouting's rhetoric and activities.

Baden-Powell's language, though, when retained in the girls' manuals, supplies a high-heroic tone unlike the conduct-manual advice in some of the new sections. Baden-Powell clothed his character-training scheme in chivalric language, imitating the high-flown romance of turn-of-the-century boys' fiction. He tells his readers, for example, that to lose their honor is to lose their life, and he impresses them with the life-or-death urgency of their spoken promise. *Scouting for Boys* treats boys as what they secretly imagine themselves to be, men. The initial translation of this book into a girls' guide is often incongruous, but the earliest Girl Scout manuals invest girls with a glamour and dignity they could not appropriate for themselves before. Baden-Powell conceives of boys and, in the revision, girls, as people of infinite resource who, once properly trained, could intervene in disasters that adults were unprepared to prevent. As Girl Scouting moves farther and farther from the Baden-Powells' book, Scout manuals lose their high seriousness and their romantic vision of their readers, expecting less daring rescues and using language more reflective of an adolescent's day-to-day life.

The ways a girl could help her country, as the title of the 1913 and 1916 manuals promised she could, range from the usual modes of influencing others, to contributing to scientific nature study, to following a curriculum for emergency preparedness. The diligent Scout could be prepared to rescue the drowning (Hoxie 92–94), administer artificial respiration (95–96), revive people rendered unconscious by sewer gas (97), and stop runaway horses, a strenuous procedure which involved "run[ning] alongside the vehicle with [a] hand on the shaft" to keep from falling, "seiz[ing] the reins with the other hand, and drag[ging] the horse's head toward you" (96). The Scout also learned the proper way to rescue people who had fallen through ice (97).

Girls could also help their country by attending to daily exercise and personal hygiene (73). Cultivating strength and health would enable a girl to "carry out all the duties of a Scout" (12), which included befriending wild birds (48), keeping careful notes on the migration patterns of local birds to increase the national knowledge base on wildlife (48–49), and learning nursing skills so that she could tend the wounded if a war occurred (11). These contributions to the adult world involved a higher level of professionalism and autonomy than was usually attributed to young girls.

Like *Scouting for Boys*, the manual promotes throughout, both in the Baden-Powell sections and the new ones, an opposition between the weak, undisciplined average person and the physically toughened, early-rising Scout who takes daily cold baths and notices the details that lead to brave rescues and Holmes-like deductions. The girl who was previously excluded from her brothers' schooling and career prospects is now treated as a potential member of a trained super race. The manual also lists two more mundane ways of benefiting the nation: caring for children and knowing and obeying the Scout Law, which exhorted girls to cultivate honor, loyalty, helpfulness, purity, obedience, and cheerfulness. These traditional expectations gained a new power by their elevation to national service.

The Girl Scout manual of 1913 repeatedly depicts "the Scout" as the highest example of bravery and resourcefulness. For example, "A Scout, of course, must have perfectly good eyesight; she must be able to see anything very quickly, and to see it a long way off" (Hoxie 72), and "All Scouts should know how to shoot . . . so as not to be at a loss for a means of defense should an emergency arise" (41–42). In addition to possessing trained eyesight and good marksmanship, "Scouts must be able to find their way by night" (62), and they must "of course, be much accustomed to the open" (15), learning camping skills and outdoor independence.

For many girls, the assumption that they could and should become proficient at shooting and develop resourcefulness out-of-doors would have been new. As Sally Mitchell writes of turn-of-the-century British girls, "prevailing gender codes barred the young lady from even imagining independence and risk" (104). Mitchell sees Scouting as adults' late recognition of (and attempt to tame) girls' yearning to be boys and incorporate boyish freedoms and exercise into their lives (119).

The 1913 and 1916 manuals, intentionally or not, make use of girl readers' identification with boys by offering scouts as role models. The manuals use the lowercased term to refer to pioneer scouts in the wilderness, medieval knights, and other romantic figures, most of them male, who braved perils, honed their wilderness survival skills, and performed difficult rescues. The texts admit the girl reader, and all Girl Scouts, to the fraternity of these admirable men. Previously, their publicly sanctioned heroes would have been nurses or wives of great men. The manuals use the genderless "Scout" in preference to the more specific "Girl Scout" to present behavioral principles such as the Scout's preeminent desire to make others happy, as in the statement, "To make others happy is the Scout's first wish" (Hoxie 16).

By the 1927 manual, however, the normative term is "Girl Scout." This manual deliberately addresses a girl audience, although it allows Girl Scouts some cross-gendered roles. The narrative presents Girl Scouting as an essentially American pursuit, with a noble lineage embracing both male and female pioneers. According to the text, Girl Scouts draw on the same courage and resourcefulness as the (male) scouts who guided the pioneers to uncivilized territory (Girl Scouts Inc. 14–15). The text also annexes famous women of the past as Girl Scouts, arguing that Sacajawea, Louisa May Alcott, and nineteenth-century physician Anna Shaw would have been Girl Scouts had the organization existed in their day (Girl Scouts Inc. 15–18).

Throughout, this manual uses such phrases as "A Girl Scout is" or "A Girl Scout naturally" to elicit the girl reader's sympathy for a devotion to domestic science (243), systematic nature study (114), patriotism, and emergency preparedness (302). This rhetorical strategy appeared in the earlier cut-and-paste manuals, but the 1927 manual most clearly articulates a sense of Americanness and a connection to all heroic Americans, whether male or female. At the same time, *Scouting for Girls* makes a point of addressing readers who are girls. The diagrams illustrating the instructions for using semaphores, rescuing drowning victims, and administering artificial resuscitation now use drawings of adolescent girls rather than the Baden-Powell drawings of boy rescuers. The 1927 book still promotes resourcefulness, a trait that later manuals would minimize, perhaps as urbanization spread and a more sheltered notion of childhood emerged in the United States. Girls in subsequent manuals, which I will not discuss here, were encouraged more explicitly in traditional women's roles and were more securely under adult leadership. Also, the later manuals treat camping and outdoor skills with less technical detail, giving the youthful reader less difficult material to master.

The technical knowledge offered to and demanded of readers differed in the boys' and girls' manuals. In general, the boys' manual demanded higher levels of skill for the various Scouting ranks and for the badges. For example, boys had to tie six different kinds of knots to become Tenderfoot Scouts; girls had to tie only four. However, girls had to produce a greater variety of dishes to earn the "cook" badge and had to demonstrate more practical nursing skills for the badges for invalid care. These gendered expectation levels characterize the entire badge system, which Baden-Powell originally envisioned as a way to motivate boys to develop job skills as well as explore new hobbies (*Scouting for Boys* 295).

Consequently, the badges available to boys include textile worker, carpenter, engineer, blacksmith, mason, and plumber, all named for job titles.

The girls' badges, on the other hand, reflect domestic careers or bear names describing a field of study rather than a job. For example, the boys' electrician badge becomes, by the 1916 manual, the girls' "electricity" badge. Some of these changes removed the gendered character of the badge: "Boatman" becomes "boatswain," and "airman" becomes "flyer" and, in 1916, "aviation." The transformation of "photographer" to "photography" and "telegraphist" to "telegraphy," however, suggests that those fields might become hobbies rather than careers.

The career badges for girls include matron housekeeper (renamed "housekeeper" in 1916), needlewoman, dairy maid, farmer, hospital nurse, and child-nurse. Other domestic badges, named for their skill areas rather than their careers, include home-nursing (new to the 1916 manual), cooking, and invalid cooking. When these topics appear in *Scouting for Boys*, they make possible a pioneer existence in which women are extraneous. For example, the boys' cook badge requires them to prepare a meal on an open fire, and the boys' tailor badge directs them to sew a Boy Scout shirt and shorts. Their nursing badge bears the name "missioner," which suggests a rugged rather than a nurturing career.

However, the girls' manuals also introduced some new badges, suggesting new expectations of girls. The girls' manuals originated a badge for personal health, requiring that girls breathe through the nose, sleep with open windows, and perform daily exercises, all according to the Baden-Powell formula. This badge has no boys' equivalent, nor does the civics badge, introduced in 1916, requiring the girl to understand the political process and know the names of her government officials. The automobiling badge, also introduced in the 1916 manual, rewarded the girl for obtaining a driver's license, being able to start a motor safely, and knowing how to extinguish fuel fires.

Girls could also aspire to status as pathfinders, pioneers, or interpreters—all originally Boy Scout badges—but these badges seem to fall into the emergency preparedness category with the badges for cyclists, swimmers, and ambulance workers. This training, though, gave the Girl Scout a certain indispensability. Pathfinders were expected to know their vicinity well enough to give directions to people who were lost, and interpreters had to know a language well enough to translate for an international visitor. Cyclists were expected to offer their bicycles and their services to government authorities in times of emergency and had to relinquish their badges when they gave up their bicycles.

The badge requirements both opened new vistas to girls, in the technological fields of electricity, telegraphy, aviation, and automotives, and confirmed them in the domestic skills they might already have learned at home, although the Scout program emphasized the same kind of expertise that the domestic science movement sought for home arts.

In addition to these new technological advances, the Girl Scouts offered members participation in military ritual, previously unavailable to girls. The military overlay on pre–World War I Scouting increased its appeal both to members and to adult supporters. Initially, talk of war preparedness fueled the British and the American Scouting movements.[9] Girls who knew they could not be soldiers were apparently eager to wear uniforms. The pictures of the Girl Scouts in the 1913 and 1916 manuals show them grimly upright in ill-fitting khaki shirts and skirts, broad-brimmed field hats, and military regalia such as the broad chevrons marking the sleeves of the captains (the titles of captain and lieutenant for troop leaders and their assistants have vanished from the program, as have the chevrons denoting the ranks). The particularly adept Girl Scout could even earn military-style medals for carrying out her duty at the risk of her life. Those medals and the Girl Scout motto, "Be prepared," imply that girls have something to be prepared for. If they are ready, something important, requiring their help and skill, will happen in their presence.

Girl Scout manuals undoubtedly reinforced traditional gender stereotypes and offered new avenues for physical and mental training for American girls. Although the rhetoric of womanly influence undercut much that was new in what the manuals and the real-world program offered adolescent girls, the manuals nonetheless provided girls with ways to imagine themselves into roles previously reserved for men. The instructional narratives and the merit badges encouraged girls to gain proficiency in lifesaving and in technical fields such as aeronautics, and to pursue knowledge of new technologies such as telegraphy, automotives, and aviation. The Girl Scout's eventual destination was still the home, but she was allowed a period of experimentation in the professional sphere. Additionally, she was given tools for self-sufficiency in the camping and pioneering experience the program provided. The manuals were important for providing a pattern for American girlhood as well: The texts gave American girls a way to envision themselves as uniquely capable, persistent, and resourceful.

Even so, Girl Scouting's attempts to address an audience of girls robbed its readership of certain revolutionary aspects of the skill-based outdoor program. In some ways, Girl Scouts lost as much as they gained when their manuals grew further away from the soldierly, heroic language of Lord Baden-Powell and became less condescending toward girls, less ready to make them "womanly." The newer manuals recognized their readers as girls and offered them a greater range of possibilities for personality and skill development, but they also proscribed for them a girls' world rather than one shared with boy peers.

How all of this affected twentieth-century American womanhood, however, requires more study. Scholarly evidence indicates that adolescent girls of the nineteenth and early twentieth centuries had far more physical freedom than most of us imagine for them. The restrictions on their activities often came with womanhood, a period that began at varying ages in different families and regions, usually arriving between ages ten and twenty. Anne Scott MacLeod calls the inevitable renunciation of girlhood freedom the "Caddie Woodlawn Syndrome": She cites memoirs, autobiographies, and novels by nineteenth- and twentieth-century women who record an abrupt transition from a tree-climbing, unsupervised childhood to a restricted, appearance-conscious womanhood.

Sally Mitchell notes a similarly short-lived period of freedom for the New Girl of the first twenty years of this century; the New Girl, Mitchell argues, could resist boundaries while in her girlhood but would have to conform to traditional gender expectations when she became a woman. In the same way, the more tomboyish activities of Scouting may have been available to some girls without the Girl Scout organization, but they did not last long into adolescence and did not receive continued official sanction. What scholars have yet to determine is whether Girl Scouting's more active pursuits stayed with former Scouts into adulthood or were left behind with other aspects of childhood.

NOTES

1. More than 6,000 British girls had enrolled themselves in the Boy Scouts before Baden-Powell's "surprise" encounter with a self-named band of Girl Scouts at the first Crystal Palace rally of Boy Scouts in 1909, two years after Baden-Powell first demonstrated his program for boys at an eight-day trial camp on Brownsea Island (Rosenthal 11, 85). After these Girl Scouts' public appearance,

Baden-Powell had his sister Agnes Baden-Powell organize a separate girls' organization, which they called Girl Guides.

2. Fern Brown's carefully researched 1996 biography for upper-elementary schoolchildren makes the point that Girl Scout biographers have made since 1928, that Low attributed Girl Scouting's success to its being "what the girls themselves wanted" (10). Brown draws on the source material that Girl Scouting's accounts of itself replay again and again: correspondence, Choate and Ferris's 1928 collection of reminiscences by Low's family, friends, and coworkers in the Girl Scouts and Girl Guides, and a biography by Low's niece and a professional writer, drawing primarily on the above sources and family legend.

3. Brown's juvenile biography nicely transmits this ethos of triumphant girl advocacy. Of Low's plans to transport Baden-Powell's program to the United States, she writes: "It would take all her strength and energy. She was deaf and frail. Yet when Daisy wanted to do something, nobody could stop her. And nobody was going to stop her now" (62).

4. For information on girls' inclination and social sanction to read boys' books, see Kimberley Reynolds's *Girls Only?* xix.

5. The differences between the Boy Scout and Girl Scout laws were few. Low substituted "A Girl Scout" for the boys' "A Scout." Her last five points were numbered differently because she placed "purity" sixth, while Baden-Powell placed the corresponding boys' rule last, probably because he added it in 1912 to the original nine. Points from *Scouting for Boys* that differ substantively are those on class, obedience, cheerfulness, and purity (or, for boys, cleanliness):

4. A Scout is a Friend to All and a Brother to Every Other Scout, no matter to what Social Class the Other belongs.

7. A Scout Obeys Orders of his parents, patrol leader, or scoutmaster without question.

8. A Scout Smiles and Whistles under all difficulties.

10. A Scout is Clean in Thought, Word, and Deed. (*Scouting for Boys*, 49–50)

The last point is identical to one the Boy Scouts of America adopted in 1911, before Baden-Powell included it (Murray 63).

The Girl Scout Laws differed more from the Boy Scouts of America's Scout Law, which had twelve items. "A Scout is Brave" and "A Scout is Reverent," like "A Scout is Clean," were additions to the Baden-Powell list of Scout attributes (Murray 59–63). The Boy Scouts of America reworded each statement so that an adjective followed "A Scout is." Some of the Girl Scouts' wording reflects the American Boy Scouts' version of the laws, as in "A Scout is Cheerful." Perhaps Low or Hoxie examined the American Boy Scout manual when writing *How Girls Can Help Their Country.*

6. Michael Rosenthal demonstrates in *The Character Factory* that Baden-

Powell intended Scouting to consume its members so that the program could reshape all of British culture and strengthen the underpinnings of the Empire.

7. Sources differ as to whose authorship dominated the manual, which mixed long excerpts from *Scouting for Boys* with new material on womanly behavior. Baden-Powell's biographers generally credit him with helping his sister, whom they suggest was overwhelmed by the writing task, but his wife Olave claims that she and her husband ridiculed the book for its Victorian outlook (O. Baden-Powell 108). Baden-Powell wrote a new Guide manual, alone, in 1918.

8. In this essay, I refer to the 1927 abridgment of the 1920 manual.

9. Rosenthal has demonstrated Baden-Powell's formulation of Boy Scouting as a way to reverse the perceived trend of degeneration in British manhood, in a period of national anxiety about Britain's military and physical fitness (131–60). Baden-Powell aimed his inclusive character-training scheme at boys too poor or poorly connected to attend public schools, where they would have imbibed such character-based virtues as physical fortitude, obedience, patriotic fervor, and a games mentality (105–6). In the United States, similar concern for national virility characterized the Roosevelt era and stimulated the growth of both the boys' and girls' Scouting programs.

WORKS CITED

Baden-Powell, Olave, with Mary Drewery. *Window on My Heart: The Autobiography of Olave, Lady Baden-Powell, G.B.E., as told to Mary Drewery.* London: Hodder, 1973.

Baden[-]Powell, Lieut. General Sir Robert, and Miss [Agnes] Baden[-]Powell. *How Girls Can Help.* Savannah: Byck, 1913.

Baden-Powell, Robert. "Can Girls Be Scouts?" *Scout* 16 May 1908: 94.

———. *How Girls Can Help to Build Up the Empire,* London: Nelson, 1912.

———. *Scouting for Boys.* 7th ed. London: Pearson, 1915.

Brown, Fern G. *Daisy and the Girl Scouts: The Story of Juliette Gordon Low.* Morton Grove: Whitman, 1996.

Choate, Anne Hyde, and Helen Ferris, eds. *Juliette Low and the Girl Scouts: The Story of an American Woman, 1860–1927.* Garden City: Doubleday for the Girl Scouts Inc., 1928.

Dyhouse, Carol. *Girls Growing Up in Late Victorian and Edwardian England.* London: Routledge, 1981.

Girl Scouts Inc. *Scouting for Girls: Official Handbook of the Girl Scouts.* Abridged ed. New York: Girl Scouts Inc., 1927.

Girl Scouts of the U.S.A. *Highlights in Girl Scouting, 1912–1996.* New York: Girl Scouts of the U.S.A., 1997.

————. *Seventy-Five Years of Girl Scouting.* New York: Girl Scouts of the U.S.A., 1986.

Hinding, Andrea, ed. *Women's History Sources: A Guide to Archives and Manuscript Collections in the United States.* New York: Bowker, 1979.

Hoxie, W. J. *How Girls Can Help Their Country.* 1913. New York: Girl Scouts of the U.S.A., 1972.

Inness, Sherrie A. "Girl Scouts, Camp Fire Girls, and Woodcraft Girls: The Ideology of Girls' Scouting Novels, 1910–1935." *Continuities in Popular Culture: The Present in the Past and the Past in the Present and Future.* Ed. Ray B. Browne and Ronald J. Ambrosetti. Bowling Green: Bowling Green State U Popular P, 1993. 229–40.

Jeal, Tim. *The Boy-Man: The Life of Lord Baden-Powell.* New York: Morrow, 1990.

Johnston, Edith D. "Juliette Low Brings Girl Scouting to the United States." Choate and Ferris 101–16.

Kerr, Rose. "Juliette Low Meets Sir Robert Baden-Powell and the Girl Guides." Choate and Ferris 81–98.

————. *The Story of a Million Girls: Guiding and Girl Scouting Round the World.* London: Girl Guides Association, 1937.

Low, Juliette. *How Girls Can Help Their Country.* Adapted from Agnes Baden-Powell and Sir Robert Baden-Powell's Handbook. New York: n.p., 1916.

MacDonald, Robert H. *Sons of the Empire: The Frontier and the Boy Scout Movement, 1890–1918.* Toronto: U of Toronto P, 1993.

MacLeod, Anne Scott. *American Childhood: Essays on Children's Literature of the Nineteenth and Twentieth Centuries.* Athens: U of Georgia P, 1994.

Macleod, David I. *Building Character in the American Boy: The Boy Scouts, YMCA, and Their Forerunners, 1870–1920.* Madison: U of Wisconsin P, 1983.

Mitchell, Sally. *The New Girl: Girls' Culture in England, 1880–1915.* New York: Columbia UP, 1995.

Murray, William D. *The History of the Boy Scouts of America.* New York: Boy Scouts of America, 1937.

Reynolds, Kimberley. *Girls Only?: Gender and Popular Children's Fiction in Britain, 1880–1910.* Philadelphia: Temple UP, 1990.

Rosenthal, Michael. *The Character Factory: Baden-Powell and the Origins of the Boy Scout Movement.* New York: Pantheon, 1984.

Shultz, Gladys Denny, and Daisy Gordon Lawrence. *Lady from Savannah: The Life of Juliette Low.* Philadelphia: Lippincott, 1958.

Springhall, John. "Baden-Powell and the Scout Movement before 1920: Citizen Training or Soldiers of the Future?" *English Historical Review* 102 (1987): 934–42.

Summers, Anne. "Scouts, Guides, and VADs: A Note in Reply to Allen Warren." *English Historical Review* 102 (1987): 943–47.

Voeltz, Richard A. "Adam's Rib: The Girl Guides and an Imperial Race." *San Jose Studies* 14.1 (1988): 91–99.

———. "The Antidote to 'Khaki Fever'? The Expansion of the British Girl Guides during the First World War." *Journal of Contemporary History* 27 (1992): 627–38.

Warren, Allen. "Sir Robert Baden-Powell, the Scout Movement, and Citizen Training in Great Britain, 1900–1920." *English Historical Review* 101 (1986): 376–98.

2

Rate Your Date

Young Women and the Commodification of Depression Era Courtship

Mary C. McComb

Every teller of fortunes knows her man—and womankind. Whether she is reading tea-leaves in a cup or spots on playing-cards or lines in your palm. . . . [s]he knows the three eternal dreams of youth—love, adventure and riches. The world is full of men and girls, adventure is around the corner, there are riches for the having. . . . This book is a guide to love, as we know it today, to adventure of the sort one finds in the association of boys and girls together, and to the riches that come in the final joint relationship in marriage and homemaking.
——Frances B. Strain, 1939

That the human race is composed of two types—male and female—is one of the fundamental facts of existence. It is a fact that at first glance may seem too obvious to mention. . . . To find happiness and satisfaction, each of these two types of being must in some way take into account the existence of the other. This implies a continuous process of adjustment. Adjustment . . . is the fundamental thread running through marriage; it is the very essence of marriage.
——Henry A. Bowman, 1942

These passages, excerpted from the introductory pages of two distinctive types of prescriptive literature that proliferated on the American cultural landscape in the 1930s and 1940s, embody the key tenets that experts expressed when addressing their young readers. Frances Bruce Strain's mass-marketed advice manual, entitled *Love at the Threshold: A Book on Dating, Romance, and Marriage* (1939), discusses issues of love, romance, and dating by directly addressing young readers. Strain professes to write from her own personal experiences and, like most manual writers, frames heterosexual romance and marriage as exciting escapades to be embarked upon by young people. Mystical images of fortune, adventure, and riches available to youths who dared to step over the threshold into the wondrous world of love are evoked in her writings. Most authors of mass-marketed manuals utilized similar rhetorical strategies and classified themselves as informal authorities on modern youth culture.

Henry A. Bowman, author of a marriage and family textbook entitled *Marriage for Moderns* (1942), employs a serious, authoritarian tone in his text. Bowman's book, written specifically for use in the classroom, emerged as a cultural form in the mid-to-late 1930s, when numerous high schools and colleges added "marriage and family" courses to their curriculums. Like most textbook authors, Bowman was a male professional with an advanced degree in sociology. *Marriage for Moderns* exemplifies the qualities found in other marriage and family textbooks in that it contains multiple allusions to the theories of Darwin and Freud which emphasize the importance of mutually exclusive gender roles.[1] Bowman, and other textbook writers of the 1930s and 1940s, relied heavily on psychological jargon, diagrams, statistical evidence, and theories of adjustment to prove their points. Textbooks from this era discussed issues of sexuality, heterosexual romance, and reproduction in a clinical manner and held an unsentimental view of courtship.

Although the language and tone used in the manuals and textbooks differ greatly, the messages contained in both types of publications prove remarkably similar. While they envision romance differently, both Strain and Bowman present marriage as the ultimate goal for happiness. Most manuals and textbooks focused on creating a sense of gender balance, which would in turn promote healthy social relations and good marriages. The authors of these texts created a hegemonic ideal of "adjusted youth" that was disseminated to young people who either read the advice books published by the popular press or received classroom instruction from textbooks regarding matters of dating, sexuality, and gender roles.

The burgeoning mass media helped to carry the messages contained in manuals and textbooks to the wider public, thereby providing a common frame of reference for Americans to consult in shaping their opinions about social norms in relation to romance, dating, and gender roles. In her text *From Front Porch to Back Seat: Courtship in Twentieth-Century America*, Beth Bailey contends that prescriptive literature came in many forms and that the rules were "constantly reiterated and reinforced. The sameness of the message was overwhelming. Popular magazines, advice and etiquette books, texts used in high school and college marriage courses, and the professional journals of educators who taught the courses all formed a remarkably coherent universe" (8). This essay examines a small constellation of texts that make up part of this universe: a collection of mass-marketed manuals and textbooks published between 1930 and 1942.[2]

During the Depression era, a psychologist named Alfred Adler gained prominence in the field of popular psychology. Adler's theories of social adjustment made such a cultural impact that historian Warren Susman has dubbed the 1930s the "Adlerian age of adjustment" (200). Self-appointed experts who wrote to a youthful audience used Adler's admonitions to advise young people to gain acceptance from their peers by being "well adjusted." Enacting the role of a well-adjusted person was upheld as the key means for achieving the coveted combined states of normalcy and popularity.[3]

This new ideal of social adjustment being equated with social success proved especially applicable to young people who were immersed in, and forced to adjust to, peer culture. Caroline Bird, in her text about the Depression, *The Invisible Scar*, argues that a lack of jobs for both adults and young people contributed to rising populations of students in high school classrooms. This led to overcrowding, a problem that was solved by segregating classrooms into age-specific domains, which, in turn, contributed to the emergence of a cohesive youth culture. Peer groups became extremely important and played a critical role in the process of socialization because most youths, from the time they entered elementary school to the day they graduated from high school or college, spent a majority of their day interacting with their peers. Paula Fass, in her writings about peer culture in the 1920s, contends that peer groups "controlled and directed habits, attitudes, and values that could not be completely directed or controlled by older and adult institutions" (57).

Although peers played a significant role in the adolescent socialization process, experts including sociologists, psychologists, educators, and etiquette writers took on the role of adult advisors to students in textbooks and advice books. Authors of the mass-marketed manuals of the 1930s and early 1940s, when dealing with sticky subjects like sexuality and dating mores, tended not to blatantly impose their own ideas about the issues on their readers. Instead of voicing rules and regulations about dating and sexual behavior, many manual writers borrowed survey methodology from sociologists, effectively utilizing expert techniques to collect, process, and report information from the peer group rather than constructing answers themselves. Therefore, young people who turned to popular publications to read expert advice on issues of gender norms, dating, necking, and petting often received responses culled from surveys of their own national peer group.[4]

The Depression era saw an emergence of surveys, polls, and sociological studies that became the predominant means of collecting "empirical" evidence about normative youth ideals and behavior. In 1935, George Gallup created the American Institute of Public Opinion, which made polling a common phenomenon in American life. Young people and the experts who tabulated and published the results of the polls entered into a dialectical relationship, where young people generated the raw data and opinions that made up the normative statistics, yet the publication of this data exposed and reinforced dominant cultural patterns onto the group that initially generated the norms (Susman 158). The publication of statistical norms and averages in the mass media created a new frame of reference for young people. The standardized, age-segregated peer group established by the organization of classrooms now became further standardized and widened to encompass the entire nation. Bailey contends, "From about the late 1930s on, many young people knew to the percentage point what their peers throughout the country thought and did. They knew what was normal" (4). This mass-mediated national standard of normalcy increasingly framed the way in which young people made personal decisions and choices.

This rise of experts, the creation of surveys to measure popular attitudes, and the publication of manuals and textbooks based on this data created a mass-mediated vision of youth that often ignored the social reality of the Great Depression. The writers who penned advice manuals and textbooks appeared to be addressing an audience of college students, yet the pecuniary crisis brought on by the Depression made attending college an upper-class luxury for both men and women (Bird 294). In the 1930s only a small minority of women, about 10.5 to 12.2 percent, attended college (Ware 18). Manual and textbook authors may have chosen to describe collegiate life because in 1920s and 1930s popular culture college students were considered to be the "fashion and fad pacesetters whose behavior, interests, and amusements were emulated by other youths" (Fass 126).[5] In this new system of mass-mediated youth culture, even if only a fraction of the population could afford to attend college, young people from all backgrounds could have access to information about campus life and customs.

The most fascinating component of the textbooks and manuals lies in the way that the experts refused to address the fact that the worst economic depression in the history of the United States was occurring while the books were being written. Some authors make passing reference to boys lacking money for extravagant dates, but, overall, they follow the standard self-help formula of placing the onus for change on individual agency. Still, cultural fears and anxieties concerning a lack of abundance, falling stocks, and the ensuing crisis of masculinity are embedded in each and every text. The men and women who wrote advice manuals and textbooks for young Americans seem to have tacitly come to the conclusion that reinforcing male dominance in gender relations would bring about an end to the crisis of masculinity and help to mediate the larger economic crisis faced by the nation.[6]

Dating and heterosexual interaction appeared to be the one arena where gender and pecuniary issues could be balanced. Most youths in the 1930s and early 1940s were not interested in forming permanent unions; instead, the objective of dating focused on achieving a level of social success and increasing one's popularity without forming emotional attachments (Cate and Lloyd 24). This promiscuous form of dating emerged, in part, because the economic reality of the Depression prevented people from settling down since they could not afford to get married.[7]

Dating, in addition to becoming a practice disconnected from emotions, was commodified and linked with the marketplace during the Depression era. Consumerism and dating had become intrinsically linked in the early twentieth century and the trend continued throughout the 1930s and early 1940s. Even with the national cash flow at an all-time low, most dates still involved a female and a male going to a public place and purchasing something: tickets to a movie or show, admission to a dance, or even a Coke at the corner store. Generally, men were expected to pay for their date's entertainment, transportation, and meals. Women were expected to repay men with varying levels of sexual favors, usually a chaste kiss good night. Dates became a cultural site where participants could work out issues associated with abundance, scarcity, and pecuniary problems without confronting the grim reality of a national economic depression. This commodified and sexualized dating scene became legitimized through its depiction in the mass media.

Women not only rewarded men with sexual favors, but young females in the 1930s and early 1940s fashioned themselves into commodified beings who existed in a heterosexual marketplace of exchange. Experts offered young readers advice on how to ensure that their "stock" ratings remained high. Even if the national economic marketplace was in disarray, young men could partake in the dating marketplace and have their pick from a bounty of female "goods." Young women who circulated in the dating marketplace and participated in the world of exchange in a passive and nonthreatening manner helped to assuage the crisis in masculinity, reaffirm traditional gender roles, and replenish a sense of abundance. Young men had copious choices of high-quality "goods" at their disposal. Males could conspicuously consume the companionship of females in the public sphere. Females, too, benefited from this public exchange because being seen in the dating marketplace advertised a young woman's popularity and caused her stock to rise, which led to her wider circulation in the marketplace. Prudent young men were able to comparison shop for good dating bargains and could easily ignore young women who failed to meet the market standards. Since marriage was still deemed the ultimate goal in mass-marketed manuals and textbooks, dating a wide variety of people became a method for "window shopping" until prosperity returned and couples could settle down.

Dating is defined in various ways by authors of manuals and textbooks. Strain's *Love at the Threshold* (1939) describes the process in the following passage:

> Besides being fun, single dating defines a person and brings out his or her capacity. Everything that he (or she) says counts. It's like selling—you must be alert to the other person's responses. An appropriate turn of phrase, and everything is won. Too much high pressure, perhaps, and everything is lost. (11–12)

The language of the marketplace permeates this passage. Strain contends that although dating can be conceptualized as a leisure pursuit, it also contains elements of serious business. While dating distinguishes people's individual traits, it also reveals their assets. The world of dating becomes a high-stakes enterprise where conversations are transformed into sales pitches. Young people learn that they must craftily market themselves in order to purchase the prize of popularity.

Sociologist Henry A. Bowman envisioned dating as a leisure activity, a source of fun and pleasure, and an essential rite of passage into adulthood. Most importantly, he conveyed the sense that dating and popularity were intrinsically linked entities:

> Dating is fun. It affords special association with a person of the opposite sex which provides elements of interest and personal satisfaction not to be found in association with one's own sex. Dating is a universal expectation; young people are expected to date when they have reached a given age. . . . *Dating may be a source of prestige, either because of the frequency with which it occurs or because of the persons dated. On the other hand it may be a source of dissatisfaction or give rise to feelings of inferiority when an individual has difficulty in dating sufficiently often or in attracting acceptable dates.* Dating is a proving ground for maturity. (212, emphasis added.)

Another sociologist, Willard Waller, studied the prestige or dissatisfaction experienced by students who participated in the world of dating at Pennsylvania State University in the mid-1930s. Students who attended the university often worked, studied, and lived on campus, meaning that they were surrounded and greatly influenced by their peer group. Many students likely imagined dating as a proving ground, not for maturity but for popularity. Waller, after tabulating his findings, coined the phrase "rating and dating" to describe college campus systems of courtship and competition for popularity. In order to discern who "rated" socially, students developed their own informal polls about the attributes of others and then constructed a hierarchical ladder where people were rated for their overall desirability. Men who "rated" were defined as "Class A Men" who usually dated "Class A Women."

A male who rated the highest level of prestige often belonged to a fraternity, possessed "smooth" manners, talked a good line, danced skillfully, dressed well, and had access to an automobile. Young women who rated "Class A" had nice wardrobes, spoke and danced well, and, most importantly, were well known as popular dates. A female student's rating depended "upon dating more than anything else; here, as nowhere else, nothing succeeds like success" (Waller 232). Waller explains that clever coeds quickly learned to "give the impression of being much sought after" even if this were contrary to fact (233). Since most university students on the campus were hyper-conscious of these social distinctions and of their own position within this tightly organized social hierarchy, they realized that *appearing* popular affected their rating, social standing, and the rung that they inhabited on the ladder of popularity. Having a high rating proved incredibly important for a young woman because being an overlooked commodity in the marketplace led to disastrous drops in a woman's stock.

Several manuals present ample evidence that the rating and dating system functioned in full force on many college campuses in the 1930s. Elizabeth Eldridge's *Co-Ediquette: Poise and Popularity for Every Girl* (1936), spends several chapters speaking to issues of rating and dating as well as to the importance of maintaining the guise of popularity. In the following passage Eldridge attempts to raise the reader's anxiety about issues that she may not have questioned before: "Perhaps it never occurred to you before to wonder whether you were popular or not. . . . But at college, all this is changed. If you can not rate a date, you are a wallflower; and any girl who has sat at home on Saturday night knows how Cinderella felt when her sisters dressed for the ball" (185).

Eldridge, a former sorority sister at a co-educational university, offered a simple solution for young women who did not rate. She advised them to study the popular girls to learn "the secrets of their success" (188). The key secret for achieving success in the rough and tumble world of rating and dating was garnering as much male attention as possible while still appearing to be a passive and nonthreatening presence. According to the expert writers of manuals and textbooks, attaining the approval of men and the envy of women caused a young woman's "stock" to rise. This social stock rose and fell due to unpredictable fluctuations in the marketplace.

Since a girl's standing in the marketplace determined her popularity and desirability as a date, she might be tempted to try to raise her own rating by bragging about her social successes. Eldridge firmly advises her young readers to forgo the temptation to discuss their other dates with the men that they are currently seeing, because in her estimation it proves a "cheap way to advertise your own popularity" (195). She counsels coeds to avoid using cunning maneuvers to temporarily enhance their ratings, but the very next section of the manual describes several strategies for attaining popularity, or at least the appearance thereof, through subversive means.

The chapter entitled "A Woman's Wiles" furnishes young coeds with multiple tactics and schemes that could be utilized to maintain an image of popularity. In order to rate and ultimately score a date, a young woman not only had to garner male attention, but also had to make her female competitors and compatriots believe that she was popular. Eldridge lists some successful maneuvers to help young women "maintain this pose," such as covering their mirror with photos of men, writing themselves letters, sending themselves flowers, and arranging to have men call them during house committee meetings (197). This investment seems extreme, but female college students were caught in a vicious cycle of having to rate in order to date and vice versa. A coed had to maintain a guise of constant male attention and approval lest her rating dip so low that she could never rate a date again.

The façade of popularity had to be maintained at all costs. If a man stood a woman up for a date, the woman was honor-bound to maintain a code of silence because advertising the fact would only lower the female's desirability rating. Most importantly, a female coed could not appear too eager to accept a date. The following scenario proves illustrative:

> On Saturday nights, the girls who do not have dates wander aimlessly from room to room watching the others dress, wondering what to do with the empty evening. Suddenly, the phone rings. There is a stampede in the house like cattle galloping across the Texas Plains as everyone dashes. A few doors open and voices call, "Was that for me?" This particular time it happens to be a male voice. One of the men at the fraternity house wants to know who hasn't a date, for he wants to "fix someone up" with one of their guests. The message is relayed from room to room. The girls look at each other blankly, and one by one they all refuse. They are eager to go out, but they are a little afraid that the man is shopping; and they would rather vegetate in boredom than admit to the voice on the other end of the wire that they have no date at that hour on Saturday night. (199)

This illuminates the key tenets of the commodified rating and dating system. Calculating young women, who recognized all other females as competitors in the dating marketplace, showed concern that men who shopped around for dates on a Saturday night might be looking for cheap goods that were left on the shelf. Enterprising females had to manipulate the marketplace to keep their stock and rating up, and accepting last-minute offers for dates lowered their own value in the marketplace. Females quickly learned to create an artificial sense of scarcity in order to keep their value high.

Strain's *Love at the Threshold* promotes the use of the scarcity model described by Eldridge. Strain contends that young women should not be too eager to date and should not fall prey to going steady because young people needed to constantly compete in the marketplace in order to keep their rating up. She states, "What's the use of keeping one's social weapons sharp and glistening when there are no opponents against whom to match one's steel? If your date is in the open field, you'll see to it that you keep in good competitive form. . . . Men like girls that other men want. . . . No, a girl must never let herself become a certainty" (Strain 23). The cold and calculating tone employed by Strain demonstrates that the one true power a young woman had in this highly competitive dating marketplace was to make herself into a scarce, and therefore more desirable, commodity. This strategy of self-commodification created a dialectical situation where young women bowed to the expert authorities and conformed to national averages while simultaneously subverting traditional gender roles by becoming savvy "economists" who actively marketed themselves in a volatile dating marketplace.[8]

The rating and dating system of the mid-1930s to early-1940s encouraged young women to remain in constant competition with one another for male approval. This factor alone positioned males in the center of female attention, making the rating and dating system a means for allaying fears generated by the Depression and the ensuing crisis in masculinity. The mass-marketed manuals indicate that young women focused incredible amounts of energy on competing with their friends and female peers to gain recognition from young men.[9]

You've Rated the Date—Now Where Do You Go?

During the Depression, the most critical social events of the season were the formal dances. These formal events provided a social stage where the intricate drama of the rating and dating system could play itself out. According to the depictions of formal dances in the manuals, the ballroom floor represented a site akin to the New York stock exchange where people could observe their peer's social status rise and plummet at alarming rates. Dance etiquette in the 1930s and early 1940s dictated that females assume a passive stance while men take on the role of actively pursuing interaction.[10] Young men, even though they were in the numerical majority on most campuses, had the opportunity to pick from a plethora of female partners. Most campus dances had a system for "cutting in" where men stood in stag lines at the edge of the floor and waited to cut in on dancing pairs by tapping the shoulder of the desired young woman. Dorothy C. Stratton's advice book, *Your Best Foot Forward: Social Usage for Young Moderns* (1940), explains that if a dance was a "cut" affair, it was generally accepted "that the girl must dance with whoever cuts in, even though she is enjoying her current partner" (149). According to advice and etiquette manuals, young women should revel in this loss of control because getting "clapped" many times in one evening was a badge of popularity. This badge advertised a young woman's high rating, guaranteeing that her stock would skyrocket.

Conversely, "getting stuck" on the dance floor with one partner and having nobody cut in was popularly perceived as a massive failure. "Getting stuck" proved to be a social nightmare for a young woman because it advertised her unpopularity in a showcase where the eyes of her peers were fixed upon her in rapt attention. Eldridge provides a worst case scenario of a young woman being guided deftly around the floor by one partner while watching out of the corner of her eye for the next man to cut in. Meanwhile, her roommate, and probable arch competitor for high ratings, is being "clapped" on the shoulder and cut in on at a breathless pace. Eldridge describes the mounting tension in vivid detail:

> Surely, someone will cut. But no one does. Around the room four times and five. What is your partner thinking? Is he casting eyes at your roommate who is surrounded by a group of eager men? Does he want to be rid of you? At last, that man in the corner is coming to your rescue; but there is no gleam of recognition in his eye as you go past, ten times, twelve. The music ends with a sudden crescendo. . . . The music starts again. He looks hopelessly about and starts dragging you around the floor once more and not even his forced politeness any longer conceals the fact that he knows that he is stuck. (202)

Men hated being stuck almost as much as women did because being seen with an obviously unpopular woman lowered a male's rating in the eyes of his peers. Also, a man was held honor bound by a code of chivalry to continue dancing with a young woman until someone cut in or she suggested that they stop. Young women had little control over who their next partner would be, but most women wanted men to cut in as often as possible. A young woman who got stuck had few options for getting herself out of the situation. She had to wait patiently and passively for another man to come to her rescue and save her from the embarrassing situation. Therefore, her plummeting stock was visible to every evaluating eye on the dance floor. Most young men knew, or could easily tell, which women were popular. Eldridge explains that men avoided dancing with unpopular women, not only because it lowered male ratings, but because they feared that "clapping [an unpopular female] is an evening's sentence" (202).

Girls with high stock ratings loved stag lines because they could enjoy having men scuffle for their attention and compete in the marketplace for the honor of dancing with a highly rated female. An unpopular young woman, also known as a "tag widow," had one of two choices: she could retreat to the dressing room or to the side of the man who brought her to the dance. Young women who got stuck and escaped to the safety of the powder room were advised by Eldridge definitely not to advertise the fact that they were stranded by the stags. Looking for comfort and commiseration within a community of other young women proved to be a dangerous option that had the potential to haunt a young woman in the future. Eldridge succinctly surmises, "Even with the girls, a prom-trotter realizes the wisdom of keeping up the fiction of her own popularity" (206).

Young women who grew tired of twirling around the dance floor or hiding in the sanctuary of the powder room could search for a more illicit brand of excitement in the parking lot. As Eldridge explains, in the 1930s cars were used not only as a convenient mode of transport, but they also served as smoking lounges and cocktail bars. She admonishes:

> Don't go into an automobile to smoke a cigarette with him and be offended if he seeks to kiss you. A college man takes your presence there as an acceptance. An automobile is also his bar; so anticipate a drinking party. You see why the sophisticated version of a wall-flower is a girl who spends all her dances on the ballroom floor. (211)

Eldridge alludes to the fact that many youths in the 1930s conceptualized their cars as "rolling parlors" that could be used as a place for sexual expression, experimentation, and even intercourse. Ellen K. Rothman explains that the automobile "provided far more privacy and excitement than either the dance hall or the movie theater, and the result was the spread of petting" (295).

Petting, meaning expressions of physical affection ranging from hand-holding to anything short of penetrative intercourse, is the only topic mentioned in every manual and textbook analyzed in this essay. Writers of both types of books expressed anxiety about the rise of youthful sexual experimentation, but when it came to discussing necking and petting, the writers' gender, more than any other factor, shaped the way in which they broached the subject. All of the experts came to the same negative conclusions about promiscuous petting, but male authors of textbooks issued earnest warnings to young women about the wily ways of men, while most female advisors relied on surveys and polls to generate data about the sexual customs, beliefs, and practices of young people.[11] Many critics of modern youthful mores blamed the concurrent rise of car culture and the commodification of courtship for making it possible for dates to occur in faraway places, beyond the chaperonage of prying parental eyes. The creators of manuals and textbooks realized that the norms for sexual expression and behavior were established by peer groups rather than authority figures, but all authors attempted to advise young people about the dangers of petting.

The highest possible price paid for promiscuous petting was a precipitous drop in a young woman's rating in the dating marketplace. Therefore, all of the authorities, male and female, place the burden of "sexual brinkmanship" squarely on the shoulders of young women. Females were held accountable for "putting the brakes on" sexual activity.[12] If they failed for any reason, it was perceived as their own fault. This issue is clearly illustrated in the following quotation from Randolph, Johnson, and Pixley's manual *Looking toward Marriage* (1942), where they issue a serious warning to young women, "There is one thing we would like to say to girls particularly—you have a grave responsibility in seeing that petting doesn't go too far. If you encourage or permit heavy petting, under the delusion that this is a short-cut to popularity, you are one of three things: vain, stupid, or ignorant" (39).

All anti-petting advocates agreed with this contention that heavy petting was a dangerous practice, yet none are quite so blunt as they in placing the onus of responsibility for sexual brinkmanship on females. Because the rating and dating system could make or break a young woman's popularity, a young woman had to maintain her balance and walk a thin line between being a "hot number" or an "icicle." Getting a reputation for being too forward or too frigid could permanently ruin a young woman's rating.

Bowman warns that young men were prone to engaging in bull sessions with their friends and that they might be tempted to tell stories, either true or fabricated, about their sexual forays with young women to gain the esteem of their peers. A young woman who was interested in keeping a high rating of dating desirability had to insure that her name did not come up too often or too seldom in young men's conversations.

Bowman acknowledges the importance of word-of-mouth advertising in the rating and dating system, but advises young women to hold onto their chastity. Female readers are duly warned that male students may try to turn the rating and dating system against those who refuse to comply with male wishes to pet:

> It is not necessary to yield merely because a boy threatens to use his influence to make it impossible for the girl to get other dates. The best he can do probably is to dissuade a few of his closest friends or fraternity brothers. In most cases he is bluffing and his bark is worse than his bite. (223)

Young women had to be careful because informal advertising was the most effective means of keeping one's stock high. If a young woman was saddled with a reputation for being an unresponsive date, her rating might plummet, never to rise again. Eldridge supports Bowman's point that young coeds had to beware of gossipy fraternity brothers. She explains that kissing a fraternity man may as well be done on the fifty yard line of the school stadium on the day of a big football game because men engage in constant bull sessions and spread the word about fast girls very quickly:

> If your date enjoys boasting, he may inspire a dangerous run of popularity for you. And if you are reckless enough to let several men from the same house make love to you, there will be an inevitable accounting; for at some bull sessions they will compare notes. Then you'll be known as a "hot edition" when all you meant to do quite innocently was insure yourself a big rush. So, it doesn't pay to kiss too lightly. (184)

Eldridge utilizes marketplace metaphors when she discusses the "inevitable accounting" of a young woman's sins and the consequential payments women had to make for kissing too freely. The hegemony of the rating and dating system forced young women to keep constant track of their status in the marketplace so that they could remain competitive commodities.

Manuals and textbooks advised young women to become obsessed with the status of their social stock and their rating in the dating market-place. The experts counseled young women to use their intelligence to charm young men, score dates, and outwit their female competitors. The academic aspects of collegiate life get pushed to the wayside in these texts in favor of promoting the endless pursuit of popularity. Female coeds who assiduously followed the advice of these adult authorities and de-voted copious amounts of time and energy to their social successes were most likely distracted from pursuing intellectual enrichment and scholarly success.

Studying, Female Academic Achievement, and the "Masculine Protest"

The depiction of college life thus far might lead the reader to wonder if young people did any studying at school. During the Depression, with so much focus on rating and dating, young women were warned that they could destroy their popularity and upset the delicate gender balance on campus by studying too much. The admonition to put the brakes on academic acceleration applied solely to women who seemed too devoted to their studies. Dedicated female students at co-educational campuses directly competed with males in the classroom setting. Expert authors expected females to remain passive and docile in the presence of males, because women were supposed to compete with *each other* for male attention, not with males for academic accolades. Aggressive female stu-dents threatened male dominance in the classroom and were seen as potentially menacing people who might decide to compete with men for employment in the limited job market. Furthermore, female students who were passionately devoted to their studies might defy gender norms alto-gether and choose never to marry. This deviant act threw the Depression-era gender balance into disarray and further contributed to the crisis of masculinity. Couples could choose to forestall marriage until prosperity returned, but the fact that women were making conscious choices not to marry deeply disturbed manual and textbook authors. These experts placed themselves at the center of debates about the education of women and took on the role of convincing defiant women to tone down their intellectual capacities and achievements.

Two writers devote several pages to warning young females not to become too "highbrow" for their male counterparts. Paul Popenoe's

Modern Marriage explains, "The average man painstakingly avoids a 'highbrow' or a girl who makes him unpleasantly conscious of her intellectual superiority. Many superior girls still pay the penalty of life-long celibacy for the spurious culture which is foisted upon them in school and college" (24). Male attention and marriage were upheld as the two prizes that young women could earn by following the rules put forth in manuals. Popenoe used the harsh statement about life-long celibacy as a shock tactic to bring academically competitive women back in line. During the 1930s, women who failed to marry were popularly perceived as lonely spinsters and pitied for their fate, so the author's comments most likely registered with young women. Popenoe's fears that women were attaining a level of education beyond what they needed to be good wives and mothers surface throughout his textbook. He believed that higher education for women further disrupted gender roles that were already woefully out of balance due to the economic instability of the Depression. Popenoe was not alone in his contentions. Strain supports his argument wholeheartedly in her section about "highbrow" types of girls, where she explains, "The highbrow girl has brains. She knows all the answers and knows them first. She can take a job, any job, and keep it. She can earn more money than her boyfriend. But her friends sometimes say, 'She's so smart, I hate her!' " (115).

Strain exposes the key fears that lie under the surface of Popenoe's text. Highbrow girls represented a challenge to male dominance in the work force that could reverberate in personal relationships if young women really did earn more money than their boyfriends. Fears about women invading the marketplace abounded during the Depression era, and working women were popularly portrayed as evil entities who took jobs that rightfully belonged to men. Being an intelligent and capable woman not only threatened male dominance, but also represented a threat to a female's popularity. Strain contends that the highbrow girl's friends secretly despised her and that boys quietly loathed her, but the situation could easily be remedied by following this sage advice:

> If girls are highbrow, they must keep it pretty dark. It's a potential sin, and if it is acute, to expose it is sure to make men take to their heels. The highbrow girl must cultivate the simple life, fun, sports, dress, new hats, love-making, to give her balance and make her an all-around woman. It takes discipline to hide a Phi Beta Kappa key and wear instead a piece of swank costume jewelry, but it pays if a woman is matrimony bound. (115)

To fulfill their natural, inborn, innate capacity as "all around" women, young females had to disguise their academic prowess and engage in superficial pastimes and displays. Popenoe and Strain place intelligence and sexual allure in binary opposition to one another, and explain that academic honors and the potential for matrimony exist in different universes. What proves most disturbing about these messages is that they were included in textbooks that were used to educate students in classrooms.[13] Young women who could potentially be liberated by earning a college degree were informed by marriage and family textbook authors that they should not overstep gender boundaries by competing academically with males. The expert authors convincingly stated their case, citing biological, statistical, and psychological models to convince young women not to challenge the shaky status quo of male dominance.

Popenoe appropriates Freudian theories to explain the inherent inadequacies of women, describing a phenomenon that he calls the "masculine protest." Women who attempted to achieve educational goals beyond their inherent capacity disrupted and distorted traditional societal and biological patterns. These attempts to defy "natural patterns" ultimately failed because women were unable to "repudiate the biological differences that underlie" these patterns (Popenoe 70). Abnormal women who failed to adjust to their proper station in life were seen as exhibiting traits of the "masculine protest." These deviant females avoided marriage or became frigid wives, exhibited stereotypically masculine behavior, and were especially prone to aggressiveness. Popenoe argues that this dangerous form of female initiative was spreading to the masses and destroying traditional ideals of masculinity. To assuage masculine fears about this impending menace, Popenoe assures young male readers that masculine women are universally hated: "Behind her back she is either laughed at, despised, or a little of each" (72).

A male-authored mass-marketed manual, George Lawton's How to Be Happy, Though Young (1942), contains several pearls of wisdom for young women who wished to pursue challenging academic goals. Lawton's book, a compilation of his responses to letters written by young people, contains a particularly telling passage where a young woman who had just won a prestigious four-year science scholarship asked if females had the capacity to succeed in male-dominated fields. To his credit, Lawton's response actually enumerates some environmental factors, such as upbringing, that led to men achieving greater success in demanding careers. Still, he contends that a young woman must learn to accept her second-class status or run the risk of being seen as a dreaded highbrow exhibiting her own masculine protest:

> You will be wise to take note that regardless of how you may compare with your husband in intelligence, and even though marriage should be a partnership, your mate will probably feel terribly deflated unless he *seems* to be doing most of the leading in family life. If you are realistic, you will be content to exert your point of view and perhaps your leadership in certain spheres without seeming to do so. (204)

Lawton assumes that the girl's main goal is marriage, so instead of offering her career advice, he tells her how to placate a threatened mate. He, like Eldridge and Strain, encourages young women to use their intelligence to manipulate men. If utilizing her intellect to charm her husband proves unfulfilling, a young woman should remind herself that "we cannot all be at the head of the procession" and that her true satisfaction and sense of achievement should come from "the degree to which you feel you have been needed by your immediate family, friends, and co-workers and have contributed to their satisfaction in life" (Lawton 205). Lawton argues that young women should not ask themselves, "How successfully have I competed with men?" Instead, they should measure their success by how useful they had been to others (205). Lawton frames the female who wishes to pursue a career in science as someone who wants to compete with men rather than as a person who desires a rewarding avocation.

Lawton's advice to play the role of a performative, other-oriented, people-pleasing female self echoes the key theses of the mass-marketed manuals and textbooks of the Depression era. This brand of prescriptive literature depicted a coherent universe and invented an intelligible vision for young readers to emulate in order to solve the crisis of masculinity created by the Depression. The expert authors of these texts recommended enacting roles and accepting norms that reinforced a model of male dominance. This model of male dominance was upheld as a means for bringing some semblance of order to the cultural chaos that ensued in the wake of the seemingly unending economic depression. The implicit message conveyed in Depression-era manuals and textbooks was that young women could play a crucial role in resolving cultural tensions by becoming preoccupied with the pursuit of popularity and by subtly shaping themselves into cultural commodities. Adjusted female readers who followed the roles presented in the manuals and textbooks learned to fashion themselves into passive products that could be purchased in the dating marketplace. The consuming desire to rate dates and to maintain high stock levels distracted young women from pursuing academic success, female friendships, and independent careers. Experts advised young female readers that they would achieve success and acceptance by coddling males rather than by competing with them. By actively adjusting their identities to fit the normative model, women could rescue emasculated men from their collective crisis and make the world safe for prosperity.

NOTES

1. Paul Popenoe's *Modern Marriage: A Handbook for Men* devotes entire chapters to outlining the binary opposition between males and females which bear titles like, "Remember, You Do Not Understand Women!", "The Femininity and Happiness of Wives," and "The Masculinity and Happiness of Husbands."

2. All of the mass-marketed manuals and marriage and family textbooks included in this analysis were published between 1930 and 1942. Although all of these texts were written during the Great Depression, few directly address the economic crisis. For a thorough list of manuals and advice books published in the twentieth century, see Deborah Robertson Hodges' *Etiquette: An Annotated Bibliography of Literature Published in English in the United States, 1900–1987.*

3. John C. Burnham's *Paths into American Culture: Psychology, Medicine, and Morals* states that during the 1920s and 1930s the general public became very concerned about standards of normalcy. He explains, "The simultaneous interest in self and interest in the abnormal reflected the common concern at the time about normality. The public in general had become vividly aware of the idea of normality when intelligence tests became standardized and widely publicized" (85).

4. In a sense, expert textbook authors and writers of mass-marketed manuals greatly resemble Roland Marchand's advertising copywriters in *Advertising the American Dream: Making Way for Modernity, 1920–1940.* Marchand contends that advertisers became "town criers" of modernity who taught people how to be consumers and how to make wise choices in an expanding marketplace. Expert manual and textbook writers utilized statistics, norms, and illustrative narrative to teach young people how to be youthful.

5. Paula Fass describes how "national agencies like movies, magazines, and advertising which spread the influence of college fashions and styles turned the idea of youth into an eminently salable commodity. A new genre, the movie about college life, flourished in the twenties, and a new technique for selling clothes that emphasized the prestige of the 'collegiate' style was introduced" (126).

6. For a detailed discussion of the crisis in masculinity see Caroline Bird's

The Invisible Scar and Winifred Wandersee's *Women's Work and Family Values, 1920–1940*. Susan Ware's *Holding Their Own* explains that married women faced intense hostility in the workplace. Polls conducted about working women found that the public believed that working women "took jobs otherwise filled by men, that a woman's place was in the home, and that children were healthier and happier" if women did not work (27).

7. Only Popenoe's *Modern Marriage: A Handbook for Men* and Bowman's *Marriage for Moderns* mention the financial burdens of marriage. This may be due to the fact that they were male authors who had fulfilled the breadwinner role in their own lives.

8. Interestingly, Caroline Bird notes, "More of my classmates [at Vassar] majored in economics than any other subject except English" (139).

9. Eldridge describes female competition in the following fashion: "The girl who shows that she has no time for other girls is at least honest. She turns her charm on and off like a faucet. She bubbles and scintillates when men are around, and she is always thoroughly disliked for it by her 'best friends.' But girls must learn to be popular with other girls as well as with men if they are going to live happily in college" (200).

10. Eldridge succinctly describes the situation: "No matter how much you believe in the equality of women, remember that on the dance floor, the man is your master" (208).

11. For the most part, female authors were reticent about raising the topic of necking and petting. Several manual writers, including Dorothy Stratton and Frances Strain, conducted elaborate surveys to collect data about dating mores. Stratton polled 6,200 college students about the rapidly changing rules about necking and petting. Strain conducted detailed surveys of over 2,000 college students about their sexual and dating practices.

12. The term "sexual brinkmanship" comes from Elaine Tyler May's *Homeward Bound: American Families in the Cold War Era*.

13. Beth Bailey critiques some college marriage and family courses for their questionable level of academic rigor. She cites evidence that "[t]he head instructor at the University of Illinois reported to colleagues that he released students from a term paper if they did six hours of baby-sitting during the term, and at Stephen's College a wedding plan was an acceptable term paper" (131).

WORKS CITED

Bailey, Beth L. *From Front Porch to Back Seat: Courtship in Twentieth-Century America*. Baltimore: Johns Hopkins UP, 1988.
Bird, Caroline. *The Invisible Scar*. New York: D. McKay, 1966.
Bowman, Henry A. *Marriage for Moderns*. New York: McGraw-Hill, 1942.

Burnham, John C. *Paths into American Culture; Psychology, Medicine, and Morals.* Philadelphia: Temple UP, 1988.

Cate, Rodney M., and Sally A. Lloyd. *Courtship.* London: Sage, 1992.

Eldridge, Elizabeth. *Co-Ediquette; Poise and Popularity for Every Girl.* New York: E. P. Dutton, 1936.

Fass, Paula S. *The Damned and the Beautiful: American Youth in the 1920s.* New York: Oxford UP, 1977.

Hodges, Deborah Robertson. *Etiquette: An Annotated Bibliography of Literature Published in English in the United States, 1900–1987.* New York: McFarland, 1989.

Johnson, Roswell H., Helen Randolph, and Erma Pixley. *Looking toward Marriage.* Boston: Allyn and Bacon, 1942.

Lawton, George. *How to Be Happy, Though Young: Real Problems of Real Young People.* New York: Vanguard P, 1942.

Marchand, Roland. *Advertising the American Dream: Making Way for Modernity, 1920–1940.* Berkeley: U of California P, 1985.

May, Elaine Tyler. *Homeward Bound: American Families in the Cold War Era.* New York: Basic Books, 1988.

Popenoe, Paul. *Modern Marriage: A Handbook for Men.* New York: Macmillan, 1940.

Rothman, Ellen K. *Hands and Hearts: A History of Courtship in America.* New York: Basic Books, 1984.

Strain, Frances Bruce. *Love at the Threshold: A Book on Dating, Romance, and Marriage.* New York: D. Appleton-Century, 1939.

Stratton, Dorothy Constance. *Your Best Foot Forward; Social Usage for Young Moderns.* New York: McGraw-Hill, 1940.

Susman, Warren. *Culture as History: The Transformation of American Society in the Twentieth Century.* New York: Pantheon Books, 1984.

Waller, Willard. *The Family; A Dynamic Interpretation.* New York: Cordon, 1938.

Wandersee, Winifred D. *Women's Work and Family Values, 1920–1940.* Cambridge: Harvard UP, 1981.

Ware, Susan. *Holding Their Own: American Women in the 1930s.* Boston: Twayne, 1982.

3

Truculent and Tractable

The Gendering of Babysitting in Postwar America

Miriam Formanek-Brunell

In the 1990s, baby boomer parents, faced with the challenge of finding reliable babysitters, often recall the responsible caretakers of their protected childhoods. But an examination of the origins of babysitting in postwar America reveals conflict between dissatisfied adolescent girls who organized babysitter unions and parents of the baby boom generation. The origins of "babysitting" began fifty years ago when high school girls in three suburban communities in the Northeast and Midwest drew upon the notion of class conflict in an effort to eliminate "exploitation," assert their "rights," and reshape the "industry." In the years after World War II, babysitting emerged as a burgeoning new service industry due to major changes in employment opportunities for women, rising affluence, a consumer culture, the baby boom, suburbanization, changing leisure patterns, child-centered families, teen culture, and the agency of adolescent girls. The 1947 babysitters' unions were short-lived, but teenage girls in other suburban communities who would shape a defiant babysitters' culture were just as angry as the activists. Teenage girls called babysitting "bratting" and referred to themselves as "bratters" ("Profession" 85).

Informed by the scholarship on women, gender, family life, labor, and youth studies, this essay focuses on the shifting boundaries between work and leisure, production and consumption, vocation and socialization in the lives of adolescent babysitters in postwar America. By examining the ways in which large numbers of girls used a traditional domain—child care—to contest prevailing constructions of gender, this essay revises the current view which maintains that *most* adolescent girls in postwar America conformed to conventional gender roles. According to historian Beth Bailey, conformist teenage girls were constrained by prevailing conservative values they also upheld (Bailey 1988). Only a small minority of adolescent girls challenged established cultural conventions argues sociologist Wini Breines (Breines 1992). However useful these studies are, they overlook the challenges to the construction of gender and the nature of feminized work presented by ordinary girls during the 1950s when nearly half of the nation's 7.9 million teenage girls worked as babysitters in the largest field of female adolescent employment.

This essay also seeks to include adolescents in the revisionist interpretation on the discourse over gender in postwar America.[1] Teenage girls who created a defiant babysitter culture were contesting the social order as we now know was the case among many of the era's mothers, fathers, and sons. Mass circulation periodicals, professional journals, the *New York Times*, teen fiction, rock 'n' roll, and a popular movie from the period reveal that between 1947 and 1960, babysitting became an arena of cultural conflict between adolescents and adults who claimed the right to establish the principles, practices, and purposes of babysitting.[2]

This study begins during the Great Depression when the need for child care was limited by decreased financial resources and depressed birth rates (Mintz and Kellogg 1988). The Second World War served to both further constrain the need for babysitters as well as to generate a demand for them. One 1943 study reported in the *Journal of Home Economics* revealed that as many as two-thirds of fourth, fifth, and sixth graders in Elmira, New York (a small city with a booming war industry) regularly cared for younger children. Like those in elementary school, high school girls also worked long and late hours for inadequate pay. For example, one girl cared for five children (between two months and nine years old) from the late afternoon until early morning (Pollock 31). Just as likely, however, adolescent girls and boys entered the traditional work force rather than babysit (Tuttle, 1993). Despite governmental attempts to conscript high school students to serve as an army of babysitters guarding the home front, one-third of all fourteen- to eighteen-year-old adolescents worked in paying jobs other than child care.[3]

Teenagers were not the only group that took advantage of expanded opportunities for employment; so did married, older, immigrant, and working-class women. In their absence, children of working mothers were cared for by grandmothers and other kin who had been the principal providers of child care. But, while Lanham Act (1940) child-care centers and federally funded Extended School Services provided for many hundreds of thousands of preschool and school-age children, many more were left without dependable care. Desperate parents granted their "latch-key" children unprecedented responsibility; others entrusted the care of their little ones to older siblings for long stretches of time (Tuttle 73). Recognizing the need to train older siblings, the New York Children's Aid Society was one of a number of organizations that offered a course on child care.

It was not until after the war, however, that the need for babysitters soared. In 1946—and during the next twenty years—nearly 76 million American babies were born to young women and men (motivated by security, optimism, and a postwar domestic ideology), all of whom were desperate for a babysitter. Rising salaries and increasing employment opportunities led many newly married middle- and upwardly mobile working-class couples to abandon cramped urban apartments for spacious suburban neighborhoods (Jackson 1985; Wright 1981).

> There are 15,000 small homes in the area and in those homes live 27,000 children, most of them toddlers. This area, a suburb of New York City, on Long Island, is officially known as Levittown, but many of us [babysitters] call it "Toddlerville". . . . Each of the 15,000 houses has an "expansion attic" where bedrooms can be added as children arrive. And how they arrive! (Church 36)

These "arrivals" presented parents with a serious problem: too many baby boomers for too few babysitters. While elementary school-age youngsters had been "minding the children" during the war, the child-centered nature of the postwar ideology effectively eliminated them as wage earners. Not so for their older sisters who were flooded with requests to baby-sit. As one adolescent explained, "I am a baby-sitter in an area where 95 percent of the residents are young married couples with small children" (Church 36). Years of declining birth rates in response to national crises had reduced the number of adolescents in the population in general and in suburbia in particular. "While there are thousands upon thousands of toddlers in Levittown, there are only a few dozen teen-age girls . . ." (Church 36). Similarly, in another "suburb of 9,000 homes there are 8,000 children [but] only about one hundred of whom were old enough for high school; most of the rest were still in playpens" (Norton 930).

The improved standard of living among many young couples was due to rising personal incomes (disposable income grew by 200 percent). But while the shortened work week provided more opportunities for leisure, parents were also more likely to be "tied down with small children—and not a grandmother, maiden aunt or sleep-in servant in sight" ("Profession" 85).[4] Increasing geographic mobility (due in part to the postwar development of a massive interstate highway system) meant that families were less likely to live near grandparents, in-laws, and other kin who now might live across the country instead of in the next block. In addition to these factors, parents were also more likely to go out for the evening and leave their children behind ". . . than was the custom years ago" (Greer and Gibbs 271, 276). One woman recalled that she answered "every R.S.V.P. invitation with an I.W.C.G.A.S. (If We Can Get A Sitter)" ("Rules" 15).

Numerous institutions and organizations came to the aid of young couples and, especially, burdened mothers. During the 1947 Christmas season several organizations offered sitting services so mothers could shop for holiday gifts ("Santa" 50). The Democratic and Republican parties, along with the Girl Scouts, offered sitting services so that mothers could get out and do their civic duty on Election Day.[5] A variety of cultural institutions also offered sitting services to patrons of the arts. In keeping with the postwar trend that de-emphasized sectarian differences and stressed common themes, neighbors in Levittown, New York, formed a Jewish-Christian sitters' exchange service.[6]

Despite attempts like these, the need for sitters was especially acute among suburban mothers. One young mother drove from Smithtown, Long Island, to New York City three times a week in order to earn a master's degree at City College. When not in school, she hired a sitter so she could go to work. Increasing numbers of mothers like her with full- or part-time jobs had also contributed to the widespread demand for babysitters. Though many women were laid off right after the war, substantially more entered the labor force thereafter. Between 1946 and 1970, the female labor force rose from 17 to 32 million. Many of those new entrants were married and many were mothers who, more often than not, held low-paying, sex-segregated jobs such as clerking, nursing, and office work. Federal social agencies expected white middle-class working mothers to hire babysitters.

Even though "[m]any more seniors than usual registered for baby-sitting" during the 1946–1947 academic year at Wellesley College, there still were not enough sitters to go around. While the placement bureau at the college had received only about forty-six annual requests for the "care of children" the decade before, by 1946 the demand had exceeded the supply: The bureau received an astounding 882 calls for babysitters. But because only 167 students were registered at the Placement Office, the staff spent hours on the telephone calling students in order to satisfy the requests of the 344 parents who lived in the vicinity. Unable to drum up enough sitters, the bureau decided instead to accept requests "insofar as there are girls available to fill them" ("Report").

In part, the demand exceeded the supply because babysitting had a poor reputation. One girl explained that "they never mentioned the dishes when they asked me to come over" (Grear 102). Others complained that parents expected caretakers to follow instructions they had never pro-vided. Often a single babysitter was left in charge of all the children of several families. Rarely did any employers even supply telephone numbers to be used in the event of an emergency. Moreover, wages were not only too low but sometimes went unpaid in full. Finally, the practice of escort-ing sitters home at night to insure their safety had not yet been instituted. These conditions are a shameful "American Custom," exclaimed a sym-pathetic reporter in 1941. "If [only] these girls could band together and fashion a set of rules . . ." (Grear 102). It had been a call to arms six years too early.

But by 1947 babysitting had become one of the fastest-growing service industries and teenage girls had forged an identity as its "workers." In their attempt to improve the conditions under which they cared for children, teenage girls in New Jersey, Massachusetts, and Michigan organ-ized babysitter unions the year following an upsurge in labor activism that rivaled the post–World War I era. Their collective protest drew upon the notion of class conflict as they sought to reshape the babysitting industry, eliminate "exploitation," and assert their "rights" as workers ("Sitter's Rights" 151). In an effort to increase and standardize wages, teenage girls in at least three states laid down the "rules for parents" (J. Ellison 36).

Through these "contracts," "codes," and "manifestoes," girls publicly articulated the complaints that had been expressed by frustrated child-care providers since the Depression ("Baby Sitters Set" 15). For example, suburban Massachusetts girls "organized" and won a "contract" with the

Auburndale Woman's Club ("Baby Sitters Win" 28). These Newton, Massachusetts, sitters demanded an hourly rate of 25 cents before midnight and 35 cents thereafter. (They also wanted 50 cents per hour for "overtime"—the period after which sitters' parents expected their daughters back home.) Sitters in Leonia, New Jersey, demanded 30 cents an hour before midnight and 35 cents an hour after midnight. For that, they would "dress, wash, and put children to bed," and that was all ("Rules" 15).

According to the fifteen-year-old business agent of the Baby Sitters' Union of Dearborn, Detroit, and Inkster, "They chisel on us to scrub floors and do dishes . . . and then pay us only a dollar to stay the whole night" (J. Ellison 37). The *Saturday Evening Post* reported that not only those in Michigan but "Sitters everywhere . . . are united in their verdict against housework" (Richards 102). Because the women who employed them often linked child care with light housekeeping, the "uniform set of working conditions" spelled out by New Jersey sitters declared that they "[would] not wash dishes except by special arrangement" ("Rules" 15). Conceiving of themselves as "skilled" industrial workers and not as dutiful daughters, sitters made it clear that "Beyond washing dishes for 15 extra cents, we won't lift a finger outside our specialty" (Richards 102).

In addition to a decent wage for services rendered, baby sitters also demanded better working conditions. In Leonia, New Jersey, sitters wanted their employers to provide "adequate heat" ("Rules" 15). Presumably, wartime rations and postwar inflation had led parents to keep thermostats turned down too low for comfort (a complaint that continued despite the fact that central heating enabled newly constructed suburban houses to be kept uniformly warm). According to fifteen-year-old Bonnie Kristoffersen of Rye, New York, "It's the limit when they don't tell you where the thermostat is and how it works, especially when it's a clock, one that goes off at 10. Some houses get so cold you have to put your coat on and roll up in blankets to keep from freezing" ("Code" 38).[7] In addition to more heat, sitters also wanted refreshments and free use of the telephone, radio, and a desk. New Jersey high school girls agreed not to entertain friends while on the job, but visits from girlfriends and boyfriends were written into the Massachusetts sitters' code ("Baby Sitters Win" 28). Finally, all agreed that when the evening came to a close, sitters must be safely escorted home ("Rules" 15).

However, while the girls sought male protection, the newsmagazines that reported on the new industry for a male readership represented babysitters as dangerously powerful. While one magazine characterized the Michigan Baby Sitters' Union as "one of the most militant of the sitters' unions," girls elsewhere were portrayed by male journalists in terms that were just as radical. One couple told a reporter for the *Christian Science Monitor* about their frightening experience with fifteen-year-old Betty Ann. "We were practically given to understand that it would be un-American and immoral for us to hire anyone one [else]. . . . [We] visualized Betty Ann parading outside the gate with a picket sign if we called in a scab" (Gross 5). Not only were teenage sitters depicted as wielding control over employers but over their children and especially sons. "Junior" appeared more often in print and in pictures than did his fictitious sister, Jane ("Entertaining" 172–73). "None of this 'wait-till-your-mother-gets home' stuff for us," Marilyn Gossman, the fifteen-year-old president of the Michigan sitters' union was purported to have said. "We require full disciplinary authority. If Junior needs a spanking, he gets it" (qtd. in J. Ellison 137).[8]

Rather than emphasizing the conflictual nature of babysitting, however, women's magazines stressed the consensual. According to an article in the *Woman's Home Companion*,

> When the union's plans were ready, she [the business agent] got herself invited to speak at the various mothers' clubs. She outlined the union's method of operation, rules and work standards to each group and asked the mothers to help with advice and comments—this was a smart move because for the first time mothers and sitters were trying to help each other. ("Sitter's Rights" 151)

In this vastly different characterization, sitters did not draw upon theories of political economy to devise a "labor code." Instead, they applied philosophical principles to develop a "Code of Ethics." Moreover, using descriptions that the editors of women's magazines probably believed their readers could understand, babysitter unions were described as a cross between a woman's club and a college sorority. "Monday evenings the union meets at Marilyn's [the business agent] house. They thrash out problems about their work and wind up with a gab session about dates, school clothes, and general frivolity. Dues are two bits a month and any surplus, after running expenses, is blown on a party" ("Sitter's Rights" 151).

Babysitter unions were short-lived. While born in a period of significant labor activism, babysitter unions also came to an end as postwar fears about communist subversion became particularly intense. Perhaps girls, their families, and prospective employers feared an association with labor union radicalism. Whatever the causes, presenting baby sitting as influenced by unionism was certainly neither helpful to the cause nor good for business. In the wake of babysitting activism, civic organizations, health departments, YWCAs, and numerous other associations nation-wide developed a course of study for the training of babysitters.[9] But to reach an audience of American mothers, experts wrote articles published in the popular magazines that were flooding American households. So did government publications such as the ninth edition of the "best seller," *Infant Care.* When it was reissued in 1951 the book included a brand new section, "You and Your Baby-Sitter." The chapter emphasized the impor-tance of informing the sitter about the location of the thermostat and providing her with lists of information and useful telephone numbers ("Infant" 46).

But the experts who emerged to standardize babysitting practices cast the sitter as a white-collar "professional" instead of as a "worker" ("Pro-fession" 85). Through advice columns, manuals, films, and vocational courses, babysitting was elevated from the ranks of industry to the status of a middle-class "career." From coast to coast, psychologists, guidance counselors, and educators writing articles for popular periodicals and professional journals argued that, as America's "youngest profession," babysitting provided adolescents with an opportunity to develop social identities as "career girls" (Bell 761). (Very seldom did experts use baby-sitting in order to glorify a maternal/domestic ethos.)

Learning how to act as the professional experts validated, required specialized training in the development of skills and sensibilities (Moore, preface; Greer and Gibbs 271). While the experts might have drawn on the unions' principles and practices, they also applied professional stan-dards of individual achievement. Articles in magazines like *Today's Health* explained that an employer's home was a sitter's "place of business" ("Fine Art" 28). Like other publications on the topic, babysitter manuals stressed the importance of punctuality, responsibility, deference, and de-pendability ("Baby Sitters Code" 539). Teen fiction was even put into service. In the short story, "Baby Sitter's Boy Friend" (first published in *Teen-Age Tales* and subsequently reprinted in *National Parent-Teacher* magazine), a babysitter, Nancy Preston, is caught in a serious dilemma. She has promised both Mrs. Cullen that she will baby sit, and Ricky

Holden, the senior she adores, a date. Coming to the realization that "she [just] could not let Mrs. Cullen down now," Nancy honors her committment to her employer and not her boyfriend (Emery 23, 37). While this story emphasized Nancy's sense of duty and obligation, it did so within the context of careerism and not family loyalty.

It would take at least a decade, however, for girls' social identity as professionals to take hold. Until then, parents derided their sitters for their selfishness. An entrepreneurial ethos disturbed one mother, who recalled her sitter: "Diane was small for her age, but surprisingly mature— at least where money was concerned. She loved the stuff. The merest hint of bonus pay, and Diane would break her date and appear at our door, urging us to depart early and stay late" (Rodgers 40). Parents typically complained that babysitters "charged too much." In the early fifties rekindled fears about the Depression and wartime rationing mingled with feelings of uncertainty about inflation and the future. The result was a noticeable decline of parents' "night out."[10] One Seattle, Washington, businessman complained that, "It costs about $5 for a couple to attend a movie. Two 94-cent tickets with all the taxes, parking expense, cup of coffee or dish of ice cream and then the [cost of a] baby-sitter" ("TV" 36). In order to cut babysitting costs, according to a University of Michigan study, some parents either stayed home and watched television or took their kids to one of the new drive-ins. But the long-term trend was decidedly in favor of what *Newsweek* in its assessment of the industry's net worth would facetiously describe as parents' "billion-dollar night out" (Brown 87).

With few other options for earning money, "sitting is the No. 1 money-making endeavor of girls between 12 and 15" (Block 38). Girls had been drawn into babysitting's informal economy because of the rewards of the postwar consumer culture. Wages earned from babysitting enabled girls to save or shop for records, clothing, and magazines now marketed just for them. "Since spending money seems to be a constant need of teenagers, this new occupation [of baby sitting] has become a thriving business, [really] a large-scale operation" (Greer and Gibbs 276). Some "Sitters save up for a spring suit, a special dress for the big dance, records, even a trip" (Stanton 151). Others were able to put aside significant contributions to college tuitions (Block 38). From age eleven to seventeen one girl earned enough money working as a babysitter (for fifty cents an hour) to pay tuition to nursing school (Church 36). Whatever they chose to spend it on, teenage wage earners could also rely less on the dictates of their parents who might have handed out an allowance but with strings attached.

The problem was, however, that the term "babysitting," which idealized postwar abundance, leisure, family, and domesticity, was a far less accurate description of sitters' social reality. So was the descriptive phrase "sitting pretty" which often appeared in magazine articles, babysitting manuals, and as titles of vocational films (Daly 156). Few teens actually spent their evenings in repose. As one contemporary explained it, "The sittees between the ages of 3 and 10 usually see the sitter as a fascinating antagonist, gifted with more energy and less authority than parents, and fair game for harassing" (Berg 98). Stories about intractable children were legion. One girl recalled that instead of "sitting in a warm, comfortable living room listening to the radio, reading, and earning money at the same time while the small charges slumber[ed] peacefully, the [four] children began slugging it out on the living-room floor" (Block 38). Some of the problems associated with child care were captured in a *Saturday Evening Post* cover illustrated by Norman Rockwell. In this narrative the babysitter obviously expects to spend the evening doing her American history homework. But the baby she is being paid to care for is inconsolable and the babysitting manual she consults is as useless as the baby's bottle (*Saturday* cover).

Mothers who had followed the advice of professionals who urged them to take "time off," often found themselves stealing "glances at the clock half-wishing they hadn't left home" (Kelder 259). Though *A Manual for Baby Sitters* (1949) described the sitter as "a strong force for happiness and stability in family life today," from the perspective of many parents, babysitters were a "strong force," but not for "happiness" (Lowndes 7). Mothers were more likely to impugn their sitters' characters than to see the problem in either personal or political terms. Yet "reading" the rebellious behavior of adolescent girls as a "text" suggests that perhaps sitters in the fifties might have conceived of themselves in subversive terms.

Unlike the activists who had drafted documents that articulated their dissatisfaction, baby sitters in the fifties expressed their resistance in more material ways. Instead of maintaining domestic order, sitters emptied the fridge, then left ". . . Coke bottles on the living-room floor" (Rodgers 40).[11] Disorderly teens also used household technologies—radios, record players, and television sets—for their own amusement and recreation.

They left a path of records on the living-room floor. Too often telephone lines were tied up by irresponsible sitters who preferred sociability to accessibility and accountability (Barclay, "Two" 40). "A Los Angeles mother lost her telephone for two years because she could not pay the long-distance bill run up by a sitter" ("Profession" 85).

Adolescent girls also expressed their resentment by drawing upon the language of their youth culture. For instance, sitters conducted "raids" on ice boxes, complained about "hour splitters" (those who did not round off to the next hour), and disparaged "wadders" (men who pressed a wad of bills "surreptitiously into her hand, as if it were something nasty that shouldn't be seen or talked about . . .") (J. Ellison 37). In a critique of permissive child rearing (promulgated by Dr. Spock whose *Baby and Child Care* had been published just one year before the sitters organized), caring for baby boomers was not "babysitting" at all, it was "bratting" (Church 37).

Despite the many drawbacks associated with babysitting, however, it enabled at least some adolescent girls to exercise their prerogatives and indulge their proclivities. A house without adults gave sitters an arena in which they could experiment. While teens in the fifties had more leisure time than those of previous generations, they also had less privacy in the suburban homes constructed with the needs of younger children in mind (May 162). As a result, "their recreation [often] took place outside the home, away from the family" (Mintz and Kellogg 167). Most typically, a babysitter would invite a girlfriend to join her at a neighbor's home which was "theirs" for the night. Far from the watchful eyes of all adults, these adolescents sought out sexual intimacy, romance, and sheer fun. Whereas in the late 1940s teenagers might have danced close to syrupy romantic ballads, the music could also get more raucous and so could the dancing. In the 1948 film classic, *Sitting Pretty*, a young suburban couple played by Robert Young and Maureen O'Hara are shocked to find that their sexually assertive babysitter (who has a crush on Robert Young) has invited her friends over to "cut a rug." They roll back the living room carpet, turn up the "hi-fi," and "jitterbug" ("Fine" 28).

While teenage girls provided the backbone of the industry, the perception that they were "not as serious about baby-sitting as they might be . . ." led some mothers gripped by the "sitter shortage" to hire adolescent boys instead (Barclay, "Boy-Sitter" 48; Greer and Gibbs 276). Boy sitters were not new; during the 1930s teenage boys who cared for the young and helped out around the house had been in great demand. (M.

Thompson 53). Teenage boys in the late 1930s had even established their own informal child-care networks. When one sitter named Lowry was unavailable, one mother explained:

> [H]e asked if we would like him to get Eddie for us. Maybe we would, but who was Eddie? Well, Eddie was Lowry's pal and he also 'minded' children. So we had Eddie. Came an evening when neither Lowry nor Eddie could come—so how about having Murray? And who, pray was Murray? Why, Murray was Lowry's brother, also a child tender with a long unblemished record. So we had Murray. (M. Thompson 24)

But forty-five male sitters "waiting for the call to duty" were no longer wanted at City College reported the *New York Times* shortly after the war ("No Men" 19). Brawny and brainy college athletes at Columbia University found jobs through the babysitter service established by the football coach. According to Coach Little (who had been a babysitter in his youth), "We've had men play in a game on Saturday afternoon, sit with a baby that night, and do a bang-up job both times" ("Ideal" 20).[12] Other Ivy League colleges also institutionalized babysitting for their college athletes. Harvard University established an employment agency so that "When parents step out in Cambridge, a Harvard athlete steps in . . ." (Richards 101).

Even though babysitting was often a petticoat monopoly, experts reported that some parents looked to adolescent boys to solve their child-care problem. According to the *Journal of the National Education Association*, "Many parents prefer them as baby sitters" (M. Thompson 565). That was especially the case for the boys who had received training in the essentials of child care taught by a variety of organizations and institutions. Instead of promoting babysitting as preparation for motherhood, vocational classes in child care offered by the Visiting Nurse Association in Needham, Massachusetts, taught boys how to diaper, feed, and burp life-sized dolls. In one month alone, the Needham facility awarded thirty-six junior high school boys their "pocket-sized certificate" ("Graduate" 107–8).

Experts felt compelled, however, to allay whatever concerns parents might have about hiring boys. The challenge they faced was reconciling prevailing constructions of gender. In the midst of broader fears about adolescent males, the first agenda was to separate the diligent from the delinquent. To this end, boy sitters were portrayed as considerate, responsible, sensible, and serious. Also described as interesting, intelligent, and "business-minded," boy sitters were unlikely to be drawn from a pool of underachieving hoodlums ("Graduate" 107–8). Still, parents clearly would not want a sitter who was more masculine than maternal. To this end, sitters were often described as possessing androgynous qualities such as "gentle determination" ("Graduate" 107–8). But if parents also had fears that their sitters were perhaps too feminine, they were reassured that "[t]here [was] certainly no doubt that they [were] entirely masculine . . . and definitely non-sissy!" (M. Thompson 24) In fact, the gender identity of little boys who shared "rough-and-tumble" adventures with their sitters would only be reinforced (Barclay, "Boy-Sitter" 48). That kind of male bonding was even celebrated in the rock 'n' roll hit, "Baby Sittin' Boogie," in which a teenage boy sings about a hip toddler, a future buddy.[13]

But elsewhere in the popular culture babies did not seem as adorable to grown men hired to care for them. Baby boomers, who loomed large in the discourse about babysitting, gave teenage girls a hard time and left grown men exhausted.[14] In a 1955 television sketch, the comedian Sid Caesar is kept on his toes. "The champ" in his charge will not "go down" for the night so that the sitter can spend his time watching a prize fight (Caesar 52). Even a light-weight ex-fighter (a veteran of 200 bouts) was no match for a four-month-old infant, according to the *New York Times*, which covered the story about a mother who failed to return home. As the former boxer explained:

> I got maybe a hundred ten pounds the best of it in the weights, but that don't help me. . . . In my time I fight over 200 fights. I fight guys like Petey Herman and Tony Canzoneri and I do pretty good. But I can't figure out this kid's style. . . . I try to rock him and he give me that clinch. I try to out-fox him but he's way ahead of me. And boy, does he fight that bottle! He knows that ain't on the up-and-up. Even when I get him flat on his back what happens? He gets up. That's discouraging. ("Veteran" 1)

At dawn, the old-time fighter conceded the match then appealed to a higher authority: the New York City Police Department ("Champ's" 27).

Beside male sitters, older, retired, widowed, or childless women provided parents with an alternative to hiring adolescent girls. Having tried out the local crop of teenage girls in Long Island, one mother turned instead to mature women she hired to watch her three young children. Though she found her sitters through informal channels, other mothers turned to the new mushrooming industry of babysitter agencies.

Employment agencies gave rise to a new professional and to her enduring stereotype in the popular culture as mature, marginal, menopausal, and masculine. Though punctual and reliable, these older sitters were presented as placing too much importance on order and regimentation. They could also be too judgmental. The writer Peter DeVries and his wife were chastised by one sitter and criticized by another. Contemptuous of the DeVries's housekeeping, one called him "Mr. Debris" (DeVries 98).

But mature sitters who had experienced the same hazards of the child-care trade as had other sitters, were a force to be reckoned with ("Profession" 79). In California, the District Appeals Court ruled that Mrs. F. Ellis could sue the four-year-old who attacked her for $10,000 in damages the sitter suffered when she broke both of her arms ("Boy" 8; Berg 52). A court in Westchester, New York, decided in favor of a sitter who had sustained injuries en route home. Under a workmen's compensation claim the court had determined that the parents were liable to pay compensation (Frey 204; "New" 35). In other parts of the country employers had faced double-indemnity penalties ("Measure" 25). As illegal employers, parents were held accountable under both workmen's compensation requirements as well as the penal provisions of the education law (Barclay, "Law" 34). To parents at the time, the litigation began to look more costly than an expensive night out. "Does it pain you to pay $1 an hour, or even more, for a baby sitter? Friend, that's nothing," explained a *Coronet* reporter who summarized the recent court rulings (Bernard 96).

In an attempt to exert a measure of control over baby sitting, teenage girls also sought legal remedies for their job-related injuries. While a Kansas family was forced to pay $500 to a teenage girl who slipped on a loose rug and broke her hip, a sitter who fell down a flight of steps was awarded $275 by a court in New Jersey. In Los Angeles, two sitters filed claims in a single week for injuries caused by rambunctious youngsters (Bernard 97). "Does your insurance cover your baby sitter?" asked *Parents' Magazine* (Berg 52). [Because] "Your baby sitter can sue you," the headline in another national periodical seemed to answer (Bernard 96).[15] Parents everywhere were being informed about sitters' rights and employers' responsibilities. Under older child labor laws that had been designed to protect children from night-time employment, babysitting was illegal. In a dozen states, laws still required (though routinely ignored) separate work permits for each employer and also placed limits on hours of work per school day. "Probably not since the days of prohibition has any law been so widely and blithely ignored as that governing the employment of part-time guardians of the young" (Barclay, "Law" 34).

Attempts to solve at least some of the problems associated with baby-sitting were undertaken by a variety of institutions and organizations. In Providence, Rhode Island, a state-wide committee consisting of representatives of the Rhode Island Congress of Parents and Teachers, the YWCA, the Girl Scouts, the Camp Fire Girls and the Bristol Police Department drew up a babysitters' code ("Baby Sitters' Code" 78). In New York City, an advisory committee on child employment established by the Board of Education studied the legal responsibilities and requirements of employers of baby sitters ("Measure" 25). The committee recommended that schools should not refer students for jobs because they could not assure either the suitability of either prospective employers or sitters ("Legal" 21).[16] The Board of Education, which mounted an educational campaign, was joined by other organizations such as the New Jersey State Safety Council, the National Safety Council, the Greater New York Safety Council and the Child Study Association, all of which issued pamphlets aimed at babysitting selection and instruction.[17]

While private and state agencies in New York tried to shape behavior, to stem the tide of law suits legislators there aimed to write new legislation. In response to a workingmen's compensation award made in nearby Westchester, Frances K. Marlatt, a Republication Assemblywoman from Mount Vernon, New York, proposed a bill to relieve parents of their legal obligations to sitters. The 1958 bill would have licensed baby sitters who, without the working papers required under child labor laws, had been committing a crime. Marlatt's bill was backed by both the Education and Labor Departments, which would have awarded badges and permits "to those qualifying as sitters . . ." ("Measure" 25).

Opposition to the proposal was led by Republican legislators who maintained that the bill "would justify invasion of the home by state officials" ("New" 35). Assemblywoman Janet Hill Gordon charged that it would open homes to inspection by a small army of state labor and education department public officials and all at the taxpayers' expense. Assemblyman Lawrence R. Rulison (a Syracuse Republican) also objected to a provision that took the authority to establish standards for babysitters out of the hands of employers and into those of state officials. "My wife is perfectly capable of setting her own standards," explained Assemblyman Rulison, himself a father of nine (Barclay, "Proposing" 49). Facing overwhelming defeat, the proposal was withdrawn and redrafted to eliminate all state regulation ("Measure 25").[18]

In a revised form the bill sailed through both houses without debate or dissenting vote. It legalized baby sitting by exempting sitters fourteen years old and older from the state's child labor laws and requirements for working papers. California and Alaska also had revised their regulations that exempted baby sitters from state statutes. Despite educators' attempts to promote babysitting as a job, the New York State law signed by Governor Harriman in 1958 declared that "baby sitting shall not be considered employment as such; thus no parent hiring a sitter will become an employer and subject to an employer's legal obligations" ("New" 35; "State" 34). Parents were protected from assuming the statutory liabilities of an employer; none would be obligated to pay workmen's compensation.

Not surprisingly, the conditions under which adolescents labored had not improved in New York or elsewhere by 1960. A survey conducted by both the YWCA and Child Labor Committee revealed that babysitters who lacked guidance and protection were still forced to "cope with abuses . . ." ("Profession" 85). What had changed, however, was the decline of the debate over babysitting and the disappearance of the history of its radicalism from the pages of popular periodicals. Parents' litany of complaints about irresponsible adolescents ceased as baby sitters seemed to inculcate a work ethic that also incorporated gender ideals. What had brought about the change in adolescent babysitters who once had been truculent but now were more tractable?

In addition to their redefined status which left them little legal recourse in at least three states, the change can also be attributed to increased competition among sitters. While labor shortages earlier in the decade had given babysitters an advantage, conditions had now become less favorable for them. In 1953 the Institute of Life Insurance had predicted that "Within the next decade many teen-agers throughout the country will no longer be able to benefit from what has been one of their most dependable and productive sources of employment—baby sitting" ("More" 25). When the adolescent population mushroomed, it generated enormous competition for jobs among the nation's estimated six million babysitters. By 1957, nearly half of all teenage girls worked as babysitters ("Profession" 85). The increased competition freed employers from their dependence on difficult sitters. With a greater choice among babysitting teens, parents were now in a better position to hire those upon whom they felt they could depend.

But girls were not only competing against each other, they were also "getting potent competition . . . from approximately 250 baby sitting agencies in the U.S. which, for a fee of 50 cents or as much as 15 percent of wages, furnish many thousands of [mature] women with full time careers." The Los Angeles Carol Agency alone had 800 registered sitters ("Profession" 79, 85). To a lesser extent girls competed with teenage boys, nearly one quarter of whom also worked as baby sitters in 1957. But this just might have been the high-water mark, as their numbers probably began to decline in the sixties. Also gone from the popular magazines were articles about the reserve army of reliable boy sitters. Boys undoubtedly continued to baby sit, but probably not nearly with the same regularity nor at the same rates seen earlier in the period.

The experts who had been providing specific instructions in babysitting at more than half of the nation's junior high schools had also had a probable impact. Sitter "employees" had received a steady indoctrination about professional responsibility by child-care experts who had provided training. Educators, social workers, and guidance counselors had urged adolescent girls to conceive of themselves as "career girls" (not workers or mothers) and of babysitting as a "profession" (not a job or their destiny). While they had not applied a revitalized maternalist ideology to justify girls babysitting, the experts seemed to have ironically contributed to a more deferential adolescent girl.

Another likely contributing factor to babysitters' docility was the impact of the popular culture in which Mary Poppins was celebrated as a new, more responsible breed of child-care provider who was neither frumpy (like the mannish sitter) nor frightful (like the rebellious adolescent girl). Babysitters also were lured into silence by a consumer culture directed at adolescent girls. Increasingly for them, earning money became the means by which they could satisfy desires stimulated by advertisers of fads and fashions in popular magazines like *Seventeen*. Teenagers who did not conform to prevailing standards were unlikely to earn even enough money to purchase a 45 rpm.

Finally, within the material culture of American girlhood, babysitting Barbie became an icon to the objectification, idealization, and gendering of babysitters. For a new generation, her child-care accessories and babysitting outfit cloaked the history of the cultural struggle initiated by adolescent girls with conceptions, expectations, and definitions of baby-sitting that differed from those of the employers and experts they had challenged. While those who followed these pioneers were less likely to organize unions and disorganize homes, baby sitting as we know it today bears the imprint of those who drew upon their youthful subculture to delineate its purposes, practices, and procedures in postwar America.

NOTES

1. For further information on the revisionist interpretation of gender discourse in postwar America, see Meyerowitz, ed., *Not June Cleaver.*

2. Research support was provided by the Princeton University Committee on the Humanities and Social Sciences, the Center for Research on Women at Wellesley College, and the University of Missouri, Kansas City. My special thanks to Research Assistants Melissa Hardin and Jane Dusselier and to the panel and participants at the 1996 Berkshire Conference on the History of Women and the National Women's Studies Association 17th Annual Conference.

3. For examples, refer to "Training High School Students for Wartime Service to Children," Washington, DC: Government Printing Office, 1943; Mary Tinley Daly, "Sitting Pretty" 156; Mary Beth Norton et al., *A People and a Nation* 818; and Karen Anderson, *Wartime Women: Sex Roles, Family Relations and the Status of Women during World War II.*

4. For more information, see "Code" 38.

5. See "Scouts to Aid Voting Mothers" 18; "Baby Sitters to Spur Voting" 18; "Baby Sitters to Aid Voters" 31; "N.Y. Young Women's Republican Club to Provide Sitters for Women Registering to Vote" 37.

6. See, for example, "Baby Sitters' Clinic Aids Church" 11; "Baby Sitters Now Help Parents Attend Church" 12; "Veterans to Test Exchange 'Sitting' " 25; and "Sunday Baby-Sitting at Church" 115.

7. See also Clark, Jr., "Ranch House Suburbia" 182.

8. See also L. Ellison, "Baby Sitter's Job" 32.

9. For additional examples, see "Will Teach Baby Sitting: Three High Schools in Rochester, N.Y.; Will Start Next Month" 17; "12 Girls are Graduated as 'Baby Sitters'; Test Skills on Life-Sized Infant Doll"; "First 'Baby Sitting' Course Graduates 19 Who are Supposed to Know All the Answers" 26; "Baby Sitters' School Awards 50 Diplomas" 24; and "Baby Sitter Drills on Safety Growing" 12.

10. J. Ellison, "Baby Sitting's Big Business Now" 39. In 1951, movie attendance declined by 20 to 40 percent in many parts of the country, which theater owners attributed to the high cost of a night out. See "TV Transforming U.S. Social Scene" 36.

11. For more information, see "Code" 38.

12. For additional information, see "Baby Sitter by the Ton" 25.

13. The lyrics and music to "Baby Sittin' Boogie" were written by Johnny Parker. It was recorded by Buzz Clifford (Columbia Records) and was on the charts for ten consecutive weeks.

14. "After watching his enormously energetic one-year-old granddaughter for five hours, a worn out grandfather declared that athletes 'Mad' Mullah and Jesse Owen could take lessons from that girl!" (Detzer 5–6).

15. Also, see "Attention" 61.

16. For further information, see "Guidance" 26.

17. For examples, see "Baby Sitting Guide Mailed in Jersey" 38; "Folder and Film Strip Aid Mother in Instructing Sitter for Junior" 32; "Safety Council Urges Talks on Baby Sitters" 30; and "Baby Sitter Manual Issued by Y.W.C.A." 64.

18. Also, see "New" 35.

WORKS CITED

Anderson, Karen. *Wartime Women: Sex Roles, Family Relations and the Status of Women during World War II.* Westport: Greenwood P, 1981.

"Attention Baby Sitters: Who Pays the Damages?" *Good Housekeeping* Sept. 1957: 61.

"Baby Sitter Drills on Safety Growing." *New York Times* 11 Nov. 1950: 12.

"Baby Sitter Manual Issued by Y.W.C.A." *New York Times* 3 Feb. 1957: 64.

"Baby Sitters by the Ton: Dodgers Football Squad to Guard 4-Year-Old on Flight." *New York Times* 1 Sept. 1948: 25.

"Baby Sitters' Clinic Aids Church." *New York Times* 13 Sept. 1948: 11.

"Baby Sitters Code." *Journal of the National Education Association* 39.7 (Oct. 1950): 539.

"Baby Sitters' Code Proposed." *New York Times* 13 Dec. 1953: 78.

"Baby Sitters Now Help Parents Attend Church." *New York Times* 18 Nov. 1950: 12.

"Baby Sitters' School Awards 50 Diplomas." *New York Times* 14 May 1948: 24.

"Baby Sitters Set Up Working Conditions Code" *New York Times* 4 Oct. 1957: 15.

"Baby Sitters to Aid Voters." *New York Times* 24 Aug. 1949: 31.

"Baby Sitters to Spur Voting." *New York Times* 19 Apr. 1947: 18.

"Baby Sitters Win Pact." *New York Times* 20 Jan. 1947: 28.

"Baby Sitting Guide Mailed in Jersey." *New York Times* 14 Oct. 1952: 38.

Bailey, Beth. *From Front Porch to Back Seat: Courtship in Twentieth-Century America.* Johns Hopkins UP, 1988.

Barclay, Dorothy. "The Boy-Sitter Takes Over." *New York Times Magazine* 26 May 1957: 48.

———. "Law Widely Ignored." *New York Times* 17 Apr. 1958: 34.

———. "Proposing B.S. for Baby Sitters." *New York Times Magazine* 6 Apr. 1958: 49.

———. "Two Problems: Teen-Agers and Baby-Sitters." *New York Times Magazine* 8 Feb. 1953: 40.

Bell, Louise Price. "Sitters Are Career Girls." *Hygeia* Oct. 1947: 761+.

Berg, Joel. "Does Your Insurance Cover Your Baby Sitter?" *Parents' Magazine and Family Home Guide* Aug. 1957: 52+.

Bernard, Will. "Your Baby Sitter Can Sue You." *Coronet* Apr. 1958: 96–98.

Block, Jean Libman. "Code for Sitters, Sittees, and Parents." *New York Times Magazine* 22 May 1960: 38.

"Boy, 4, Liable in Suit: Child Who 'Threw' Baby Sitter to Floor Subject to Action." *New York Times* 28 Feb. 1953: 8.

Breines, Wini. *Young, White, and Miserable: Growing Up Female in the Fifties.* Boston: Beacon P, 1992.

Brown, Standford. "Boom in Baby-Sitting, Our Billion-Dollar Night Out." *Newsweek* 3 Dec. 1956: 87–88.

Caesar, Sid. "So I'm a Baby Sitter?" *Coronet* June 1955: 52.

"Champ's Mother Found." *New York Times* 28 Dec. 1950: 27.

Church, Phyllis. "If I Were a Parent." *American Magazine* June 1951: 36+.

Clark, Clifford, Jr. "Ranch House Suburbia." *Recasting America: Culture and Politics in the Age of Cold War.* Ed. Lary May. Chicago: U of Chicago P, 1989. 171–91.

"Code for Sitters, Sittees—and Parent." *New York Times Magazine* 22 May 1960: 38+.

Daly, Mary Tinley. "Sitting Pretty." *Parents' Magazine and Family Home Guide* Sept. 1949: 156.

Detzer, Karl. "My Day with Susan." *Reader's Digest* Apr. 1953: 5–6.

DeVries, Peter. "They Also Sit." *New Yorker* 20 Mar. 1948: 98.

Ellison, Jerome. "Babysitting's Big Business Now." *Saturday Evening Post* 20 Nov. 1948: 36+.

Ellison, Lawrence Frank. "Baby Sitter's Job." *New York Times Magazine* 23 Jan. 1949: 32.

Emery, Anne. "Baby Sitter's Boy Friend." *National Parent-Teacher* Oct. 1959: 23+.

"Entertaining a Baby-Sitter; Leave Something for Nibbling." *Good Housekeeping* May 1949: 172–73.

"The Fine Art of Baby Sitting." *Today's Health* Mar. 1952: 28–30.

"First 'Baby Sitting' Course Graduates 19 Who Are Supposed to Know All the Answers." *New York Times* 23 Dec. 1947: 26.

"Folder and Film Strip Aid Mother in Instructing Sitter for Junior." *New York Times* 4 Oct. 1955: 32.

Frey, Richard. "Your Baby Sitter and the Law." *Good Housekeeping* Apr. 1953: 51+.

"Graduate Course in Baby-Sitting." *Life* 12 Apr. 1954: 107–8.

Grear, Isabel Wiley. "An American Custom We're Not Really Proud Of!" *American Home* June 1941: 102.

Greer, Carlotta C., and Ellen P. Gibbs. *Your Home and You*. Boston: Allyn and Bacon, 1965.

Gross, Edwin A. "Baby Sitters I Have Known." *Christian Science Monitor* 10 Apr. 1948: 5.

"Guidance for Mothers Asked." *New York Times* 3 Mar. 1953: 26.

"Ideal Baby-Sitting Service—Columbia." *New Yorker* 29 Oct. 1949: 20–21.

" 'Infant Care' Is Out in Revised Edition." *New York Times* 14 Oct. 1951: 46.

Jackson, Kenneth T. *Crab-Grass Frontier: The Suburbanization of the United States*. New York: Oxford UP, 1985.

Kelder, Robert J. "Know Where You Stand with Your Sitter." *Better Homes and Gardens* Apr. 1951: 259.

"Legal Guide Urged for Teen 'Sitters'." *New York Times* 25 Feb. 1953: 21.

Lowndes, Marion. *A Manual for Baby Sitters*. 1949. Boston: Little, Brown, 1961.

May, Elaine Tyler. *Homeward Bound: American Families in the Cold War Era*. New York: Basic Books, 1988.

"Measure to License Baby Sitters Is Killed on State House Floor." *New York Times* 7 Mar. 1958: 25.

Meyerowitz, Joanne, ed. *Not June Cleaver: Women and Gender in Postwar America, 1945–1960*. Philadelphia: Temple UP, 1994.

Mintz, Steven, and Susan Kellogg. *Domestic Revolutions: A Social History of American Family Life*. New York: Free P, 1988.

Moore, Mary (Purlong). *The Baby Sitter's Guide*. New York: Thomas Y. Crowell, 1953.

"More Rivalry Due for Baby-Sitters." *New York Times* 9 Nov. 1953: 25.

"New Baby-Sitter Bill Goes to Governor; Would Free Parents from Legal Claims." *New York Times* 25 Mar. 1958: 35.

"N.Y. Young Women's Republican Club to Provide Sitters for Women Registering to Vote." *New York Times* 9 Oct. 1949: 37.

"No Men Are Wanted." *New York Times* 4 Aug. 1947: 19.

Norton, Mary Beth, et al., *A People and a Nation: A History of the United States*. Vol. II. Boston: Houghton Mifflin, 1994.

Parker, Johnny. "Baby Sittin' Boogie." Berg Reiss Music, 1960.

Pollock, Kathryn M. "Helping the Mother-Aides." *Journal of Home Economics* 35.1 (June 1943): 31.

"Profession of Baby Sitting." *Life* 29 July 1957: 79–86.

Report, Placement Office, Wellesley College. 1 July 1946–30 June 1947.

Richards, Virginia. "This Baby-Sitting Business." *Coronet* Apr. 1949: 101–5.

Rodgers, Mary Augusta. "We Love Our Babysitters . . . But Please, No Bongo Drums." *Good Housekeeping* Aug. 1960: 40+.

"Rules for Baby Sitters." *New York Times* 4 Oct. 1947: 15.

"Safety Council Urges Talks on Baby Sitters." *New York Times* 22 Mar. 1956: 30.

"Santa Claus Sitters for Hire." *New York Times* 16 Nov. 1947: 50.

Saturday Evening Post 8 Nov. 1947: cover.

"Scouts to Aid Voting Mothers." *New York Times* 18 Oct. 1947: 18.

"Sitter's Rights." *Woman's Home Companion* Feb. 1948: 150–53.

Stanton, Barbara. "Baby Sitters United." *Woman's Home Companion* Mar. 1947: 150–51.

"State Exempts Sitters from Child Labor Laws." *New York Times* 17 Apr. 1958: 34.

"Student Agency for Baby Sitters Sets up Code and Minimum Fees." *New York Times* 19 Feb. 1951: 25.

"Sunday Baby-Sitting at Church." *Good Housekeeping* Jan. 1958: 115.

Thompson, Margaret. "Boys as Mother-Helpers." *Parents' Magazine* Aug. 1939: 24+.

Thompson, Nellie Zetta. "Baby-Sitting Is Growing Up." *Journal of the National Education Association* 40 (Nov. 1951): 565.

"Training High School Students for Wartime Service to Children." Washington, DC: Government Printing Office, 1943.

Tuttle, William M., Jr. *Daddy's Gone to War: The Second World War in the Lives of America's Children.* New York: Oxford UP, 1993.

"TV Transforming U.S. Social Scene; Challenges Films." *New York Times* 24 June 1951: 1, 36.

"12 Girls Are Graduated as 'Baby Sitters'; Test Skills on Life-Sized Infant Doll." *New York Times* 23 Dec. 1948: 17.

"Veteran of 200 Bouts Is Flattened in First Baby-Sitting Engagement." *New York Times* 26 Dec. 1950: 1.

"Veterans to Test Exchange 'Sitting'." *New York Times* 2 Jan. 1947: 25.

"Will Teach Baby Sitting: Three High Schools in Rochester, N.Y., Will Start Next Month." *New York Times* 2 Oct. 1948: 17.

Wright, Gwendolyn. *Building the Dream: A Social History of Housing in America.* New York: Pantheon, 1981.

4

Female Juvenile Delinquency and the Problem of Sexual Authority in America, 1945–1965

Rachel Devlin

Something about school always makes me want to say no. It's the authority there. I know, it represents Father to me. (Qtd. in Coolidge 630)

—Anne, age fifteen, to her psychoanalyst

On October 29, 1951, the pictures of three white, middle-class teenage girls from a suburb outside of Boston appeared in *Time* and *Newsweek*. Both magazines showed the girls smiling broadly while holding up lingerie, clothing, and pearls for the cameras, a cigarette dangling from each of their gloved hands. The place was a New York City police station; the pictures were taken while the girls, age fifteen, sixteen, and seventeen, were being arraigned for theft, running away, and "immorality." According to the magazines, the girls had stolen $18,000 from a safe in the house of a family where they were babysitting, jumped on a bus and headed for New York. "Ravenous for excitement," one reporter tells us, they first "engaged in a surrealistic shopping spree" and afterward went to several night clubs, picking up men and dropping outrageous tips to doormen and taxicab drivers along the way ("Little Women" 24). Their plan had been to buy a car and drive to Mexico, but they were spotted outside their hotel the next day by a detective carrying their description. The girls "seemed unconcerned about their plight" and told the photographers to take some "real cheesecake pictures" ("Three" 38). Both magazines ended their stories with what was called the "curtain line of the week": As the flashbulbs went off, one of the girls admonished reporters, "don't tell my father I've been smoking. He'd kill me if he knew" ("Three" 38).

One of the great contradictions of the postwar period was that the relationship between fathers and daughters appeared increasingly strained as the era of "family togetherness" progressed. James Gilbert has shown how concern about juvenile delinquency during the 1950s reflected the widespread apprehension that new forms of youth culture—including aggressive music, the dominance of working-class fashions and interest in "souped-up" cars—threatened traditional, middle-class social values (15). The female juvenile delinquent, however, posed a specific kind of challenge to America's postwar culture that has not been investigated by historians: She became a site for the expression of cultural anxiety about the authority of the family generally and of fathers specifically. Female juvenile crime began to be interpreted as a crisis stemming from the dynamics of a girl's relationship with her father, both as a parent and authority figure. I shall argue that this crisis reflected and helped produce postwar tensions concerning the appropriate nature of the father-daughter relationship in a society where girlhood was increasingly marked by social and sexual precocity and where female juvenile crime was visibly and dramatically on the rise.[1]

Searching for the causes of youthful behavior that seemed delinquent and destructive, many social commentators turned to psychoanalytic theories of adolescent development. After World War II, psychoanalysis enjoyed an unprecedented level of popularity in America, bringing ideas about Oedipal disturbance and the psychodynamics of adolescent hostility to bear on the study of juvenile crime (Hale 276–99). However, while psychoanalysis influenced ideas of youthful misbehavior, its theories proved to be particularly useful for describing and coming to terms with female delinquency. Indeed, while sociologists and criminologists continued to do much of the research on male juvenile delinquency, female delinquency became almost the exclusive preserve of the psychoanalysts.[2] The psychoanalytic paradigm for understanding female misbehavior was especially attractive during this period because it managed simultaneously to express anxieties about the social meaning of female delinquency yet contain the meaning of that behavior safely within the matrix of the family—a feat accomplished at the very moment when teenage girls threatened to break free from the family in new ways. Explaining the cause of delinquency in terms of a psychologically inescapable familial event—most importantly the Oedipus complex—rearranged but essentially left intact the critical importance of fathers to girls' social and sexual prospects: It simply rested on a language of "psychosexual" development rather than custom. This discursive construction of adolescent behavior implied that female rebellion was less an act than an "acting-out" of anger directed at her father, less an autonomous form of expression than a reaction to her familial circumstances.

Despite the fact that female delinquency received a great deal of attention from psychoanalysts, the female juvenile delinquent is a largely forgotten artifact of the postwar period. Taking their cue from Paul Goodman, who polemically declared, "our 'youth troubles' are 'boys' troubles,'" (13) most chroniclers of the period describe female rebellion as only incipient in nature and largely hidden from view. General histories of juvenile delinquency have not considered female delinquency separately, and have enhanced the sense that juvenile crime was almost entirely male by limiting discussion of postwar juvenile delinquency theory to the sociological perspective. Similarly, Wini Breines's account of white middle-class girlhood in the fifties looks exclusively at sociological and autobiographical accounts, and hence concludes that, when "defiance was . . . portrayed" young white women were "invisible" (130). The contradictory responses of the media to female delinquency during the period, which alternately sensationalized and ignored the problem, has contributed to confusion about the extent of adolescent female misbehavior and the cultural role that it played. At the very moment when *Popular Science Monthly* was attempting to use ratios of male to female delinquency to begin an empirical investigation of "why girls are so good," other national magazines were agonizing over climbing female arrest rates and reporting ever more vicious crimes perpetrated by girls (Robbins and Robbins 158).

Although girls of all ethnicities and from virtually every background were perceived to be "juvenile delinquents" when they broke the law, most of the girls who came under the purview of the juvenile court and eventually found their way into state-funded clinics were from working-class families. Because female juvenile delinquency was most often described in terms of the dynamics of familial relationships, however, it was generally represented as a problem that erupted regardless of other social conditions. Nevertheless, the types of familial dynamics thought to give rise to delinquency differed across class and racial lines. This essay argues that the mass media played a significant role in associating psychoanalytic explanations of juvenile delinquency exclusively with the white, middle-class family, thus rendering the notion of "Oedipal conflict" itself constitutive of class and racial identity.

The beginning and ending dates for this investigation encompass the years of the cold war, the period that historian Elaine Tyler May has called the era of "domestic containment" (14). The years between 1945 and 1965 were characterized by unprecedented levels of consumption, anxieties about the potential for nuclear destruction, and threats of Communist subversion. The purposes of domesticity were harnessed to the political ends of the cold war, and a stable, emotionally fulfilling family was depicted as a bulwark against the dangers of the outside world. This era has been described as a time of apparent calm, when girls' discontent percolated just below the surface, only to explode with the political and social movements of the 1960s (Breines 1). After 1965 "teen culture" was superseded by the "counterculture" as baby boomers began to question the ideological perspectives of their parents. Reflecting these changes, theorists of juvenile delinquency in the late 1960s began to shift their attention from youth culture and the family to issues of poverty, drugs, and race; and in the mid-1960s New York City dismantled the juvenile court system and replaced it with the family court system. Yet the boundaries that separate these two periods are not quite as rigid as they might appear. The staid familial containment of the 1950s was constantly in danger of collapsing under the weight of its contradictory imperatives and the ongoing rebellions these imperatives engendered: The emergence of the female juvenile delinquent was testimony to the profound difficulties that the ideal of cultural containment faced even at the height of its influence.

Girls, Delinquency, and the National Media

According to the Children's Bureau, which collected and analyzed juvenile court statistics annually, overall juvenile delinquency rates increased markedly during World War II, declined somewhat in the years immediately following, and then from 1949 onward steadily increased each year (U.S. Children's Bureau 1940–1965). Whether or not the postwar increase in juvenile delinquency warranted the sense of crisis that it engendered is unclear. For example, in New York City the overall crime rate for children under sixteen was significantly lower in 1950 than it had been in 1907 (Gilbert 68). In contrast, however, the rate of *female* juvenile delinquency in New York City, in relation to the rate of male delinquency, increased each year over the course of the first half of the twentieth century. In the first decade of the Children's Court in New York, 1902–1912, the ratio of delinquent boys to girls was approximately 60:1; by 1932 it had dropped to 8:1 (Maller 10–18).[3] Nationally, the Children's Bureau statistics revealed a less dramatic though similar pattern. Throughout the 1930s and early 1940s, the ratio of male to female delinquents remained approximately 6:1; after World War II, the ratio began to narrow. By 1949 girls represented one out of every four juvenile court cases, with the ratio continuing to move unevenly downward throughout the postwar period.

The question of female arrest and detention rates was distinctly colored by shifts in the definition of crime, the extent of surveillance, and the means of enforcement, all of which differed according to the legal and social practices of every state. Thus, a national average ratio of male to female delinquents of 4:1 included Oklahoma, where girls made up half of all juvenile arrests and Puerto Rico, where boys' cases outnumbered girls' by 19 to 1. In general, the ratio was lower in the midwestern states and a bit higher in cities on the East and West Coast (Children's Bureau 4). The overall shift in figures, however, was national in scope, the bare numbers revealing at their simplest that more girls were getting into trouble with the law in the postwar period than ever before. Even though the nature of female delinquency changed over the twenty-year period between 1945 and 1965, the bulk of female crimes were and continued to be status crimes of some sort rather than violations of the penal code; that is, they were acts considered to be criminal because of the age at which they were committed rather than the nature of the act itself. The number of girls arrested for larceny stayed between 13 and 15 percent of all crimes committed after the war, while "ungovernability," running away, sex offenses, and truancy comprised the dominant acts for which girls found themselves under the purview of the court.[4]

Some sociologists and criminologists sounded a note of alarm about the shift in the nature of female crime and the shrinking male-to-female ratio, calling it "striking" that the number of girls' cases continued to climb in relation to boys' (Barron 55). But most sociologists simply ignored these shifts, employing the logic that because girls *only* made up one out of every four juvenile court cases, juvenile delinquency was in effect male (Children's Bureau 1955). The irony of this interpretation, however, was that any sociologist or criminologist worth his credentials knew that most girls who came to the attention of social agencies, youth bureaus, and even the police were never referred to the juvenile court, no matter the infraction. Local police and social agencies had a variety of ways of "sheltering" girls from the judicial system in order to keep their misdeeds, as the saying went, "off the blotter" (Murphy 184). For instance, a former chief policewoman from Philadelphia told the Subcommittee on Juvenile Delinquency that girls' cases were routinely "adjusted" rather than treated as arrests: Out of 3,077 girls that came to the attention of the local police, only 151 were actually arrested. Most cases were simply handled by policewomen who made "home visits" and worked with the girls' parents directly, rather than going through the justice system (United States. Cong. Senate 35). "Adjustment," to the police, meant handling a case informally or discreetly either to spare the girl the experience of going to court or to safeguard her reputation; in effect girls' behavior was literally "adjusted" or changed in order to fit the normative fiction of what that behavior was supposed to look like and (statistically) reflect. In one police department the resistance was so great that a juvenile court judge had a girl come before him who had eleven separate police contacts before she was ever referred to the court: "In each instance she had been given a 'sermon' and released" (Murphy 185). Other police departments handled the problem of female delinquency by classifying cases under different names. As one police officer testified before the subcommittee, when a girl got into trouble in Louisiana, the police often recorded the case under the category of "dependency and neglect," so that the behavior would "reflect on the parents" rather than the girl herself (United States. Cong. Senate 31).[5]

The disparity between the actual number of girls who came to the attention of local agencies and the official national delinquency statistics, as well as the confused way in which information about female misbehavior was received and interpreted, speaks not only to the way in which that behavior was occluded by juvenile justice authorities, but also to the ways in which the meaning of that behavior was problematic, uncertain, and dangerous within the cultural context of postwar America. On the one hand, the partial nature of the information that was made available, especially by the police, suggests that a great deal of all kinds of behavior remained hidden from view. On the other, the rise in female delinquency rates clearly reflected an enhanced form of attention, an attempt to rigidly control juvenile social and sexual behavior. Whatever the reality of the situation, it is clear that girls were engaging in behavior that they *knew* would be considered either delinquent or threatening—behavior that the community-at-large branded unacceptable or even deviant (Gilbert 70–71).[6] Hence, the motley array of uses and repressions of official information about female juvenile delinquency rested upon both timeworn assumptions about female passivity and family-centered dependency as well as "shocking" examples of blatant revolt, alienation, and disregard for the law. The result was a constant sense of public incredulity about the female delinquent, a perception that effectively distanced her behavior as strange, while simultaneously employing it as an occasion to reflect upon the particular problems of the postwar American culture.

During the war, much attention was focused on the girls who flocked to soldiers' camps, variously called "Victory Girls," "Khaki Wakies," and "Amateur Girls" (D'Emilio and Freedman 261). The accompanying rise in sexual delinquency set off a wave of alarm, encouraged in large part by the single-minded crusade for publicity initiated by the chief of the FBI, J. Edgar Hoover. Yet when Hoover drew a general portrait of juvenile delinquency, he was equally emphatic about the concomitant rise in female crime (as opposed to promiscuity), and especially liked to employ stories about girls' misdeeds, jolting his readers into the realization of children's capacity for lawlessness. "If the violence of boys is alarming, the increasing wartime waywardness of teen-age girls is tragic," he began in an article for *American Magazine* entitled "Wild Children" (104). A girl named Jenny, he claimed, was the "apparent chief" of a gang of kids that stole a car and "set out on a wild trip to the Southwest" during which they "stole other cars, stole gasoline, slept in abandoned farms, [and] held up a liquor store" (103). Mary, another "ringleader" of a group of youngsters involved in ten burglaries, was remarkable for her ingenious methods of breaking into apartments: "[S]he would . . . slip her light sweater under the door, push the inside key out so that it would fall on the sweater, draw the sweater (with key) out from under the door, and unlock the door" (104). These, among other stories, served to illustrate the alarming dimensions of the delinquency problem—the extent of societal disruption made palpable by the fact that girls in particular had somehow slipped beyond the bounds of control, their "wildness" signifying the breakdown of the boundaries of gender as much as of civil behavior.

After the war, reports of teen-age female violence and gang activity began to punctuate accounts of the national juvenile crime wave, enhancing anxieties about the potential for adolescent female criminality. A favored way of dramatizing the scope of the juvenile delinquency outbreak was simply to list events and scenarios, one after the other, without situating the discussion within any particular framework. One *Newsweek* report, under the heading "The Kids Grow Worse" contained postings of different events across the nation. At one location, "police noted with alarm that girls were imitating their boy friends, organizing gangs of their own—uniformed in tight blue jeans and leather jackets" while at another there were "reports of a girl gang which overpowered other girls and cut off their hair" ("Kids Grow" 26). A year earlier, *Newsweek* had also reported that "[i]n Utah, a 14-year-old gun moll, after exchanging shots with policemen, complained: 'I hate cops; I wish I had got me one'" ("All Our" 28). A similar list published in *Time* magazine included the announcement that a "student riot brimmed over into the streets in front of The Bronx's Walton High. . . . [A] harried school official could think only of keeping the news from the press. . . . And this at a girls' school . . . where the situation is described by teachers and students as a 'powder keg' with girls arming themselves with knives" ("The New" 68). The stories, embedded in sequential headlines from around the country, were rarely elaborated upon, and the lack of explication or contextual surrounding served to highlight the violent nature and irrationality of the crimes. Moreover, the situational disorientation and terse descriptions occluded class and racial distinctions, effectively implicating girls in general without actually classifying who was being described.

If the perception that girls were "imitating their boy friends," or acting more like boys, surprised and bothered social commentators, it also reinforced the notion that the juvenile delinquency crisis reflected profound cultural disorientation. As the line between "high-jinks" and delinquency—between adventurousness and crime—became increasingly thin, so too did the line between traditionally male and female anti-social behavior (Gilbert 12). In 1958 James Farrell, the author of *Studs Lonigan* (1935), a book that chronicled the adventures of Studs, a sometime juvenile delinquent during the 1910s and 1920s, wrote an article for *Coronet* magazine that compared "the condition of youth today" to his own time (72). Farrell was predictably nostalgic: In his day boys fought with their fists and stayed mostly on the right side of the law. But the most profound and surprising difference between the two historical moments, was, to him, the transformation in teen-age girls. "Most of the girls in my old neighborhood were what we called 'good girls,' though a few were promiscuous. Most of the girls did not drink . . . but violence on the part of girls, or the formation of such things as girl gangs would have created a sensational shock" (73).[7] Indeed it is the unsettling sight of what he called "confused" girls, "half-children, half-adult" (77) that he saw as the weakest link in American society, evidence of a civilization failing to live up to its own values. "The emotions and budding minds within their flowering bodies," he wrote, "are too choked for one to know with sure confidence whether or not they have the potentialities to take their place as mothers, wives and citizens in the America we want to build to a higher peak of freedom and civilization" (77). Farrell pointed to the sense of underlying psychological and social confusion by adding the indiscriminate description: "Questioned by a judge as to why they did certain things, they repeatedly say: 'I don't know' " (77). The girls' confusion about their own behavior (interpreted here by Farrell as a fact rather than a strategy with which to respond to a judge) was characterized as emblematic of postwar social dislocation or disorientation; the reference to the mutually defining trilogy of mother, wife, and citizen provided a backdrop of lost womanhood and, by association, social stability.

The impression that girls were becoming more "tough," "hardened," and "vicious" was widespread (Sullivan 139). Moreover, there were several studies done during the period that contributed to the aggregate sense of social disorientation and increasing violence by reporting that many middle-class girls who never came to the attention of the authorities experimented with some form of delinquency during their adolescent years. In 1945 Austin Porterfield asked a group of college students in Fort Worth, Texas, to report what "delinquencies" they had committed while they were in high school (none of them had ever been officially charged as a juvenile delinquent). Women reported a rather surprising array of pranks and "acts of public annoyance," including "painting and flooding rooms" (18 percent), setting off fireworks in public buildings (9 percent), throwing "spitwads at others' displeasure" (30 percent), reckless driving (23 percent), trespassing (17 percent), and using abusive language (37 percent) (39–41).[8] Capitalizing on the unfamiliarity of middle-class female delinquency, articles like the one that appeared in the *Ladies' Home Companion* with the title "Nice Girls Can Be Delinquent," pointed directly to the difficulty of the concept; "nice" was no longer functioning as the obverse of working class. "This shockingly true story," the subtitle promised, "shows how young girls from good homes went terribly wrong" (Morgan

48). The sense that middle-class girls were increasingly likely to take part in behavior that had been not only male but more often working-class contributed to the perception that delinquency resulted from psychological rather than social problems. As Martha Eliot, chief of the Children's Bureau put it: "Gradually we have seen that it is not the neighborhood alone that causes juvenile delinquency. . . . [S]ome of the most serious acts of delinquent behavior have been committed by children from so-called good families and good neighborhoods" (qtd. in United States. Cong. Senate [1953] 14).

As female teenage rebellion began to be associated with psychological "confusion," delinquency was increasingly attributed to anger at adults (and by extension adult norms). Robert Lidner, commenting on a particularly violent crime committed by two teenage girls, claimed that "the brute fact of today is that our youth is no longer in rebellion, but in a condition of downright active and hostile mutiny" (qtd. in "Rebels" 64). Although Lidner, author of *Rebel without a Cause*, tended toward the hyperbolic, his interpretation of the state of youth captured the general sentiment that juvenile delinquency was a product of "deep-lying emotional tensions and stresses" which, in some way, reflected ominously on the character of postwar society as a whole (64). Within this context, the classic conflict between generations took on the quality of a war, and attributes that were especially taboo during the conversion to a peacetime social economy during the 1950s, like restlessness and aggression, lay at the heart of fears about juvenile misbehavior, regardless of sex (Hale 233). As concerns about anger, discontent, and aggression escalated, the interpretation and categorization of more traditional forms of female misbehavior, like sex offenses, began to be shaped by these more general anxieties; in the process, promiscuity was integrated into a comprehensive framework premised on the idea of the fundamental role of hostility.

This view of female delinquency as a complicated brew of confusion and hostility, however, established a vexed relationship between girls and authority figures, particularly fathers. The difficulty of describing and coming to terms with female misbehavior stands in sharp contrast to the relative ease with which social commentators linked male juvenile delinquency to specific social and familial conditions. Sheldon and Eleanor Gluek conducted the most extensive and meticulous research on juvenile delinquency during the 1950s. They compared characteristics of delinquents and non-delinquents, including physical traits, home life, and personality type, reaching a composite picture of each through statistical difference. They concluded that boys who tended to become delinquent had "an exceptional need for change, excitement and risk" and were less inhibited by the desire to please adults (*Family* 31). Parental attitudes of the delinquent boys were characterized primarily by lack of ambition and secondarily by erratic discipline. Most mothers of delinquent boys, the Glueks found, were overly lax, while a considerable proportion of both parents swung "erratically from laxity to over strictness without apparent reason" (*Delinquents* 66). The perception that boys needed to be handled more firmly and consistently was echoed by judges in adolescents' court who embraced the "back to the woodshed movement" and believed that middle-class fathers in particular allowed their sons too much "individualism" ("All Our" 28). Judge Samuel S. Leibowitz, Senior Judge of Brooklyn's Kings County Court, issued the simple edict in America in 1958, "PUT FATHER BACK AT THE HEAD OF THE FAMILY" ("Put Father" 682). A "permissive psychology," he complained, "where Johnny is rarely if ever disciplined [has] resulted in the confused, rebellious, unhappy teen-agers who flood our courts" (682).

Although not all authorities believed the problem of male juvenile delinquency could be solved so simply, the causes and cures of female rebellion were inevitably portrayed as subtle, difficult, and elusive. Delinquents in general were considered to be "confused," but the response that female delinquency demanded, the appropriate *authoritative* attitude it required, was never fully identified and only partially explained. Both the phenomenon and its solution remained unfocused and unresolved—a source of ongoing consternation rather than a call to renewed standards of conduct. In a series on juvenile delinquency called "The Shame of America," the *Saturday Evening Post* told the story of a girl named Florence—a case study in the dire results of paternal restrictiveness. Florence's father demanded that she "be circumspect in her behavior in every way" (Clendenen 18). She "wasn't permitted to attend dances even when they were sponsored by the high school" and "had been forbidden to wear lipstick." His authoritarian approach, the article explains, backfired when she eventually lashed out at him by realizing his worst fears. When the *Saturday Evening Post* caught up with her she was in a state training school for girls. "She had been sent there as an incorrigible after she ran away from home, got involved with several men and learned about beer joints and narcotic peddlers" the article reports, concluding that "heavy use of rod not only failed to keep Florence on the straight and narrow path but obviously had driven her away from it" (18). Hence the ills of repression, represented here by an antiquated notion of paternal duty, are obvious in the extremity of their results. But in describing paternal behavior through negative example, popular discourses on female juvenile delinquency failed to put forward definite solutions, leaving open the question of appropriate paternal behavior. If traditional paternal authority was to be abandoned, what was to take its place? Beyond permissiveness, what was to define the substance of paternal involvement? Acting as a sort of hidden reference point, this question haunted the problem of female delinquency.

Psychoanalysis and the Law: Girl's Term

The history of a juvenile court created specifically for wayward girls in New York City just after the war illustrates some of the ways in which definitions of female delinquency were transformed during this period. The Wayward Minor Court came to be known as "Girl's Term" after 1945, following the jurisdictional and legal expansion of the court's activities, most importantly the addition of two amendments to the Wayward Minor Act of 1925, under which the court operated (Fischer 141).[9] Girl's Term was (and remained) an "experimental" tribunal for teenage girls (Tappan 1). The court developed out of what was once a juvenile subsection of the Women's Night court, a court that dealt primarily with prostitution; in 1936 the court began meeting one day a week "to establish a new technique for handling wayward minors" (Tappan 42). The court grew steadily, and in 1944, partly in response to the problem of the "bobby socks girls," was established as a special Wayward Minor Court. The Wayward Minor Statute defined any person between the ages of sixteen and twenty-one to be legally "wayward" who was addicted to drugs, associated with "dissolute persons," was a prostitute, or was "willfully disobedient to the reasonable and lawful commands of parent." The subdivisions added to the statute in 1945 designated that anyone who "deserts his or her home" or so deports "himself or herself as to willfully injure or endanger the morals or health of himself or herself or others" was a wayward minor (Fischer 137). Girl's Term was designed to be a social court, or a socio-legal tribunal—that is, a court that used the most up-to-date psychiatric methods to diagnose and then rehabilitate what were described in 1955 as "the sexually promiscuous girls, the runaway, the undisciplined, defiant youngster, the neglected girl" (Fischer 21). Girls were brought in by their parents in 98 percent of the cases, and the sitting magistrate decided the case based on interviews with the girls, her relatives, and the attendant social worker, when available. As a socialized court it was meant only to serve this narrow function, and girls who committed any other criminal act appeared in other courts (Fischer 21).

While many people had advocated the use of psychiatric clinics in juvenile courts prior to the Second World War, very few courts actually employed them for anything except diagnostic purposes until the late 1940. Their founding, in many instances, was in direct response to the difficulty involved in interpreting and disposing of female juvenile delinquency cases (Kross 6). Hence the growth of psychoanalysis within the court system happened in a particularly gendered way. Proponents of the use of psychology or psychotherapy for the interpretation and rehabilitation of male juvenile crime often had to contend with accusations of "coddling" and "soft pedaling" in addition to a general discomfort with the incomprehensible jargon of psychoanalysis (Blanshard 60). Many complained that the use of the social sciences in the courtroom, with regard to boys, compromised the adjudication of guilt or innocence, thereby infringing upon the rights of parents, children, and especially the community at large (Connecticut 4). With girls, however, the most apparently natural, the most obvious form of intervention consisted of psychological case histories and treatment. The public dimensions of the punishment of crime were almost entirely absent in relation to female delinquency. Girls committed what were considered "private" crimes of a personal nature, and thus the public's ability to fully comprehend the nature of their rehabilitation did not seem necessary.

With the introduction of the court clinic and the influence of psychoanalysis, the case histories of girls brought to the attention of Girl's Term changed markedly. The typical delinquent who was described in 1939 as "fresh, impudent, disrespectful, lazy or otherwise beyond control" (New York City. Magistrates' Courts 21) had, by 1955, metamorphosed into a girl whose emotional makeup was "defensive, hostile, provocative and challenging," often with a few "violent temper tantrums" (New York City Youth Board 55) thrown into the mix. This is not to say that the *same* behavior merited wholly different observations during the two historical periods, but rather that the social meaning of delinquency underwent a transformation. "Freshness" and "impudence" represented an affront to a system of manners, with connotations of shamelessness, immodesty, rudeness, or audacity. The descriptions of defensiveness, temper tantrums, and hostility in the case histories of the 1950s, on the other hand, were perceived as demonstrations of blatant ill will, belligerence, even rage—all of which were informed by aggressive drives and, to a lesser extent, the potential for violence. This distinction is important insofar as it speaks to the particular ways in which demonstrations of anti-social behavior were perceived as threatening after World War II and the extent to which female *discontent*, especially within the context of the family, became particularly noticeable, if not central, to the definition of delinquency itself. From this psychoanalytic point of view, all female misbehavior became symptomatic of aggression and revolt that took as its point of reference not the disdain for authority that it once did, but the feelings of fear and antagonism that were supposedly born out of a state of psychic confusion about self in relation to authority figures.

Aggression, revolt, and "reactivity" were perceived in several different ways, but almost always in relationship to an underlying insecurity. As one court psychiatrist put it, "whether we think of aggression as a fundamental human drive or as a reaction to deprivation, it must be agreed that the aggression in the form of antisocial behavior is reactive" (Kaufman 169). A typical case reviewed in the 1950s by Girl's Term involved Jerry, who had been brought in by her father for staying out late and drinking. Jerry's father was much preoccupied with his new girlfriend, and thus, according to the psychiatric interviews, "Jerry expressed considerable feeling around what she saw as her father's rejection of his role as father" (New York City Youth Board 36). In response to this situation, according to the diagnosis, Jerry was "threatened seriously by adolescence and her repression of sexual content was prominent . . . [with] evident confusion in her psychosexual identification" (36). The most striking aspect of this diagnosis was that it was based on the *repression* of sexuality, as opposed to illicit indulgence, which originally constituted the legal grounds (especially in the Wayward Minor Act) for the intervention of the court in the first place. The fear here was not that Jerry was on the path to immorality, but that her disturbed relationship with her father was blocking the road to sexual maturity.

Psychoanalysis and the "Wayward Girl"

The crux of the postwar psychoanalytic understanding of female child and adolescent development, as construed by prominent psychoanalysts like Helene Deutsch, her disciple Peter Blos, Phyllis Greenacre, and others, was the defining nature of the Oedipus complex.[10] Successful navigation of the adolescent (as opposed to the infantile) Oedipal stage, often called the "second edition of the Oedipus complex," dictated whether or not a girl accepted her feminine nature—a nature that was described as passive, masochistic, and, most significantly, erotic (Deutsch 91–107). Girls who did not achieve these qualities usually suffered, in the eyes of these psychoanalysts, from a form of Oedipal disturbance, which resulted in regression to a pre-Oedipal, infantile relationship with their mothers. Insofar as passivity, femininity, and the erotic were understood as mutually determinative, the failure of one implied the failure of the other; this understanding rendered an aggressive personality and the suppression of mature sexuality synonymous. Casting the meaning of "acting-out" behavior within the constellation of the Oedipal family dynamic, particularly as it related to the father's role in female development, was not, however, the foregone conclusion of the psychoanalytic explanation of delinquency. Rather, this Oedipal explanation was the particular conclusion of the postwar psychoanalytic analysis of the American family. Contemporary psychiatrists and psychoanalysts working out of court clinics, hospitals, and to a limited extent in private practice, observed what they often described as a peculiarly American family constellation disabled by psychoses resulting from Oedipal disturbance. While Oedipal problems differed in their manifestation, they nonetheless shared one compelling concern: A sense of disappointment in the American father, born primarily out of a perception of his passivity and renunciation of emotional involvement within the family (Bibring 278–84). Paternal failure, often described as incapacity, was evinced by the sense or fact of his absence: emotional distance, literal neglect or cruelty in the form of the removal of love and affection, experienced inevitably by his daughter as indifference.

A good example of the ideas that informed the psychoanalytic discourse on female delinquency in case histories like those from Girl's Term is found in an article which appeared in *The Psychoanalytic Study of the Child* in 1957. Delinquent girls, Blos observed, were invariably "fixated" at a pre-Oedipal level, unable to progress through and then surmount the adolescent Oedipal stage to become a sexually mature young adult. "It is my impression," he said, "that this type of delinquent did not only experience an Oedipal defeat at the hands of a—literally or figuratively—distant, cruel or absent father, but, in addition, she also has witnessed her mother's dissatisfaction with her husband; both mother and daughter share their disappointment" (237). Blos charted two types of possible "acting out" behaviors in reaction to paternal disappointment, which, as a pair, formed the psychological foundation for a whole spectrum of female delinquencies. The first scenario was one in which the failure of the father to fulfill his daughter's expectations, highly romanticized or erotic in nature, impelled the girl to search for some kind of partner who served "to surmount in fantasy [her] oedipal impasse" (237). Blos termed this behavior "pseudoheterosexuality" (237) and included within its reach precocious sexuality and promiscuity. The alternative scenario was one in which the daughter, suffering from the "painful rejection" by her father, assumed "the masculine role" by identifying with him as opposed to her mother, thereby remaining in a pre-Oedipal relationship with the mother and failing to progress into the Oedipal situation with the father. The most prevalent form of delinquency arising from this scenario was stealing, an act considered to be aggressive and "masculine" in nature. In this schema, then, antisocial behavior in all its guises was linked to a single adolescent Oedipal moment: In the first case the girl circumvented the Oedipal by maintaining a "pseudo" or "illusory oedipal situation" through the substitution of one or many men for the Oedipal father; in the second, the girl fled the Oedipal by denying its existence and retreating to a pre-Oedipal relationship with her mother, unthreatened by the spectre of heterosexual desire.

Although a father might play various roles in his daughter's life, his presence was depicted as *critical* because he validated and encouraged her sexual development; hence, his failings in relationship to his daughter were erotic by definition. One clinical vignette, in which a girl was found "hobnobbing with questionable characters" and "running off to teen-age clubs and bars," described the culpable father as "blind" to his daughter's "pretty face" and unresponsive to "the girl's charm and beauty" (Ackerman 46). This kind of prescribed erotic recognition, however, was an unstable and precarious concept, prompting many psychoanalysts to define unhealthy forms of erotic father-daughter relationships. For instance, when describing cases where fathers were all too aware of their daughter's charm and beauty, a form of erotic recognition was prescribed in contradistinction to "seductiveness," no matter how difficult it might be to locate the exact nature of that difference (Coolidge 611). Yet in a culture invested above all in the attainment of "mature heterosexuality," the danger of overt paternal desire lay not in the threat of incestuous attachment, but in the uncanny similarity between the overly attentive father and the father who was immune to his daughter's adolescent sexual transformation. That is, a father's failure to cope with his own sexual impulses towards his maturing daughter incited a jealous attitude towards a daughter's boyfriends, which in turn caused the father to be restrictive about his daughter's dating and antagonistic towards any sign of her sexual maturity.

A good example of such an analysis involved a case referred to the Judge Baker Guidance Center in Boston. Anne, the daughter of an Italian immigrant who worked in a factory, had been referred to the clinic for stealing lipstick on several occasions. At the time of the incidents, her father, according to the psychiatrist's analysis, "had been expressing his negative feeling with increasing intensity . . . [and] there was constant evidence of an underlying seductive attitude (Coolidge 612). The father's "negativity" about Anne manifested itself in his constant criticisms, suspiciousness about dating and the demand that she abstain from feminine adornment: "He demands that Anne . . . wear tailored, unfrilly clothes, and scorns lipstick and fingernail polish" (616). The psychiatrist found this rigidity significant, and reported that "when Anne's classmates began wearing lipstick, it took a great deal of courage on her part and much arguing before he accepted her wish to wear it" (616). The diagnosis did not conclude that the father's "seductive attitude" was pathological, but rather that his refusal to allow Anne to progress at a rate commensurate with her classmates had, as in Jerry's case, arrested her heterosexual development, resulting in "ambivalency in her sexual identification." Gender confusion presented itself in the simultaneous tendency to dress boyishly—"Anne appears in slacks, her brother's jacket, and men's socks, size 11" (616)—and to steal cosmetics (a sign of her desire to be feminine).

The influence of the psychoanalytic paradigm for understanding female delinquency can hardly be overstated. Its reach crossed boundaries of disciplines and institutions, affecting the interpretation and treatment of girls across race and class, and serving to define "girlhood" in a way that superseded other forms of classification. Yet despite their general currency, psychoanalytic explanations of female rebellion were deployed, in their popular guise, as a vocabulary with which to construct and comment upon the white, middle-class suburban family at mid-century. As popular articles and a whole string of films on juvenile delinquency began to take their cue from psychoanalytic theories of adolescent development, those theories became constitutive of the white middle-class father-daughter relationship, a way to evoke and flesh out the characteristics of class identity. This development is especially significant in light of the fact that most of the girls that came before the courts and upon whom most case histories were based were from the working class. Hence, the ways in which theories of female juvenile delinquency were deployed by the media reflect assumptions—perhaps desires—about the nature of middle-class family life and its particular relationship to psychoanalytic concerns.

This middle-class psychoanalytic portrait was achieved mostly through the use of contrast and elision. Sidney Poitier became the iconic black male "juvenile delinquent" in *Blackboard Jungle*, although his character owed much more to ideas about the nature of racial struggle in the 1950s than to theories of adolescence.[11] But the black female delinquent was rarely portrayed at all, either in film or in the popular press.[12] Moreover, while white working-class female juvenile delinquents did appear in print and in film, they occupied different discursive contexts from middle-class girls. Much of that difference was construed in terms of the father-daughter relationship. Although *Rebel without a Cause* and *The Wild One* were the most famous, a whole host of low-budget, quick releases attempting to capitalize on the public interest in juvenile delinquency appeared in the 1950s, a surprising number of which were about female juvenile delinquents. *Teenage Devil Dolls, Naked Youth, Girl's Town, Teenage Crime Wave, Hot Car Girl, Reform School Girl, Teenage Doll,* and *So Young So Bad*, to name just a few, were all about girl "J. D.'s." Like the boys in delinquency films, many of these girls saw themselves as betrayed by the adult world. As "Silver" the tough reform school girl in the film *Girl's Town* (1959) said to the school matron, "you created such a great world. Too bad we don't appreciate it." Yet the picture of female adolescent defiance that was projected on screen was divided along class lines by juxtaposing, among other things, the type of family life that was constitutive of each. When working-class girls appeared in these films, their fathers were *invariably* absent (at times through death or divorce, at others he simply did not appear); when middle-class girls were delinquents, fathers were present, but weak, ineffectual, or somehow disappointing to their daughters. The plots associated with middle- and working-class female rebellion in film were inflexible on this point; and though paternal absence was or could be obliquely associated with Oedipal disturbance, it was only between middle-class girls and their fathers that Oedipal struggle was dramatized.

Probably the most suggestive and difficult father-daughter encounter to be portrayed in popular culture occurs in *Rebel without a Cause*: Judy, arrayed in a strikingly suggestive sweater, is rebuffed by her father while attempting to kiss him. Trying simultaneously to fend her off and establish his authority, he nevertheless exposes his own quandary with the self-defeating response, "you're getting too old for that, kiddo." When Judy tries to kiss him again, he actually slaps her face. "Don't worry dear, it's just her age" observes her mother as Judy runs out of the room crying. "Yeah, the atomic age!" quips her little brother, shooting his toy gun. An age, in both senses of the word, that makes this father-daughter scene explosively difficult to navigate, and, most importantly, for which no answer is given. The indeterminacy of Judy's problem with her father is only enhanced by the relative clarity of Jim's struggle with his. Jim has one demand of his father: that he stand up to his shrewish wife, that he behave like a man. The movie ends with the famous scene at the planetarium in which Jim's father, inauspiciously arrayed in bathrobe and slippers, promises to be as "strong" as Jim needs him to be. Gathered around are Plato's black caretaker and the perceptive police detective from the first night at the juvenile detention center. Missing are Judy's parents. What, one is left to wonder, would Judy's father offer her?

The popular suggestions and silences about female rebellion combined to produce a perspective on the father-daughter relationship that was dictated by the difficult imperatives of the Oedipus complex. The Oedipal relationship became, in effect, the tie that bound father and daughter ever more closely together during a historical moment when the authority of fathers was threatened by the apparent social and sexual sophistication of teenagers and ideologies of familial egalitarianism. Yet the effect of the popular representation of Oedipal conflict, I would argue, did not so much resolve the problem of the father-daughter relationship as render its eroticism manifest, however difficult and disruptive that eroticism might have been to the postwar, middle-class American family. In the process, a girl's rebellion became tied not to an angry but nevertheless autonomous self, but rather to a self-defining relationship with her father. The adolescent girl could clearly rebel from dominant, middle-class norms—but the constant invocation of the etiology of Oedipal disturbance linked the nature and meaning of that rebellion inextricably to her father, and thus brought her, full circle, back home.

NOTES

1. For an analysis of the ways in which gender roles were perceived to be converging in the 1950s, see Joanne Meyerowitz, ed., *Not June Cleaver: Women and Gender in Postwar America, 1945–1965* and Wini Breines, *Young, White, and Miserable: Growing Up Female in the Fifties*. On changes in conventions of dating and sexual codes of youth, see Beth L. Bailey, *From Front Porch to Back Seat: Courtship in Twentieth-Century America*. For juvenile delinquency statistics, U.S. Department of Health, Education and Welfare, Children's Bureau, *Juvenile Court Statistics*.

2. A 1965 survey of the sociological literature on juvenile delinquency found that sociologists had minimized the incidence of female delinquency and ignored its role in American society. See Nancy Jo Barton, "Disregarded Delinquency: A Study of Self-Reported Middle-Class Female Delinquency in a Suburb." While there were a few articles that dealt with female delinquency in the *American Journal of Sociology*, the *American Journal of Orthopsychiatry* actually printed more articles on female than male delinquency between 1945 and 1965.

3. The statistics for New York reflect, at least in part, the growth of a juvenile justice system prepared to handle adolescent girls. In Chicago, for example, where the juvenile justice system was older, the male to female delinquency ratios were less uneven at the turn of the century and therefore underwent less change over time. See Sophonisba P. Breckinridge and Edith Abbott, *The Delinquent Child and the Home*.

4. For an in-depth discussion of the difficulty of legally classifying a girl as a sex offender, see Paul Tappan, *Delinquent Girls in Court*.

5. The police were not the only or even the most important contributors to what one sociologist called the "mirage" of juvenile delinquency statistics. Local child-serving agencies played a critical role, primarily by using the procedure of referral to juvenile court selectively. Sociologist Edward Schwartz found that in 1945 children's agencies in Washington, DC, handled five times as many girls' cases without referral to the court as boys' cases, regardless of the type of delinquency committed.

6. For more information, see Gilbert 70–71.

7. The reality of girl gangs, the extent of their activities, and their interdependence with boy gangs was contested on a number of levels: Many, if not most, journalists, sociologists, and criminologists either dismissed the possibility of genuine female gang activity, or simply limited discussions to "gang-girls," usually called "debs"—girlfriends of boys in boy gangs. In the early sixties a few sociologists, impressed by the extent of female gang delinquency, attempted to perform some controlled scientific investigations into female gang behavior in working-class neighborhoods in Los Angeles and Boston. But such studies were rarely well funded and remained outside of the dominant concerns of sociological

inquiry. See Nancy Jo Barton, "Disregarded Delinquency: A Study of Self-Reported Middle-Class Female Delinquency in a Suburb."

8. Original percentages included decimal figures. Figures have been rounded off at plus or minus 0.5 percent.

9. Sources for history and philosophy of Girl's Term court include: Anna M. Kross, *Procedures for Dealing with Wayward Minors in New York City* (1936), New York City, Magistrates' Courts, Probation Bureau, *The Wayward Minor's Court: An Evaluative Review of Procedures and Purposes, 1936–1941,* Paul Tappan, *Delinquent Girls in Court* and Bernard Fischer, *Justice for Youth, the Courts for Wayward Youth in New York City.*

10. On the psychoanalytic portrayal of "normal" female adolescent development during the period, see Helene Deutsch, *The Psychology of Women,* volume 1 and Phyllis Greenacre, *Trauma, Growth, and Personality.* For overviews of postwar developments in psychoanalysis, see Leo A. Spiegel, "A Review of the Contributions to a Psychoanalytic Theory of Adolescence," Irene Josselyn, "The Ego in Adolescence," and Elisabeth R. Geleerd, "Some Aspects of Ego Vicissitudes in Adolescence."

11. Black delinquency, both male and female, tended to be linked either to racial prejudice or to activity in the civil rights movement in the South. See Hans von Hetig, "The Criminality of Colored Women," Joseph S. Himes, "Negro Teen-Age Culture," and Walter Chivers, "The Negro Delinquent." Alternatively, in the sociological imagination, black female delinquency was linked to the problem of the "matriarchal family." See E. Franklin Frazier, *The Negro Family in the United States,* and Harry Shulman, *Juvenile Delinquency in American Society.* On this question see also Robin D. G. Kelley, *Race Rebels: Culture, Politics, and the Black Working Class.*

12. Douglas Sirk's film *Imitation of Life* (1959) is an important exception; it was not, however, specifically about juvenile delinquency. Significantly, the silence about the black female delinquent occurred when she comprised one of the fastest growing groups of juvenile delinquents during the period. In Connecticut black female cases jumped from 17 percent in 1944 to 26 percent of total female cases in 1960 (Connecticut Juvenile Court).

WORKS CITED

Ackerman, Nathan W. "Sexual Delinquency among Middle Class Girls." *Family Dynamics and Female Sexual Delinquency.* Ed. Otto Pollak. Palo Alto: Science and Behavior Books, 1969. 45–50.

"All Our Children." *Newsweek* 9 Nov. 1953: 28–30.

Bailey, Beth L. *From Front Porch to Back Seat: Courtship in Twentieth-Century America.* Baltimore: Johns Hopkins UP, 1988.

Barron, Milton L. *The Juvenile in Delinquent Society*. New York: Knopf, 1954.

Barton, Nancy Jo. "Disregarded Delinquency: A Study of Self-Reported Middle-Class Female Delinquency in a Suburb." Diss. Indiana University, 1965.

Bibring, Grete L. "On the 'Passing of the Oedipus Complex,' in a Matriarchal Family Setting." *Drives, Affects and Behavior: Essays in Honor of Marie Bonaparte*. Ed. Rudolph M. Loewenstein. New York: International Universities P, 1953. 278–84.

Blanshard, Paul. *Probation and Psychiatric Care for Adolescent Offenders in New York City*. New York: Society for the Prevention of Crime, 1942.

Blos, Peter. "Preoedipal Factors in the Etiology of Female Delinquency." *The Psychoanalytic Study of the Child* 12 (1957): 229–49.

Breckinridge, Sophonisba P., and Edith Abbott. *The Delinquent Child and the Home*. New York: Charities Publication, 1912.

Breines, Wini. *Young, White, and Miserable: Growing Up Female in the Fifties*. Boston: Beacon, 1992.

Chivers, Walter. "The Negro Delinquent." *Yearbook of the National Probation Association*. New York: National Probation Association, 1942. 56–59.

Clendenen, Richard, and Herbert W. Beaser. "The Shame of America." *Saturday Evening Post* 8 Jan. 1955: 17+.

Connecticut Juvenile Court. *Annual Report*. 1944–1965.

Coolidge, John C. "Brother Identification in an Adolescent Girl." *American Journal of Orthopsychiatry* 24 (1954): 611–45.

D'Emilio, John, and Estelle Freedman. *Intimate Matters: A History of Sexuality in the United States*. New York: Harper and Row, 1988.

Deutsch, Helene. *The Psychology of Women*. New York: Grune and Stratton, 1944.

Farrell, James T. "What Makes Them That Way?" *Coronet* 43 (1958): 71–80.

Fischer, Bernard C. *Justice for Youth, the Courts for Wayward Youth in New York City*. New York: Bureau of Public Affairs, 1955.

Frazier. E. Franklin. *The Negro Family in the United States*. New York: Citadel P, 1948.

Geleerd, Elisabeth R. "Some Aspects of Ego Vicissitudes in Adolescence." *Journal of the Psychoanalytic Association of America* 9 (1961): 263–83.

Gilbert, James. *A Cycle of Outrage: America's Reaction to the Juvenile Delinquent in the 1950s*. New York: Oxford UP, 1986.

Gluek, Sheldon, and Eleanor Gluek. *Delinquents in the Making: Paths to Prevention*. New York: Harper and Row, 1952.

———. *Family Environment and Delinquency*. Boston: Houghton Mifflin, 1962.

Goodman, Paul. *Growing Up Absurd: The Problems of Youth in an Organized Society*. New York: Vintage, 1960.

Greenacre, Phyllis. *Trauma, Growth, and Personality*. London: Hogarth, 1953.

Hale, Nathan. *The Rise and Crisis of Psychoanalysis in the United States: Freud and the Americans, 1917–1985*. New York: Oxford UP, 1995.

Hetig, Hans von. "The Criminality of Colored Women." *University of Colorado Studies in the Social Sciences* 1 (1936–1946): 231–34.

Himes, Joseph S. "Negro Teen-Age Culture." *Annals of the American Academy of Political and Social Science* 338 (Nov. 1961): 91–101.

Hoover, J. Edgar. "Wild Children." *American Magazine* 136 (1944): 40+.

Josselyn, Irene. "The Ego in Adolescence." *American Journal of Orthopsychiatry* 24 (1954): 223–37.

Kaufman, Harvard S. "Aggression in the Girl Delinquent." American Journal of Orthopsychiatry 15 (1945): 167–71.

Kelley, Robin D. G. *Race Rebels: Culture, Politics, and the Black Working Class.* New York: Free P, 1994.

"The Kids Grow Worse." *Newsweek* 6 Dec. 1954: 26.

Kross, Anna M. *Procedures for Dealing with Wayward Minors in New York City.* New York: Works Progress Administration for the City of New York, 1936.

"Little Women." *Time* 29 Oct. 1951: 24.

"Major Crime Wave Due, Says Hoover." *New York Times* 11 Dec. 1945: 23.

Maller, J. B. "The Trend of Juvenile Delinquency in New York City." *Journal of Juvenile Research* 17 (1933): 10–18.

May, Elaine Tyler. *Homeward Bound: American Families in the Cold War Era.* New York: Basic, 1988.

Meyerowitz, Joanne, ed. *Not June Cleaver: Women and Gender in Postwar America, 1945–1960.* Philadelphia: Temple UP, 1994.

Morgan, Murray. "Nice Girls Can Be Delinquent." *Woman's Home Companion* Apr. 1955: 48–64.

Murphy, Fred J. "Delinquency Off the Record." *Society's Stake in the Offender.* New York: National Probation Association, 1946. 179–95.

"The New Three R's." *Time* 15 Mar. 1954: 68–69.

New York City. Magistrates' Courts. Probation Bureau. *Justice for the Wayward Minor Girl in the City Magistrates' Courts of New York: Facts and Figures for 1939.* 1941.

———. *The Wayward Minor's Court: An Evaluative Review of Procedures and Purposes, 1936–1941.* 1941.

New York City Youth Board. Monograph 3. *Reaching Adolescents Through a Court Clinic.* 1955. 21–56.

Porterfield, Austin L. *Youth in Trouble: Studies in Delinquency and Despair.* Forth Worth: Leo Ptishman Foundation, 1946.

"Put Father Back." *America* 15 Mar. 1958: 682.

"Rebels or Psychopaths?" *Time* 6 Dec. 1954: 64.

Robbins, Jhan, and June Robbins. "Why Girls Are So Good." *Popular Science Monthly* Jan. 1958: 158–61.

Schollsman, Steven, and Stephanie Wallach. "The Crime of Precocious Sexuality:

Female Juvenile Delinquency in the Progressive Era." *Harvard Educational Review* 48 (1978): 65–94.

Schwartz, Edward E. "The Delinquent in the Community." *Social Correctives for Delinquency.* New York: National Probation Association, 1946. 157–81.

Shulman, Harry. *Juvenile Delinquency in American Society.* New York: Harper and Brothers, 1961.

Spiegel, Leo A. "A Review of the Contributions to a Psychoanalytic Theory of Adolescence." *Psychoanalytic Study of the Child* 6 (1951): 375–93.

Sullivan, Katharine. *Girls on Parole.* Cambridge: Houghton Mifflin, 1956.

Tappan, Paul W. *Delinquent Girls in Court.* New York: Columbia UP, 1947.

"Three Smart Girls." *Newsweek* 29 Oct. 1951: 38.

United States. Cong. Senate. *Hearings before the Senate Subcommittee to Investigate Juvenile Delinquency.* 1944–1955.

U.S. Department of Health, Education and Welfare, Children's Bureau. *Juvenile Court Statistics,* 1946–1965.

Part II

The Girl Consumer

5

Little Girls Bound

*Costume and Coming of Age
in the "Sears Catalog"
1906–1927*

Rhona Justice-Malloy

As a young girl growing up in rural Indiana, I spent many lonely summer afternoons gazing at the glossy pages of the latest "wish book." The *Sears Catalog* was a great source of entertainment and information for me. Like all kids, I loved the pages of toys and games. Perhaps because I was a girl, the sections on home furnishings and appliances held an even greater interest. They informed me of the ideal of comfort and domestic effi- ciency that would make any house a home. My daily chore was doing the family dishes after dinner. How I longed for the latest dishwasher. I lusted after all the newest kitchen gadgets, the stoves and self-defrosting refrig- erators, the electric fry pans and no-stick cookware.

As the oldest child and only girl, I learned the domestic skills of canning and cleaning from my mother and grandmother. While not deprived of modern conveniences, we often made do with hand-me-down pressure cookers and baby bottle sterilizers. I yearned to be modern. In the rural Midwest the standard for modernity in those pre–mall super- store days was the *Sears Catalog*. From it I learned what I thought was the decor of the modern home. A daughter of the rising middle class, I studied taste in home decorating. From the pictures of living rooms and bedrooms coordinated in tasteful avocado and gold, I practiced choosing pleasant patterns and colors. I discovered fabric patterns and La-z-boys, pleated curtains and valances, Singer sewing machines and Kenmore appliances.

There was also a secret side to my gazing at those beautiful pages. On the verge of puberty, I was introduced to training bras and sanitary belts, girdles and garter belts and Clingalon hose. I looked in amazement at the conical shaped brassieres, high heels, and coordinated outfits with gloves and purse to match. All that I knew and understood about personal fashion came from those pages.

I even practiced my domestic and fashion skills. When my mother finished with the catalog, I carefully cut out the photos of underwear models for my paper dolls. Those beautiful models bound in elastic girdles and eighteen-hour bras became my standard of perfect woman-hood. They possessed the body I longed to achieve. I cut out ensembles, perfectly coordinated, for my paper dolls to wear. Sometimes I cut out husbands and children, though they were not nearly as interesting to me, for my bound beauties. I clipped out furniture and the newest, most efficient appliances. I designed rooms, fully furnished with lamps, rugs, and sofas. I found that I could furnish an entire domestic world from the catalog's pages. I spread them out under the dining room table, where I could protect them from my younger brothers.

When I became a teenager, with a bit of money of my own earned from selling vegetables from my garden, I ordered clothes, underwear, and bathing suits from the wish book. What a memorable day when I became a "junior" and ordered my first training bra and garter belt. While British designer Mary Quant and Yardley defined the youth move-ment in fashion on Carnaby Street in London, I was still ordering from the Chicago-based catalog, as were most of my friends. As much as we loved *Vogue* and *Seventeen*, the *Sears Catalog* was one of few available sources of merchandise and, by extension, an expression of fashion. Per-haps more than any other mail-order catalog, *Sears* shaped our ability to function as consumers. My girlfriends and I started off with little spend-able cash, but our consumer patterns were influenced by the merchandise in those pages as well as our ideas of the perfect, tastefully decorated home, functional kitchen, and well-dressed family.

I was fascinated with all the varieties of underwear for women and the "training" versions offered for young girls. There were brassieres, dress shields, garter belts, sanitary belts, girdles of all varieties. There were panties, camisoles, and a kind of bloomer called "petti-pants." There were half-slips, full slips, nursing and training bras. For every article of under-clothing offered to the adult woman, a junior counterpart existed. They were generally smaller, softer, and daintier, but their power to bind a girl's body and engage her mind was no less efficient. I was unaware then that the reason I was so fascinated by the training bras and other items of underwear is that they are in many ways the bindings that hold together a culture's image of what it means to be a girl looking forward to growing into a woman. We know to be true to what we understand; we know what we are by what we wear under our outer disguise, by how we are bound by our underwear.

Generally in our culture, the wearing of a brassiere, the binding of the breasts, is a sign of maturity for a girl or young woman, as is binding the abdomen with girdles, control-top panty hose, and lycra panties. While there may be times when such binding is necessary and appropriate, why do we, as women and girls, cherish and anticipate this restriction? What does the binding of the young body mean and what can it tell us about our culture? What is this potency of the young female body and why is it so powerful that it must be contained? How are we, as girls, taught the etiquette and practice of this binding? How are we taught to accept it? Most importantly, how do these bindings give shape and validity to the way we move our bodies?

Movement is a basic element of life itself, and as women, our practices of binding affect movement. What is that effect and how has it changed over time? I am concerned here with what a given social order perceives as beautiful and natural and how it schools its young females in ways to achieve that perception.

I will explore this theme not from my own experience but from what might have been a girl's experience growing up from 1906 to 1927. Though this girl lived in a time earlier than my own, she may have grown up as I did, in the rural Midwest, the daughter of a middle-income family, com-fortable yet economical. Perhaps her people were farmers. The house was kept up not by servants but by mothers and daughters. She and her family were educated and not entirely unsophisticated. They went to the movies. They knew Mary Pickford and Cecil B. De Mille. They were well aware of the great Paris clothiers. They even knew of cubism and the tango. But when they shopped for the newest sewing machine, most efficient washing machine, or a new porcelain kitchen stove, they looked to Sears.

That girl probably learned, just as I did, of becoming a woman in body and spirit from those very same catalog pages. What did it mean to her to be bound and corseted? The pages of *Sears* can give us a better understanding of her experience.

In 1906, Sears was the largest mercantile institution in the world. Their mail-order catalog offered thousands of products for the home and farm. An entire family and estate could be clothed and furnished from its pages. It gave testimony to the fashion and consumer preferences of the day. It offered not just what Sears hoped consumers would want and buy but what they did indeed want and buy, which makes the catalog an important tool for studying the relationship between costume, culture, and consumerism.

But we must be careful not to assume that we will learn much simply by gazing at the *Sears Catalog*, except to reinforce the aesthetic prejudices of our own time. We need to have a method of viewing, if we want to take meaning from clothing. I propose a method of looking at the historical design of clothing for girls and young women in a way that will tell us something of what their culture believed was natural and beautiful. I also believe that the growing girl learns from the culture itself to prefer and desire what her culture considers natural and beautiful, specifically in fashion clothing, and more generally in the art of design. It is quite easy to observe a figure, such as the S-shaped, corseted silhouette of the Gibson Girl of 1908, and call it "unnatural." Of course, so it is from our viewpoint. But as Anne Hollander reminds us, though images and styles change throughout history they do fulfill a fundamental visual need— "the need to see the human world, both known and imagined, in the forms of lifelike images" (xii). In other words, in 1908, the Gibson Girl appeared natural and beautiful even if her naturalness was imagined by that specific culture and designed by its preferences.

Indeed, clothing is much more than fashion design. In many ways clothing defines who we are as a culture and how we move as individuals within our culture. It informs the way we see ourselves and others. It dictates how we move within our personal and private spaces, as well as in the public realm.

While Hollander is discussing the relationship between clothes and visual art, she makes a further point in *Seeing through Clothes* that is pivotal to the methodology of this essay: "Considering their importance for the individual self-image, it might seem right to think of clothes as entirely social and psychological phenomena, as tangible and three-dimensional emotions, manners, or habits" (xv). Hollander contends that clothes, like paintings, present themselves to the eye immediately and totally. It is the image itself that first strikes the observer. To approach the visual aspect of clothing merely as a social or psychological construct is essentially to destroy it. We must understand that we take in a visual subject through the eye before we scrutinize it with our brains. Preference must first be given to the act of seeing, since this act mediates between being and knowing. Hollander writes: "Because they share in the perpetually idealizing vision of art, clothes must be seen and studied as paintings are seen and studied—not primarily as cultural by-products or personal expressions but as connected links in a creative tradition of image-making" (xvi).

Image-making and consumerism go hand in hand. In many respects marketing depends on image-making. Advertising is nothing but image-making. So, when we study girls' culture and the influences of fashion design, where better to look than to *Sears Catalog*? After all, by 1906, this mail-order operation boasted that it was the largest in the country. Not only can we learn about how the girl's body was shaped in the early part of the twentieth century by reviewing the *Sears Catalog*, we can also learn what merchandise was available to help her achieve that body. We can understand how the visual ideal was marketed and consumed. Because of the wide range of merchandise offered, we can also look at all types of products that affected how the young girl used her body to accommodate herself to society's ideals and to prepare herself for the physical appearance she aspired to achieve as she grew into womanhood. Domestic artifacts, such as those found in the *Sears Catalog*, tell us how that look was reinforced and finally achieved. These were the products used by young women and girls in their daily life.

How might we analyze the images of girls and young women in the *Sears Catalogs*? How can we interpret the effect of fashion design on their bodies?

A large number of works, commencing with James Laver's *Modesty in Dress* (1969), have been published recently which contemplate the body, especially the female body, in its relation to motion and its place in culture.[1] One such work, *Space, Time, and Perversion: Essays on the Politics of Bodies* by Elizabeth Grosz, is among a sizable collection of others. Despite the new scholarship, Grosz admits: "The tools and techniques by which we can think corporeally are still in the process of being developed. Only recently has the body been understood as more than an impediment to our humanity; and it is even more recently that feminists have come to regard women's bodies as objects of intense wonder and productivity." (3).

Center, Point, and Sphere

The model of the human body in culture that I will use is based upon the work of August W. Staub, who began his studies of bodies in space as early as 1973 in a book on theatrical directing. In his recent paper, "The Body Enthymemic: Center, Sticking Point, and Sphere," Staub resists the idea that the body can be "read" because motion itself is the defining rhetoric of the body. To read a body as a site of meaning is to deny its most basic element—action. Further, he argues that the meaning of human gesture and motion, indeed the body itself, is locked within a culture. Staub, like Hollander, contends that the body must be granted its local nature. He proposes a method of studying the body he calls a kino-rhetorical approach. What Staub offers is a systemic way of discussing the meaning of movement that acknowledges the particular and local influence of a given culture. He writes:

> [H]uman motion grows out of the body, which has limitations on what it can do. Once we recognize these limitations and understand how they are applied, we can greatly enlarge our understanding of how a given culture behaves physically and what drives the culture to do as it does. ("Body" 2)

Staub's methodology is particularly helpful because it allows students of motion, gesture, and clothes to avoid translations of a system into "our own or of judging and adapting another culture's system to our own concept of the beautiful and the graceful" ("Body" 3). Instead, what Staub and Hollander encourage the scholar to do is to find a way to view a given culture with as little prejudice as possible. This is not easy to do, and girl's culture in particular presents unusual challenges. We must first recognize that the culture of girls is constantly in a state of flux. From the ages of seven to seventeen, the girl grows and her body experiences major transformations. To attempt to pin down her culture or her body at one particular site or to attempt to read her in one particular syntax is not, I think, particularly enlightening.

So, what is a kino-rhetorical approach to the body? It begins with three kinetic figures Staub calls center, sticking point, and kinesphere. Center is the easiest to understand. We all have a sense of center because we are all subject to gravity, and our bodies are poised upon a fulcrum of gravitational distribution or else we would never be able to stand upright. While every person has a center of gravity, the exact location varies according to body type and size. The search for center is complicated not only by body type but by the conceits imposed from cultural influences, especially fashion. For instance, the Gibson Girl of the early twentieth century is deliberately thrown off center by the fashionable S-shaped posture. Today, many young girls have difficulty using center flexibility because they have been taught to "stand up straight and pull in their tummies." The result of learning that cultural lesson too well is that they are convinced that they should not relax their center even to gain the flexibility to control all of the powerful forces stored therein. This contemporary restriction on center is made in the name of physical beauty and is an example of how a local culture can affect how a person moves (with more or less power) and, thus, how a girl produces power with her body.

All societies must give some attention to center, but some cultures stress another bodily theme: the sticking point. This is defined as the movement of a part of the human body to a point at which it cannot progress further, unless it moves in another direction or another bodily part is moved. Perhaps the simplest example is the raising of the hand, palm forward, until it sits upright on the wrist. The hand cannot be moved any further, unless the arm or the whole upper body is moved. An attempt to move beyond the sticking point will throw the entire body off balance.

The most protean of the body's figures is the kinesphere. Staub takes this term from Rudolph Laban's *The Mastery of Movement.* Contemporary sociologists and psychologists use the term "personal space." Architects speak of proxemics. The Laban term is useful because of its movement implications. Personal space or the kinesphere is that space surrounding our bodies that we require in order to feel individualized, in order to spread ourselves out. The kinesphere varies greatly both geographically and culturally. It is also portable. We move in it and we carry it about with us. Among the more famous acknowledgments of the kinesphere is Leonardo da Vinci's famed icon of man encircled.

Girls' Bodies and Bindings: "Sears Catalog," 1906–1909

Using center, sticking point, and kinesphere as descriptive tools, I shall turn to girls' and women's fashions as found in *Sears Catalog*, 1906–1909, and in particular what these catalogs tell us about how girls were bound physically in the early twentieth century.

It is striking that the early catalogs made little distinction between girls' and women's fashion. Girls' clothing for the ages of five and under was featured in the infant's section. From ages seven to fourteen, girls' and women's clothes were placed side by side. In short, in the catalogs there was no long period of girlhood. From age seven on, a girl was simply portrayed as a small woman. This concept was made clear by the fact that styles for older girls were called "misses" and were sometimes also featured for slender or petite women.

The fact that girls were considered simply "little" women was made clear in the design of underwear. In 1906, the basic undergarment was the corset, which was intended to force the girl into being a woman, to "train your child's figure when young" (*Sears*, 1906, 1017). The assumption was that the woman was already present in the girl, but was not sufficiently disciplined to have a culturally beautiful body. The corsets that offered "to train" the bodies of girls twelve to seventeen years were virtually identical to those shown for women.

The corset of 1906 rode just at or below the nipple line. It did not hang from the shoulders but was laced either in front or back or fastened with hooks. Bone and steel stays were sewn vertically into the corset so that it thrust the sternum and bosom forward to its sticking point: the point where the sternum could not be thrust any further forward. The waist was pinched to an extremely narrow sticking point, just slightly larger than the circumference of the neck. The bones and steel then pressed on the pelvic region, forcing it backward to its sticking point. The final effect on the kinesphere was the famous S-shape we call the Gibson Girl. The corsets designed for "misses" or young women repeated this same shape. Those designed for younger girls were modified only in that they rode a bit higher under the arms because there was less bosom to thrust up, and they were not cinched so tightly around the waist because the waist was already smaller.

The way the corset rearranged large sticking points in the sternum and pelvis, so that the upper body was pushed dangerously forward of center, emphasized a tendency to move leading with the breasts. In order to balance the forward thrust, women would have to push the pelvis back, making the breasts and buttocks exaggerated and lacking in a relationship to center. The female body was at once idealized and weakened; in order to reinforce the cultural ideal, young girls were made to bypass any sense of center by the age of six or seven. Early in life the girl's body was literally thrown off-center by her corset. She spent the years as she matured into womanhood learning to compensate for this instability.

Wearing of the corset was augmented by all manner of trusses, supports, and braces to "improve" the posture. The body braces were said to "restore a woman's general health, well being and comfort" (*Sears* 1908, 805) and could be worn over or under her corset. Such braces were also popular for children, young girls, and growing women to ensure a "healthy posture." In short, they were intended to aid in maintaining the S-curve kinesphere and to substitute for the lack of balance brought on by being deprived of a reasonable use of center.

Even with the strict bracing and corseting, if the slender young woman was not able to achieve the proper roundness, there were many products she might employ to achieve the figure desired. There was the "Famous H. and H. Bust Form," described as giving the "natural" breast. This was a single pad made of rubber in the approximate shape of a half-moon. It was slipped inside the front of the corset to achieve the desired mono-bosom effect. The goal was to make cleavage undetectable. As advertised in the 1908 catalog: "The celebrated H. and H. Bust Forms are now so perfect that they cannot be detected from the natural bust, whether by sight or touch. . . . Positively the only device which perfectly simulates flesh and blood" (794). It was especially appealing to the young or slender lady: "Why then wear heavy pads, wire forms or be flat chested, all of which are so unnatural and plainly detected when so natural a form is within your reach?" (794).

If the young lady needed some help from behind, she might have added a bustle to her underwear, which was used to "add grace and symmetry to the figure, allowing the skirt to hang in graceful folds" (*Sears*, 1908, 998). Instead of the wire bustle, she might have tried a "hip form petticoat" designed for the slender woman. It produced "a well-rounded, graceful figure, such as nature herself intended" (*Sears*, 1908,

1114). The bustle, which was attached to the inside of the petticoat skirt, was presented with the argument that "there is no more excuse for an angular, ungraceful form" (*Sears*, 1908, 1114).

All of this complicated underwear functioned to remake the body into the ideal woman by changing the relationship of her sticking points (specifically breasts and buttocks) to her center so that a "beautiful" S-shaped kinesphere could be achieved. At the same time, the underwear hid those physical aspects (legs, stomach, separated breasts, menstrual processes) which might give a lie to the idealized shape of a woman's body-space. The girl's body parts, breasts, hips, and waist, were hidden before they were fully formed, essentially robbing her of a legitimate sense of what it felt like to be centered physically. While the underwear bound the young girl's body so that it was "trained" into a new use of center and sticking points, the outer garments were designed to structure to the fullest extent the S-shape of the kinesphere.

The gathered bodice or blouse was designed to give a distinct mono-bosom look. To enlarge on the full-blown bosom, the shoulder was increased with puffed "leg-o'-mutton" sleeves. Skirts were generously curved at the hip. Hems were full and ankle-length for women, slightly shorter for young women. Skirts for girls of age six or seven were just below the knee. Collars were often yoked and high and the hair was worn high on the head. Each of these fashion features contributed to maintaining the ideal of a girl, beautiful but ethereal, not firmly planted on her feet. In an age where boys were taught to "stand up straight on their own two feet," girls were encouraged to float in an S-shaped kinesphere, to be "flighty" creatures.

The young girl's hem met her sphere about three-quarters of the way down her body just at the knees. Her hair was worn closer to the skull. However, the huge bows and ribbons she wore extended out toward her kinesphere. In preparation for her role as a young woman, all the outer garments and accessories followed the lead of the underwear by throwing a girl's body off center. Adding to this effect, hair ribbons and flounce petticoats under draped skirts supported the impression that she floated within her personal space as did her older sister. From an early age, girls learned that they must be light on their feet. They were taught to glide across a room. These lessons were reinforced by the fashions they wore. Girls were not boys; they would not grow up to stand on their own two feet.

The corset especially restricted movement in the shoulders. In costume design for film and theatre it is known that generally the higher a garment is cut under the arms, the greater the range of movement in the shoulders. When we look at the designs of 1908, we notice that the garments, like the corset, were cut low under the arms, thereby severely limiting the range of motion of the shoulder. If the girl wished to move her arm at all she moved from her elbow rather than her shoulder. Thus, the elbows were bent toward the edge of her personal space, further stabilizing her. Conventional costume theory has regarded the Gibson Girl shape as a restrictive one, but when we look at it in terms of center, sticking point, and sphere we can see that although there were definite limitations to the range of movement, it also had its means of compensating and finding movement and stability because people, no matter what the cultural ideal, must move.

When we examine the actual poses of the girls in the catalogs of 1906–1908, we discover that the S-shaped form was symmetrical and balanced and had a kind of kino-rhetorical logic. While it was not easy for the young woman to raise her arm at the shoulder, domestic appliances were designed in a way that made such movement rarely necessary. The latest in washing machines offered in the 1908 catalog was called "The Superba Ball Bearing Washing Machine" which used a hand-operated mechanism that swung from side to side with a limited range of motion. Its advertisement in the catalog featured a drawing of a young girl operating the machine as her proud mother looked on; the caption read: "Mother goes right on with her regular work while her little helper finds it so easy to swing the Superba to an fro that she is glad to do it." (*Sears*, 1908, 583). The point is that aspects of a culture do not exist in isolation. What was worn on the body had a direct influence on the design of objects that surrounded that body. This is important to the development of the young girl because she inhabits a world of objects designed to accommodate the mature female form. Over time, this worldview will teach the young girl to perceive those forms as natural, desirable, and beautiful, and she will learn to accommodate those preferences. The practice of Chinese foot binding is a striking example of how an aesthetic preference literally crippled the feet of girls and young women. Yet, they somehow came to accept the practice as attractive and desirable.

It is impossible to tell to what extent fashion influences culture or culture influences fashion. Still, an apparent relationship exists between the two in an array of cultural artifacts. For example, the S-shaped sphere is repeated again and again in the pages of the *Sears Catalog*. No doubt, the young girl, scrutinizing the pages of hair brushes, home remedies, and appliances, would at least subliminally have come to recognize this shape as realistic and appropriate as an ideal towards which she should aspire.

The pages of the 1908 catalog are constantly reminding us of the silhouette worn by young women of the day. For example, the Oxford Cylinder Talking Machine featured a bell, called a "flower horn," which mimicked the shape of the young woman's skirt (194). The "flower horn" was named after an organic or "natural" shape. It does not seem unreasonable to assume that the bell shape of the skirt was considered to be organic and aesthetically desirable. This is but one of many examples of how the shape worked its way back and forth from what was worn on the young woman's body to the objects she used in her daily life.

The idealized female body was repeated again and again, as in the shape of the double-globed banquet or parlor lamps (*Sears*, 1908, 363), in the cupid-faced "boudoir alarm clock" (*Sears*, 1908, 344), and in the mirrored hall rack (*Sears*, 1908, 422). The "rose" pattern on the handle of the silver stocking darner resembled the mono-bosomed bodice (*Sears*, 1908, 328) as did the baby's "Birthday Souvenir Spoon" (*Sears*, 1908, 328). As the girl lived with these images and artifacts she learned to see them as beautiful. She also learned how to achieve the visual preference of form by watching older females whose dress and manners reinforced the preferred shape.

Transitions in Girls' Sticking Points, Centers, and Spheres: "Sears Catalog," 1917

Although the *Sears Catalogs* of 1906 and 1908 featured clothing and accessories for young women and girls, it is apparent that the target consumer of the catalog as a whole was the man of the house, with many more pages devoted to farm implements, and animal medicines than to women's clothing and toiletries. In 1917 all this changed. This was the year the United States entered World War I, and Sears was quick to pick up on the fact that women would be the active consumers of goods while their men were off to war. Many young women would fill the jobs vacated by the men fighting in Europe. These young women would earn their own money; many would make good wages. After their obligations to domestic expenses were met, they would find themselves with spendable cash, money to be spent on luxuries, money to be spent on fashion.

The first page of the 1917 catalog offers testimony to the recognized importance of the consumer power of women:

OF SPECIAL INTEREST TO WOMEN

To the women of America we could well dedicate the larger part of this 1,490-page book. To their buying intelligence is largely due our success—our rise from an obscure beginning twenty-two years ago to a foremost position among merchandising institutions. . . .

And now we come with this new catalog displaying the seasons' offerings fresh from the hands of the designers. We call special attention to the first 300 pages with their fashionably made suits, new models in full flaring coats and skirts, dresses in delightful patterns, blouses in dainty new materials, hats in new shapes and beautiful color combinations, dainty undergarments, correctly fitting corsets in the latest models, pretty neck wear, stylish gloves and hair ornaments—everything for women, misses, growing girls and small children right down to the new born babe. (1)

The catalog delivered on its claim to offer value, variety, and fashion. The volume began with color plates of juniors' and misses' spring dresses. "Juniors" was a new market category for girls aged thirteen to nineteen. Seven full pages offered hats for girls and young women. These pictures show active girls—no longer posing prettily as they did in 1908. The models for youth fashions were shown pursuing a variety of activities. They held in their hands tennis rackets, golf clubs, riding whips, and yo-yos. They were often seen with bicycles or in the stable with a favorite quarter horse. This change in physical activity meant that there was a rearrangement of the female center and shape. The new visual preference reflected a desire for mobility and action. Girls were no longer floating within their spheres. They were on the move at home and in public.

Dresses were categorized by where they were worn. "Working dresses" were featured, as well as "porch dresses." The young woman of 1917 spent much of her time out-of-doors or generally away from the home. One would expect that in 1917, on the verge of women's suffrage and in the midst of World War I, clothing would be by necessity less restrictive. However, the fashions marketed in the 1917 *Sears Catalog* show this was not the case. Even though young women had entered into public life, the professions and sports, their clothing was in fact hardly less restrictive. Corsets continued to restrict the body while high-heeled shoes threw it off center and sheer stockings exposed it. Anne Hollander observes, "Corsets, famous for being discarded, were in fact simply remodeled; pressure was applied by tough elastic material rather than wholly by steel and canvas. Shoes had higher heels than ever . . ." (338). Everything contributed to the vulnerability and instability of the young woman's body. However, as in earlier periods, young women showed a remarkable ability to adapt to the restrictive requirements of fashion while pursuing activities they enjoyed such as sports and dancing.

When we closely consider the female body of 1917 in terms of shape, it becomes apparent that this was truly a period of transition. Underwear and outerwear seemed at odds. The corseted, streamlined body revealed a form that had a relatively stable center—erect and in a neatly stacked vertical line. In underwear we see a shape that was nearly a perfect cylinder. When we look at the fully clothed body, we see a seemingly contradictory shape that was formed more like a pyramid than a piston. The shoulders were narrow, while the hips were quite full. The mid-calf hemline enhanced the triangular silhouette. Center, therefore, was shifted much lower on the body, allowing for increased freedom of movement. Indeed, what we observe are centers, sticking points, and especially kinespheres that more closely resemble those of the males of the culture.

Sticking points shifted from the torso as seen in the S-shaped silhouette of 1908, to the extremities—particularly the hands and feet. This shift was important because it described young women who "did" things for themselves. They were active participants, rather than passive spectators or objects to be observed. In contrast to the girls of 1908, whose hands were often hidden behind the waist (accentuating the elbows), the girls of 1917 were shown with their hands in front of them. Many girls and women held objects in their hands, such as spades, shears, and watering cans. We also see an emphasis on the feet and ankles. Most often girls were shown in a stance with one foot flat on the floor and the other pointed, working the sticking point at the ankle. This working of the joints in the legs attests to the fact that the girl of 1917 was a mover, active with her hands and her feet, able to move about with relative ease at home and in public.

In 1908, a young woman's garments rooted her within her sphere, but she did not move freely within it. Her sphere was a defining space in which to pose. In 1917, the young woman's hands extended out toward the edge of her sphere. Her feet and toes were pointed to delineate her personal space. She often held a parasol which described the edge of her sphere or could be used to puncture it. Golf clubs, tennis rackets, and riding whips served the same function. In 1917, the young woman moved freely within her sphere and her stance implied movement. She reached for a bird in flight (*Sears*, 1917, 6) or butterflies floated just beyond her reach (*Sears*, 1917, 2). Rather than merely posing for the picture, the young woman, we feel, is caught in a moment of action. She was a working girl.

Young girls and women continued to be heavily corseted. The corset rode well below the breasts and extended nearly to the knees. It did not pinch the waist but rather confined the hips. Sitting would have been uncomfortable. Specially designed corsets, which freed the hip bones for some motion, were advertised for the active girl because they gave "ideal support for dancing, skating and sport wear of all kinds" (*Sears*, 1917, 125). There were special corsets for children up to twelve years old as well as for growing "misses" from twelve to seventeen. The effect of the corset was to slim the hips, loosen the waist, and create a nearly cylindrical or piston-type shape, one that approached the ideal male shape. The breasts appeared unbound or the young lady might have worn a "bust confiner," also called a "brassier," although, in this period of transition, the mono-bosom and mono-buttock were still seen.

Underwear for young women was still constrictive. Outerwear was more relaxed. Dresses were belted, but the waist was not cinched. Drap-ing, tiers, and tunics created fullness at the hip line, which seemed contra-dictory to the hip-confining corsets worn underneath. While the transi-tion from off-centeredness to a more centered body was gradual, it was no less necessary if young women were to perform their new wartime tasks. Though the underwear remained restrictive, outerwear relaxed. The sticking point of the bosom was brought closer to center as were the buttocks. The changes were especially apparent in girls' clothing, where a more relaxed quality led to a mid-calf hemline. Girls could "stand on their own two feet" and move about with greater ease than a decade earlier, but their underwear still "bound" them to the social ideal of beauty.

The style of many domestic utensils mirrored the shape and sphere we see in fashions for young women and girls. It pointed towards the sleek shapes in clothing by 1927. In general, bottles for medicines and toiletries were simpler in design with fewer curves. The design patterns on cloth were often more geometrical, based on stripes, squares, and plaids rather than curved patterns. Women's necklaces, called "La Valliers," featured a triangular or tear-drop style (*Sears*, 1917, 546). The patterns for silverware were streamlined and simpler. Phonographs no longer sported the Flower Horn. They were simple boxes with the speaker mechanism contained within (*Sears*, 1917, 798). Just as in the 1900–1910 decade, we find that the artifacts of daily life, especially those associated with girl's and young women's lives, echoed in shape the idealized female form, reinforcing the ideal as natural, lovely, and inevitable. Of course, this was the new ideal of a young woman with a greater range of movement available than ten years earlier.

The most striking resemblance to the new shape can be seen in the form of the oil lamps, also known as hurricane lamps (*Sears*, 1917, 1198). Their shape, narrow on top and widening toward the bottom, was similar to the ideal female silhouette. This shape was seen often in the design of the electric light bulb (*Sears*, 1917, 1199) as well as hanging lamps (*Sears*, 1917, 1200). Just as in 1908, it becomes clear that the form of the sphere inspired design far beyond clothing.

Radical New Spheres, Points, and Centers: "Sears Catalog," 1927

The changes in girls' fashion brought by World War I were followed by even more drastic design changes. By 1927 men had returned home to their jobs. Women had earned the right to vote. The standard for fashion radically shifted. To be beautiful, a woman had to look young. To be feminine, she needed to be slim. The *Sears Catalog* reminded her of this in descriptions from corsets to coats. In 1927, we find the following:

> Is she as Young as She Looks? . . . [W]omen today are more youthful looking than were women of the same age just a few years back. They realize today as never before that it is wise to guard that youthful look, not only for the sake of appearance, but also for better health. Many smart women nowadays are careful not to overeat—they exercise moderately, and last, but very important, they buy their foundation garments from Corsetry Headquarters, in other words, from Sears. (108)

For the mature woman the emphasis on youth is striking. The new, flatter, less-rounded shape, the tomboy look, signaled a complete discarding of the ideals of feminine beauty held by the prewar culture. Now, girls could be girls, and women must also emulate girls. The catalog directed much of its appeal toward young people in general. There were clear delineations between clothing for girls, young women, and mature women. The "co-ed" emerged as a formidable consumer.

The female body shape of 1927 was radically different from those of

1908 or 1917. It was cylindrical, free of any curves whatsoever. The look of outerwear was streamlined and simple, but underwear, though different, was as binding as ever. Women and girls continued to be bound by corsets. The difference from earlier periods is that the corsets and other underwear hung from the shoulders rather than cinched at the waist. When clothes hang from the shoulders a wider range of movement is possible, as is exemplified by modern "sack dresses." Accompanying greater freedom of movement was an impulse toward sexual equality because the young woman's clothing "hung" on her body as the young man's suit "hung" on his. When the young woman was shaped more like a boy, she might be included in the activities previously reserved for boys.

The catalog offered many new choices in underwear for the young woman, though corsets still played an important role. Young women who were corseted were no longer called "misses"; they became "co-eds" (*Sears*, 1927, 109). Little girls were referred to as "schoolgirls" (*Sears*, 1927, 164). "To be smartly dressed you must be correctly corseted," the catalog proclaimed (*Sears*, 1927, 108). The corset rode under the arms, from above the breasts to about mid-thigh. The object of the corset was to flatten the breasts and abdomen and narrow the hips. The desired look was slender and boyish without any curves. Shoulders, bosom, waist, and hips were of equal circumference, forming a silhouette that was a perfect cylinder. The preference for a boyish shape implied a seeming paradox in terms of the girl's relationship to her maturing body. It told her that the outward appearances of her femininity (growing breasts and hips) were to be disguised, even de-valued. But it also offered her at least some of the freedoms that come with being a boy—these would be freedoms of activity and productivity.

A brassiere was shown featuring a bandeau style that bound the bosom. "Brassieres should conform to the natural outlines of their figure—their chief purpose is to hold the flesh immovable . . ." (*Sears*, 1927, 136). The "Boysform Brassiere" was popular as it gave "your figure that smart boylike flat appearance that so many women desire" (*Sears*, 1927, 137). Corsets, brassieres, chemises, and slips were offered for girls, young women, and mature women. All of the underwear, regardless of the age or size of the wearer, was designed to produce the curveless body, the ideal boyish look predicted by the smaller hips of 1917.

The new freedom of movement was deceptive in that the hemline was fairly short, falling barely to the knees. Since the garment hung from the shoulders and was not cinched at the waist, raising the arms above the head would pull the entire dress up exposing the garters and stockings and perhaps some bare flesh. So if the daring young woman wanted to emphasize her femininity she might have raised her arms in the wild "flapping" of the Charleston to expose her garters and bare flesh. In this way she could be active and feminine at the same time.

All dresses sported a dropped waist that rode just at the hips. Since the hips were generally confined by the corset, the final effect was slimming and sleek but did not allow for much bending either at waist or hips. Movement was restricted to the vertical. The body became a piston. The men of 1927 were also piston-shaped, an acknowledgment of the new machine age. Art deco, futurism, and Russian constructivism were all art movements glorifying the piston and the gear.

Once again, the restraining preferences of clothing design were overcome by the young woman without denying her desire to be fashionable. The limited range of movement was solved in two ways. For the young woman, knickers were offered as appropriate wear for activities such as sports. Bloomer dresses were introduced for younger girls ages seven to nine. They were intended "To fill a long felt need. . . . Appropriately designed for the little girl who is not quite ready for the styles that 'big sister' can wear" (Sears, 1927, 80). Appreciating the girl's and young woman's inclination to participate in sports and other vigorous activities, Sears marketed products, such as bloomers, that allowed girls to engage in such activities. In this case, the tendency to be active directly affected the design of clothing.

It becomes apparent in the comparison of styles over a period of twenty years that fashion is not evolutionary. Clothing for the young female body does not necessarily evolve neatly from the most restrictive to the least restrictive. Despite the influences of the feminist movement, clothing for young women and girls continued to bind the body and confine the range of movement. That confinement had been reconfigured but it was no less powerful. We might expect that after her accomplishments in the work place during World War I, her improved opportunities in education and public life, the fashionable young woman of 1927 would be portrayed as an active, professional woman of the world. This was not the case. In 1917, the girls were drawn or photographed with all manner of tools in their hands; they read, gardened, played the piano, participated in sports. In 1927, the girls carried fashion accessories in their hands. Clearly the emphasis was on style rather than utility. The "co-ed" was always shown carrying gloves, an elegant purse, mesh bag, or even a compact. She often carried a fur or a long scarf. From her stylish and mandatory hat to the accessories in her hands the final effect was one of an elegant ensemble. The young woman once again became a form to be taken in by the observer. The things she carried in her hands were not objects of work or agency, they were not tools of industry. Rather she carried in her hands the accessories that completed her "look." Like the obedient child, she was to be seen rather than heard. She was also obviously posing for the photographer or illustrator. (See figures 5.1–5.4.)

If she was naturally slim and small-busted, the styles of 1927 may have been fairly comfortable. However, if the young woman was large-busted or overweight, she would have been bound and corseted aggressively, restricting her ability to move as much as her Gibson Girl sister. So, while these styles insinuated freedom of movement, they did not always deliver such freedom.

Again, it is evident that the cultural preference for a certain shape repeats itself throughout the artifacts of a culture. The art of fashion design not only shapes the young woman's body, it also shapes the things that surround her. This visual reinforcement of design teaches girls how to grow to be beautiful women. It instructs her eye to see the desired shape in decor and then to repeat that shape in the form of her own body. The geometric design of the cylindrical shape can be seen in a variety of domestic goods. The electric washing machine was shaped in a perfect cylinder. Bottles and other toiletries such as perfume atomizers showed a sleek design of oblong or rectangular shapes. Furniture such as radios, phonographs, and pianos tended to be economical and square or rectangular in shape. Jewelry, especially watches, were often seen in a rectangular or oval shape and the wire mesh handbags so popular in 1927 were also in a rectangular shape. Tableware, eating utensils, and fine silverware offered styles based on geometrical shapes rather than on the curved ones seen earlier in 1917. The new machine age was not just an idea. It became a visual and tangible element of its culture.

"Fashion," we are told, "is an important influence on what we wear and what we think. It is part of the social world we inhabit; we constantly meet with references to it; we are surrounded by shops which sell it; and we judge clothes by its standards" (Rouse 68). My point in this essay has been to analyze how young girls learn to accept the fashions of a given culture and how those girls accept and, most importantly, value that fashion as a standard for behavior, specifically movement.

So, then, as a student of human movement, what generalizations dare

5.1. Sears Catalog, 1909. Courtesy of *Everyday Fashions 1909–1920 as Pictured in Sears Catalogs* by Joann Olian, Dover Publications, Inc., NY: 1995.

5.2. Sears Catalog, 1917. Courtesy of *Everyday Fashions 1909–1920 as Pictured in Sears Catalogs* by Joann Olian, Dover Publications, Inc., NY: 1995.

5.3. Sears Catalog, 1917. Courtesy of *Everyday Fashions 1909–1920 as Pictured in Sears Catalogs* by Joann Olian, Dover Publications, Inc., NY: 1995.

5.4. Sears Catalog, 1927. Courtesy of *Everyday Fashions of the Twenties as Pictured in Sears and Other Catalogs.* Ed. Stella Blum, Dover Publications, Inc., NY: 1981.

I make? I am amazed by the resiliency of women's bodies. Pregnant or pubescent we move and act with strength and effectiveness regardless of how we bind our bodies. And, in all fairness, we must admit that we willingly do this to ourselves and our daughters. How many of us bind our daughter's feet for ballet lessons? How many of us bind their bodies in biker's pants and prom dresses?

And now in 1997, I still live in the rural Midwest. I teach theatre and movement at a major Midwestern university. I have a nine-year-old daughter. I do not receive a *Sears Catalog* because it is no longer the important source of fashion ideas it once was. Nearly every week though I do receive a *Victoria's Secret* catalog. This is of great interest to her. And I wonder what does she see. She comes home from tap-dancing class and basketball practice and swipes my catalog and gazes at the wonder bras and the corsets and the stiletto heels. How will she reconcile these contradictions between what she recognizes as fashion and her personal need for self-expression? How will she move within the kinesphere these fashions create? How do I, even now, bind her little body? And how will she bind it herself? I am convinced she will bind herself in some way because a society defines itself by its bounds and boundaries. I await with great interest the first decade of the new millennium to see for myself the new bindings and boundaries of beauty in young girls.

NOTE

1. See Barnard, Craik, Gallop, Rouse, Horn, and Savigliano.

WORKS CITED

Barnard, Malcolm. *Fashion as Communication*. London: Routledge, 1996.
Blanchard, Phyllis. *The Adolescent Girl: A Study from the Psychoanalytic Viewpoint*. New York: Dodd, Mead, 1924.
Craik, Jennifer. *The Face of Fashion: Cultural Studies in Fashion*. London: Routledge, 1994.
Gallop, Jane. *Thinking through the Body*. New York: Columbia UP, 1988.
Grosz, Elizabeth. *Space, Time, and Perversion: Essays on the Politics of Bodies*. New York: Routledge, 1995.
Hollander, Anne. *Seeing through Clothes*. New York: Viking, 1978.

Hood, Mary G. *For Girls and the Mothers of Girls; A Book for the Home and the School Concerning the Beginnings of Life*. Indianapolis: Bobbs-Merrill, 1914.

Horn, Marilyn J. *The Second Skin: An Interdisciplinary Study of Clothing*. Boston: Houghton Mifflin, 1981.

Laban, Rudolph. *The Mastery of Movement*. 3rd edition. London: MacDonald and Evans, 1971.

Laver, James. *Modesty in Dress: An Inquiry into the Fundamentals of Fashion*. Boston: Houghton Mifflin, 1969.

Richmond, Winifred. *The Adolescent Girl: A Book for Parents and Teachers*. New York: Macmillan, 1925.

Rouse, Elizabeth. *Understanding Fashion*. London: BSB Professional Books, 1989.

Savigliano, Marta E. *Tango and the Political Economy of Passion*. Boulder: Westview, 1995.

Sears, Roebuck Catalog. Chicago: Sears, 1906.

Sears, Roebuck Catalog. 1908. Ed. Joseph J. Schroeder, Jr. Northfield: Digest Books, 1969.

Sears, Roebuck Catalog. Chicago: Sears, 1909.

Sears, Roebuck Catalog. Chicago: Sears, 1917.

Sears, Roebuck Catalog, 1927. Ed. Alan Mirken. New York: Crown, 1970.

Staub, August W. "The Body Enthymemic: Center, Sticking Point, and Sphere." Paper delivered to the International Federation of Theatre Research, Toronto, 1996.

6

"Teena Means Business"

Teenage Girls' Culture and "Seventeen" Magazine, 1944–1950

Kelly Schrum

> Teena means business—don't pass her by. You can't afford to overlook the high school girl. . . . She's an important girl and bound to be quite a woman. Sell her now—for now and the future—in the magazine she reads and believes—SEVENTEEN.
> —Promotional Flyer, Ellis Collection

Seventeen magazine made its debut in September 1944 amidst economic, social, cultural, and institutional changes that provided the basis for an emerging concept of the "teenage girl."[1] The magazine's editors and publishers invested substantial resources in interpreting and promoting their definition of the prototypical teenage girl, "Teena." Slogans such as "Teena means business" had multiple interpretations: Teena meant advertising revenues for *Seventeen* as well as sales and profits for businesses that marketed to her, but she also had a future as a thoughtful, determined person with a mind of her own. *Seventeen* magazine was instrumental in developing the image of the teenage girl as a consumer of the magazine and the products advertised within its covers, but also as a member of society. It invested the teenage girl with two separate, yet related, identities: the image of a consumer for manufacturers, business-men, and advertisers; and the image of a teenage girl for girls themselves. This essay begins by exploring the broader societal changes that led to the rise of teenage culture and *Seventeen*'s place within that culture. Deepening our understanding of consumer culture by focusing on the formation of an age- and gender-segmented market, it then analyzes *Seventeen*'s role in developing images of teenage girls through promotional materials, relationships with advertisers, and editorial content.

Seventeen magazine built on late nineteenth- and early twentieth-century developments in publishing. By the late nineteenth century, popular magazines had become commercial products that effectively blended editorial and advertising content. By the twentieth century, magazines catered to a world in which the reader was perpetually enticed and unfulfilled as advertisers began to focus on creating and appealing to consumer anxiety.[2] The multiple roles of magazines blurred further through design techniques such as ad-stripping and editorial advertisements. *Seventeen* used both techniques while professing to teach teenage girls fashion sense and consumer skills. To be effective, these strategies relied on a magazine's ability to target an increasingly homogeneous readership whose members were likely to purchase similar products.[3] Teenage girls proved to be such a group.

Why media devoted attention to teenage girls during World War II— a time of instability, international insecurity, and mass destruction— must be addressed within the larger context of the national emergence of teenage consumer culture. The most noticeable change was economic growth. After the lean years of the 1930s, the United States economy leaped into wartime production as federal expenditures rose from $8.8 billion in 1939 to almost $100 billion in 1945 (Kurian 13–14; Blum 91–92). Although production of civilian goods had slowed in 1942, supplies remained, and by spring 1944, when shortages were most apparent, the peak of wartime production had passed. Even during shortages, retail sales increased because employment opportunities and real wages rose and translated into consumer buying power for men, women, and children (Hartmann 4; Honey 54–59; Williams 122).

Advertising also did not suffer unduly, during the war or after. Throughout *Seventeen*'s early years, consumer goods and advertising budgets multiplied. Between 1939 and 1956, the number of national advertisers and brands merchandised grew rapidly, as did advertising expenditures (Peterson 20–26). Rather than risk accusations of unpatriotic behavior during rationing, advertisers attempted to funnel consumer desire into postwar purchases. One advertisement explained that consumers could not lose: "Lucky gals may find some Featherknits at their favorite shops. Plucky gals will be glad to wait for Victory" (Featherknit 141). Such appeals were successful in both respects as sales and profits remained high during the war and climbed even higher after its end. By 1945, Americans consumed many more goods than before the war. These conditions opened the doors for *Seventeen*.

Economic prosperity translated into consumer power for teenagers as well as adults and provided the material base for an evolving teen consumer culture. With rising incomes and limited durable goods, more money was available for amenities. Through increased allowances and work, teenagers secured more spending money collectively than in previous years and as a poll in the mid-1940s found, the vast majority of youth felt satisfied with the size of their discretionary spending budgets. *Business Week* wrote in 1946 that the teenage market was undoubtedly accelerated by the wartime economy and exclaimed, "Teen-age Market: It's 'Terrif'" ("Teen-age Market" 72).[4]

But economic prosperity and teenagers' enhanced buying power alone cannot explain the emergence of a defined teenage culture. Other factors include teenagers' decreasing presence in the full-time work force and greater high school attendance. These trends enhanced the separation of teenagers from the adult world and increased the potential for a distinct, age-specific identity dependent on peers. In the decades preceding World War II, the number of adolescents who worked full-time declined due to mechanization, efforts of child labor reformers, and the Depression. Although government officials, educators, and social scientists watched the rise in youth employment during the war with alarm, the long-term decline resumed after 1945. Combined with compulsory education laws, this led to greater high school enrollment.[5]

The remarkable growth of high school attendance affected the formation of teenage culture as the proportion of fourteen- to seventeen-year-olds who attended high school grew from 11 percent in 1900, about 630,000 students, to almost 80 percent in 1940, over seven million students. Enrollment for girls roughly equaled that of boys (Fass *Damned* 124, 407–8; Thompson 20; United States 372).[6] By the 1940s, the majority of American teenagers attended high school and a shrinking minority worked full-time. High school, although regulated and supervised by adults, was the central meeting place for teenagers, an arena for teenage interaction and peer influence. Advertisers and mass media helped create, and profited from, this group and the subculture developing around it.[7]

The influence of school and peers, combined with the growing prominence throughout the early twentieth century of professionals who advised on family life and child-rearing practices, decreased parental authority (Fox, "Epitaph"; Kett). Social critics bemoaned these changes and castigated teenage culture and juvenile delinquency as their consequences. They also blamed these developments on the rising number of women in the work force, although mothers of *Seventeen* readers usually did not work.[8]

Even when family life was not radically altered, teenagers began to rely more heavily on their peers and on commercial popular culture, such as movies and music, for guidance and entertainment. Teen canteens, teen- and community-organized places to dance and socialize, became popular during the war and, like music and movies, contributed to the teenager's designated role as consumer. *Seventeen* encouraged all these habits through monthly movie and music columns, as well as articles about popular teen canteens and how to start one. Soft drink companies heavily promoted teen canteens as well in order to enhance business (Ugland 313). Academics and others involved with youth noted this growth of mass-produced, group-oriented entertainment popular among teenagers and worried over the loss of creative, individual entertainment.

While these teenagers were not the first youth to evoke adult concern, they were younger than those previously studied. "Youth" aged eighteen to twenty-four emerged in the 1920s as a distinct cultural entity, recognized in part by their trend-setting fashions.[9] Estelle Ellis, the first promotional director at *Seventeen* magazine, noted, "They're growing older, younger," and by the late 1930s and early 1940s, the emerging image of the teenager, between the ages of thirteen and eighteen, embodied the new youth (Ellis, Interview). In the early years of teenage consumer culture, advertisers and clothing manufacturers experimented with a wide variety of appellations for this group including "teenster" and "Petiteen." This attention to teenagers and interest in their sobriquets and habits marked the consumer-oriented transition from youth to teenager. The word "teenager" described a group defined by high school attendance. In the 1940s, however, this definition expanded, along with teenagers' growing economic power, to include participation in specific leisure activities, styles, and fashions that attracted national media and business attention. *Seventeen* capitalized on this attention in promoting teenage girls as a subculture.

Studying this subculture serves to balance a gender bias common in the literature about youth and youth culture. While recent work, such as Grace Palladino's *Teenagers*, addresses the lives of teenage girls as well as boys, much of the literature does not. Joseph Kett acknowledged in his innovative 1977 history of adolescence in the United States that his primary focus on males reflected his attempt to trace past discussions of youth, which were historically of boys (7). In the 1950s, as teenage culture became a widespread, national obsession, scholars and media continued to write predominantly about males, as reflected in James Gilbert's work on societal response to juvenile delinquency and male youth culture. Rock and roll, drag racing, and rebellion were the territory of boys.[10]

As in Kett's book, most twentieth-century literature on boys emphasized education, work, independence, rebellion, and financial responsibility. The scant literature on female adolescents addressed issues of behavior, appearance, and relationships and idealized teenage girls for their domesticity and dependence on consumer goods to alleviate feelings of inferiority (Silverman 12; Lynd and Lynd 159–67). These anxieties deepened as teenage girls were identified and targeted as a viable consumer group by *Seventeen* and its advertisers who depended on those insecurities and used them to help shape the teenager's consumer identity. The magazine cultivated concern about appearance, grooming, clothes, posture, figure, and weight, and offered products and advice as remedies.

Seventeen was not the first publication to notice teenage girls. Magazines such as *Parent's*, *Ladies' Home Journal*, and *Good Housekeeping* started monthly columns about, and sometimes for, teenage girls in the late 1930s. With names like "Sub-Deb" and "Teens of our Times," these columns recognized the teenage audience, but were confined to adult magazines. Although they spread information about teen social life and contributed to the definition of teenagers as a separate social category, these publications did not speak specifically to teenagers (Ugland 361–79).[11]

It was not until *Parent's* magazine attempted to reach this market in July 1941, with *Calling All Girls*, that an entire magazine focused on "girls and sub-debs." The magazine offered thirty-two pages of "girl comics" and a distinct tone, clearly articulated in its initial editorial message, "Well, girls, at last we have a magazine of comics, and stories and things that is published just for us! . . . Don't you think we should all get together to boost our own magazine? We want all the girls we know to read it, too, don't we?" (*Calling All Girls* July 1941: inside cover). The magazine addressed dating, beauty, fashion, and manners in addition to the comics, and circulation eventually reached a respectable 500,000. But the average age of readers was thirteen and the magazine never gained readership among high school girls. *American Girl,* the Girl Scout magazine, did not attract the general population of teenagers either and its circulation hovered around 200,000 ("*Seventeen*" 19).

In comparison, *Seventeen* reached the teenage market far more successfully. The first issue in September 1944 sold out quickly—400,000 copies in six days. Circulation exceeded one million copies by February 1947 and two-and-a-half million by July 1949. *Seventeen* declared that through copies shared with friends and family, it reached over half of the six million teenage girls in the United States (*Seventeen* Mar. 1947: 2; Ellis Collection). The magazine's readers were mostly white middle- and upper-middle-class; 63 percent of their fathers worked as business executives, owners, professionals, or in other white-collar occupations and an additional 19 percent earned their living as skilled workers. This reader cohort was more heterogeneous than the very exclusive band of debutantes who had previously received sole media attention, but it still did not represent the entire population of teenage girls in the 1940s. In spite of this demographic reality, *Seventeen* claimed to be the voice of the aggregate population of teenage girls and declared itself the cultural mediator between the "American teenage girl" and advertisers, manufacturers, and mass media in general (Benson and Benson, *Life with Teena* 18).[12]

Those who did read *Seventeen* liked the magazine because it attempted to make its readers better teenagers rather than instant adults. Helen Valentine, *Seventeen*'s first editor-in-chief, envisioned a magazine that would treat teenage girls seriously and respect what she perceived to be their emotional and intellectual needs. In addition to helping the teenage girl negotiate her way through the market and choose her first lipstick, Valentine wanted to teach her a "concern for how we are as persons, for how we relate to family and friends, how we present ourselves. But also a deep concern for what's happening in the world politically and socially. As women, as full human beings, to be part of the greater human struggle" (Ellis, "Reaching Women").[13] Many teenage girls appreciated this effort. One teenager wrote to *Seventeen* exclaiming, "Congratulations for being smart enough to realize that we can take a dose of seriousness along with the more pleasurable fashions, beauty articles, etc." (June 1945: 150). One admirer particularly appreciated the age-appropriateness, "Puleez, SEVENTEEN, always stay seventeen. That is, some of these so-called magazines for the high school crowd we pick up either have us in the Fifth Grade having our pigtails pulled or seated at a bar in some swanky nightclub, fluttering eyelashes at some Navy lieutenant" (Nov. 1944: 7). This comment captures part of *Seventeen's* successful formula and illustrates the degree to which teenage girls saw their age group as socially and culturally distinct.

Physically larger than today's magazine, *Seventeen* was initially 10⅜ by 13⅛ inches, printed on quality, thirty-five pound paper. The reader, first attracted to the colorful cover that promised "Young fashions and beauty, movies and music, ideas and people," would pause to view either a head-and-shoulder or full-body photograph of an innocent-looking, neatly dressed, young, white model, occasionally accompanied by a similar male or female model. The cover model and background promoted each month's theme and advertised clothing and accessories. The reader then turned past two full-page advertisements to find the contents and store locations of the cover fashions. She also found section headings, dividing the entire magazine into well-defined categories such as "What You Wear," "How You Look and Feel," "Getting Along in the World," "Your Mind," and "Having Fun." Whether the girl then turned straight to a seductive article or slowly wandered through the magazine's collage of images, colors, and words, she entered a world of advertising and advice, shopping and responsibility. Advice appeared in the voice of a big sister or aunt—older and experienced, yet friendly and concerned. For only fifteen cents, *Seventeen* offered moments of enjoyment for the curious and many hours of thorough reading for the dedicated.

The staff of *Seventeen* carefully shaped the public image of the teenage girl as her perceived power as a consumer increased and competition for the money she spent intensified. Among those charged with helping define and harness the teenage girl's consumer identity was a recent college graduate who, through a chance meeting with Valentine, began a career in promotion that continued for over fifty years. Estelle Ellis explained her prime responsibility as *Seventeen's* promotional director as one of translation: to translate *Seventeen's* editorial message, readers, and readers' buying power for the advertising industry, business, and retailers. "Of course the emphasis was on consumption—the buying power of this age group," she reflected, "to prove that this magazine had marketing power because it could move people to believe in it enough to want to buy the products that were in that magazine, whether it was editorial content or ads" (Ellis, "Reaching Women"). The significant amount of money Triangle Publications spent to create and distribute its image, attract advertising, and strengthen the teenage market attests to their seriousness in achieving this goal.[14]

Ellis's promotional materials from the first six years of *Seventeen*'s history, 1944–1950, provide a unique glimpse of this transition during the formation of the teenage girl's consumer identity. She designed these materials to convince the business community to invest money in the magazine and in marketing to teenage girls, and she always emphasized girls' value as consumers—how many there were, how much money they spent annually on clothes, shoes, hats, cosmetics, and shampoo, and how to reach them. She also presented the teenage girl as responsible, a future voting, consuming citizen with a family to shop for and an eye on world politics.

Ellis based the "ideal teenage girl" on her own personal impressions and experiences. It was over a year after the initial planning meetings and six months after *Seventeen*'s first publication that the magazine undertook its first substantial market research in 1945 entitled *Life with Teena: A Seventeen Magazine Survey* to study, personalize, and package the teenage girl as a consumer. *Seventeen* embodied the results in a prototypical teenage girl they created and named "Teena." As with contemporary sociological and psychological studies of girls, market researchers assumed that teenage girls invested substantial time and energy in commercial self-improvement by purchasing fashion and beauty products. The survey examined Teena's family, educational background, future plans, and favorite types of entertainment, but focused primarily on clothes, cosmetics, and personal grooming items. The most detailed section surveyed recent purchases and brand preferences. A follow-up study in June 1946, *Life with Teena, Volume II—Food*, expanded to include teenage girls who did not read *Seventeen* and surveyed teenagers' food consumption habits, specifically focusing on name brand recognition of, and preferences for, packaged food.

Many of the promotional materials *Seventeen* sent to retailers, advertising agencies, and manufacturers or published in advertising trade journals emphasized the teenage girl's decision-making and purchasing power. Ellis combined slogans with census and consumer information on the six million girls between the ages of thirteen and eighteen who spent two billion dollars annually on food, clothing, cosmetics, and entertainment. One sales pitch read, "Teena is a good listener. . . . Tell her your sales story! Teena, the high school girl has a mind of her own—but it's open to suggestions. . . . At a fast-growing fashion-conscious age, Teena and her teen-mates comprise a market . . . that is strong in its buying power and positive in its brand preferences" (Ellis Collection).

In the promotional materials, Ellis also emphasized *Seventeen*'s success with the teenage reader, both as a magazine through editorial content and as a venue for distributing advertising messages. A 1946 campaign contained "love letters" written to *Seventeen* primarily from manufacturers, retailers, and advertising agencies. The letters applauded the magazine's marketing success: "The ad we ran in Seventeen made mail order history for Neiman-Marcus" (Ellis Collection). These testimonials were sent out to convince other advertisers of teenage girls' buying power and of *Seventeen*'s role as the appropriate avenue for reaching their pocketbooks. Figure 6.1 illustrates this use of the magazine's promotional success with the question, "When is a girl worth $11,690,499?" (Ellis Collection). It declared that the teenage girl was "worth" almost twelve million dollars because businesses were willing to invest that much into selling her their products. She was worth this to advertisers because she purchased the magazine and the products advertised in it.

Ellis's promotional materials repeatedly emphasized readers' devotion to the magazine and belief in what they read there: "A dress is a dress is a dress until you see it in SEVENTEEN!" because "naturally, Teena finds the answer to her needs and wants in the magazine she reads and believes—SEVENTEEN" (Ellis Collection). But this message had to be carefully constructed. *Seventeen* strove to persuade the advertisers that Teena could be convinced to buy almost anything, but had to avoid the dangers in promoting the image of purely irrational, silly girls. When it came to the magazine, therefore, *Seventeen* claimed, "There's nothing fickle about our girl Teena. . . . She's sold on SEVENTEEN—sold solid on everything in it" (Ellis Collection). It connected Teena as an individual to Teena as a generic member of a broader category and magnified each teenage girl's individual buying power through her collective strength.

Promotional materials emphasized girls' independence from adults and children as well as their dependence on peers and group pressure. Ellis always implied, and often explicitly stated, that teenage girls bought as a group—an advertisement strategically placed between its covers would sell to not just one girl, but the whole crowd. If Teena liked it, all six

When is a girl worth $11,690,499?

seventeen

—the magazine that keeps pace with each new generation of teens

6.1. _Seventeen_ Promotional Campaign, 1946. Estelle Ellis Collection, Archives Center, National Museum of American History, Permission No. 9709213.

million teenage girls would. "Teena is a copycat—what a break for you!" The copy continued, "She and her teen-mates speak the same language . . . wear the same clothes . . . use the same brand of lipstick" (Ellis Collection). When addressing advertisers, _Seventeen_ therefore highlighted the developing intensity of peer groups, especially in the high school, and the increasing role friends played in behavior and consumer decisions.[15]

At the same time the magazine depended on advertisers' belief in the reliability of teenage girls as a unified market, it strove to combat negative stereotypes of swooning bobby-soxers. In an attempt to develop positive images of the teenage girl as a valuable member of society, Ellis highlighted one of _Seventeen_'s editorial messages—that the teenage girl cared about her world and would one day be a responsible citizen and therefore a responsible consumer. A March 1946 promotion emphasized that "Seventeeners are intensely curious about the place in the world they're slated to inherit. Adult-level articles on politics, civics and world affairs are featured regularly" (Ellis Collection). In combination, these promotional materials represented the identity *Seventeen* magazine presented to the advertising and business world: an intelligent yet impressionable, consumption-oriented, economically powerful, peer-dependent, teenage female consumer.

Beyond selling the teenage girl as consumer to attract advertising, *Seventeen* had a vested interest in shaping her image in the advertising content. To further its vision, as well as attract revenue, the magazine created an advertising advisory board to encourage age-appropriate advertisements and unite advertising and editorial content into a seamless product. The magazine tried to build a wholesome image and quickly earned a reputation for strict standards regarding advertisements and products (Ellis Collection; Ellis Interview; "*Seventeen*" 20).[16] This was not easy in the beginning, but *Seventeen* worked quickly to replace advertisements it considered inappropriate. Success in this area was significant because the promotion department convinced advertisers to create special images and copy for *Seventeen* and the teenage market that required substantial investment of money and resources. Willingness to make such an investment demonstrated advertisers' considerable interest in the female teenage market.

To help advertisers create the advertising *Seventeen* desired, the advisory board produced a booklet entitled "Who Is Teena? Judy Jeckyll or Formalda Hyde?" that recommended ways to bridge the gap between editorial and advertising content. The cover (figure 6.2) pictured a girl split in half. One half was Teena, the ideal *Seventeen* teenager in a sweater and skirt with long, straight hair and no make-up. The other half depicted her opposite—a girl in a slinky evening gown and fishnet stockings with lipstick, rouge, big earrings, and hair piled on her head. The booklet asked why advertisers tried to attract the teenage girl with slang or sell her on "glamor girls who piled on the warpaint . . . wore bird nest hair-do's and sprouted claw-y fingernails" (Ellis Collection). *Seventeen* preferred a "wholesome" teenage girl, neither her mother nor her younger sister, who dressed neatly and conservatively for high school and dates. This idealized, wholesome girl, who was always white, quiet, and virginal, excluded many real-life teenage girls who were nevertheless supposed to identify with, and aspire to, this image.

One of *Seventeen*'s primary concerns in constructing this image was the negotiation and control of teenage girls' sexuality. Girls were supposed to think about being attractive and highlighting their feminine qualities, but not about wearing fishnet stockings or big earrings. General fear of

WHO IS TEENA ?

Judy Jeckyll
or Formalda Hyde ?

6.2. *Seventeen* Booklet for Advertisers, n.d. Estelle Ellis, Personal Collection.

conspicuous sexuality, combined with the wartime panic over female sex delinquents, led the magazine to be even more cautious in shaping Teena's sexuality.[17] The magazine tried to manage her sexuality without compromising sexual allure. The sweater and skirt implied white, middle- to upper-middle-class girls who controlled their sexuality, used it only to attract men, and then safely tucked it away for the postnuptial bedroom.

These efforts to encourage a more homogenous, sexually attractive but controlled teenage image were fairly successful. Teen cosmetics and back- to-school dresses replaced movie fan magazine holdovers, such as sexy make-up and blond hair dye, in *Seventeen*'s advertising pages. Slang use and advertisements for older women appeared less frequently. Advertise- ments for shoes with four-inch spiked heels, like the one named "Jr. Skyscraper" (Mandel's 138), gradually gave way to ones for flat or low- heeled shoes, such as the "American Revolution" in low heels (Toni Drake 88). The switch to low heels further symbolized Teena's conserva- tive, controlled sexuality, never flashy or loud.

To further ensure controlled sexuality, perfume advertisements quickly toned down their appeal from Varva perfume's 1944 slogan, "She's Var- vacious. Her presence is dynamic . . . her attraction undeniable . . . her impression unforgettable," accompanied by a sexy woman wearing an evening dress and long gloves (figure 6.3), to Beau Catcher Perfume (figure 6.4). The teenager in the 1945 Beau Catcher advertisement was still trying to lasso a man (literally), but wearing a short polka dot skirt and a pony tail, the copy read, "It's the saucy scent that won't take 'no' for an answer . . . fills your date book." Both were trying to catch men, but while the Beau Catcher wanted dates, the Varvacious woman was looking for a longer evening. Teena was undeniably the former, longing for a prom date who would admire and marry, but not kiss, her.

The promotion department accomplished many of its goals. Although some advertisers initially doubted the economic viability of the female teenage market, within two years advertisers purchased more ad lineage in *Seventeen* than in all other youth magazines combined ("*Seventeen*" 19– 20; Ellis Collection). Estelle Ellis and her staff successfully encouraged advertisers not only to purchase space in *Seventeen*'s pages but to invest money into redesigning their advertisements or creating entirely new advertising campaigns. *Seventeen* controlled what products it would and would not accept, a formidable feat for a new publication, and worked to shape the image of teenage girls as consumers. While the teenage girl's identity, as displayed in advertisements, varied, it was consistently con-

6.3. Varva Perfume Advertisement in *Seventeen*, 1944. The Schlesinger Library, Radcliffe College.

Vigny's

Beau Catcher Perfume

fills your
date book

It's the saucy scent
that won't take "no"
for an answer

$3.75, $7.50, $12.50,
$22.50, $45.00
by the dram $1.50
plus federal tax

6.4. Beau Catcher Advertisement in *Seventeen*, 1945. The Schlesinger Library, Radcliffe College.

sumer-oriented. The editorial message was less uniformly and more subtly so.

As *Seventeen* negotiated with advertisers, it also negotiated with readers, responding to them but ultimately controlling the final product. In such a young publication with a newly defined market, boundaries were unclear and the editorial and advertising pages sometimes worked together and at other times offered multiple messages for broader appeal. Valentine and the editorial staff worked as hard to create an image of the teenage girl for readers and for society at large as the promotional staff did to attract advertisers. This editorial task was complicated by a desire to help girls forge their own way through their problems and the world, and, at the same time, a wish to communicate directly with girls as responsible young women.

Seventeen's relationship with its readers is difficult to assess. The magazine welcomed, even solicited, readers' comments and reactions to the magazine. In response to reader requests, the magazine added a fiction component and a section entitled "It's All Yours," with stories, poems, and pictures created by teenagers. Readers themselves often articulated both sides of the conflicting messages within the magazine and demonstrated the diversity of its audience. Their responses serve as a gauge of teenage girls' responses, a glimpse at how they consumed and reacted to *Seventeen* and how the magazine utilized or ignored their requests.[18] The magazine listened to their compliments and complaints in shaping and reshaping the image of the teenage girl it displayed for reader consumption, even as it maintained control of that image.

Valentine envisioned a magazine that would speak to all female teenage readers, to the studious future doctor as well as the future homemaker—a magazine that combined "boys and books, clothes and current events, people and politics, cooking and careers" (*Seventeen* Sept. 1944: 33). Inherent in such a vision was some degree of conflict—cooking and careers were not always compatible.[19] On one level, *Seventeen* was primarily a fashion and beauty magazine that cultivated insecurity and the constant need for personal improvement, similar to its advertising content. But true to the editor's promise, *Seventeen* also recommended books on inflation and atomic energy, offered articles on politics and world affairs, and encouraged its readers to take responsibility for themselves and become active, questioning citizens. The result was a kind of civic consumerism, combining one's democratic role as active citizen with one's duty as a responsible and active consumer. This discussion occurred within a sheltered, limited world, but even within it, not all was uniform. A close examination of *Seventeen*'s major themes—fashion and beauty, boys, education, and politics—reveals that the magazine did not attempt to portray teenage girls as solely one-dimensional or homogenous. To appeal to the interests of all its readers, the magazine offered a variety of messages that remained open to multiple interpretations.

In controlling that image, *Seventeen* was no exception to the general emphasis of women's magazines on fashion, beauty, health, and the continual need to improve oneself; its innovation was in the group of consumers it targeted. Cosmetics and the pursuit of beauty were commercial industries by the late nineteenth century and by 1921 were firmly rooted in American culture with the first Miss America beauty pageant. Also well established long before *Seventeen* was the notion that beauty was available for the price of hair products, deodorant, or cosmetics. The fashion industry depended on feelings of inadequacy and the potential for redemption through consumption. In *Seventeen*'s first issue, 70 percent of the total paid and editorial advertising pages were for bras, girdles, hair and nail products, make-up, or shoes. Within five years, that total soared to 88 percent.[20] On the editorial side, *Seventeen* contained articles such as "Year-Round Beauty" that encouraged concern with personal beauty: "You want to be more attractive—you and every woman between the ages of four and eighty-eight! You want Tom to be pleased with the way you look, and Joe and Eric and Ted. And you want to be pleased with yourself! This isn't vanity. It's perfectly natural and we're all for it" (July 1944: 41). The professed ultimate goal of this obsession—to free oneself from these petty worries and focus attention on others—was rather flimsy, given that once insecurity was cultivated, few could escape its lingering doubts. Sometimes *Seventeen* informed readers that all problems could be corrected or camouflaged through fashion tricks or commercial products, and other times it emphasized general health, cleanliness, and exercise. The overarching theme, however, was still concern with one's physical appearance, a message woven deeply into the magazine's editorial and advertising pages.[21]

Teenagers responded in a variety of ways—some applauded, some criticized, but most accepted the critical importance of beauty. Many teenagers wrote that *Seventeen*'s advice had changed their habits forever: "Believe me—I decided maybe I'd better make some repairs on myself and I must admit they've helped" (Nov. 1944: 4). But not all teens accepted the fashion and beauty advice unquestioningly and one responded to an article on Christian Dior and the "New Look," "Nauseating! That's the only way to describe the replicas of the clothes our mothers wore twenty years ago" (Nov. 1947: 4). She was not questioning the desire for beauty, however, but the path toward attaining it, and the magazine continued the quest for beauty within its pages.

Seventeen did not always agree with its readers. A telling example of teenagers' resistance to *Seventeen*'s advertising and editorial message that did not elicit change involved girdles. *Seventeen*'s early market research showed that the majority of readers did not wear girdles; in fact 74 percent did not even own a girdle and another 19 percent owned only one (Benson and Benson, *Life with Teena* 53). *Seventeen*, however, strongly encouraged wearing a girdle through articles and advertising. "A Fine Figger—Or Else" (Jan. 1946) and "Wear a Girdle" (Oct. 1946) reinforced the message that "Girdles help the adolescent silhouette take shape.... *Seventeen* feels strongly about this." Girdle advertising copy similarly tried to convince teenage girls that their figures, though young, required improvement: "Some of you may not have had to figure on your figure much as yet.... [But] even the youngest of us needs a kind but firm control to mould [sic] us and hold us in the way we should go" (Flexnit Foundations 13).

Seventeen readers responded in a variety of ways. One mother wrote thanking *Seventeen* for her daughter's conversion, but more teenagers wrote in disagreement: "I definitely do not agree with your article, 'Wear a Girdle'.... I feel that there are many girls, including myself, who do not need one.... Hence I say: girdles...fooey!" (Jan. 1947: 4). Thus, fashion and beauty advice, prevalent throughout each issue and often fueling feelings of insecurity, was complex and questioned by readers. The number of manufacturers producing girdles for teenagers continued to rise in the late 1940s. Combined with the "New Look" that dictated a tiny waist and exaggerated female figure, girdle use probably increased among teenagers. But teenage girls were not passively accepting all fashion mandates, and even a magazine that continued to promote girdles had to register its readers' dissent.

Articles, advertisements, and letters on dating, kissing, and marriage continued the trend towards offering multiple messages on a topic. According to studies conducted in the late 1930s and early 1940s, teenage girls were deeply concerned about male-female relationships. *Seventeen* both fueled and countered this interest by encouraging dating but emphasizing tame sexuality. "Good" girls in the 1940s were advised to snare or catch a boyfriend or date, but always passively. *Seventeen* counseled girls to combine physical attractiveness with strong moral virtues. Starting in April 1945, the magazine devoted an annual issue to the theme "Boy meets Girl," in addition to articles on how to converse with and attract boys and the ubiquitous teenage romance fiction. *Seventeen* encouraged teenage girls to concentrate their energy on boys and to attract male attention, but strongly discouraged necking, petting, going steady, or early marriage (May 119; McCracken 144–46).[22]

Teenagers did not always agree. Again *Seventeen*'s editors allowed them an outlet to voice their dissent, but did not alter the magazine's message. A 1942 *Fortune* survey of teenagers' attitudes showed that although girls condemned necking on a moral basis more frequently than boys, they participated in roughly equal numbers, 71 percent for boys and 63 percent for girls ("Fortune" 14).[23] Teenagers expressed these feelings in letters to *Seventeen*: "In the gang I go with, the boys are really swell. At least I thought so until I read your article. We are actually wicked enough to believe in necking. And, hold your hat, I really enjoy it!" (Oct. 1945: 6). *Seventeen*, however, continued to discourage kissing in articles such as "No for an Answer" (Aug. 1945) and "How to Say No Nicely" (Aug. 1947).

The continual focus on boys advised girls not to talk too much, but rather to ask the boy about himself and to always sound interested. "How to Win Men and Influence Statistics," in April 1949, gave opposing advice. Ignore the statistics that college-educated women never marry, *Seventeen* warned, and never change just to attract a boy. A girl cannot please every man she meets, "So why not decide to suit yourself and be sure of pleasing one person at least?" (171). In response to these and similar conflicting messages, one reader wrote, "A girl's life is not centered around boys all the time, just pleasing them and living for them" (Sept. 1945: 6).

Beyond dating and kissing, marriage dawned as an increasingly imminent prospect for teenagers. The median age at first marriage for females fell from 22.0 in 1890 to 21.5 in 1940 and 20.3 in 1950. The median age for males at first marriage also declined from 26.1 in 1890 to 24.3 in 1940 and 22.8 in 1950 (United States 19).[24] *Seventeen*'s editorial message not to marry young was increasingly in conflict with its proliferation of wedding-related advertisements for engagement rings, hope chests, silver, linen, china, and carpets. Such advertisements always emphasized the wisdom of planning young, starting a hope chest and silver collection in preparation for the inevitable, much anticipated, heterosexual marriage.

Seventeen further complicated its messages in 1948 with a new "Food and Home Doings" section and articles on choosing silver patterns and filling hope chests, but it continued to encourage education over early marriage. Not only was seventeen too young to marry, *Seventeen* opined, but the magazine also urged readers to plan education and careers. As the debate regarding the validity of academic education versus domestic training for women raged,[25] the magazine validated all options. *Seventeen* encouraged those with aptitude for college to continue their education and printed articles on choosing a college and financing higher education. Although career articles often highlighted traditional female jobs such as teaching, nursing, and secretarial work, some discussed new opportunities for women in publishing and banking. "So You Want to be a Scientist?" informed readers that, "Women are discovering a 'new' industry for themselves." The article continued, "[W]omen have been showing themselves to be just as brightly intelligent about aerodynamics and isotopes, equations and Bunsen burners, as the next man" (Sept. 1951: 144–45, 190). College bound or not, the message that work might be a necessity was also clearly stated: "A girl who plans to mark time in a job until marriage, or thinks a bridal veil cancels jobs forever, is flouting the statistics. Over a third of the women in America who are of working age work for a living" (Ellis Collection). These messages reflected options open to some women and encouraged well-informed decisions, but the emphasis on college and professional careers reflected the experiences of Helen Valentine and the editorial staff. They were predominantly college-educated women who often continued to work after marriage and children. As a whole, however, career articles did not overshadow *Seventeen*'s emphasis on cleaning, decorating, shopping, cooking, or planning parties. But they did signify—and help legitimate—new opportunities for women.

The issue was further clouded by messages that reinforced good study habits and continued education, but projected negative images of smart women. In one Singer advertisement, " 'The Brain' learns an angle *not* in the geometry book. Carol is our Valedictorian and a math shark, but as my brother Boz remarked—'too bad she dresses like the square root of pi' " (May 1946: 37). After learning the secrets of Singer's teenage sewing course, Carol received the desired male attention. A comical rendition of prom disasters, "How Not to Get Another Prom Bid," however, rendered the bookworm with glasses doomed because of her intelligence: "Big books and words denote a brain/ All beaux will fear to date again" (Apr. 1946: 125). The first girl ended up with dates *in spite* of her intelligence because she learned to dress well while the second lost out completely. *Seventeen* was both encouraging and discouraging regarding education and careers. It responded to requests for college and career advice, yet continued to project negative stereotypes of intelligent women. This attempt to appeal to a wider range of girls and expand their ideas of women's opportunities did not challenge the cultural norms that shaped women as consumers.

Beyond beauty, careers, and relationships, *Seventeen* attempted to bolster teenage girls' responsibility as individuals and citizens. "We expect you to run this world a lot more sensibly than we have," the editors declared in April 1945 as war in Europe approached an end (59). Such pronouncements can easily be dismissed as hypocritical cover for advertising and promotion of consumerism, but to assume that any women's magazine could only teach fashion denies *Seventeen*'s breadth and depth of coverage of world affairs and politics. It also assumes a disinterested reception on the part of readers. The New Year's editorial letter in January 1945 criticized the intolerant or those with a "terrific preoccupation with the way your hair curls" and declared, "Here is our world, sick and in need of healing. Here are you—the generation whose gigantic job it will be to bring us back into a balance of sanity. . . . Never for a moment think: I'm only a girl in my teens, what can *I* do? You can do plenty" (49). This message criticized a sole preoccupation with curls if it precluded citizenship, but did not challenge the importance of fashion and beauty. It reflected the assumption that teenage girls needed encouragement to care about their world, as well as the belief that they could and should care.

The theme of personal responsibility resonated throughout the first six years of *Seventeen* among all the beauty and fashion, with the goal of cultivating responsible, democratic, consuming citizens. This theme was prevalent in American society throughout the war. It was every person's patriotic duty to purchase war bonds and to pay regulated prices. Hoarding goods or paying inflated prices was un-American and undemocratic. After the war, *Seventeen* continued to link the themes of responsibility with consumption and to encourage both separately. The proportions were unbalanced in favor of gratuitous consumerism, but to conclude that it was merely a token attempt to appear non-frivolous is to assume that the serious content meant nothing for the girls who read the magazine. In contrast, there is ample evidence that in addition to praise from national service organizations, teachers, and parents, many teenagers supported these efforts. The enormous growth and circulation figures attest to the popularity of the magazine as a whole, and readers' letters printed in the magazine were disproportionately in favor of teaching teenagers about the problems and complex issues of the world and in encouraging them to participate actively. Whether this imbalance demonstrates the actual proportion of letters received or an editorial bias in favor of these responses, it reflects at a minimum a strong editorial commitment to personal responsibility in national and world affairs and support among readers.

There were, of course, dissenting voices. Occasionally *Seventeen* printed letters complaining about the editorial content, "Why, oh why, must you print articles on world affairs in a magazine that a girl looks to for advice on clothes, charm and personality?" (June 1945: 150) or "I think you should have more articles on dates and shyness.... Stories like those on Atomic Energy are *very* boring." *Seventeen* editors took this criticism seriously and replied, "If enough world citizens are similarly bored by atomic energy, we fear that teen-agers may find themselves with no dates left to worry about" (Apr. 1946: 4). But other teenage girls praised the effort: "Although I am thirteen, I feel that I am not too young to think seriously about the part I am to play in the great postwar world" (Dec. 1945: 6). Another reader agreed, "Seven out of ten teen-age girls don't know half as much as they should about world affairs.... Seventeen can and *must* create a teen-age interest in world affairs" (Aug. 1945: 4). These and similar letters attest that at least some teenage girls were serious, concerned individuals who wanted the magazine that claimed to represent them to reflect their values and discuss world issues. Few read only the serious articles; they could have read other magazines or newspapers if this was their sole desire. But *Seventeen* strove to attain a balance between fun and substantive material and most readers consumed the magazine for this combination, some asking for more, some less, of each.

The world in which *Seventeen* appeared was not comforting, but the magazine did not encourage its readers to ignore disturbing issues. The first issue was published eight months before the end of World War II in Europe and almost a year before the United States dropped an atomic bomb on Hiroshima. Although *Seventeen* readers themselves may not have been as affected by shortages and working mothers as other teens, the war's psychological impact was apparent in articles on postwar peace, dangers of wartime inflation, and war refugees. *Seventeen* readers responded with letters, donations, and volunteer work.

Atomic energy also captured public attention in 1945. The article "Atomic Energy . . . Fearful Miracle" (Feb. 1946) explained how atomic energy was produced and discussed its potential uses, both destructive and beneficial. In May 1946, *Seventeen* recommended the book *One World or None: A Report to the Public on the Full Meaning of the Atomic Bomb.* Warning the reader to expect big words and scientific terms, the reviewer emphasized its importance: "This is a book you must read, think about and discuss. You've absolutely got to realize that the problems presented in it are your own, not those of other people. You are a citizen of the world; you must bear the responsibility" (May 1946: 14).[26] *Seventeen's* editors always treated war issues seriously and encouraged education, individual responsibility, and action.

Stressing this theme of responsibility, *Seventeen* strongly encouraged political involvement and knowledge of current events. It advised young women to develop political acumen in preparation for their role as voting citizens: "You're not old enough to vote—but you certainly can *think!*" The article "Straw Vote" furthered the connection between good citizenship and good consumerism when it compared voting to dress shopping (Oct. 1944: 10). With a five-point plan for choosing a candidate that advised teenagers to research important issues, study past records of candidates and party platforms, and analyze campaign speeches, a wise shopper could easily apply her skills to become a wise voter.

Voting and democracy, as well as pride in America and the right to buy goods, were common themes throughout this period, a reflection of both lingering war rhetoric and the beginning of the cold war. Discussions of tolerance and prejudice appeared throughout *Seventeen's* first six years— a call for tolerance that encouraged cultural homogenization and often denied ethnic differences. But *Seventeen* did not interpret this declaration of equality as a challenge to its own pages that continued to picture only white models. T. F. in Chicago responded to the article "What Kind of World," "I'm a Negro, and my people are one of the many victims of prejudice. The article didn't exactly make 'life beautiful,' but it did help me to see through a lot." She then asked, "Could you have an article written on the part the colored boys are taking in this war? They're not all smiles the way pictures show them. They work hard. They sweat and shed blood, too. They give their lives, and above all, they're humans"

(Apr. 1945: 7).[27] This girl's poignant letter exemplified the complexity of racism and the ideals of tolerance versus acceptance. The writer simultaneously accepted the magazine's affirmative message and recognized the shallowness of such messages of harmony and unity.

So who were these consumers of *Seventeen* magazine and how did the magazine influence their lives? Their world was changing and increasingly reflected the role of high school and peers, as well as that of mass media like *Seventeen*. Although their family life may not have changed drastically during the war, they were still affected by the important issues of the day. They looked to their contemporaries for what to wear and how to behave, but also wanted advice from respected sources other than parents or teachers. Teenagers wanted guidance in fashion and dating etiquette, but also in becoming teenagers. *Seventeen* worked hard to address these issues and to communicate with teenagers seriously about the problems central to their lives. Although the advice was often similar to that given by teachers, parents, and professionals, its delivery in a teen-oriented package was both more acceptable and rooted in consumerism.

Seventeen magazine was a product of the 1940s. Manufacturers, advertisers, and businesses were interested in teenage girls and what they consumed. *Seventeen* actively recruited and shaped that energy and served as both creator of and vehicle for the teenage girl's consumer identity. It played a significant role in identifying and constructing teenage girls as a distinct group through negotiations among the magazine's staff and with advertisers over the teenage girl's identity. This discussion continued within its pages over how to appeal to a large audience's diverse interests and goals. The bulk of the magazine focused on fashion and beauty, but it was also a magazine designed to respect teenage girls' concerns and intelligence and to encourage their self-awareness as a group. While these intentions were occasionally inconsistent, *Seventeen* attempted to display them all.

Sometimes political messages merged with the dominant fashion and consumer-oriented aspects of the magazine and sometimes they simply appeared side-by-side. In one vivid example, an editorial Christmas letter (Dec. 1944) expressed sorrow over the war while the editorial advertisement on the opposite page displayed a colorful holiday dress with the caption, "As long as no one seems to be looking at the Christmas cards anyway, we might as well tell you that the bold-checked basque-bodice dress . . . is $14.95" (Dec. 1944; 48–49). What message the reader grasped from these two pages is difficult to assess—perhaps a message of peace, an idea for a party dress and new hair style, or a feeling that sadness existed but was potentially alleviated by pretty dresses. It is possible that the focus on good citizenship was simply a shallow attempt to fill pages and appear respectable, a façade over the desire to sell products. Or that the magazine was in transition, trying alternative approaches to create a successful, marketable product. Most likely, Seventeen offered myriad messages intending to appeal to readers with varying interests with the ultimate aim of cultivating consuming citizens who voted responsibly with their dollars and their ballots.

These possibilities are not mutually exclusive. Seventeen magazine helped shape a new market from 1944 to 1950 and therefore played the role of advertiser, translator, and advisor for their version of the teenage girl. It experimented with content and style and rarely offered a solid, unified image of the quintessential teenager for simple digestion. It was necessarily fluid in these attempts, experimenting with various voices in pursuit of a successful balance. It did not conclusively answer many of the questions it raised. Whether the hard work and intelligence that helped one achieve a dream of college and a science career would necessarily scare away dates, or why it was important to be beautiful and sexy to get dates, but not to kiss them, remained for the reader to decide. It also did not radically alter its message in response to readers' requests. This mixture was dominated by fashion, beauty, style, and the redemptive value of consumption, yet clear in its moral advice to vote, think, and participate as a responsible citizen.

Consumer culture for teenage girls was a primary beneficiary in this interchange. Manufacturers, retailers, and advertisers who targeted teenage girls reaped large profits and, although advertisements were increasingly age-appropriate, they never substantively adjusted their image of the teenage girl from a swooner to a serious individual. Their goal was to sell; their means were the creation and marketing of products designed specifically for teenage girls. It is difficult to know whether the girls themselves benefited from the attention—from clothes and products designed for their changing bodies or the magazine that claimed to represent and reach over half of them. What is clear is that Seventeen's messages were significant for the millions and millions of teenage girls who continued to consume the magazine and praise its efforts. Teenagers read, however quickly or thoroughly, the medley of messages and learned something beyond style as they adapted new information to their changing value systems. They neither accepted nor rejected all. Through the process, manufacturers, advertisers, and *Seventeen* magazine capitalized on an enormous, wealthy, newly defined market and in turn helped define that market. They also articulated a complex, multifaceted set of identities of the teenage girl as consumer and citizen.

NOTES

1. Although "girl" does not necessarily describe thirteen- to eighteen-year-old females well, its use is so prevalent in my sources that I have chosen to use it throughout this essay.

2. Advertising and editorial content are more inseparable today. See Fox and Lears, especially essays by Lears and Wilson; Fox, "Epitaph"; Steinem; and Lynd, "People."

3. For further information, see Peterson; Damon-Moore.

4. See also Ugland 195–96.

5. The number of gainfully employed youth dropped from an estimated 2.4 million to 1 million between 1920 and 1940 (Ugland 152).

6. Of *Seventeen* readers, 97 percent attended school, and 82 percent of those attended public school (Benson and Benson, *Life with Teena* 12).

7. For further information, see Fass, *Damned* 168–221; Kett 234–38; Lynd and Lynd 181–224. Although Fass discusses college youth in the 1920s, a similar cycle was repeated with high school students in the 1940s.

8. Although the press glorified "Rosie the Riveter" as a housewife working only for the duration, most women workers during the war had worked previously (Honey 19–20; Hartmann 16–18). On women who stayed home during the war, see Chafe; Hartmann 22; Campbell 167; Anderson 104.

9. See also Fass, *Damned* 119–26; Ugland 348.

10. Gilbert mentions the importance of teenage girls as consumers to the overall development of teenage culture, but focuses on male teenagers. Palladino includes teenage girls in her study and similarly argues that *Seventeen* was an important force in developing teen consumer culture. Her argument that teenage culture was adult-directed until the rise of rock 'n' roll in the mid-1950s, however, does not allow space for teenagers' agency in creating teen culture.

11. General press stories such as "Life Goes to a Slumber Party" and "Teen-Age Girls" showed girls chatting, giggling, and shopping.

12. *Seventeen* printed letters from African American, Jewish, Catholic, and international readers, but these were not the majority of readers.

13. Ellis Interview.

14. After spending over $150,000 to establish its image, *Seventeen* successfully sued a clothing manufacturer over the attempted use of its name (Triangle 8).

15. Benson and Benson asked about friends' influence on shopping decisions.

Eighty-seven percent helped friends shop; 76 percent helped friends purchase clothing (Benson and Benson, *Life with Teena* 27).

16. *Seventeen* retains that reputation today by rejecting advertisements for liquor, cigarettes, and birth control (McCracken 143).

17. On juvenile and sex delinquency, see Ugland 219–86 and Costello.

18. The literature on cultural interpretations of popular texts and reader response is complex and contentious. I found ample evidence to support the theory that popular culture's ambiguity and contradictions allow for oppositional reading and individual interpretation. Though problematic, I have tried to understand how teenage girls read and responded to *Seventeen* through their published letters (original letters no longer exist). My interviews with Estelle Ellis and women who worked at *Seventeen* in the 1940s, however, led me to believe that editors read the letters seriously and tried to print a representative sample (Ellis Interview; Sladkus Interview; Eisman Interview; Foley Interview).

19. According to Meyerowitz's work on postwar American culture, this was not uncommon: "[D]omestic ideals coexisted in ongoing tension with an ethos of individual achievement that celebrated non-domestic activity" (231).

20. These figures are based on ads of a quarter-page or larger.

21. Articles consistently asked whether one was too tall, too short, too fat, or too thin. Just right was never an option.

22. On dating practices, see Rothman; Fass, *Damned* 260–90.

23. Kinsey reported that 88 percent of girls and 93 percent of boys aged sixteen to twenty petted by the late 1940s (Rothman 300).

24. May argues that rising marriage rates reflected attempts to achieve "domestic containment," in response to changing roles of women and an increasingly threatening world.

25. Hartmann 101–16; Fass, *Outside In* 156–88.

26. Boyer.

27. I found no article on black soldiers. And despite the emphasis on equality, no fiction or articles promoted dating between black and white or Jewish and Christian teenagers.

WORKS CITED

Anderson, Karen. *Wartime Women: Sex Roles, Family Relations, and the Status of Women during World War II*. Westport, Conn.: Greenwood, 1981.

Beau Catcher. Advertisement. *Seventeen* Apr. 1945: 30.

Benson and Benson, Inc. *Life with Teena: A Seventeen Magazine Survey*. Princeton: Triangle Publications, 1945.

———. *Life with Teena, Volume II-Food: A Seventeen Magazine Survey*. Princeton: Triangle Publications, 1947.

Blum, John. *V Was for Victory: Politics and American Culture during World War II.* New York: Harcourt Brace Jovanovich, 1976.

Boyer, Paul. *By the Bomb's Early Light: American Thought and Culture at the Dawn of the Atomic Age.* New York: Pantheon, 1985.

Campbell, D'Ann. *Women at War with America: Private Lives in a Patriotic Era.* Cambridge: Harvard UP, 1984.

Chafe, William. *The Paradox of Change: American Women in the Twentieth Century.* New York: Oxford UP, 1991.

Costello, John. *Virtue under Fire: How World War II Changed Our Social and Sexual Attitudes.* Boston: Little, Brown, 1985.

Damon-Moore, Helen. *Magazines for the Millions: Gender and Commerce in the Ladies' Home Journal and the Saturday Evening Post, 1880–1910.* Albany: State U of New York P, 1994.

Eisman, Alberta. Telephone Interview. 11 Dec. 1994.

Ellis, Estelle. Personal Interview. 15 Nov. 1995.

———. "Reaching Women: Magazines, Muscles, and Make-up." National Museum of American History Conference. 7 Mar. 1993.

Ellis Collection, National Museum of American History, Archives Center. Series 1, Boxes 1–8.

Fass, Paula. *The Damned and the Beautiful: American Youth in the 1920s.* New York: Oxford UP, 1977.

———. *Outside In: Minorities and the Transformation of American Education.* New York: Oxford UP, 1989.

Featherknit. Advertisement. *Seventeen* Mar. 1945: 14.

Flexnit Foundations. Advertisement. *Seventeen* July 1945: 13.

Foley, Gina. Telephone Interview. 7 Jan. 1995.

"Fortune Survey-Part II," *Fortune* Dec. 1942: 8–18.

Fox, Richard Wightman. "Epitaph for Middletown: Robert S. Lynd and the Analysis of Consumer Culture." Fox and Lears 101–41.

Fox, Richard Wightman, and T. J. Jackson Lears, eds. *The Culture of Consumption: Critical Essays in American History 1890–1980.* New York: Pantheon, 1983.

Gilbert, James. *A Cycle of Outrage: America's Reaction to the Juvenile Delinquent in the 1950s.* New York: Oxford UP, 1986.

Hartmann, Susan. *The Home Front and Beyond: American Women in the 1940s.* Boston: Twayne, 1982.

Honey, Maureen. *Creating Rosie the Riveter: Class, Gender, and Propaganda during World War II.* Amherst: U of Massachusetts P, 1984.

Kett, Joseph. *Rites of Passage: Adolescence in America 1790 to the Present.* New York: Basic, 1977.

Kurian, George Thomas. *Datapedia of the United States, 1790–2000.* Lanham, MD: Bernan, 1994.

Lears, T. J. Jackson. "From Salvation to Self-Realization: Advertising and the Therapeutic Roots of the Consumer Culture, 1880–1930." Fox and Lears 1–38.

"Life Goes to a Slumber Party." *Life* 4 Jan. 1943: 72–75.

Lynd, Robert S. "The People as Consumers." 1933. United States. President's Research Committee on Social Trends. *Recent Social Trends in the United States, Vol. II.* New York: Arno, 1979. 857–911.

Lynd, Robert S., and Helen Merrell Lynd. *Middletown: A Study in Modern American Culture.* 1929. New York: Harvest/Harcourt Brace Jovanovich, 1956.

Mandel's of CA, Jr. Skyscraper. Advertisement. *Seventeen* Feb. 1945: 138.

Marchand, Roland. *Advertising the American Dream: Making Way for Modernity, 1920–1940.* Berkeley: U of California P, 1985.

May, Elaine Tyler. *Homeward Bound: American Families in the Cold War Era.* New York: Basic, 1988.

McCracken, Ellen. *Decoding Women's Magazines: From Mademoiselle to Ms.* New York: St. Martin's, 1993.

Meyerowitz, Joanne. "Beyond the Feminine Mystique: A Reassessment of Postwar Mass Culture, 1946–1958." *Not June Cleaver: Women and Gender in Postwar America, 1945–1960.* Ed. Joanne Meyerowitz. Philadelphia: Temple UP, 1994. 229–62.

Palladino, Grace. *Teenagers: An American History.* New York: Basic, 1996.

Peiss, Kathy. "Making Faces: The Cosmetics Industry and the Cultural Construction of Gender, 1890–1930." *Genders* 7 (Spring 1990): 143–69.

Peterson, Theodore. *Magazines in the Twentieth Century.* 2nd edition. Urbana: U of Illinois P, 1964.

Rothman, Ellen. *Hands and Hearts: A History of Courtship in America.* New York: Basic, 1984.

"*Seventeen*: A Unique Case Study." *Tide* 15 Apr. 1945: 19–20.

Silverman, Sylvia. *Clothing and Appearance: Their Psychological Implications for Teen-Age Girls.* New York: Bureau of Publications, Teachers College, Columbia U, 1945.

Sladkus, Ingrid. Telephone Interview. 10 Dec. 1994.

Steinem, Gloria. "Sex, Lies, and Advertising." *Ms* July–Aug. 1990: 18–28.

"Teen-Age Girls: They Live in a Wonderful World of Their Own." *Life* 11 Dec. 1944: 91.

"Teen-Age Market: It's 'Terrif.'" *Business Week* 8 June 1946: 72.

Teentimer OHriginals. Advertisement. *Seventeen* Sept. 1944: 2.

Thompson, Warren. "Adolescents According to the Census." Annals of the American Academy of Political and Social Science. *Adolescents in Wartime* 236 (Nov. 1944): 17–25.

Toni Drake. Advertisement. *Seventeen* Sept. 1947: 88.

Towle Sterling. Advertisement. *Seventeen* Nov. 1949: 33.

Triangle Publications, Inc. vs. Hanson, et al. 16 May 1946. Opinion #953.

Ugland, Richard. *The Adolescent Experience during World War II: Indianapolis as a Case Study.* Diss. Indiana University. Ann Arbor: UMI, 1977. 78-5584.

United States Department of Commerce. Bureau of the Census. *Historical Statistics of the United States: Colonial Times to 1970 Part I.* Washington, DC: US Bureau of Census, 1975.

Varva. Advertisement. *Seventeen* Nov. 1944: 12.

Williams, Faith. "The Standard of Living in Wartime." Annals of the American Academy of Political and Social Science. *The American Family in World War II* 229 (Sept. 1943): 117–27.

Wilson, Christopher. "The Rhetoric of Consumption: Mass-Market Magazines and the Demise of the Gentle Reader, 1880–1920." Fox and Lears 39–64.

7

"Anti-Barbies"

*The American Girls Collection
and Political Ideologies*

Sherrie A. Inness

When Felicity debuted in 1991, a coming-out party was held for her at Williamsburg. The cost was $50 per child and $30 per adult, plus the regular admission price to Colonial Williamsburg.[1] Despite these high prices, the nine original sittings sold out in less than thirty-six hours. The schedule was then altered to include an additional twenty-four sittings in eight days. Over six thousand girls came, from forty-nine states (Evans C5). Counting parents, the party's list of guests swelled to over eleven thousand (Mehren E5). No, Felicity was not the deb sensation of the moment: Felicity was a doll. Her coming-out party was just one example of the zeal demonstrated by the youngsters who flock to purchase Felicity and her pals, Kirsten, Addy, Samantha, and Molly, the dolls that comprise the American Girls collection.

My curiosity about the American Girls and their manufacturer, Pleasant Company, was originally piqued when a friend's daughter, Anne, asked whether she could have an American Girl of Today™ for her eighth birthday. Anne felt so strongly about the doll that she begged for it in August, although her birthday was not until January. Blanching at the $82 basic price of the American Girl of Today™, my friend told her daughter the doll was just too expensive. After Anne's mother vetoed the purchase, I continued to wonder why Anne was so fixated on this doll that she still slept with the American Girl catalogue under her pillow every night.

I turned to the Summer 1996 catalogue from Pleasant Company for some answers.[2] What I discovered was a world of conspicuous consumption that would make Thorstein Veblen roll over in his grave. I could purchase, for starters, the five historical dolls known as the American Girls, which would set me back $82 each, unless I decided to splurge and buy a doll with her six hardcover book set. Then the price would escalate to $144. These prices, of course, do not include the small kit of optional accessories for each doll (another $20), the American Girls books, activity books, the American Girl magazine, American Girls trading cards, and read-along audio cassettes. Then, if I still had credit, I could pick up a few furnishings, such as a pint-sized Windsor writing chair ($55), a trestle table with two chairs ($75), a tilt-top tea table and chairs for $98, and a double desk ($68) for Addy. If I wanted to rack up charges on my credit card further, I could buy a set, composed of one particular doll, her six books, and all her accessories. Felicity's complete collection retails for $995, with gift wrapping $80 extra (12); Molly's is $895 (52). Addy, an ex-slave living in Philadelphia, has a complete collection that costs $995 (32).

If these items were a trifle high for my professor's salary, I could still purchase a friendship quilt for a mere $18, a patriotic party dress for $20, a Victorian valise for $18, or classic brown oxfords for $8, to mention just a few of the lower-priced items from the American Girls' well-stocked households. If my home were still not overflowing with a surfeit of American Girl paraphernalia, I could buy bookmarks, balloons, buttons, stationery, doll dress patterns, cookbooks, craft books, paper dolls, and theater kits. I could also purchase outfits, including a sailor suit ($95), a birthday sundress ($50), or a prairie school dress ($80), to let a little girl fantasize she was her favorite American Girl. Finally, there is the doll that originally sent me on my quest through Pleasant Company's catalogue. If the historical dolls seem too old-fashioned for your modern girl, there is always the American Girl of Today™ doll.[3] The consumer can chose from a wide variety of skin, hair, and eye color combinations, thus personalizing the doll and presumably making her look as much like the owner as possible. You can buy lots of cool stuff for your American Girl of Today™: in-line skating gear ($28), swim set ($22), ballet costume ($24), patio furniture ($70), or the complete American Girl of Today™ birthday collection for $235, which, at this point, was beginning to look like a bargain.

I was overwhelmed by the prices and the tremendous number of items for sale in the catalogue, but I was also curious. Who would purchase the expensive items? Was the business in peril because of prices that were far beyond the reach of many parents and grandparents? I discovered that far from being a financial flop, Pleasant Company is "a publishing and marketing phenomenon" (Lombardi 23).[4] In 1986, the company had a modest 1.8 million in sales, but that figure grew to over 49 million in 1990 (Evans C5). Sales were 65 million in 1992 (Neal 33). Then sales hit 150 million in 1993, and they have kept on growing (Mehren E5), making the company what one writer calls the "premier doll-maker of the '80s and '90s" (Newmark E4). The dolls, books, and other items have been widely praised. "If you don't know about the American Girls Collection," wrote one person, "you're missing a line of high-quality toys and accessories for young girls that really delivers on the promise to entertain and educate" ("Calling" 22). This comment is not uncommon, as the company has received an overwhelming amount of good press.

But is there another side to this doll and book manufacturer? Are the Pleasant Company productions promoting empowering images of girls or do the products convey more socially conservative messages? These are two of the questions that this essay seeks to answer by exploring the political ideologies with which the American Girls are inevitably inter-twined. Although I shall discuss the dolls and other assorted American Girls items, I am chiefly concerned about the books because of the major role books play in girls' development.[5] As girls' culture historian Sally Mitchell writes, "I believe that reading . . . has an effect on girls' inner lives, their personal horizons and standards, their image of self and poten-tial" (6). Because of the significant role that reading plays in girls' lives and its ability to teach lessons that girls view as "truthful" (especially in a historical series like the American Girls), the lessons conveyed by the American Girls books need to be carefully scrutinized.

Selling History

Before we can turn to examine the American Girls, we need to know a little more about their background. The five historically based dolls were created by Pleasant Rowland, who wished to create what one writer called "anti-Barbies . . . dolls that could teach American history, family values, and self reliance" (Dumaine 106). Rowland wanted to move away from the "Barbies that wore spiked heels, drove pink Corvettes, and looked as if they belonged in strip joints" (Dumaine 106). What resulted in 1985 was Pleasant Company and the American Girls. Each girl has her own distinct character. Felicity lives in colonial Williamsburg. Kirsten emigrates from Sweden to America in 1854. Addy grows up as a slave during the Civil War before she and her mother escape and flee to Philadelphia. Samantha is a well-off Victorian girl. Molly is a nine-year-old growing up in 1944. The adventures of the individual girls are chronicled in a series of six books—marketed at seven- to eleven-year-old girls—which can either be bought separately or accompanying the American Girls dolls. The books themselves have been very successful, with four million volumes selling by 1991 (Evans C5) and seven million copies by 1992 (Neal 35). Twenty million copies had been sold by 1994 (Mehren E5).

The American Girls books are far from alone as a popular twentieth-century series aimed at girl readers. Many other companies have published similar series. For instance, the Stratemeyer Syndicate published dozens of popular series for both boys and girls, the most popular being Nancy Drew.[6] The famous sleuth had numerous chums, including Ruth Fielding, Grace Harlowe, the Greycliff Girls, and the Glenloch Girls, just to name a few of the girls featured in series early in this century. Today, series novels appear everywhere. It is hard to avoid the Baby-Sitters Club and Sweet Valley High books, whose sales have been phenomenal.[7] Over forty-one million copies of the Baby-Sitters books sold by 1991 (Simpson 89). By 1995, the series had sold over 130 million copies, while the Sweet Valley High books also racked up large sales (Lodge, "A Baby-sitter" 28). When compared to the long-running success of the Nancy Drew books or the huge sales of the Baby-Sitters Club or Sweet Valley High books, the American Girls pale in comparison. But, although the American Girls do not yet have the durability of Nancy Drew or the same popularity as the Baby-Sitters, Pleasant Company's historical series with its dolls and their accompanying accouterments is still important to study because of the messages it conveys about the socialization of girls today.

The popularity of the American Girls items is partially explained by the fact that the books and dolls lie at the heart of a carefully planned and executed advertising campaign.[8] One of the reasons for the success of Pleasant Company is its astute use of direct marketing. In 1986, the company's catalogue went to 500,000 people ("New Company" 37). In 1991, the company sent out over sixteen million catalogues (Evans C5). By 1994, over twenty-nine million catalogues were mailed out in the course of the year (Lodge, "American Girls" 35). The majority of the advertised products, except for the books and crafts books, are available only from the catalogue. Rather than hindering the sales of the dolls, books, and accessories, marketing them through catalogues seems only to increase sales by perpetuating the notion of the exclusivity of the American Girls collection, an image the company seeks to maintain given the high cost of its goods, which are marketed towards upper-middle-class families, presumably because only they would be able to afford items such as a tall-post bed with tester for Felicity for $98 or Samantha's "elegant Victorian steamer trunk" for $175 (*Pleasant*, Summer 1996, 43). Pleasant Company has also sought to increase its marketing share by using an advertising strategy that is aimed at the girl consumers reading the books. For instance, the books all contain a card to send to Pleasant Company in case a reader wants more information about the American Girls. The advertisement announces, "The books are the heart of The American Girls Collection, but they are only the beginning. There are also lovable dolls that have beautiful clothes and lots of wonderful accessories" (n.p.). Needless to say, the girl (or her mother) is supposed to go from buying a $12.95 book to plunking down $60 for Samantha's brass-plated bed or perhaps a cool $150 for Molly's "glamorous but sturdy" locker (*Pleasant*, Summer 1996, 53). And this, as we know, is only the start of the buying frenzy that might seize little Matilda or Georgina. Along with a highly successful advertising campaign, Pleasant Company spreads its name in many other ways, including through the magazine *American Girl*, which has over 400,000 subscribers (Mehren E5). The company is even trying to establish historical museums that would be modeled after the residences of the American Girls and would be targeted primarily at young girls, the readers of the books (Lombardi 23). In these and other ways, Pleasant Company ensures that its name and products get out to millions of doting, well-off parents and grandparents.

As I mentioned, the Pleasant Company juggernaut has met with largely positive reviews. For instance, Emily Prager writes in the *New York Times* about the collection: "I could just feel how much fun these things would be if I was 7 again. I got chills. There is also a full line of period clothing little girls can buy so they can dress just like their dolls. Bliss" (48). Felicity Evans also praises the dolls: "[M]any parents . . . are delighted to find dolls with fewer endowments than Barbie and more pizzazz than a Cabbage Patch" (C5). Despite the overwhelming praise of Pleasant Company, its products have met with some criticism. One commentator writes about the Felicity books that they are "a cross between 'Little Women,' fourth-grade American history and junior bodice rippers without the bodice part" (Prager 48). Cynthia Dockrell observes:

> [T]he American Girls Collection is both boon and bane to parents of girls from about ages 6 to 12. Aimed at upper-middle-income families, says public affairs manager Julia Prohaska, the products have "lasting value," which accounts for their high prices. But because the books can be found in most elementary school libraries—and because the big glossy catalogs have a way of showing up on a female child's doorstep almost as soon as she is born—few youngsters fail to meet these characters eventually. (34)

Although these toys carry a more socially acceptable educational message than Barbie, they are also products that are sold with a calculating eye on the upper-middle-class pocketbook. They are far beyond the wallets of many parents.

As for the American Girls themselves—what cultural work do they perform? Even these dolls, which appear much more desirable to many parents than a Barbie, are operating to enforce gender-specific behaviors. Although the ideology passed on by the American Girls about women's socially desirable roles might appear more subtle than the messages conveyed by Barbie, the American Girls are no less imbued with ideology, and the messages they convey are not always as liberating to girls as the messages might first appear. It seems almost sacrilegious to suggest that the American Girls books could convey ideological messages that are less than desirable since Pleasant Company *does* support girls' intellectual and emotional growth, something I strongly approve of. As Rowland states, "We're in the little girl business, not the doll business. We want to have a positive impact on their lives" (qtd. in Dumaine 106). No doubt, the American Girls books and dolls can and do have positive effects on young girls. For instance, the American Girls provide role models of girls who act in a heroic fashion, and girls desperately need such models. I also believe the company possesses a genuine desire to provide girls with stronger role models than those found in Barbie and other similar fashion dolls, a laudable goal in a country where many dolls "promote self-fulfillment for girls through superficial, sweet maternity and very earnest materialism" (Formanek-Brunell 1). It is important, however, also to acknowledge that some of the children's toys and books that are touted by parents and educators as being praiseworthy are conveyers of ideologies that those same people might or might not favor. The American Girls collection, despite its positive qualities, still suggests numerous traditional ideas about how girls and women should act, behave, and look. The American Girls also convey a variety of ideological messages about how girls should mature into women; these messages, while not necessarily harmful, need to be examined to understand how girls are being socialized not only by the American Girls Collection but by girls' culture in general.

Politics and Children's Literature

> The values which shape a book are the author's politics. The promulgation of these values through publication is a political act. . . . [M]ost of what children read is filled with ideology, whatever the source, purpose, and mode of expression, whether consciously promulgated by the authors or not. (Sutherland, "Hidden Persuaders" 157)

When discussing politics and children's literature, one is commonly met by disbelief; people refuse to believe there is any connection between children's literature and politics. Nothing could be further from the truth, as Peter Hunt, a theorist of children's literature, points out: "rather like A. A. Milne's Christopher Robin saying his prayers, children's books may look sweet and innocent, but they cannot be—and nor can their critics" (154). People often wish to view children's literature and children's culture as politically and ideologically neutral or naive. Seeking to return to the "innocent" years of their own childhoods, adults find it deeply distressing to imagine that there never was a Golden Age of childhood when children could escape the ideological assumptions of our culture. Such a Golden Age has never and will never exist, since children's literature and culture are imbued with ideology. "As with discourse in general, the discourses of children's fiction are pervaded by ideological presuppositions, sometimes obtrusively and sometimes invisibly" (Stephens 1–2). When we think about it, the ideological nature of children's fiction and culture should not surprise us; after all, childhood is the period when young people are learning how to be what society regards as correctly socialized women and men, and much of their play, including their reading, is aimed at achieving this goal. As John Stephens writes in *Language and Ideology in Children's Fiction* (1992), "children's fiction belongs firmly within the domain of cultural practices which exist for the purpose of socializing their target audience" (8). Although he is discussing fiction in particular, the same idea applies to children's toys, which are often developed to teach children about a culture's values. Dolls, for instance, have always contained messages about the cultures that produced them.[9] As Formanek-Brunell notes, "Gilded Age dolls . . . reflected conspicuous consumption, ritual, and display, [while] Progressive Era dolls encapsulated the values of 'scientific motherhood' espoused by urban and middle-class professionals" (3). More contemporary examples of toys that carry a clear ideological message are G.I. Joe and Barbie. Each teaches a different message about how men and women should act. Their accessories reflect the different expectations for each gender: G.I. Joe touts a rifle, Barbie nothing more lethal than a curling iron. G.I. Joe lurks in the trenches, not the mall. Ideological and political messages pervade children's literature and toys, even the playthings that appear most innocuous.

When discussing the politics of children's culture, it is useful to turn to Robert D. Sutherland's influential essay "Hidden Persuaders: Political Ideologies in Literature for Children" (1985).[10] He describes the pervasive nature of ideology in children's literature:

> Like other types of literature, works written especially for children are informed and shaped by the authors' respective value systems, their notions of how the world *is* or *ought to be*. These values—reflecting a set of views and assumptions regarding such things as 'human nature,' social organization and norms of behavior, moral principles, questions of good and evil, right and wrong, and what is important in life—constitute authors' ideologies. (143)

He continues, "Like other writers, authors of children's books are inescapably influenced by their views and assumptions when selecting what goes into the work (and what does not) . . ." (143). Although he is writing about literature, his ideas are also applicable to children's toys, which, as I have already stated, are deeply influenced by adult ideologies about how children should mature. Sutherland suggests three forms that ideology adopts: the politics of advocacy, attack, or assent. All three political forms appear in the American Girl products, demonstrating the pervasive nature of ideology in girls' culture.

Politics of Advocacy

The first political form discussed by Sutherland is the politics of advocacy, which he describes as "pleading for and promoting a specific cause, or upholding a particular point of view or course of action as being valid and right" (145). He argues that "the politics of advocacy serves the aims of indoctrination, *urging* a particular value system or course of action, or attempting to enforce conformity to a set of behavioral norms" (146). As is evident from Sutherland's description, the politics of advocacy, as well as the politics of attack and assent, can be positive. There are numerous values, such as the importance of politeness and a strong work ethic, that we might want to encourage, but we also need to recognize how the politics of advocacy can work to affirm values with which we disagree. Sutherland provides an example of the politics of advocacy in the Alger books: "Implicit in these books is a belief in, and advocacy of, a 'bound to rise' philosophy, upholding America as a land of opportunity, wealth as a measure of success, and capitalism as an economic system" (145–46). These Algeresque ideas may be promoted and supported by some people, while others might be equally critical of them.

The positive aspects of the politics of advocacy are evident in the American Girls books. For example, Pleasant Company is engaged in a form of revisionary history that offers girls new stature: "in the wake of the new feminist movement, advocacy may be seen in the large number of works which are recovering the historical achievements of women and presenting young readers with new models of behavior that reject or modify traditional gender roles" (Sutherland 146). The books are not only presenting girls' history, but also actively promoting it, a worthwhile change from the typical elision of girls that happens in most history texts.

Another example of the positive side of the politics of advocacy is that the American Girls collection does address and promote issues of multicultural understanding. For instance, in *Kirsten Learns a Lesson: A School Story* (Shaw, 1986), the title character befriends a Native American girl. Kirsten must address the distrust felt by many settlers toward Native Americans when she and Singing Bird become friends. Kirsten recognizes that the settlers' arrival has resulted in a scarcity of food for the Native Americans. It is clear that we as readers are supposed to sympathize with the Native Americans, not the settlers. Although Native Americans are being represented in a positive light and not portrayed as wild "Injuns" as they might have been earlier in the century, it is also crucial to note that the politics of advocacy can function to show just an opposite view: Instead of the Indians being the "bad guys," now it is the settlers. Such black and white thinking does not show children the true complexity of historical change and can provide them with a distorted picture of American history.

What aspects of history the American Girls series do or do not endorse have become particularly important because of the American Girls' entrance into the classroom. In 1994, Pleasant Company introduced a school curricula package, called "America at School," which is used in two thousand third- through fifth-grade classrooms (Lombardi 23). The package includes "a copy of each of the five school-centered novels, a teacher's guide, 20 activity cards, 10 poster maps of the U.S. at various points in history and two 62" × 48" wall charts illustrating changes in America and its schools over 225 years. In addition, schools can buy or rent the American Girl Collection's dolls and 'realia'" (Lodge, "American Girls" 35). Undoubtedly, the quality of the America at School activities is high, but that is not my primary concern. What does it mean that a toy and book company is also making school curriculum units? What does it mean when a product heavily targeted at a youth audience is available for a school to display? Does it not imply that the values and ideas embodied in the American Girls should be accepted as historical fact? What Pleasant Company chooses to advocate or not to advocate becomes part of the school curriculum in thousands of schools, a frightening proposition that shows the increasing ability of companies to sell their products in classrooms as "fact."[11]

Politics of Attack

The politics of attack is what Sutherland calls "the reverse side of coin" to the politics of advocacy (147). He writes, "The politics of attack is generated by the authors' sense of amusement, outrage, or contempt when they encounter something that runs counter to their concepts of right and wrong, good and evil, justice, fair play, decency, or truth" (147). As with the politics of advocacy, the politics of attack can benefit young readers. Girls need to recognize that some actions are not generally tolerated by the larger society and deserve censure. For instance, our society as a whole would approve of condemning murder and stealing in children's books. Likewise, advocating racism and the persecution of minorities would be considered by many educators and parents as reprehensible in contemporary children's books. The difficulty lies in who should decide what is or is not to be attacked. For example, children's literature published in Nazi Germany commonly portrayed Jews as evil beings, scarcely human, who preyed on upstanding Aryans. Today, many people would consider such a biased portrayal inappropriate, but, when the books were written and published, many Germans accepted this view of the world as perfectly acceptable and "normal." Although visiting the local bookstore today, one might not discover a children's book that is as virulently anti-Semitic as those produced in World War II Germany, it remains crucial for readers to think about how the politics of attack functions, along with *who* and *what* are being attacked.

Like the politics of advocacy, the politics of attack appears frequently in the American Girl books, often to teach behavioral messages that have broad appeal. In *Meet Felicity: An American Girl* (Tripp, 1991), there are numerous examples of the politics of attack when Felicity falls in love with a horse, Penny, owned by a drunken brute, Jiggy Nye, who will not part with his property. Felicity borrows a pair of breeches from her father's apprentice, Ben, so that she is free to ride Penny secretly. Ulti-mately, Felicity helps Penny to escape so that the horse can leave its ill-tempered master. In *Changes for Felicity: A Winter Story* (Tripp, 1992), Felicity's adventures continue. She has to help Penny give birth to a foal and discovers Jiggy Nye in debtors' jail, where she brings him medicine and a blanket, despite her fear that he might hurt Penny. The politics of attack is clear in Felicity's adventures. Drunkards are cruel, mean-spirited people. People who abuse animals are obnoxious, as are debtors. People who are bad to children, as is Jiggy, deserve to be punished. Although some of these messages might be positive, it is all too easy to recognize how quickly these statements of "fact"—this is the way the world operates—can be universalized by girl readers to be applicable in all cases. Should the readers shun all alcoholics as "bad" because of what many physicians consider a medical illness? Should all debtors, which includes most members of our American society, be disparaged equally?

Another series of American Girls books in which the politics of attack plays a prominent role is the one that focuses on the adventures of Addy Walker. The books repeatedly attack the evils of slavery. In *Meet Addy: An American Girl* (Porter, 1993), Addy lives with her family, who are slaves to Master Stevens. At his plantation Addy is subject to unspeakable indignities. She is whipped when she refuses to let go of her father, who has just been sold. The most horrific scene is when she is forced to eat the tobacco worms she overlooks as she searches for them in the field: "The overseer forced open her mouth and stuffed the still-twisting and wiggling worms inside" (23). Slavery continues to be portrayed in a grim fashion even after Addy and her mother have escaped and settled in Philadelphia. In *Addy's Surprise: A Christmas Story* (Porter, 1993), Addy and her mother live in poverty, unable to afford even a lamp to cast light on Addy's mother's sewing (she works as a seamstress). It remains evident, however, that Addy's life is far better than her former life as a slave, which is why she and her mother donate their entire small savings account to help newly freed blacks. In the Addy books, the politics of attack is used to point out the many evils of slavery, certainly a goal that many people, including myself, would praise. But we still need to be aware of how politics functions in literature, even if we agree with the ideas being expressed. Only keen awareness of ideology in girls' fiction and culture will help make us as educators, parents, and scholars more aware of how girls are socialized in our culture, both in positive and negative ways.

Politics of Assent

In many ways, the politics of assent is more insidious than the politics of advocacy or attack because the politics of assent is often hidden. The politics of assent, according to Sutherland, works to affirm "ideologies generally prevalent in the society" (151). "The politics of assent not only affirms the status quo but continually reinforces it," he argues. "By inhibiting change and supporting tradition, it has great potential impact on the shape of society—for good or ill" (155). Sutherland's description points out some of the disturbing aspects of the politics of assent. Since the politics of assent is invisible and considered "natural," observers often fail to recognize how the politics of assent functions. It is far more difficult to be unobservant of the politics of advocacy or attack, which tend to be more blatant and openly visible.

The politics of assent is omnipresent in the American Girls collection. One way the politics of assent appears is through the overwhelming American-centric view of the books, dolls, and other items. For example, a T-shirt that the company markets reads "Proud to be an American Girl!" (*Pleasant*, Fall 1996, 1). Not only are all the dolls American, but the books repeatedly suggest that American ways are best. In *Changes for Felicity*, the title character works in her father's store so that he can serve as a commissary agent for the Patriots. A clear assumption is made that the American cause is more just than the British. Similarly, in the books that focus on Kirsten's adventures, it is evident that she traveled to

America because her family believed it to be superior to her home country. In *Changes for Molly: A Winter Story* (Tripp, 1988), a chapter's title is
"Hurray for the U.S.A.!" (1). Children's literature critic Jerry Griswold
points out that "America's sense of national identity is intimately connected to its children's books" (13). Although he is writing specifically
about nineteenth- and early twentieth-century literature, his words are
also applicable to the American Girls series, which help to build up an
American identity that stresses the importance and centrality of the
United States. The politics of assent is apparent in that this vision of
America as superior to other countries becomes so naturalized that people
assume it is simply the "truth." Because of the American-centric attitude
of the American Girls collection (which is revealed even in the name of
the collection itself), it would be unlikely for girls to carry away any belief
from reading the books and playing with the dolls other than that America is superior to other nations.

Another way that the politics of assent functions in the American Girls
collection is by presenting the collection as "real" history. Although the
collection itself does not state that it is factual, "true" history, in many
ways the illusion is constructed that the books are "real." For example,
Pleasant Company sells what it describes as "historically accurate reproductions" (*Pleasant*, Summer 1996, 5). The books conclude with "a peek
into the past," a section of pictures and prose that records information
about life in a particular period. Real images from the time are used,
making the entire story seem more historically realistic. "A peek into the
past" also confuses the line between what is fiction and non-fiction. And,
as I have mentioned already, the American Girls appear in classrooms
across America, working to legitimate the collection as "real history." The
issue here is not the reality of history. Any astute cultural critic today
recognizes that *all* history is a form of story-telling. What I am concerned
about is that Pleasant Company (or any other company) helps to form
young girls' notions about what constitutes history, a trend that can have
disturbing effects. Since the books and dolls present a rather limited
discussion of race and ethnicity (mainly in regards to Addy[12]), girl readers
might assume that the early United States was largely white, with a few
blacks thrown in, but with no Hispanics, Asians, or the many other
groups that made up America. Since the American Girls, except for Addy,
are relatively well off, they affirm that Americans have always been pros-
perous, ignoring the countless immigrants who have had to labor in

poverty. Addy serves to support the reverse stereotype that African Americans are generally poverty-stricken. There are a few supporting characters who are also poor. In *Meet Samantha: An American Girl* (Adler, 1986), well-off Samantha meets Nellie, the nine-year-old who works as a servant at a neighbor's house. Samantha and Nellie form a friendship that continues throughout the series. In *Samantha Learns a Lesson: A School Story* (Adler, 1986), Nellie describes her family all living in one room in which "the air always smelled bad" (7). Nellie tells Samantha about the terrible working conditions at a factory where Nellie worked, a place where the "machines got fuzz and dust all over everything" (47). But poverty never remains a problem for long in the American Girls' world. In *Changes for Samantha: A Winter Story* (Tripp, 1988), Nellie solves her problems with poverty. When her parents die, she moves in with Samantha and her well-off aunt and uncle. As is clear from Samantha's stories, the American Girls collection does sometimes address poverty, but it never is an issue as important as attending tea parties or receiving a doll as a present.

The politics of assent also functions in the American Girls through the books' repeated emphasis on a conservative ideology about what it means to be a girl or woman. A caveat to include at this point is that I do not believe the Girls convey *only* conservative notions about gender roles. The books often emphasize that girls can be as outspoken and intelligent as boys. Still, Pleasant Company is by no means challenging many gender stereotypes about how women and girls should look and behave. What does it suggest that *every* American Girl doll (including the contemporary ones) has long hair? Although this might appear to be a small concern, it is more significant than it may first appear. Hair represents much more than merely a way to keep one's scalp warm, as Frigga Haug observes: "Hair long ago lost its function of mere protection . . . and has become a symbol of femininity and masculinity" (111). The inevitable long hair of the American Girls serves as a subtle reminder that girls and women should have long hair. The politics of assent works to show long hair as only "natural" on women and implies that short hair is unfeminine. The American Girls collection supports traditional notions of feminine beauty standards in other ways. The catalogue sells a hair care kit, complete with "a styling cape, misting bottle, doll hairbrush, 12 hair rollers, and packet of end papers" (*Pleasant*, Summer 1996, 55) so that the young owner can give her doll "American curls" (55). Girls are already being taught that primping and excessive preoccupation with appearance are issues that require special attention. From looking at these examples, it becomes evident that the American Girl collection adheres to a fairly traditional ideology about how girls should look.

Other evidence of the politics of assent working in the American Girls books supports the stereotype that girls are concerned about insignificant issues. In *Meet Molly: An American Girl* (Tripp, 1986), Molly has a number of small, harmless adventures. She daydreams about being Cinderella for Halloween, but settles for dressing as a hula dancer. She refuses to eat her turnips until her mother doctors them up by adding butter, sugar, and cinnamon. She gets into a fight with her brother, Ricky. In *Molly Learns a Lesson: A School Story* (Tripp, 1986), Molly is involved in ordinary events, such as having to take part in a multiplication bee, which she dreads. In *Molly Saves the Day: A Summer Story* (Tripp, 1988), she encounters more small adventures. She attends Camp Gowonagin, where she battles with her fear of swimming under water, catches poison ivy, and leads her team to victory while playing color guard. Although one could argue that all of these events are common in a girl's life, the politics of assent works to naturalize the events to make them seem like they are the "reality" of a girl's life. Of course, not all the books emphasize the minor events in a girl's life. Addy escapes from slavery and Kirsten needs to cope with a long, arduous ship journey, and she has to handle the sorrow of having her friend, Marta, die from cholera. In *Changes for Kirsten: A Winter Story* (Shaw, 1988), Kirsten also has to deal with the hardships that result from her house burning down. But the American Girls still spend a great deal of time pursuing traditional girl activities, like cooking, playing with dolls, buying new clothing or dressing up in it— activities that work to demonstrate the "natural" roles of the woman as nurturer and caregiver, not roles I view as negative, but which I am concerned about because the politics of assent tends to present such roles as being the "natural" province of women and girls.

The Politics of Girls' Culture

This essay has focused primarily on how the politics of advocacy, attack, and assent function in the American Girls books; my argument, however, has broader implications, applying to all books that girls (and boys) read. It is impossible to escape ideology in girls' books. Think about how the politics of advocacy appears in the Sweet Valley High books, which support the notion that teenage girls should want to be popular cheerleaders rather than studious bookworms. Consider the ideology of assent as it appears in L. M. Montgomery's *Anne of Green Gables* (1908) when the book presents it as entirely "normal" that Anne, as a girl, should stay to take care of her adopted family member, Marilla, rather than pursue her career as a teacher. These are two examples of many that show how ideology is inevitably interwoven in girls' reading and needs to be considered to understand the messages, both implicit and explicit, being conveyed to girls by books.

As educators, scholars, and parents, we need to be aware of how ideology functions not just in the books girls read but in girls' culture in general. This is especially critical because we live in a culture where women are still second-class citizens, and they begin to learn about their inferior status as very young girls. When girls discover what society expects from them, a dramatic form of reverse learning occurs, during which girls' test scores in mathematics and science drop, and many girls decide to become nurses rather than physicians, or elementary school teachers rather than college professors, or legal secretaries rather than lawyers.[13] Also, a large number of young women get pregnant and drop out of school while they are still in their teens. Even after the feminist movement of the late 1960s and early 1970s, which supposedly taught women and girls that they could be and do whatever they desired, an alarming number of girls are still trapped in the same roles as their mothers or grandmothers were. One of the reasons many girls are ensnared in such roles at early ages is that girls' culture is still largely directed at turning girls into women who are mothers and caretakers rather than rocket scientists and engineers. If one doubts this, just take a stroll down the girls' aisle of a local toy store; how many baby dolls are present? How many doll scientists or engineers? Because of the overwhelming influence of girls' culture not only on girls but on future women, feminist scholars and anyone else interested in changing gender roles need to scrutinize girls' culture with greater care.

Whether it is analyzing today's dolls, Disney films, television shows aimed at girls, recess games, girls' fashion, or other areas, the possible subjects for study are many. Girls' lunch boxes, magazines marketed for girls, girls' horse books, baby dolls, cookbooks, make-up for girls: These are only a few of the items of girls' culture that could be studied. For far too long, girls' culture and the items that compose it have been considered frivolous and unimportant. Who wishes to think about the appeal of horse stories or stuffed animals to girls if one can instead study the impact of drugs or alcohol on adults? Girls have long been marginalized because of their gender and age, making them some of the most disregarded individuals in our culture. It is more than time to alter this belief and recognize that girls' culture deserves attention.

Flipping through the fall 1996 edition of the Pleasant Company catalogue, I remain ambivalent about the company. Browsing through the American Girl of Today™ section, I notice new items: a complete miniature Macintosh computer, which really works, a Kwanzaa outfit, Hanukkah gifts, and a Chinese New Year outfit, or a wheelchair for an American Girl. But, among the new additions, there is also a cheerleader outfit including "pompons to lead the wave!" (68). For me, these varied items represent the different sides of Pleasant Company, which attempts to create a more diverse, empowered image of girldom, but also remains invested in traditional ideology about what girls are supposedly all about.

NOTES

1. If these prices seem high, consider the weekend tour package at Williamsburg designed for American Girls fans. A family of four can have a tour of the city, two nights' lodging including a tavern dinner, breakfast, afternoon tea, and etiquette lessons for a cool $470 to $648 ("Family" 51).

2. The correct name is Pleasant Company, *not* the Pleasant Company.

3. Articles that discuss the new contemporary line of American Girl dolls include Hellmich and Newmark.

4. Additional information about the American Girls collection and its tremendous success can be found in "Calling"; Dockrell; Dumaine; Lenhard; Lodge, "American Girls"; and Mehren.

5. For more information about girls' popular reading, see Clark; Inness; and Mitchell.

6. More information about the Stratemeyer Syndicate can be found in Billman and Johnson.

7. For additional information on the Sweet Valley High series and the Baby-Sitters Club books, see Dougherty; Huntwork; Lodge, "A Baby-sitter"; and Simpson.

8. Advertising is only one way that Pleasant Company promotes the American Girls. The books themselves help to sell the dolls and their accessories. For instance, in *Meet Felicity: An American Girl* (Tripp, 1991), the title character "[wears] her coral necklace for good luck" (50). Not surprisingly, a coral bead

necklace is included in Felicity's accessories. This is one example of the many times that the books mention and even picture the items that the catalogue sells.

9. Laura Starr, a doll collector from 1909, wrote, "history could be taught by means of dolls. The future historian will have no difficulty in reconstructing our age if he finds merely a few toys in dusty garrets or museums" (qtd. in Formanek-Brunell 6). Certainly, the American Girls would convey a great deal about the current values our society holds.

10. For another important essay about the pervasive nature of ideology in children's literature, read Hollindale.

11. Even the mere presence of the American Girls in the classroom acts to legitimize the collection to parents who assume that educators support the dolls and their accompanying books.

12. See, for instance, the description of Addy's problems with the racist attitudes of Northerners in *Happy Birthday, Addy! A Springtime Story* (Porter, 1994).

13. I am not suggesting that there is anything wrong with being a nurse, elementary school teacher, or legal secretary. They are, however, stereotypically women's jobs, which are often less prestigious and well paid than men's.

WORKS CITED

Adler, Susan S. *Meet Samantha: An American Girl.* Madison: Pleasant, 1986.
———. *Samantha Learns a Lesson: A School Story.* Madison: Pleasant, 1986.
Billman, Carol. *The Secret of the Stratemeyer Syndicate: Nancy Drew, the Hardy Boys, and the Million Dollar Fiction Factory.* New York: Ungar, 1986.
"Calling All Girls." *Parents* Apr. 1990: 22.
Clark, Beverly Lyon. *Regendering the School Story: Sassy Sissies and Tattling Tomboys.* New York: Garland, 1996.
Dockrell, Cynthia. "Dolls and Cents." *Boston Globe* 10 June 1996: 34+.
Dougherty, Steve. "Heroines of 40 Million Books, Francine Pascal's *Sweet Valley Twins* Are Perfection in Duplicate." *People Weekly* 11 July 1988: 66–68.
Dumaine, Brian. "How to Compete with a Champ." *Fortune* 10 Jan. 1994: 106.
Evans, Felicity. "American Girls to Treasure." *Washington Post* 27 Aug. 1991: C5.
"Family Traveler." *Family Fun* May 1996: 51.
Formanek-Brunell, Miriam. *Made to Play House: Dolls and the Commercialization of American Girlhood, 1830–1930.* New Haven: Yale UP, 1993.
Griswold, Jerry. *Audacious Kids: Coming of Age in America's Classic Children's Books.* New York: Oxford UP, 1992.
Haug, Frigga, ed. *Female Sexualization: A Collective Work of Memory.* London: Verso, 1987.
Hellmich, Nanci. "A Doll for Today's American Girl." *USA Today* 25 Sept. 1995: D1.

Hollindale, Peter. "Ideology and the Children's Book." *Signal* 55 (Jan. 1988): 3–22.

Hunt, Peter. *Criticism, Theory, and Children's Literature.* Cambridge: Basil Blackwell, 1991.

Huntwork, Mary M. "Why Girls Flock to Sweet Valley High." *School Library Journal* 36.3 (1990): 137–40.

Inness, Sherrie A. *Intimate Communities: Representation and Social Transformation in Women's College Fiction, 1895–1910.* Bowling Green: Bowling Green State U Popular P, 1995.

Johnson, Deidre. *Edward Stratemeyer and the Stratemeyer Syndicate.* New York: Twayne, 1993.

Lenhard, Elizabeth. "Playing with the Past." *Atlanta Constitution* 24 Sept. 1993: G1+.

Lodge, Sally. "The American Girls Put the Past in Pastime." *Publishers Weekly* 8 Aug. 1994: 35–36.

———. "A Baby-sitter Birthday." *Publishers Weekly* 4 Sept. 1995: 28–29.

Lombardi, Kate Stone. "Pleasant Company Museum Proposal Stirs Community." *Publishers Weekly* 10 Apr. 1995: 23.

Mehren, Elizabeth. "Playing with History." *Los Angeles Times* 28 Nov. 1994: E1+.

Mitchell, Sally. *The New Girl: Girls' Culture in England, 1880–1915.* New York: Columbia UP, 1995.

Montgomery, L. M. *Anne of Green Gables.* 1908. New York: Bantam Books, 1984.

Neal, Mollie. "Cataloger Gets Pleasant Results." *Direct Marketing* May 1992: 33–36.

"New Company to Launch Collection of Girls' Historical Fiction and Toy Reproductions." *Publishers Weekly* 22 Aug. 1986: 36.

Newmark, Judith. "Doll Makes Child into 'American Girl' Herself." *St. Louis Post-Dispatch* 29 Nov. 1995: E4.

Pleasant Company Catalogue. Fall 1996.

Pleasant Company Catalogue. Summer 1996.

Porter, Connie Rose. *Addy's Surprise: A Christmas Story.* Middleton: Pleasant, 1993.

———. *Happy Birthday, Addy! A Springtime Story.* Middleton: Pleasant, 1994.

———. *Meet Addy: An American Girl.* Middleton: Pleasant, 1993.

Prager, Emily. "Adventures in History: Dolls with a Past." *New York Times* 21 May 1995: 45+.

Shaw, Janet Beeler. *Changes for Kirsten: A Winter Story.* Madison: Pleasant, 1988.

———. *Kirsten Learns a Lesson: A School Story.* Madison: Pleasant, 1986.

———. *Kirsten Saves the Day: A Summer Story.* Madison: Pleasant, 1988.

———. *Meet Kirsten: An American Girl.* Madison: Pleasant, 1986.

Simpson, Janice C. "Adventures in Baby-Sitting." *Time* 28 Jan. 1991: 89.

Stephens, John. *Language and Ideology in Children's Fiction*. London: Longman, 1992.

Sutherland, Robert D. "Hidden Persuaders: Political Ideologies in Literature for Children." *Children's Literature in Education* 16.3 (1985): 143–57.

Tinkler, Penny. *Constructing Girlhood: Popular Magazines for Girls Growing Up in England, 1920–1950*. London: Taylor & Francis, 1995.

Tripp, Valerie. *Changes for Felicity: A Winter Story*. Middleton: Pleasant, 1992.

———. *Changes for Molly: A Winter Story*. Madison: Pleasant, 1988.

———. *Changes for Samantha: A Winter Story*. Madison: Pleasant, 1988.

———. *Meet Felicity: An American Girl*. Middleton: Pleasant, 1991.

———. *Meet Molly: An American Girl*. Madison: Pleasant, 1986.

———. *Molly Learns a Lesson: A School Story*. Madison: Pleasant, 1986.

———. *Molly Saves the Day: A Summer Story*. Middleton: Pleasant, 1988.

8

Boys-R-Us

Board Games and the Socialization of Young Adolescent Girls

Jennifer Scanlon

In a 1973 volume of *Ms.* magazine, Letty Cottin Pogrebin introduced a checklist for parents who wanted to buy nonsexist toys for their children. An acceptable toy would be "respectful of the child's intellect and creativity, nonracist, moral in terms of the values it engenders, and nonsexist in the way it is packaged, conceived, and planned for play" (48). One of the board games she recommended was Life, a Milton Bradley product, as it encouraged all players to pursue lives of their own, money of their own, careers of their own.

Now, readers, as the instructions on a game might tell you, advance twenty years. Enter the 1990s, a mall, Anytown U.S.A. A parent looking for nonsexist toys for children might, at a Toys-R-Us store, find a few toys and games that Pogrebin would approve of. The game of Life remains popular, and consumers can find numerous trivia games, memory games, and games of skill on the shelves. Unfortunately, however, mall toy stores rely heavily on gender stereotypes for their displays, layout, advertising, and, most importantly, products. This essay looks at four gender-specific board games directed at young adolescent girls, examines their messages in light of Pogrebin's now twenty-five-year-old suggestions, and brings to light issues about a much-neglected period in girls' lives, early adolescence, and a much-neglected area of popular culture or leisure studies, gender-specific games.

The least gender-specific toys and games in the stores are, arguably, those in the baby and toddler section. Primary colors predominate in these toys, and customers purchase chunky trains and boats for baby girls or boys. Sex-typing occurs quickly as you move either down the aisle or up in age, as trucks become masculinized, dolls feminized. Pastels replace primary colors in girls' toys, and the packaging, game boards and pieces, even the cover photographs become feminized. For boys' toys, camouflage greens and browns replace soft colors, and war toys and sports equipment fill the shelves. And now you arrive at these four games for young adolescent girls, where the players featured on the game boxes, girls only, dress in feminine clothing and wear heavy make-up and jewelry, even though the suggested starting age for the games is eight.

Heart-Throb: The Dream Date Game, and Sweet Valley High: Can You Find a Boyfriend in Time for the Big Date? are both produced by Milton Bradley, subsidiary of Hasbro, a company with $410 million in annual sales. Hasbro, with no women on its board of directors, produces board games for children and adults as well as a range of other products from teething rings to women's undergarments, baby pacifiers to girls' nightwear. The second two games, Girl Talk: A Game of Truth or Dare, and Girl Talk: Date Line, are produced by Western Publishing Company, which has annual sales of $495 million and produces, among other things, board games for children and adults, gift wrap and novelties, stationery, and books (Dun and Bradstreet 813, 1831).

Not surprisingly, these four games invite girls to enter the consumer marketplace by encouraging players to use products such as clothing and make-up to enhance their looks. Another game for young adolescent girls, Meet Me at the Mall, more blatantly emphasizes the consumer side of things; players run around the mall, visiting stores like The Gap and Benetton, trying to outbuy the competition. For the four games discussed in this chapter, though, players must obtain boyfriends rather than consumer goods. Whether a girl steals one from a friend, wins one through her own matchmaking skills, or reads one in her future, a boyfriend rather than a career or a life remains the player's central goal.

A curious consumer might wonder whether the pursuit of a boyfriend is in fact a typical adolescent girl's primary goal. Unfortunately, researchers have not adequately studied the activities of young adolescent girls. Adolescence and pre-adolescence have most often been described as periods of conflict, with juvenile delinquency and violence the most frequently covered behaviors. Violence within this group, specifically male violence, receives the most attention from the media as well as from scholars. With this emphasis on delinquency and violence, both defined in male terms, issues in girls' lives are often overlooked (Coleman and Hendry 53–58). The recent debate over the proposed segregated schooling of African American males, in order to meet their needs, largely ignores the needs of young African American women and exemplifies this trend (Goodman A21).

Feminist scholars, however, recently began to take notice. As one puts it, we need to focus on the larger issue of adolescent culture rather than on delinquency and focus on what girls are doing, what their lives are like. Young adolescence may be redefined, in fact, not as violence versus lack of violence but as peer identity versus isolation. For girls, this often means close ties to the consumer culture rather than to so-called rituals of resistance (McRobbie 8; Coleman and Hendry 53).

A quick review of the literature on adolescence reveals the problem. A recent handbook for parents about middle-school children encourages straight talk with children about the many issues that affect their lives. The book urges parents to examine questions of racial, ethnic, and cultural diversity, but it never discusses gender as a category of difference (Berla et al. 83). This is distressing when we know that during adolescence children become acutely aware of themselves as gendered beings, both biologically and socially. The exclusion of gender issues is typical, as is the tendency, when researchers do mention girls, to discuss them in relation to boys and in terms of dating or mixed-sex social encounters. Research virtually ignores girls' same-sex activities, an important aspect of pre-adolescent and adolescent growth.

Of course, gender is a crucial element in adolescent development for girls and boys. In no other period of life except infancy do so many biological changes occur so quickly, and many of those biological changes are sex-specific (Montemayor et al. 9). Those who study adolescence, however, argue that social expectations, even more than physical changes, shape gender roles (Huston and Alvarez 158). When young people respond to peers and television as socializing influences, they often become increasingly intolerant of deviations from traditional sex role norms; surprisingly enough, peers often promote more traditional roles than do parents. Stereotypical attitudes about girls and boys, while not born in adolescence, often solidify at this age into hard and fast rules rather than simple observations (Montemayor et al. 13; Coleman and Hendry 123; Chandler 150).

The implications of this rigid agenda for girls are dramatic. Studies show that girls' academic and career ambitions actually decline in early adolescence when they internalize the notion that females should achieve less than males. During this period females and males both come to view math, science, and computer skills as male domains (Huston and Alvarez 158, 169). Teachers and educational programs as well as the family encourage such messages. Girls also learn by early adolescence that in order to be defined as successful they must please others, putting the needs of others first. Girls have few illusions about how this translates into real life experiences. Sadly, while cognitive developments that take place in early adolescence can encourage children to look at roles, including gender roles, in a flexible way, social constraints encourage them to limit their thinking and conceptualize gender roles in highly conformist and predictable ways (Huston and Alvarez 173). For girls this translates to the rule that they must get a boyfriend, keep a boyfriend, and learn dependence on males to be successful in life (McRobbie xvii; Newman and Newman 150–51; Chandler x).

While children repeatedly get these messages at home and in school, they get them from popular culture as well. Widely documented studies of television's influence on gender role socialization reveal the connections between television watching and the likelihood that children and teenagers will have stereotypical beliefs about gender roles (Comstock 160–75). Adolescence heightens sensitivity about gender, and numerous studies demonstrate the extent of gender stereotyping on contemporary television. Males are overrepresented two or three to one in commercial television, and the voice-over in commercials remains male 90 percent of the time. This is significant, of course, as children in the United States watch an average of 40,000 commercials per year (Comstock 188). In addition to television, magazines and fiction addressed to pre-adolescent and adolescent girls stress traditional gender roles, the importance of girls' bodies, and the overwhelming and incessant need to find a boy. Magazines, for example, provide constant reminders that a girl must consciously and continuously cultivate sexual attractiveness, her greatest asset. Magazines, teen formula romance fiction, and other commercial enterprises replay the messages that come, in other forms, through the family and school.

However, unlike family or school, leisure pursuits like reading magazines or playing games do not appear to be coercive. Simply because of this, they demand attention. Associated with freedom, leisure activities for girls often carry heavy ideological messages wrapped in the context of an escape from limits (McRobbie 88). These activities define girlhood in class-, race-, and behavior-specific ways. Three out of four teen fashion magazines in the United States, with a combined circulation of almost four million, portray young American women as white, very feminine, carefree, boy-crazy virgins. A recent issue of *Teen* featured liposuction and plastic surgery as options for those readers dissatisfied with their bodies. *Sassy*, noted for its initial frank discussions of adolescent sexuality, bent to pressure and omitted much of what made it controversial and, not coincidentally, a favorite among many young women craving honest discussion of their needs. These forms of popular culture, rather than an escape from limitations, provide clear and limited definitions of what it means to be a girl.

Board games, another form of popular culture, are a significant aspect of same-sex play for girls. Girls do not play them with boys, nor do they play them to get boys' attention. As the back covers of the games illustrate, girls play in the company of other girls, often in the privacy of one of their bedrooms. The picture on the back of Heart-Throb is typical: four girls in a bedroom, one of them on the bed, the others lounging on the carpeted floor. The game board sits on the floor, and the background features a telephone, a radio/tape player, and a bowl of popcorn. In fact, three of these four covers show a telephone, a radio/tape player, and popcorn, which is, of course, a low-calorie snack. In this sacred space girls learn to define themselves. Real boys do not invade this very feminine scene, but the idea of boys takes up a good deal of space, as each game encourages girls to think about themselves in relation to boys. By playing these board games, girls learn a central rule: they need boys to complete their self-definition.

The four games featured here offer young adolescent girls a wide variety of messages, all of them gender specific. From the uniformly "pretty" boxes to the uniform goal of getting a guy, the games promote traditional gender role behaviors, emphasize clear messages about race, class, and sexual orientation, and encourage play that is decidedly humdrum if not outright insulting to any young adolescent's intelligence. They clearly fail Letty Pogrebin's test for nonsexist toys, but the ways in which they do so and fail young women in the process is worth examining further.

All of these board games promote the idea that the central object in a girl's life is to get a guy. In Sweet Valley High, girls literally race around the school trying to retrieve a boyfriend, a teacher chaperon, and all the accessories needed for a big date. In the process of trying to get it all done first, girls can steal other girls' boyfriends or fight over boyfriends; such behaviors receive rewards.

In Heart-Throb, each player chooses which boy she would like to have ask her out and guesses which boys her competitors will choose. The game pieces include 60 boyfriend cards, each picturing a different boy, and 162 personality cards, which reveal both good and bad qualities of boys. In Girl Talk: Date Line, players match up girl and boy cards they hold in their hands in order to create successful dates. While they travel around the board, trying to set up a date, the players date as well; if they do not secure a date for the imaginary characters they hold in their hands, they themselves must go stag or settle for a blind date.

In Girl Talk: A Game of Truth or Dare, the initial focus seems different. Girls spin a wheel and then must reveal a secret or do a stunt. Many of the stunts are unrelated to getting a boyfriend and include doing sit-ups or sucking a lemon. Others, however, clearly promote the overall gender-enforcing plan and include pretending to put on make-up, calling a boy and telling him a joke, rating your looks from one to ten, or revealing what you would like to change about your looks. Anytime a girl does not complete the required stunt, she must peel off a red zit sticker and wear it on her face for the rest of the game. The game's instructions warn that the zit sticker must be visible: It cannot go under the chin or behind the ear.

The end goal of this game is to collect one of each of the fortune cards, which fit into four categories: Marriage, Children, Career, and Special Moments. However, dependency on boys or men dictates girls' experiences in each of the four categories except Children. Under Marriage, two possible fortunes are "You will marry _____'s boyfriend" or "You will meet your future husband while working together at _____ fast-food restaurant." Under Career, you could receive "After three weeks on your first job as a _____ (profession), you will meet the man that you will eventually marry," or "You will take a job as a carhop just to get a date with a certain boy who drives a _____." Finally, under Special Moments, fortunes include "A tall, dark, and handsome policeman will stop you for speeding and give you a ticket, but will make up for it by asking you for a date," or "While visiting a dude ranch, your horse will bolt and you will be rescued by a ranch hand who looks just like _____ (actor)." In the category of Special Moments, with twenty-four possible cards, seven are specifically about boys, but only one portrays a girl having a special moment with a girlfriend.

Each of these four games portrays girls in strictly feminine terms and boys in strictly masculine terms, with little overlap in traditional definitions. In the Sweet Valley High game, for example, students vote Jessica Most Popular Girl in the school; she is also, not coincidentally, co-captain of the cheerleading squad. Elizabeth, Jessica's sister, receives an award for her newspaper column, a gossip column called "Eyes and Ears." The names used in the Sweet Valley game indicate which girls and boys are popular and which are not. The nerdy and nonmasculine boy is called Winston Egbert; Winston prefers feminine activities like talking and being gentle to masculine qualities like playing football and being aloof. The desirable boys in Sweet Valley, Todd Wilkins and Bruce Patman, do masculine things like skiing and driving expensive sports cars.

Names are used as indicators of appropriate levels of feminine or masculine qualities in Girl Talk: Date Line as well. When players land on a date space, they choose two of the character cards in their hand and set them up for a date. When they put the cards together in a microphone machine, girls discover whether or not the date they choreographed went well. The characters Gert and Homer stand out as nerds in appearance, name, and behavior. Both Gert and Homer wear glasses, but none of the many popular characters wear glasses, and the popular people have names like Nicole and Drew, Stephanie and Matt.

In Girl Talk: Date Line, Homer's personality profile reveals that he loves the computer club and collecting bugs but hates sports and school dances. Boys clearly should love sports, including the sport of pursuing girls at dances, whether or not they actually like to dance. Gert, the girl without make-up and hence without much personality, loves Latin and algebra, hates rock music and gym class. Obviously girls should not have academic aspirations. The attributes of the popular people in Girl Talk: Date Line confirm clear rules about what it means to be a girl or boy. Stacie loves talking on the phone and shopping but hates greasy hair and book reports. Tina loves pizza and make-up but hates computers and report cards. Eric, on the other hand, loves tennis and water skiing, hates shopping malls. Matt loves math and football, hates double-dating (wants to be in control?) and haircuts.

In Heart-Throb, girls and boys behave in gender-specific ways in dating. When the players choose which of the boys in the boyfriend cards they would like to date and which they think the other players will choose, it seems that at last girls are making choices. In actuality, though, the rules state that three boys from the boyfriend cards ask the girls first to dance, then to go on a date, then to go steady. The girls must choose from among the three boys. Players have some very limited choices: They can choose which boy they want, but they cannot choose not to accept a dance, a date, or a steady boyfriend. Refusing the advances of all three boys is not an option, regardless of how uninviting they appear in their personality cards.

These board games clearly promote male privilege, then; they also promote the privileges of race, wealth, and heterosexuality. In the four games, virtually all of the characters are white. In Sweet Valley High, located in California, all of the students are fair-skinned, and the only ones with names that deviate from the most popular or trendy, which include Ken—who does in fact look like Barbie's counterpart—are the names of the nerdy characters, but Winston remains, nevertheless, a Waspy nerd. In Heart-Throb, a game with sixty boyfriend cards, not one of the boys even has an ethnic-sounding name. The only feature that distinguishes a few, and makes them appear somewhat "different," is the appearance of dark sunglasses. In Girl Talk: Date Line, the trendy names include, for the girls, Danielle, Tina, Allison, and Stephanie, and for the boys, Drew, Trent, Eric, and Brad. This game, interestingly enough, features one African-American boy but no African-American girls; one wonders who players match him up with for a date.

In addition to the privilege of race, the characters in these games have the privilege of social class. The Sweet Valley High game goes the furthest with this: One character gets rewarded for giving her housekeeper the day off and making her own bed, another for donating a large sum to charity, a third for taking everyone for a ride in her new sports car. In each of the other games, the girls shown playing the games or the character pieces in the games dress well, have access to income to buy clothing and make-up, and have private space all their own. No apartment living for these girls; they relax in their suburban bedrooms with plush carpet or scoot around town in their very own vehicles.

These board games promote the social control of girls' sexuality as well, with heterosexuality consistently privileged. In three of the four games, the only object is either to secure a boyfriend for oneself or secure one for others. The fourth clearly favors marriage and children as the end goal in life. Each game encourages competition among girls for boys, as girls steal others' boyfriends or find warnings in the instructions, as they do in the Sweet Valley game, that they need to keep an eye on their thieving girlfriends. Girls play these games together, but rather than promoting positive female culture or solidarity, the games teach girls that they cannot trust each other when it comes to their primary life definition: boys. The directions in the Sweet Valley game specify that girls can never have more than one boyfriend at a time; if they pick up a second, they must discard one. In Girl Talk: Date Line, the directions actually state in writing that players should not attempt to match up a girl with a girl or a boy with a boy for a date. According to these games, all girls, even the nerdy ones, can look forward to a shared future. What the games encourage players to share, however, is not the ability to laugh, intelligence, or even stereotypical nurturing qualities; instead, players share a future that must, apparently at any cost, include a man.

These four games rely on stereotypes about girls that stray far from the goal of promoting more egalitarian, difference-respecting play experiences. The games suggest that their characters represent the "ordinary" adolescent in the United States. Virtually all young adolescents, the games would have us believe, are white, long-haired, fair-haired, blemish-free, wealthy, heterosexual, and well dressed. The overall message does not necessarily suggest that all adolescent girls think the same way, because aside from their desire to secure a boyfriend we or the players learn little about what interests girls. What ties young adolescent girls together, through these games, is simply that they must acquire a boyfriend.

Interestingly enough, the stars of these games, the girls featured on the covers and on the boards and playing pieces, do not closely resemble the voluptuous and flashy young women of the teen magazines. In fact, they seem far closer to the "average" than that. It would be a mistake to think for a moment, though, that they represent anything but a carefully crafted version of the ideal, of the "average" ideal. Perhaps girls read fashion magazines and wish they could have the beautiful looks of the models. Perhaps when they play the board games they wish they could be the average girl, fit easily into developing peer norms, and blend into their settings as easily as the girls on the game boxes seem to blend into theirs. The games present a message just as damaging as that of the magazines, though, because if the game characters represent the norm, the average, they must represent the attainable. The truth remains that white wealthy heterosexuality is not the norm, not what young girls have in common.

Unfortunately, however, most adolescents share a strong desire to meet the established, if largely unattainable, norm.

The final way in which these games fail Letty Pogrebin's test and, in so doing, fail real girls' needs, is that they completely fail to challenge girls' intellects or inspire their creativity. Researchers have revealed that girls' games often provide fewer intellectual challenges than do boys' games. Girls, more restricted in their play than boys in terms of movement and noise, learn to appreciate indoor activities, in smaller groups, and at lower skill levels (Rivers et al. 105–7). The few board games we have focused on match those findings.

The most insulting of the four games is Girl Talk: Date Line. Girls match couples up and then hope that the date takes place. In fact, though, the individual qualities players match up do not determine whether or not the date takes place. Instead, a continuously running cassette tape determines everything. While the game instructs players that if the two individuals seem compatible the date will happen, sheer luck actually determines the course of action. If a player is fortunate enough to put her two characters in the microphone machine when the tape is about to play a successful date scenario, she wins. If not, she loses.

The next two games provide little more of a challenge. In Heart-Throb girls choose which boy they prefer, then they guess which boy their friends will prefer. A simple guessing game, Heart-Throb is packaged as though it contains something of consequence. Girls could easily play the same game, if they wished, using a magazine with pictures of boys in it; they hardly need the game board or pieces. Sweet Valley High is essentially a memory game. Girls have to remember in which classroom the corsage card sits, in which classroom their boyfriend sits. This game hardly differs from any matching game with cards played by young children, except for the ideological messages reinforcing gender and other stereotypes.

Girl Talk: A Game of Truth or Dare is the most sophisticated and potentially challenging of these board games. Girls actually do things in this game; they move around, they talk to each other, they share secrets. Were the end goals not so blatantly sexist, the packaging not so stereotypically feminine, and the zit stickers not so offensive, this might not be a bad game.

Games encourage players to develop particular skills. By encouraging large group play in a variety of settings, many boys' games urge them to achieve success in the world at large. Most girls' games, however, prepare girls for a life in one setting, the home, by emphasizing verbal skills in small groups rather than large ones, and by taking place indoors. Interestingly enough, although the object of many of the girls' games is to secure a boyfriend, the verbal skills emphasized do not apply to him. In other words, girls learn to talk to each other about boys, but they do not learn to communicate with those boys.

Further research may reveal that girls use these games in subversive as well as stereotypical ways or that, like the latest fashions, these trendy games spend more time in closets than they do in the center of girls' play areas. For the many girls who do play them as designated, however, these sex-stereotyped games promote damaging stereotypes, passive rather than active play, and skills that fall short of girls' cognitive abilities. The games assume that all girls share a common future of domestic work, subservience to men, and limited life experience. They also further the likelihood of such a future by failing to encourage intellectual growth. In an advice book for girls published in 1936, Mary Brockman wrote that "boys don't want girls to talk too much or try to appear too wise.... [T]hey want girls to know when to sit back and look interested" (173). Apparently, the lesson lives on. These board games, as much a part of the toy-store world of the 1990s as they were of the 1970s, frame a world of limited possibilities for girls.

WORKS CITED

Berla, Nancy, Anne Henderson, and William Kerewsky. *The Middle School Years: A Parents' Handbook.* Columbia, MD: National Commission for Citizens in Education, 1989.

Brockman, Mary. *What Is She Like? A Personality Book for Girls.* New York: Scribner's, 1936.

Chandler, E. M. *Educating Adolescent Girls.* London: Allen, 1980.

Coleman, John C., and Leo Hendry. *The Nature of Adolescence.* New York: Routledge, 1990.

Comstock, George. *Television and the American Child.* San Diego: Academic, 1991.

Dun and Bradstreet. *America's Corporate Families.* Parsippany: Dun and Bradstreet, 1992.

Goodman, Ellen. "Girls Fail Too." *Washington Post* 7 Sept. 1991: A21.

Huston, Aletha, and Mildred Alvarez. "The Socialization Context of Gender Role Development in Early Adolescence." *From Childhood to Adolescence: A Tran-*

sitional Period? Ed. Raymond Montemayor, Gerald Adams, and Thomas Gullotta. Newbury Park: Sage, 1990. 156–79.

McRobbie, Angela. *Feminism and Youth Culture: From "Jackie" to "Just Seventeen."* Boston: Unwin Hyman, 1991.

Montemayor, Raymond, Gerald Adams, and Thomas Gullotta, eds. *From Childhood to Adolescence: A Transitional Period?* Introduction. Newbury Park: Sage, 1990.

Newman, Barbara, and Philip Newman. *Adolescent Development.* Columbus: Merrill, 1986.

Pogrebin, Letty Cottin. "Toys for Free Children." *Ms.* Dec. 1973: 48+.

Rivers, Caryl, Rosalind Barnett, and Brace Baruch. *Beyond Sugar and Spice: How Women Grow, Learn, and Thrive.* New York: Putnam, 1979.

Part III

Re-imagining Girlhood

9

The Flapper and the Chaperone

*Cultural Constructions of
Identity and Heterosexual
Politics among Adolescent
Mexican American Women,
1920–1950*

Vicki L. Ruiz

Imagine a gathering in a barrio hall, a group of young people dressed "to the nines" trying their best to replicate the dance steps of Fred Astaire and Ginger Rogers. This convivial heterosocial scene was typical of the lives of teenagers during the interwar period. But along the walls, a sharp difference was apparent in the barrios. Mothers, fathers, and older relatives chatted with one another as they kept one eye trained on the dance floor. They were the chaperones—the ubiquitous companions of unmarried Mexican American women. Chaperonage was a traditional instrument of social control. Indeed, the presence of *la dueña* was the prerequisite for attendance at a dance, a movie, or even church-related events. "When we would go to town, I would want to say something to a guy. I couldn't because my mother was always there," remembered María Ybarra. "She would always stick to us girls like glue. . . . She never let us out of her sight."[1]

An examination of events like this one reveals the ways in which young Mexican women in the United States between the wars rationalized, resisted, and evaded parental supervision. It offers a glimpse into genera-

9.1. My mother Erminia Ruiz as a young woman, c. 1941.

tional conflict which goes beyond the more general differences in accul-turation between immigrants and their children. Chaperonage existed for centuries on both sides of the political border separating Mexico and the United States. While conjuring images of patriarchal domination, chap-eronage is best understood as a manifestation of familial oligarchy whereby elders attempted to dictate the activities of youth for the sake of family honor. A family's standing in the community depended, in part, on women's purity. Loss of virginity not only tainted the reputation of an individual, but of her kin as well. For Mexicano immigrants living in a new, bewildering environment filled with temptations, the enforcement of chaperonage assumed a particular urgency.[2]

Historians Donna Gabaccia and Sydney Stahl Weinberg have urged immigration historians to notice the subtle ways women shaped and reshaped their environments, especially within the family. In addition, path-breaking works by Elizabeth Ewen, Andrew Heinze, and Susan Glenn examine the impact of U.S. consumer culture on European immigrants.[3] Indeed, while some Mexican American youth negotiated missionary idealizations of American life, other teenagers sought the American dream as promised in magazines, movies, and radio programs.

Popular culture could serve as a tool for literacy. While mothers may have viewed romance magazines, like *True Story*, as giving their daughters "bad ideas,"[4] the following passage taken from my interview with Jesusita Torres poignantly reveals a discourse of discovery:

> I started reading in English. I remember when I started reading the love story books ..., I started understanding. But I never knew the end of it. You know why I never knew the end of the story? [VR: Why?] Because ... when you turn the page and at the end it says "cont." like in continue, I never knew what it meant. So one day I discovered it myself. I was reading and I always wanted to know the end of the story. I wanted to know so bad so I continued flipping the pages, then I looked ... the same name of the story and it said the same word "cont" ... I learned that. And then from then on ... I finished the stories. ... To me that was something ... you see, I did not have anybody to say: "Look, you look at the page and you continue."[5]

The transmitters of Americanization, including mass culture, could influence women in many ways—from fantasy to lived experience, from hegemonic presence to small, personal victories. I am reminded of the words of George Lipsitz, "Images and icons compete for dominance within a multiplicity of discourses." He continues, "consumers of popular culture move in and out of subject positions in a way that allows the same message to have widely varying meanings at the point of reception." Or as Indonesian poet, Nirwan Dewanto stated, "the struggle for our survival in the information era is not to be won where information originates, but where it arrives."[6]

Confronting "America" began at an early age. Throughout the Southwest, Spanish-speaking children had to sink or swim in an English-only
environment. Even on the playground, students were punished for con-
versing in Spanish. Admonishments, such as "Don't speak that ugly language, you are an American now. . ," not only reflected a strong belief in
Anglo conformity but denigrated the self-esteem of Mexican American
children.[7] As Mary Luna stated:

> It was rough because I didn't know English. The teacher wouldn't let us
> talk Spanish. How can you talk to anybody? If you can't talk Spanish and
> you can't talk English. . . . It wasn't until maybe the fourth or fifth grade
> that I started catching up. And all that time I just felt I was stupid.[8]

Yet, Luna credited her love of reading to a Euro-American educator who
had converted a small barrio house into a make-shift community center
and library. Her words underscore the dual thrust of americanization—
education and consumerism. "To this day I just love going into libraries.
. . . [T]here are two places that I can go in and get a real warm, happy
feeling; that is, the library and Bullock's in the perfume and make-up
department."[9]

Racial/ethnic women struggled with boundaries and made decisions as
individuals, family members, neighbors, and peers. The following works
in Asian American history seem especially enlightening. Taking into account a buffet of cultural choices emanating from Japanese communities
and U.S. society at large, Valerie Matsumoto's study of Nisei women
teenagers before the Second World War elegantly outlines the social
construction of the Nisei world. Matsumoto emphasizes the agency of
adolescents in creating and nurturing their own youth culture. Along
similar lines, Judy Yung in *Unbound Feet* beautifully details the work and
leisure activities among Chinese American teenagers in San Francisco.[10]

For Mexican Americans, second-generation women as teenagers have
received scant scholarly attention. Among Chicano historians and writers,
there appears a fascination with the sons of immigrants, especially as
pachucos.[11] Young women, however, may have experienced deeper generational tensions as they blended elements of americanization with Mexican expectations and values. This essay focuses on the shifting interplay
of gender, cultures, class, ethnicity, and youth and the ways in which
women negotiate across specific cultural contexts, blending elements as
diverse as celebrating Cinco de Mayo and applying Max Factor cosmetics.

In grappling with Mexican American women's consciousness and agency, oral history offers a venue for exploring teenage expectations and for preserving a historical memory of attitudes and feelings. In addition to archival research, the recollections of seventeen women serve as the basis for my reconstruction of adolescent aspirations and experiences (or dreams and routines).[12] The women themselves are fairly homogeneous in terms of nativity, class, residence, and family structure. With two exceptions, they are U.S. citizens by birth and attended southwestern schools. All of the interviewees were born between 1908 and 1926.[13] Although three came from families once considered middle class in Mexico, most can be considered working class in the United States. Their fathers' typical occupations included farm worker, miner, day laborer, and railroad hand. These women usually characterized their mothers as homemakers, although several remembered that their mothers took seasonal jobs in area factories and fields. The most economically privileged woman in the sample, Ruby Estrada, helped out in her family-owned hardware and furniture store. She is also the only interviewee who attended college.[14] It should be noted that seven of the seventeen narrators married Euro-Americans. Though intermarriage was uncommon, these oral histories give us insight into the lives of those who negotiated across cultures in a deeply personal way and who felt the impact of acculturation most keenly. Rich in emotion and detail, these interviews reveal women's conscious decision-making in the production of culture. In creating their own cultural spaces, the interwar generation challenged the trappings of familial oligarchy.

Chicano social scientists have generally portrayed women as "the 'glue' that keeps the Chicano family together" as well as the guardians of traditional culture.[15] Whether one accepts this premise or not, within families, young women, perhaps more than their brothers, were expected to uphold certain standards. Parents, therefore, often assumed what they perceived as their unquestionable prerogative to regulate the actions and attitudes of their adolescent daughters. Teenagers, on the other hand, did not always acquiesce in the boundaries set down for them by their elders. Intergenerational tension flared along several fronts.

As in the case of U.S. teenagers, in general, the first area of disagreement between an adolescent and her family would be over her personal appearance. As reflected in F. Scott Fitzgerald's "Bernice Bobs Her Hair," the length of a young woman's tresses was a hot issue spanning class, region, and ethnic lines. During the 1920s, a woman's decision "to bob or not bob" her hair assumed classic proportions within Mexican families.

After considerable pleading, Belen Martínez Mason was permitted to cut her hair, though she soon regretted the decision. "Oh, I cried for a month."[16] Differing opinions over fashions often caused ill feelings. One Mexican American woman recalled that as a young girl, her mother dressed her "like a nun" and she could wear "no make-up, no cream, no nothing" on her face. Swimwear, bloomers, and short skirts also became sources of controversy. Some teenagers left home in one outfit and changed into another at school. Once María Fierro arrived home in her bloomers. Her father inquired, "Where have you been dressed like that, like a clown?" "I told him the truth," Fierro explained. "He whipped me anyway. . . . So from then on whenever I went to the track meet, I used to change my bloomers so that he wouldn't see that I had gone again."[17] The impact of flapper styles on the Mexican community was clearly expressed in the following verse taken from a corrido (ballad) appropriately entitled, "Las Pelonas" (The Bobbed-Haired Girls):

> Red Banannas [sic]
> I detest,
> And now the flappers
> Use them for their dress.
> The girls of San Antonio
> Are lazy at the *metate.*
> They want to walk out bobbed-haired,
> With straw hats on.
> The harvesting is finished,
> So is the cotton;
> The flappers stroll out now
> For a good time.[18]

With similar sarcasm, another popular ballad chastised Mexican women for applying make-up so heavily as to resemble a piñata.[19]

The use of cosmetics, however, cannot be blamed entirely on Madison Avenue ad campaigns. The innumerable barrio beauty pageants, sponsored by mutualistas (mutual aid societies), patriotic societies, churches, the Mexican Chamber of Commerce, newspapers, and even progressive labor unions, encouraged young women to accentuate their physical attributes. Carefully chaperoned, many teenagers did participate in community contests from La Reina de Cinco de Mayo to Orange Queen. They modeled evening gowns, rode on parade floats, and sold raffle tickets.[20] Carmen Bernal Escobar remembered one incident where, as a contestant, she had to sell raffle tickets. Every ticket she sold counted as a vote for her in the pageant. Naturally the winner would be the woman who had accumulated the most votes. When her brother offered to buy twenty-five dollars worth of votes (her mother would not think of letting her peddle the tickets at work or in the neighborhood), Escobar, on a pragmatic note, asked him to give her the money so that she could buy a coat she had spotted while window-shopping.[21]

The commercialization of personal grooming made additional inroads into the Mexican community with the appearance of barrio beauty parlors. Working as a beautician conferred a certain degree of status, "a nice, clean job," in comparison to factory or domestic work. As one woman related:

> ... I always wanted to be a beauty operator. I loved makeup; I loved to dress up and fix up. I used to set my sisters' hair. So I had that in the back of my mind for a long time, and my mom pushed the fact that she wanted me to have a profession—seeing that I wasn't thinking of getting married.[22]

While further research is needed, one can speculate that neighborhood beauty shops reinforced women's networks and became places where they could relax, exchange *chimse* (gossip), and enjoy the company of other women.

During the 1920s, the ethic of consumption became inextricably linked to making it in America.[23] The message of affluence attainable through hard work and a bit of luck was reinforced in English- and Spanish-language publications. Mexican barrios were not immune from the burgeoning consumer culture. The society pages of the influential Los Angeles–based *La Opinion*, for example, featured advice columns, horoscopes, and celebrity gossip. Advertisements for make-up, clothing, even feminine hygiene products reminded teenagers of an awaiting world of consumption.[24] One week after its inaugural issue in 1926, *La Opinion* featured a Spanish translation of Louella Parsons' nationally syndicated gossip column. Advertisements not only hawked products but offered instructions for behavior. As historian Roberto Treviño related in his recent study of Tejano newspapers, "the point remains that the Spanish-language press conveyed symbolic American norms and models to a potentially assimilable readership."[25]

Advertisements aimed at women promised status and affection if the proper bleaching cream, hair coloring, and cosmetics were purchased. Or as one company boldly claimed, "Those with lighter, more healthy skin tones will become much more successful in business, love, and society."[26]

A print ad [in English] for Camay Soap carried by *Hispano-America* in 1932 reminded women readers that "Life is a Beauty Contest."[27] Flapper fashions and celebrity testimonials further fused the connections between gendered identity and consumer culture. Another promotion encouraged readers to "SIGA LAS ESTRELLAS" (FOLLOW THE STARS) and use Max Factor Cosmetics. It is important to keep in mind that Spanish-language newspapers filtered to their readers not only the iconography of U.S. popular culture, but also their perceptions of gender relations within that culture. For example, an advertisement for Godefroy's "Larieuse" hair coloring featured an attractive woman in profile smiling at the tiny man cupped in the palm of her hand. The diminutive male figure is shown on bended knee with his hands outstretched in total adoration. Now does this hair coloring promotion found in the February 8, 1938, issue of *La Opinion* relay the impression that by using this Anglo product, Mexican women will exert the same degree of power over their men as their Anglo peers supposedly plied?[28]

These visual representations raise all sorts of speculation as to their meaning, specifically with regard to the social construction of gender. I cannot identify the designers of these layouts, but the architects are less important than the subtle and not-so-subtle messages codified within the text. Mexican women interpreted these visual representations in a myriad of ways. Some ignored them, some redefined their messages, and other internalized them. The popularity of bleaching creams offers a poignant testament to color consciousness in Mexican communities, a historical consciousness accentuated by Americanization through education and popular culture.[29]

Reflecting the coalescence of Mexican and U.S. cultures, Spanish-language publications promoted pride in Latino theater and music while at the same time celebrating the icons of americanization and consumption. Because of its proximity to Hollywood, *La Opinion* ran contests in which the lucky winner would receive a screen test. On the one hand, *La Opinion* nurtured the dreams of "success" through entertainment and consumption, while on the other, the newspaper railed against the deportations and repatriations of the 1930s.[30] Sparked by manufactured fantasies and clinging to youthful hopes, many Mexican women teenagers avidly read celebrity gossip columns, attended Saturday matinees, cruised Hollywood and Vine, and nurtured their visions of stardom. A handful of Latina actresses, especially Dolores del Rio and Lupe Velez whetted these aspirations and served as public role models of the "American dream."

As a *La Opinion* article on Lupe Velez idealistically claimed, "Art has neither nationalities nor borders."[31]

In her essay "City Lights: Immigrant Women and the Rise of the Movies," Elizabeth Ewen has argued that during the early decades of the twentieth century "the social authority of the media of mass culture replaced older forms of family authority and behavior." Ewen further explained that the "authority of this new culture organized itself around the premise of freedom from customary bonds as a way of turning people's attention to the consumer market place as a source of self-definition."[32] Yet, Mexican women had choices (though certainly circumscribed by economic considerations) about what elements to embrace and what to ignore. As George Lipsitz reminds us in *Time Passages*, "hegemony is not just imposed on society from the top; it is struggled for from below, and no terrain is a more important part of that struggle than popular culture."[33] Mexican American women teenagers also positioned themselves within the cultural messages they gleaned from English- and Spanish-language publications, afternoon matinees, and popular radio programs. Their shifting conceptions of acceptable heterosocial behavior, including their desire "to date," heightened existing generational tensions between parents and daughters.[34]

Obviously, the most serious point of contention between an adolescent daughter and her Mexican parents regarded her behavior toward young men. In both cities and rural towns, close chaperonage was a way of life. Recalling the supervisory role played by her "old maid" aunt, María Fierro laughingly explained, "She'd check up on us all the time. I used to get so mad at her." Ruby Estrada recalled that in her small southern Arizona community, "all the mothers" escorted their daughters to the local dances. Estrada's mother was no exception when it came to chaperoning her daughters. "She went especially for us. She just sit there and take care of our coats and watch us." Even talking to male peers in broad daylight could be grounds for discipline.[35] Adele Hernández Milligan, a resident of Los Angeles for over fifty years, elaborated:

> I remember the first time that I walked home with a boy from school. Anyway, my mother saw me and she was mad. I must have been sixteen or seventeen. She slapped my face because I was walking home with a boy.[36]

Describing this familial protectiveness, one social scientist remarked that the "supervision of the Mexican parent is so strict as to be obnoxious."[37]

Faced with this type of situation, young women had three options:

they could accept the rules set down for them; they could rebel; or they could find ways to compromise or circumvent traditional standards. "I was *never* allowed to go out by myself in the evening; it just was not done," related Carmen Bernal Escobar. In rural communities, where restrictions were perhaps even more stringent, "nice" teenagers could not even swim with male peers. According to Ruby Estrada, "We were ladies and wouldn't go swimming out there with a bunch of boys." Yet, many seemed to accept these limits with equanimity. Remembering her mother as her chaperone, Lucy Acosta insisted, "I could care less as long I danced." "It wasn't devastating at all," echoed Ruby Estrada. "We took it in stride. We never thought of it as cruel or mean. . . . It was taken for granted that that's the way it was."[38] In Sonora, Arizona, like other small towns, relatives and neighbors kept close watch over adolescent women and quickly reported any suspected indiscretions. "They were always spying on you," Estrada remarked. Women in cities had a distinct advantage over their rural peers in that they could venture miles from their neighborhood into the anonymity of dance halls, amusement parks, and other forms of commercialized leisure. With carnival rides and the Cinderella Ballroom, the Nu-Pike amusement park of Long Beach proved a popular hang-out for Mexican youth in Los Angeles.[39] It was more difficult to abide by traditional norms when excitement loomed just on the other side of the streetcar line.

Some women openly rebelled. They moved out of their family homes and into apartments. Considering themselves free-wheeling single women, they could go out with men unsupervised as was the practice among their Anglo peers. Others challenged parental and cultural standards even further by living with their boyfriends. In his field notes, University of California economist Paul S. Taylor recorded an incident in which a young woman had moved in with her Anglo boyfriend after he had convinced her that such arrangements were common among Americans. "This terrible freedom in the United States," one Mexicana lamented. "I do not have to worry because I have no daughters, but the poor *señoras* with many girls, they worry."[40]

Those teenagers who did not wish to defy their parents openly would "sneak out" of the house in order to meet their dates or to attend dances with female friends. Whether meeting someone at a drug store, roller rink, or theater, this practice involved the invention of elaborate stories to mask traditionally inappropriate behavior.[41] In other words, they lied.

In his study of Tucson's Mexican community, Thomas Sheridan related the following saga of Jacinta Pérez de Valdez:

> As she and her sisters grew older, they used to sneak out of the house to go to the Riverside Ball Room. One time a friend of their father saw them there and said, "Listen, Felipe, don't you know your daughters are hanging around the Riverside?" Furious, their father threw a coat over his longjohns and stormed into the dance hall, not even stopping to tie his shoes.... Doña Jacinta recalled. "He entered by one door and we left by another. We had to walk back home along the railroad tracks in our high heels. I think we left those heels on the rails." She added that when their father returned, "We were all lying in bed like little angels."[42]

A more subtle form of rebellion was early marriage. By marrying at fifteen or sixteen, these women sought to escape parental supervision; yet, it could be argued that for many of these child brides, they exchanged one form of supervision for another in addition to the responsibilities of child-rearing.[43] In her 1933 ethnography, Clara Smith related the gripping testimony of one teenage bride:

> You see, my father and mother wouldn't let us get married.... Mother made me stay with her all the time. She always goes to church every morning at seven-thirty as she did in Mexico. I said I was sick. She went with my brothers and we just ran away and got married at the court.... They were strict with my sister, too. That's why she took poison and died.[44]

One can only speculate on the psychic pressures and external circumstances which would drive a young woman to take her own life.

Elopement occurred frequently as many parents believed that no one was good enough for their daughters. "I didn't want to elope ... so this was the next best thing to a wedding," recalled María Ybarra as she described how the justice of the peace performed the ceremony in her parents' home. "Neither my Dad or my Mom liked my husband. Nobody liked him," she continued. "My husband used to run around a lot. After we got married, he did settle down, but my parents didn't know that then."[45] One fifteen year old locked her grandmother in the outhouse so she could elope with her boyfriend. Indeed, when he first approached her at a San Joaquin Valley migrant camp asking if he could be her *novio*, she supposedly replied, "No, but I'll marry you." Lupe was just that desperate to escape familial supervision.[46]

If acquiescence, apartment living, early marriage, or elopement were out of the question, what other tactics did teenagers devise? The third alternative sometimes involved quite a bit of creativity on the part of young women as they sought to circumvent traditional chaperonage. Alicia Mendeola Shelit recalled that one of her older brothers would accompany her to dances ostensibly as a chaperone. "But then my oldest brother would always have a blind date for me." Carmen Bernal Escobar was permitted to entertain her boyfriends at home but only under the supervision of her brother or mother. The practice of "going out with the girls," though not accepted until the 1940s, was fairly common. Several Mexican American women, often related, would escort one another to an event (such as a dance), socialize with the men in attendance, and then walk home together. In the sample of seventeen interviews, daughters negotiated their activities with their parents. Older siblings and extended kin appeared in the background as either chaperones or accomplices. Although unwed teenage mothers were not unknown in Mexican barrios, families expected adolescent women to conform to strict standards of behavior.[47]

As can be expected, many teenage women knew little about sex other than what they picked up from friends, romance magazines, and the local theater. As Mary Luna remembered, "I thought that if somebody kissed you, you could get pregnant." In *Singing for My Echo*, New Mexico native Gregorita Rodríguez confided that on her wedding night, she knelt down and said her rosary until her husband gently asked, "Gregorita, *mi esposa*, are you afraid of me?" At times this naiveté persisted beyond the wedding. "It took four days for my husband to touch me," one woman revealed. "I slept with dress and all. We were both greenhorns, I guess."[48]

Of course, some young women did lead more adventurous lives. A male interviewer employed by Mexican anthropologist Manuel Gamio recalled his "relations" with a woman he met in a Los Angeles dance hall. Though born in Hermosillo, Elisa "Elsie" Morales considered herself Spanish. She helped support her family by dancing with strangers. Although she lived at home and her mother and brother attempted to monitor her actions, she managed to meet the interviewer at a "hot pillow" hotel. To prevent pregnancy, she relied on contraceptive douches provided by "an American doctor." Although Morales realized her mother would not approve of her behavior, she noted that "she [her mother] is from Mexico. . . . I am from there also but I was brought up in the United States, we think about things differently." Just as Morales rationalized her actions as "American," the interviewer perceived her within a similar, though certainly less favorable, definition of americanization. "She seemed very coarse to me. That is she dealt with one in the American way. . . ." Popular corridos, such as "El Enganchado" and "Las Pelonas," also touched on the theme of the corrupting influence of U.S. ways on Mexican women.[49] If there were rewards for women who escaped parental boundaries, there were also sanctions for those who crossed established lines.[50]

Women who had children out of wedlock seemed to be treated by their parents in one of two ways—as pariahs or as prodigal daughters. Erminia Ruiz recalled the experiences of two girlhood friends:

> It was a disgrace to the whole family. The whole family suffered and . . . her mother said she didn't want her home. She could not bring the baby home and she was not welcome at home. . . . She had no place to go. . . . And then I had another friend. She was also pregnant and the mother actually went to court to try to get him to marry her. . . . He hurried and married someone else but then he had to give child support.[51]

In another instance, Carmen and her baby were accepted by her family. She was, however, expected to work in the fields to support her infant. Her parents kept a watchful eye on her activities. When Diego, a young Mexicano immigrant, asked Carmen out to dinner, her baby became her chaperone. "[My mother] said to take the baby with you. She was so smart so I wouldn't go any farther than the restaurant. At first, I was ashamed but [he] said, 'Bring him so he can eat.' " Before Carmen accepted Diego's proposal of marriage, she asked him for his family's address in Mexico so she could make sure he was not already married. "I told him I wouldn't answer him until I got an answer." Diego's mother replied that her son was single, but had a girlfriend waiting for him. Carmen and Diego have been married for over fifty years.[52]

Carmen's story illustrates the resiliency and resourcefulness of Mexican American women. Her behavior during her courtship with Diego demonstrates shrewdness and independence. Once burned, she would be nobody's *pendeja* (fool).

Yet, autonomy on the part of young women was hard to win in a world where pregnant, unmarried teenagers served as community "examples" of what might happen to you or your daughter if appropriate measures were not taken. As an elderly Mexicana remarked, "Your reputation was everything."[53] In this sense, the chaperone not only protected the young woman's position in the community, but that of the entire family.

So, chaperonage exacerbated conflict not only between generations but within individuals as well. In gaily recounting tales of ditching the dueña or sneaking down the stairwell, the laughter of the interviewees fails to hide the painful memories of breaking away from familial expectations. Their words resonate with the dilemma of reconciling their search for autonomy with their desire for parental affirmation. It is important to note that every informant who challenged or circumvented chaperonage held full-time jobs, as either factory or service workers. In contrast, most woman who accepted constant supervision did not work for wages. Perhaps because they labored for long hours, for little pay, and frequently under hazardous conditions, factory and service workers were determined to exercise some control over their leisure time. Indeed, Douglas Monroy has argued that outside employment "facilitated greater freedom of activity and more assertiveness in the family for Mexicanas."[54]

It may also be significant that none of the employed teenagers had attended high school. They had entered the labor market directly after or even before the completion of the eighth grade. Like many female factory workers in the United States, most Mexican operatives were young, unmarried daughters whose wage labor was essential to the economic survival of their families. As members of a "family wage economy," they relinquished all or part of their wages to their elders. According to a 1933 University of California study, of the Mexican families surveyed with working children, the children's monetary contributions comprised 35 percent of total household income.[55] Cognizant of their earning power, they resented the lack of personal autonomy.

Delicate negotiations ensued as both parents and daughters struggled over questions of leisure activities and discretionary income. Could a young woman retain a portion of her wages for her own use? If elders demanded every penny, daughters might be more inclined to splurge on a new outfit or other personal item on their way home from work or even more extreme, they might choose to move out taking their pay checks with them. Recognizing their dependence on their children's income, some parents compromised. Their concessions, however, generally took the form of allocating spending money rather than relaxing traditional supervision. Still, women's earning power could be an important bargaining chip.[56]

On one level, many teenagers were devoted to their parents as evident (at least, in part) by their employment in hazardous, low-paying jobs. For example, Julia Luna Mount recalled her first day at a Los Angeles cannery:

> I didn't have money for gloves so I peeled chiles all day long by hand. After work, my hands were red, swollen, and I was on fire! On the streetcar going home, I could hardly hold on my hands hurt so much. The minute I got home, I soaked my hands in a pan of cold water. My father saw how I was suffering and he said, "*Mi hija*, you don't have to go back there tomorrow," and I didn't.[57]

On the other hand, adolescents rebelled against what they perceived as an embarrassingly old-fashioned intrusion into their private lives. When chastised by her aunt for dancing too close to her partner, Alma Araiza García would retort, "I am not going to get pregnant just by leaning on his cheek, okay?"[58] They wanted the right to choose their own companions and to use their own judgment.

Chaperonage triggered deep-seated tensions over autonomy and self-determination. "Whose life is it anyway?" was a recurring question with no satisfactory answer. Many women wanted their parents to consider them dutiful daughters, but they also wanted degrees of freedom. While ethnographies provide scintillating tales of teenage rebellion, the voices of the interviewees do not. Their stories reflect the experiences of those adolescents who struggled with boundaries. How can one retain one's "good name" while experiencing the joys of youth? How can one be both a good daughter and an independent woman?

To complete the picture, we also have to consider the perspective of Mexican immigrant parents, who encountered a youth culture very different from that of their generation. For them, courtship had occurred in the plaza; young women and men promenaded under the watchful eyes of town elders, an atmosphere in which an exchange of meaningful glances could well portend engagement. One can understand their consternation as they watched their daughters apply cosmetics and adopt the apparel advertised in fashion magazines. In other words, "If she dresses like a flapper, will she then act like one?" Seeds of suspicion reaffirmed the penchant for traditional supervision.

Parents could not completely cloister their children from the temptations of "modern" society, but chaperonage provided a way to monitor their activities. It was an attempt to mold young women into sheltered young matrons. But one cannot regard the presence of la dueña as simply an old-world tradition on a collision course with twentieth-century life. The regulation of daughters involved more than a conflict between peasant ways and modern ideas. Chaperonage was both an actual and symbolic assertion of familial oligarchy. A family's reputation was linked to the purity of women. As reiterated in a Catholic catechism, if a young woman became a "faded lily," she and her family would suffer dire consequences.[59] Since family honor rested, to some degree, on the preservation of female chastity (or vergüenza), women were to be controlled for the collective good, with older relatives assuming unquestioned responsibility in this regard. Mexican women coming of age during the 1920s and 1930s were not the first to challenge the authority of elders. Ramón Gutiérrez in his path-breaking scholarship on colonial New Mexico uncovered numerous instances of women who tried to exercise some autonomy over their sexuality.[60] The Mexican American generation, however, had a potent ally unavailable to their foremothers—consumer culture.

U.S. consumerism did not bring about the disintegration of familial oligarchy, but it did serve as a catalyst for change. The ideology of control was shaken by consumer culture and the heterosocial world of urban youth. As previously indicated, chaperonage proved much easier to enforce in a small town. Ruby Estrada described how a young woman would get the third degree if caught with a potential boyfriend alone. "And they [the elders] would say what are [you] doing there all alone. . . . Yeah, what were you up to or if you weren't up to no good, why should you be talking to that boy?"[61]

In contrast, parents in the barrios of major cities fought a losing battle against urban anonymity and commercialized leisure. The Catholic church was quick to point out the "dangerous amusement" inherent in dancing, theater-going, dressing fashionably, and reading pulp fiction. Under the section, "The Enemy in the Ballroom," a Catholic advice book warned of the hidden temptations of dance. "I know that some persons can indulge in it without harm; but sometimes even the coldest temperaments are heated by it."[62] Therefore, the author offered the following rules:

(1) If you know nothing at all . . . about dancing do not trouble yourself to learn (2) Be watchful . . . and see that your pleasure in dancing does not grow into a passion. . . . (3) Never frequent fairs, picnics, carnivals, or public dancing halls where Heaven only knows what sorts of people con-

gregate. (4) Dance only at private parties where your father or mother is present. . . . [63]

Pious pronouncements such as these had little impact on those adolescents who cherished the opportunity to look and act like vamps and flappers.

Attempting to regulate the social life of young parishioners, barrio priests organized gender-segregated teen groups. In Los Angeles, Juventud Católica Feminina Mexicana (JCFM) had over fifty chapters. In her autobiography *Hoyt Street*, Mary Helen Ponce remembered the group as one organized for "nice" girls with the navy blue uniform as its most appealing feature. The local chapter fell apart during World War II as young women rushed off to do their patriotic duty at "canteens," preferring to keep company with "lonely soldiers" than to sitting "in a stuffy church while an elderly priest espoused the virtues of a pure life." Too young for the USO (United Service Organizations), Ponce enjoyed going to "las vistas," usually singing cowboy movies shown in the church hall after Sunday evening rosary.[64] Priests endeavored to provide wholesome entertainment, showing films approved by the Legion of Decency. Movies in parish halls also served other purposes. The cut-rate features, like church *jamaicas*, raised money for local activities and provided a social space for parishioners. In an era of segregated theaters, church halls provided an environment where Mexicanos and their children could enjoy inexpensive entertainment and sit wherever they pleased.[65]

Even within the fish bowl of church-sponsored functions, romance could blossom. In Riverside, Frederico Buriel kept going to the movies held every Sunday night at Our Lady of Guadalupe Shrine so he could chat with the pretty ticket seller, Eusebia Vasquez. Theirs, however, was not a teenage courtship. When they married, she was thirty-seven, he forty-three.[66]

Parents could also rely on Catholic practices in the home to test the mettle of prospective suitors. When Fermin Montiel came to call on Livia León in Rillito, Arizona, her parents instructed him to join them as they knelt to recite the family rosary. In Livia's words: "It was a real education for him to be told it was rosary time."[67]

As a manifestation of familial oligarchy, chaperonage crossed denominational lines. Protestant teens, too, yearned for more freedom of movement. "I was beginning to think that the Baptist church was a little too Mexican. Too much restriction," remembered Rose Escheverria Mulligan.

Indeed, she longed to join her Catholic peers who regularly attended church-sponsored dances "I noticed they were having a good time."[68]

As mentioned earlier, popular culture offered an alternative vision to parental and church expectations, complete with its own aura of legitimacy. While going out with a man alone violated Mexican community norms, such behavior seemed perfectly appropriate outside the barrio. Certainly Mexican American women noticed the less confined lifestyles of their Anglo co-workers who did not live at home and who went out on dates unchaperoned. Some wage-earning teenagers rented apartments, at times even moving in with Anglo peers. Both English- and Spanish-language media promoted a freer heterosocial environment. Radios, magazines, and movies held out images of neckers and petters, hedonistic flappers bent on a good time. From Middletown to East Los Angeles, teenagers across class and ethnicity sought to emulate the fun-seeking icons of a burgeoning consumer society.[69]

Even the Spanish-language press fanned youthful passions. On May 9, 1927, La Opinion ran an article entitled, "How do you kiss?" Informing readers that "el beso no es un arte sino una ciencia" (kissing is not an art but rather a science), this short piece outlined the three components of a kiss: quality, quantity, and topography. The modern kiss, furthermore, should last three minutes.[70] Though certainly shocking older Mexicanos, such titillating fare catered to a youth market. La Opinion, in many respects, reflected the coalescence of Mexican and American cultures. While promoting pride in Latino theater and music, its society pages also celebrated the icons of Americanization and mass consumption.

Mexican American women were not caught between two worlds. They navigated across multiple terrains at home, at work, and at play. They engaged in what I have termed cultural coalescence. The Mexican American generation selected, retained, borrowed, and created their own cultural forms. Or as one woman informed anthropologist Ruth Tuck, "Fusion is what we want—the best of both ways."[71] These children of immigrants may have been captivated by consumerism, but few would attain its promises of affluence. Race and gender prejudice as well as socio-economic segmentation constrained the possibilities of choice.

The adult lives of the seventeen narrators profiled in this essay give a sense of these boundaries. Most continued in the labor force, combining wage work with household responsibilities. Their occupations varied from assembling airplanes at McDonnell-Douglas to selling clothes at K-Mart.[72]

Seven of the seventeen narrators married Euro-American men; yet, their economic status did not differ substantially from those who chose Mexican partners.[73] With varying degrees of financial security, the majority of the narrators are working-class retirees whose lives do not exemplify rags to riches mobility, but rather upward movement within the working class. Though painfully aware of prejudice and discrimination, many people of their generation placed faith in themselves and faith in the system. In 1959 Margaret Clark asserted that the second-generation residents of Sal si Puedes (a northern California barrio) "dream and work toward the day when Mexican Americans will become fully integrated into American society at large."[74] Perhaps, as part of that faith, they rebelled against chaperonage.

Indeed, what seems most striking is that the struggle over chaperonage occurred against a background of persistent discrimination. During the early 1930s, Mexicans were routinely rounded up and deported and even when deportations diminished, segregation remained.[75] Historian Albert Camarillo has demonstrated that in Los Angeles restrictive real estate covenants and segregated schools increased dramatically between 1920 and 1950. The proportion of Los Angeles area municipalities with covenants prohibiting Mexicans and other people of color from purchasing residences in certain neighborhoods climbed from 20 percent in 1920 to 80 percent in 1946. Many restaurants, theaters, and public swimming pools discriminated against their Spanish-surnamed clientele. In southern California, for example, Mexicans could swim at the public plunges only one day out of the week (just before they drained the pool).[76] Small-town merchants frequently refused to admit Spanish-speaking people into their places of business. "White Trade Only" signs served as bitter reminders of their second-class citizenship.[77]

Individual acts of discrimination could also blunt youthful aspirations. Erminia Ruiz recalled that from the ages of thirteen to fifteen, she worked full-time to support her sisters and widowed mother as a doughnut maker. "They could get me for lower wages." When health officials would stop in to check the premises, the underage employee would hide in the flour bins. At the age of sixteen, she became the proud recipient of a social security card and was thrilled to become the first Mexican hired by a downtown Denver cafeteria. Her delight as a "salad girl" proved short-lived. A co-worker reported that $200 had been stolen from her purse.[78] In Erminia's words:

> Immediately they wanted to know what I did with the $200.00. I didn't
> know what they were talking about so they got . . . a policewoman and they
> took me in the restroom and undressed me. [Later they would discover
> that the co-worker's friend had taken the money.] I felt awful. I didn't go
> back to work.[79]

Though feeling deeply humiliated, Erminia scanned the classified ads the
next day and soon combined work with night classes at a storefront
business college.[80]

During the course of her adolescence, Erminia Ruiz was the sole
breadwinner. Even so, familial oligarchy significantly influenced her actions. For Erminia, there was no dueña because she was not allowed to
date period. However, she found ways to have a social life. On weekend
evenings, she had to meet her dates at the drug store or sneak out to go
with girlfriends to the Rainbow Room.[81]

Mexican American adolescents felt the lure of Hollywood and the
threat of deportation, the barbs of discrimination and the reins of constant supervision. In dealing with all the contradictions in their lives,
many young women focused their attention on chaperonage, an area
where they could make decisions. The inner conflicts expressed in the
oral histories reveal that such decisions were not made impetuously. Hard
as it was for young heterosexual women to carve out their own sexual
boundaries, imagine the greater difficulty for lesbians coming of age in
the barrios of the Southwest.

Although only one facet in the realm of sexual politics, chaperonage
was a significant issue for teenagers coming of age during the interwar
period. The oral interviews on which I relied represented the experiences
of those who were neither deported nor repatriated. Future studies of
chaperonage should examine the experiences of those adolescents whose
families returned to Mexico. This physical uprooting, no doubt, further
complicated the ways in which they negotiated across shifting cultural
terrains. For example, in Mexico were young women expected to tolerate
even more stringent supervision? Did they, in essence, return to the ways
of their mothers or did they adopt distinctive patterns of behavior de-
pending on which side of the political border they found themselves?

Coming of age during the interwar period, young women sought to
reconcile parental expectations with the excitement of experimentation.
Popular culture affirmed women's desire for greater autonomy and in
hearing its messages, they acted. Chaperones had to go. In studying the

interwar generation, a pattern emerges regarding the presence of *la dueña*. Although still practiced in some areas, chaperonage appeared less frequently after World War II. By the 1950s chaperonage had become more a generational marker. Typically only the daughters of recent immigrants had to contend with constant supervision. Mexican Americans relegated chaperonage to their own past, a custom which as parents, they chose not to inflict upon their children. Family honor also became less intertwined with female virginity, but the preservation of one's "reputation" was still a major concern.[82] Some Mexican American women found themselves invoking the threats of their mothers. María de las Nieves Moya de Ruiz warned her daughter Erminia that if she ever got into trouble and disgraced the family, she would be sent packing to a Florence Crittenden Home for Unwed Mothers. During the 1960s and 1970s, Erminia repeated the exact same words to her teenage daughters. Chaperonage may have been discarded, but familial oligarchy remained.[83]

In challenging chaperonage, Mexican American teenagers did not attack the foundation of familial oligarchy—only its more obvious manifestation. (It would take later generations of Chicana feminists to take on this task.) Chaperonage, however, could no longer be used as a method of social control, as an instrument for harnessing women's personal autonomy and sexuality. Through open resistance and clever evasion, daring young women broke free from its constraints. Their actions represent a significant step in the sexual liberation of Mexican American women.

NOTES

1. Interview with María Ybarra, December 1, 1990, conducted by David Pérez.

2. For colonial New Mexico, Ramón Gutiérrez convincingly demonstrates how family honor was tied, in part, to women's *vergüenza* (literally, shame or virginity). See Ramón Gutiérrez, "Honor, Ideology, and Class Gender Domination in New Mexico, 1690–1846," *Latin American Perspectives* 12 (1985): 81–104. I contend that since mothers and elder female relatives played major roles in enforcing chaperonage, strict supervision of daughters related more to what I term "familial oligarchy" than to patriarchal control.

3. Donna R. Gabaccia, *From Sicily to Elizabeth Street* (Albany: SUNY Press, 1984); Sydney Stahl Weinberg, "The Treatment of Women in Immigration History: A Call for Change," in *Seeking Common Ground*, ed. Donna Gabaccia (Westport: Greenwood Press, 1992), pp. 3–22; Stuart Ewen and Elizabeth Ewen,

Channels of Desire (New York: McGraw-Hill, 1982); Elizabeth Ewen, *Immigrant Women in the Land of Dollars* (New York: Monthly Review Press, 1985); Susan A. Glenn, *Daughters of the Shtetl* (Ithaca: Cornell University Press, 1990).

4. Interview with Erminia Ruiz, February 18, 1993 conducted by the author. In 1919 *True Story Magazine* began an industry of romance and scandal magazines; by 1929 this publication had over two million subscribers. See Joanne J. Meyerowitz, *Women Adrift: Independent Wage Earners in Chicago, 1880–1930* (Chicago: University of Chicago Press, 1988), pp. 129–133.

5. Interview with Jesusita Torres, January 8, 1993, conducted by the author.

6. George Lipsitz, *Time Passages: Collective Memory and American Popular Culture* (Minneapolis: University of Minnesota Press, 1990), p. 13; Nirwan Dewanto, "American Kitsch and Indonesian Culture: A Sketch," paper presented at the Third Annual International Symposium: American Studies in the Asia-Pacific Region (April 3, 1992), Tokyo, Japan. For a comprehensive examination of the impact of mass culture on immigrants and their children, see Lizbeth Cohen, *Making a New Deal: Industrial Workers in Chicago, 1919–1939* (Cambridge: Cambridge University Press, 1990).

7. Ruth Tuck, *Not with the Fist* (New York: Harcourt, Brace, 1946; rpt. Arno Press, 1974), pp. 185–188; Vicki L. Ruiz, "Oral History and La Mujer: The Rosa Guerrero Story," in *Women on the U.S.-Mexico Border: Responses to Change* (Boston: Allen and Unwin, 1987), pp. 226–227; interview with Belen Martínez Mason, Volume 23 of *Rosie the Riveter Revisited: Women and the World War I Work Experience*, ed. Sherna Berger Gluck (Long Beach: CSULB Foundation, 1983), pp. 24–25; Ruiz interview (1993); interview with Ruby Estrada, August 4, 1981, conducted by María Hernández, "The Lives of Arizona Women" Oral History Project (On File, Special Collections, Hayden Library, Arizona State University), p. 6. For a scholarly overview of the educational experiences of Spanish-speaking children in southwestern schools, see Gilbert González, *Chicano Education in the Era of Segregation* (Philadelphia: Balch Institute Press, 1990).

8. Interview with Mary Luna, Volume 20 of *Rosie the Riveter Revisited*, p. 10. During the 1940s, bilingual education appeared as an exciting experiment in curriculum reform.

9. Luna interview, p. 9.

10. Valerie J. Matsumoto, *Farming the Home Place: A Japanese American Community in California, 1919–1982* (Ithaca: Cornell University Press, 1993); Judy Yung, *Unbound Feet: A Social History of Chinese Women in San Francisco* (Berkeley: University of California Press, 1995).

11. Mauricio Mazón's *The Zoot Suit Riots* (Austin: University of Texas Press, 1984) and the Luis Valdez play and feature film, *Zoot Suit*, provide examples of the literature on *pachucos*.

12. I would like to introduce these women by grouping them geographically.

María Fierro, Rose Escheverria Mulligan, Adele Hernández Milligan, Beatrice Morales Clifton, Mary Luna, Alicia Mendeola Shelit, Carmen Bernal Escobar, Belen Martínez Mason, and Julia Luna Mount grew up in Los Angeles. Lucy Acosta and Alma Araiza García came of age in El Paso and Erminia Ruiz in Denver. Representing the rural experience are María Arredondo, and Jesusita Torres (California), María Ybarra (Texas), and Ruby Estrada (Arizona). As a teenager, Eusebia Buriel moved with her family from Silvis, Illinois, to Riverside, California. I appreciate the generosity and long-standing support of Sherna Gluck who has given me permission to use excerpts from the *Rosie* interviews. This sample also does not include oral interviews found in published sources.

13. The age breakdown for the seventeen interviewees are as follows: nine were born between 1908 and 1919 and eight between 1920 and 1926. This sample includes some who were chaperoned during the 1920s and others who were chaperoned during the 1930s and 1940s. The sample does not represent a precise generational grouping, but instead gives a sense of the pervasiveness and persistence of unremitting supervision.

14. Estrada interview, pp. 2, 15, 17, 19.

15. George J. Sánchez, " 'Go after the Women': Americanization and the Mexican Immigrant Woman 1915–1929," in *Unequal Sisters: A Multicultural Reader in U.S. Women's History*, 2nd ed., eds. Vicki L. Ruiz and Ellen DuBois (New York: Routledge, 1994) p. 285.

16. F. Scott Fitzgerald, *Flappers and Philosophers* (London: W. Collins Sons, 1922), pp. 209–246; Emory S. Bogardus, *The Mexican in the United States* (Los Angeles: University of Southern California Press, 1934), p. 741; Martínez Mason interview, p. 44. During the 1920s, Mexican parents were not atypical in voicing their concerns over the attitudes and appearance of their "flapper adolescents." A general atmosphere of tension between youth and their elders existed—a generation gap which cut across class, race, ethnicity, and region. See Paula Fass, *The Damned and the Beautiful: American Youth in the 1920's* (New York: Oxford University Press, 1977).

17. Interview with Alicia Mendeola Shelit, Volume 37 of *Rosie the Riveter*, p. 18; Paul S. Taylor, *Mexican Labor in the United States*, Volume II (Berkeley: University of California Press, 1932), pp. 199–200; Interview with María Fierro, Volume 12 of *Rosie the Riveter*, p. 10.

18. Manuel Gamio, *Mexican Immigration to the United States* (Chicago: University of Chicago Press, 1930; rpt. New York: Arno Press, 1969), p. 89.

19. Taylor, *Mexican Labor*, Vol. II, pp. vi–vii.

20. Rodolfo F. Acuña, *Community under Siege: A Chronicle of Chicanos East of the Los Angeles River, 1945–1975* (Los Angeles: UCLA Chicano Studies Publications, 1984), pp. 278, 407–408, 413–414, 418, 422; *FTA News*, May 1, 1945; Interview with Carmen Bernal Escobar, 15 June 1986, conducted by the author.

21. Escobar interview, 1986.

22. Sherna B. Gluck, *Rosie the Riveter Revisited: Women, the War and Social Change* (Boston: Twayne, 1987), pp. 81, 85.

23. See Roland Marchand, *Advertising the American Dream: Making Way for Modernity, 1920–1940* (Berkeley: University of California Press, 1985).

24. For examples, see *La Opinion*, September 26, 1926; *La Opinion*, May 14, 1927; *La Opinion*, June 5, 1927; *La Opinion*, September 9, 1929; *La Opinion*, January 15, 1933; *La Opinion*, January 29, 1938.

25. Vicki L. Ruiz, " 'Star Struck': Acculturation, Adolescence, and Mexican American Women, 1920–1940," in *Small Worlds: Children and Adolescents in America*, eds. Elliot West and Paula Petrik (Lawrence: University Press of Kansas, 1992): 61–80; Roberto R. Treviño, "*Prensa Y Patria*: The Spanish-Language Press and the Biculturation of the Tejano Middle Class, 1920–1940," *Western Historical Quarterly*, Vol. 22 (November 1991): 460.

26. *La Opinion*, September 29, 1929.

27. *Hispano-America*, 2 July 1932. I thank Gabriela Arredondo, a doctoral student at the University of Chicago, for sharing this advertisement with me.

28. *La Opinion*, June 5, 1927; *La Opinion*, February 8, 1938.

29. Richard A. García, *Rise of the Mexican American Middle Class: San Antonio, 1929–1941* (College Station: Texas A&M Press, 1991), pp. 118–119; Treviño, "*Prensa Y Patria*," pp. 459–460.

30. For examples, see *La Opinion*, September 23, 1926; *La Opinion*, September 24, 1926; *La Opinion*, September 27, 1926; *La Opinion*, September 30, 1926; *La Opinion*, June 4, 1927; *La Opinion*, February 27, 1931; and *La Opinion*, August 17, 1931.

31. The quote is taken from *La Opinion*, March 2, 1927.

32. Ewen and Ewen, *Channels of Desire*, pp. 95–96.

33. Lipsitz, *Time Passages*, p. 16.

34. The struggles young Mexican American women faced just to talk freely with men and to attend the movies unchaperoned stand in stark contrast to their Euro-American peers who had passed first base and were headed toward greater liberties, like having a drink in a bar without tainting their reputations. See Mary Murphy, "Bootlegging Mothers and Drinking Daughters: Gender and Prohibition in Butte, Montana," *American Quarterly*, 46:2 (June 1994): 174–194.

35. Martínez Mason interview, pp. 29–30; Ybarra interview; Escobar interview; Fierro interview, p. 15; Estrada interview, pp. 11–12; Interview with Erminia Ruiz, July 30, 1990, conducted by the author; Ruiz interview, 1993, conducted by the author; interview with Alma Araiza García, March 27, 1993, conducted by the author.

36. Interview with Adele Hernández Milligan, Volume 26 of *Rosie the Riveter*, p. 17.

37. Evangeline Hymer, "A Study of the Social Attitudes of Adult Mexican Immigrants in Los Angeles and Vicinity: 1923" (M.A. thesis, University of South-

ern California, 1924,; rpt. San Francisco: R and E Research Associates, 1971), pp. 24–25. Other ethnographies which deal with intergenerational tension include Helen Douglas, "The Conflict of Cultures in First Generation Mexicans in Santa Ana, California" (M.A. thesis, University of Southern California, 1928); and Clara Gertrude Smith, "The Development of the Mexican People in the Community of Watts" (M.A. thesis, University of Southern California, 1933).

38. Escobar interview, 1986; Estrada interview, pp. 11, 13; interview with Lucy Acosta, conducted by Mario T. García, October 28, 1982 (On File at the Institute of Oral History, University of Texas, El Paso), p. 17.

39. Estrada interview, p. 12; Shelit interview, p. 9; Antonio Ríos-Bustamante and Pedro Castillo, *An Illustrated History of Mexican Los Angeles, 1781–1985* (Los Angeles: Chicano Studies Research Center, UCLA, 1986), p. 153.

40. Paul S. Taylor, "Women in Industry," Field Notes for his book, *Mexican Labor in the United States, 1927–1930,* Bancroft Library, University of California, 1 box; Richard G. Thurston, "Urbanization and Sociocultural Change in a Mexican-American Enclave" (Ph.D. dissertation, University of California, Los Angeles, 1957; rpt. San Francisco: R and E Research Associates, 1974), p. 118; Bogardus, *The Mexican,* pp. 28–29, 57–58.

41. Martínez Mason interview; Ruiz interviews (1990, 1993); Thomas Sheridan, *Los Tucsonenses* (Tucson: University of Arizona Press, 1986), pp. 131–132.

42. Sheridan, *Los Tucsonenses,* loc. cit.

43. Interview with Beatrice Morales Clifton, Volume 8 of *Rosie the Riveter,* pp. 14–15.

44. Smith, "The Development of the Mexican People," p. 47.

45. Ybarra interview. Ethnographies by Smith, Thurston, and Douglas refer to elopement as a manifestation of generational tension.

46. Discussion following my presentation of "The Flapper and the Chaperone" at the Riverside Municipal Museum, May 28, 1995.

47. Shelit interview, pp. 9, 24, 30; Ruiz interviews (1990, 1993); Escobar interview; García interview; Martínez Mason interview; Hernández Milligan interview, pp. 27–28; interview with María Arredondo, 19 March 1986, conducted by Carolyn Arredondo; Taylor Notes.

48. Interview with Julia Luna Mount, November 17, 1983, conducted by the author; Fierro interview, p. 18; Luna interview, p. 29; Ruiz interview (1993); Gregorita Rodríguez, *Singing for My Echo* (Santa Fe: Cota Editions, 1987), p. 52; Martínez Mason interview, p. 62.

49. "Elisa Morales," interview by Luis Recinos, April 16, 1927, Biographies and Case Histories II folder, Manuel Gamio Field Notes, Bancroft Library, University of California; Taylor, *Mexican Labor,* Vol. II, pp. vi–vii; Gamio, *Mexican Immigration,* p. 89.

50. Ruth Alexander in her study of wayward girls in New York City illuminates this balancing of boundaries among teenagers. See " 'The Only Thing I

Wanted Was Freedom': Wayward Girls in New York, 1900–1930," in West and
Petrik, *Small Worlds*.

51. Ruiz interview (1993).

52. Carmen and Diego are pseudonyms used to ensure the privacy of the
family. Carmen's oral interview is in the author's possession.

53. Discussion following my presentation, of "The Flapper and the Chaperone," May 28, 1995.

54. Douglas Monroy, "An Essay on Understanding the Work Experiences of
Mexicans in Southern California, 1900–1939," *Aztlán*, 12 (Spring 1981): 70. Feminist historians have also documented this push for autonomy among the daughters of European immigrants. See Peiss, *Cheap Amusements*; Glenn, *Daughters of
the Shtetl*; E. Ewen, *Immigrant Women*; and Alexander, "The Only Thing I
Wanted Was Freedom."

55. Heller Committee for Research in Social Economics of the University of
California and Constantine Panuzio, *How Mexicans Earn and Live*, University of
California Publications in Economics, XIII, No. 1, Cost of Living Studies V
(Berkeley: University of California, 1933), pp. 11, 14, 17; Taylor Notes; Luna Mount
interview; Ruiz interviews (1990, 1993); Shelit interview, p. 9.

56. These observations are drawn from my reading of the seventeen oral interviews and the literature on European immigrant women.

57. Luna Mount interview.

58. García interview.

59. Rev. F. X. Lasance, *The Catholic Girl's Guide and Sunday Missal* (New
York: Benziger Brothers, 1905), Esther Pérez Papers, Cassiano-Pérez Collection,
Daughters of the Republic of Texas Library at the Alamo, San Antonio, Texas,
pp. 279–280.

60. Gutiérrez, "Honor, Ideology," pp. 88–93, 95–98.

61. Estrada interview, p. 12. Focusing on the daughters of European immigrants, Elizabeth Ewen has written that "the appropriation of an urban adolescent
culture" served as "a wedge against patriarchal forms of social control." This
holds true, to some degree, for the women profiled here. But, for Mexican Americans, the underlying ideological assumption was familial oligarchy rather than
patriarchy. See Ewen and Ewen, *Channels of Desire*, p. 95.

62. Lasance, *Catholic Girl's Guide*, pp. 249–275. (Quote is on p. 270.)

63. *Ibid.*, p. 271.

64. George J. Sánchez, *Becoming Mexican American: Ethnicity, Culture, and
Identity in Chicano Los Angeles, 1900–1945* (New York: Oxford University Press,
1993), p. 167; Mary Helen Ponce, *Hoyt Street* (Albuquerque: University of New
Mexico Press, 1993), pp. 258, 266–271 (quote is taken from p. 258). "Las vistas"
is slang for the movies.

65. Ponce, *Hoyt Street*, p. 266. Discussion following my presentation of "The

Flapper and the Chaperone," May 28, 1995. Comment provided by Rose Medina. *Jamaicas* are church bazaars or festivals.

66. Interview with Eusebia Buriel, January 16, 1995, conducted by the author; interview with Ray Buriel, December 21, 1994, conducted by the author.

67. Patricia Preciado Martin, *Songs My Mother Sang to Me* (Tucson: University of Arizona Press, 1992), pp. 19–20.

68. Interview with Rose Escheverria Mulligan, Volume 27 of *Rosie the Riveter*, p. 24.

69. Taylor Notes; Monroy, "An Essay on Understanding," p. 70; Rosalinda González, "Chicanas and Mexican Immigrant Families 1920–1940: Women's Subordination and Economic Exploitation," in *Decades of Discontent: The Women's Movement, 1920–1940*, eds. Lois Scharf and Joan M. Jensen (Westport: Greenwood Press, 1983), p. 72; Vicki L. Ruiz, *Cannery Women, Cannery Lives: Mexican Women, Unionization, and the California Food Processing Industry, 1930–1950* (Albuquerque: University of New Mexico Press, 1987), pp. 10–12, 17–18; Ruiz interview (1990); John D'Emilio and Estelle B. Freedman, *Intimate Matters: A History of Sexuality in America* (New York: Harper and Row, 1988), pp. 233–235, 239–241.

70. *La Opinión*, May 9, 1927.

71. Tuck, *Not with the Fist*, p. 134.

72. Only two achieved a solid, consistent middle-class standard of living. Six of the thirteen California women took their place at the shop floor in the aerospace, electronics, apparel, and food processing industries. Two became secretaries and one a sales clerk at K-Mart. One has been a farm and nursery worker since the age of nine. The remaining three narrators are homemakers.

73. Among the husbands of the California women, many were skilled workers in the aerospace industry and the highest occupation for a spouse was firefighter.

74. Margaret Clark, *Health in the Mexican American Culture* (Berkeley: University of California Press, 1959). p. 20.

75. Between 1931 and 1934 an estimated one-third of the Mexican population in the United States (over 500,000 people) were either deported or repatriated to Mexico, even though many were native U.S. citizens.

76. Albert Camarillo, "Mexican American Urban History in Comparative Ethnic Perspective," Distinguished Speakers Series, University of California, Davis (January 26, 1987); Rodolfo Acuña, *Occupied America: A History of Chicanos*, 2nd ed. (New York: Harper and Row, 1981), pp. 310, 318, 323, 330–331; Shelit interview, p. 15.

77. Paul Taylor, *Mexican Labor in the United States*, Vol. I (Berkeley: University of California Press, 1930, rpt. Arno Press, 1970), pp. 221–224; Arredondo interview; Ruiz interviews (1990, 1993).

78. Ruiz interview (1993).

79. *Ibid.*

80. *Ibid.*

81. *Ibid.*

82. Acosta interview; Tuck, *Not with the Fist*, pp. 126–127; Thurston, "Urbanization," pp. 109, 117–119; Ruiz interviews (1990, 1993).

83. Ruiz interviews (1990, 1993); personal experience of author.

10

Fictions of Assimilation

Nancy Drew, Cultural Imperialism, and the Filipina/American Experience

Melinda L. de Jesús

I was raised a parochial school, steel-town girl, the third of four sisters, in one of the "gritty cities" of eastern Pennsylvania in the 1970s. My girlfriends and I, like countless others across the United States, shared a love of "Abba" and "The Bay City Rollers," "The Brady Bunch" and "The Partridge Family," Leif Garrett and Andy Gibb, clogs and "Bonne Bell Lipsmackers." We held myriad sleepovers where we never really slept, logged endless hours talking on the phone; we hated our piano teachers, babysat, and shopped at the mall. We read *Seventeen* magazine and religiously attended Girl Scout meetings. Forever clad in our boring parochial school plaid uniforms (complete with Peter Pan collar blouses), we were besotted with our young female lay teachers who wore stylish platform shoes and let us try them on. We were into "Godspell" and CYO activities, and some of us wanted to be nuns.

Between third to fifth grades we began that awkward transition between girlhood and womanhood, and our first inklings of adolescence were characterized by anxiety over menstruation, bras, body hair, and breasts. Moreover, what had once been a relentless competition *with* boys for academic and athletic superiority turned into a confusing competition *between* girls for boys' attention. In response we immersed ourselves in the world of Nancy Drew: unflappable, sophisticated Nancy always out-smarted the boys and got things done. She exhibited the supreme confidence that we lacked yet so desired.

Our love for Nancy bordered on obsession: we reveled in the minute details of her life and would devour each of her mysteries, frantically trading them with each other while keeping careful track of which mysteries remained unread. We were devout fans of her television show and used our Nancy Drew lunch boxes with pride. Thus, Nancy Drew Mystery books provided a communal experience for us pre-adolescents. Through the familiar, lulling surety of these formulaic mysteries—Nancy's predictable "adventures" were always capped with her triumphant successes—we vicariously explored adulthood even as we clung, however tenuously, onto the more neatly delineated life we were leaving behind—the safety of girlhood.

However, there is an interesting complication to these wistful reminiscences. My fellow acolytes in the cult of Nancy Drew—Joni, Cindy and Mary Jo, Tina, Patti and Diane, Suzanne, Pam, Carla, and Molly—were all of Pennsylvania Dutch, Irish, Italian, German, or Slovak descent. I was the only Filipina—indeed the only girl of color in my parochial elementary school, my family the only "non-white" family in my entire neighborhood. Thus, I am forced to ask: How did the specificity of white consciousness impact the construction of our girls' culture? Did race make a difference in terms of my relationship to Nancy Drew? I believe so. While my girlfriends and I gleaned important messages about female agency through reading Nancy Drew books, my close identification with the girl super sleuth had a specific impact upon my psyche as a Filipina, which I shall explore in this essay.

Feminist assessments of the fictional teen detective Nancy Drew depict her as an important role model for generations of American women. Like many girls, my love of Nancy Drew was a maternal legacy; however, my mother is a Filipina raised during the American regime in the Philippines. What enabled both my mother and me to identify so strongly with this blond-haired, blue-eyed sleuth and her exciting adventures? Below I explore the parameters of my mother's and my own investment in Nancy Drew. Highlighting the Filipina American experience and drawing upon Filipino American history and feminist criticism, I delineate how "The Nancy Drew Mystery Stories"—a cultural phenomenon steeped in and intent upon defending WASP values, introduced to the islands via the imposed American educational system—furthered the aims of "benevolent assimilation" in the Philippines through American cultural imperialism and internal colonization.[1]

In the Shadow of the "Famous Girl Detective"

As my sisters had done before me, from about third through fifth grade I was obsessed with reading every single volume of "The Nancy Drew Mystery Stories." Like many generations of American girls, I would voraciously devour one satisfyingly hair-raising mystery a day, content in the knowledge that my idol, the shrewd, fashionable, "titian-haired" Nancy, along with trusty side-kicks, Bess and George, would be around tomorrow with yet another mystery to solve. Moreover, after grueling indoor soccer practices on Tuesday nights, I remember begging my father to rush me home so I would not miss the new "Hardy Boys/Nancy Drew" television program. During this period, prior to moving onto the infamous Judy Blume books, I read several other detective series—the Bobbsey Twins, the Hardy Boys, Cherry Ames, Vicki Barr, Judy Bolton, and the Dana Girls—yet Nancy reigned supreme. She held an important place in my imagination and became an impossible role model of brains, guts, and honor combined with impeccable manners and style. So great was her imprint upon me that as an angst-ridden sixteen year old, I wrote the following poem:

> *Fuck off, Nancy Drew*
> Fuck off, Nancy Drew
> and your famous father, Carson Drew
> the prominent lawyer of River Heights
> and your housekeeper, Hannah Gruen
> who has loved and cared for you since your mother died
> and your perfect boyfriend, Ned Nickerson
> the scholar athlete of Emerson College
> Were you ever suicidal?
> Did you ever shoplift?
> Ever run off to Phillipsburg, NJ
> to drink Molsons in the parking lot of some dingy warehouse?
> What did you do when your blue roadster broke down
> or when there were no more mysteries to be found?
> You had all the answers—
> but the questions aren't the same anymore!
> You outsmarted Mrs. Tino,

saved Bess from the abductors
And never smeared your mascara.
Your clothes were always impeccable
though your hair changed like the weather—
titian, strawberry blond, auburn.
You deceived me—
you and your two best friends,
Bess and George, the sycophants.
Life was one big party for you, Nancy
But not for me.
All your problems solved within two hundred pages.
Did you ever lose your virginity?
Did you ever get drunk and throw up?
Did you ever fight with your dad and wish he were dead?
Nancy, you never told us
that detectives could feel so shitty.
I always believed that you were real
But you never lived outside "The Nancy Drew Mystery Series."
Now I'm left to solve it all by myself
Me, famous girl detective
In my own shiny blue roadster
Without a damn clue at all.

While certainly melodramatic, the poem illustrates how my strong identification with Nancy turned to bitter disillusionment about her and her simple world as I aged. Outgrowing and discarding childhood idols is a part of adolescence; yet, in retrospect, given my training as a literary and cultural critic, an Asian American feminist and scholar, it seems improbable that I could have identified so deeply with Nancy Drew. Thus, the real mystery alluded to in the last four lines of my poem would be the following: How did a brown Pinay[2] like myself come to identify so much with this WASP girl detective? Furthermore, how could my valorization of Nancy Drew as role model ever lead me to a coherent sense of self as a *Filipina American* feminist? These are not rhetorical questions when one begins to consider the intense cultural dominance of the United States in the Philippines and how "The Nancy Drew Mystery Stories," imported as part of the American-imposed educational system, functioned as one aspect of "social engineering" in the Americanization of Filipino culture.[3]

Importing the Stars and Stripes: Education and Cultural Imperialism

As civilian government replaced military rule in the islands after the Philippine-American War, an intensive program of social engineering was enacted by the United States government. Its goal, the complete Americanization of the entire population, was promulgated by the arrival of hundreds of American teachers to the islands (called "Thomasites") whose "mission was to impart Western civilization to Filipinos under a policy of 'benevolent assimilation' and political tutelage" (Chan 17). The American public school system introduced throughout the islands revised existing Filipino educational models and curriculum and mandated English as the official language of instruction.[4] Thus, "infected with colonial culture and with grand illusions about the United States, Filipinos soon started to migrate to what they had been taught to think of as the land of opportunity and fair play" (Espiritu 3). These Filipino laborers, recruited in the 1920s and 1930s for cannery and field work, unlike most Asian immigrants, were thoroughly Americanized.

Unfortunately, the optimistic *manongs*[5] arrived in the United States during a period of intense anti-Asian sentiment, and, although wards and nationals of the United States at the time, found themselves subjected to the same patterns of Asian exclusion suffered by Chinese, Japanese, Koreans, and Asian Indians before them. Politically disenfranchised—denied land ownership, citizenship, and education—and mired at the bottom of the labor market in "stoop labor," *manongs* endured racist stereotyping as "savages" and "sex-crazed monkeys" who threatened white female purity and thus were subject to miscegenation laws.[6] The harsh discrepancy between the Filipino dream of America and the reality of Filipino reception in America is summed up by author Carlos Bulosan in his 1943 novel, *America Is in the Heart*. Fraught with images of deracination, homelessness, despair and loneliness, poverty and disillusionment, Bulosan's book describes the migratory, violent lives of the *manongs* through a mind-numbing catalog of place names, murders, beatings, and riots. It fascinates me to think of Bulosan and my mother as contemporaries of sorts, subjects of the same Americanization process that engenders within them the same dream. While she, a well-to-do *mestiza* in Baguio dreams of becoming American, Bulosan, subjected to the brutal migratory life of the *manong* farmworker, continues to search for the America he had been promised back in the islands.

Nancy Drew, Mom, and Me

My mother, Eloisa, passed on her love of Nancy Drew to my sisters and me. We all admired Nancy Drew's image as the smart, level-headed, feisty girl detective, fearless, gracious, and well dressed. For my mom, the image of American girlhood freedom was especially attractive: Nancy drove herself about unchaperoned and lived an exciting, adventure-filled yet wholesome life, far beyond the reality of patriarchal Filipino society (which dictated Filipina responsibilities to home and to the Church), and also beyond the realities of the Japanese occupation. Underscoring these qualities, however, my mother insisted that Nancy had one overriding attraction: "She was American, and everyone wanted to be American."

However, mom's family had not always embraced Americanization. Her maternal great-uncle, Maximo Angeles, fought alongside Emilio Aguinaldo, leader of the Filipino revolutionary nationalistic group, *Katipunan*, for Filipino sovereignty, first against Spain (1896) and later against the United States in the Philippine-American War (1898–1901). By the time of my mother's childhood in Baguio (c. 1932–1944), the family's legacy of resistance had changed radically. Her father, José Domingo, was a staunch supporter of American innovation, investments, and culture. Mom attended a private school run by the Belgian Missionary Canonesses of St. Augustine; there she raided the school's library for the Bobbsey Twins and Nancy Drew mysteries and later for those by Zane Grey, Louisa May Alcott, Frances Hodgson Burnett, and Sir Walter Scott. Mom was discouraged from reading vernacular Ilocano or Tagalog magazines and fondly remembers reading the *Saturday Evening Post*.

My mother's family's paradigmatic shift from resisting the imposition of American culture via imperialism to valorizing/reifying the importation of American culture, I believe, is cemented in the following story. After the liberation from Japanese occupation, U. S. soldiers came by to ask my grandfather what his children might need. The next day, servicemen returned with American cultural artifacts: V-discs (special records shipped to the troops), magazines, and books. It is telling that my mother remembers being thankful not for the food and clothing the Americans would supply, but for the American culture denied her during the occupation.

Here the process of Americanization is completed: Recapturing the Philippines, Americans re-established cultural supremacy and the war-weary Filipinos were thankful.[7]

Mom taught English and home economics at Holy Family College in Baguio before her marriage and relocation to the United States in 1958. In this sense, what had been for my mother a desired, imagined construct (Nancy Drew's American lifestyle) became a reality for me: As part of my family's first American-born generation, the literal terrain of "The Nancy Drew Mystery Stories" became my own. Indeed, the fictional "River Heights" could easily be my own hometown along the Lehigh River, complete with the requisite winding backroads, quaint towns, and mysterious mansions. Thus mom's vision of American girlhood was truly realized for her daughters; her sharing of her love of Nancy Drew mysteries only reinforced this fact.

Recently, I asked my mother if she remembered being bothered by the fact that Nancy was a "white girl." Mom maintained that she never noticed Nancy's whiteness; she "just became her." For me, however, growing up in a racially segregated community, my reading and identifying with Nancy Drew entailed complex negotiations with my "American" and "Filipino" identities that resulted in the negation of myself as Filipina in order to be the "American girl." For both of us, then, identifying with Nancy Drew entailed an erasure and subsuming into whiteness, an integral process of internal colonization that I describe in the next section.

Fictions of Assimilation: Nancy Drew and Hegemonic Feminism

Carolyn Heilbrun writes in "Nancy Drew: A Moment in Feminist History": "[Nancy's] class and the fact of her ready money and upper-middle-class WASP assumptions are what make her an embarrassment today. The question is, should we therefore dismiss her as predominantly an embarrassment, a moment in the history of feminism of which we are now ashamed?" (18). Answering her own question, Heilbrun admonishes that "there is a danger that we critics, with our close analytical machinery and our explorations of social and economic conditions, will damage the original Nancy Drew books . . . looking for things that they do not and cannot offer, while failing to see and praise their real qualities" (19). She and other authors in the collection entitled *Rediscovering Nancy Drew*

(1995) maintain that we can appreciate Nancy Drew for what she inspired, and that what might be construed as Nancy's shortcomings in our current political climate should not negate our love for her. Heilbrun allows, "By the 1990's we have learned that no woman can speak for all women. Certainly Nancy Drew cannot speak for women of color or poor women" (20); nevertheless, reading "The Nancy Drew Mystery Stories" as a tool of American cultural imperialism, a fiction of assimilation imported to the Philippines as part of the "civilization" process, radically complicates such feminist desire for nostalgia. Indeed, how benign are these texts when they are employed to inculcate a desire for American culture and whiteness? Given the reality of forced cultural assimilation in the Philippines, how can we begin to assess the value of Nancy Drew as a feminist role model for Filipinas or other women of color?

I contend that Heilbrun's recuperation of the image of Nancy Drew, while seeming to gesture towards consciousness of race and class differences, once again inscribes the imperialistic stance of the United States in relation to the Filipina American experience. The ease of this racist stance is compounded when we consider how the realities of Filipina American culture often conspire to prevent recognition and resistance to modes of hegemonic feminist domination. Pinay feminist Delia D. Aguilar writes:

> What I am attempting to stress here is that our colonial mentality makes it almost second nature for us to assume the persona of our colonizer. Consequently, our susceptibility to conceptions of shared sisterhood among all women merely acts to reinforce our neocolonial standing. . . . This can explain our inability as Filipinos, unless residence in the U.S. and elsewhere has educated us, to discern racism in the conduct of those whose mission is to uplift and enlighten us. (10)

She exhorts Filipinas to reject the "colonial predisposition toward self-erasure," as well as the "unrehabilitated colonial outlook" which "makes us very vulnerable to the influx of ideas . . . the uncritical acceptance of which could signify nothing more than a feminist replication of neocolonialism" (8). Through her pointed consideration of Filipina American realities, Aguilar emphasizes how Filipina feminism demands a mode of vigilance and resistance to both internal colonialism (colonialist mentality) and to a hegemonic feminism which seeks to incorporate us and erase our very existence within its blinding whiteness. Moreover, Aguilar makes clear that feminists like Heilbrun must begin to acknowledge how simplistic invocations of "sisterhood" merely accentuate hegemonic feminism's complicity in maintaining white dominance. Thus, a truly "global" feminist theory would incorporate attention to the circulation of ideologies as well as to the complex personal negotiations we ourselves make within competing modes of power—for example, patriarchy, white supremacy, compulsory heterosexuality, classism, and imperialism.

For Filipinas, Nancy Drew books, circulated by the grade school and public libraries established by the American-imposed educational system and also readily available in local bookstores, become one of the means by which the Americanization of Filipino culture is accomplished. As fictions of assimilation, imported by American colonizers to promulgate American cultural dominance in the islands, Nancy Drew books inculcate affiliations with and yearnings for an American femininity implicitly valorized as "white." Emphasized throughout these books is the pervasive positing of WASP culture and values as "normative." In this sense, it is easy to see how Nancy Drew functions as another facet of cultural imperialism through engendering childhood identifications with and strong desires *to be* Nancy Drew.

Revisiting River Heights: Rereading "The Mystery at Lilac Inn" and "The Clue of the Leaning Chimney"

Scholars of children's serial detective fiction have analyzed "The Nancy Drew Mystery Stories'" place within the Stratemeyer Syndicate. Founded by Edward Stratemeyer in the early 1900s, this virtual empire of children's serial novels was produced with factory-like efficiency by the Syndicate's hired stable of ghostwriters (and continues this same process today).[8] The Stratemeyer Syndicate created almost all of the most popular children's series books (Nancy Drew, the Hardy Boys, the Bobbsey Twins), controlling the series fiction market as well as the imaginations of generations of ten- and eleven-year-olds who read them. The implicit goal of Stratemeyer series books was to inculcate American children into middle-class values and behavior, even as librarians decried their "racy" plots—yet how did these same goals translate to colonies of the United States? What are the implications of these texts within the economy of cultural persuasion in the Philippines which was based on capitulation to American ideologies? Specifically, what vision of America is available in "The Nancy Drew Mystery Stories"? How did Nancy Drew books promulgate American cultural values and expectations of social relations?

Bobbie Ann Mason in *The Girl Sleuth* (1995) sums up the world of Nancy Drew in the following way:

> Thus, the original Nancy Drew[9]—first thirty-five or so volumes which accumulated throughout the 1930s, 1940s, and 1950s—portrays a fading aristocracy, threatened by the restless lower classes. . . . When minorities know their place, Nancy treats them graciously. . . . Nancy's job is to preserve the class lines, and for her the defense of property and station are inextricably linked with purity and reputation. She defends beautiful objects, places, and treasures from violence. . . . (73)

Mason's reading seemed harsh until I myself reread *The Mystery at Lilac Inn* (1930). Seeking to discern the overall vision of America and American girlhood in "The Nancy Drew Mystery Stories," I was astounded by what I found versus what I had remembered. My gentle remembrance of Nancy as a thoughtful, modest young woman was replaced by a snobbish, icy Daddy's girl. Less American girl-next-door than Carson Drew's confidante and hostess, she epitomizes WASP privilege and its wealthy suburban lifestyle. *The Mystery at Lilac Inn* details not only Nancy's search to find Emily Crandall's stolen fortune in jewels, but also describes the sleuth's irksome search for a temporary housekeeper.

Nancy's interactions with possible housekeepers demonstrates how the series' authors reinscribed the racist politics of the period: white is right and non-WASPS are unattractive or suspicious. The first example below is a very stereotypical description of an African American woman whom Nancy dismisses in disgust:

> As she opened the door her heart sank within her. It was indeed the colored woman sent by the employment agency, but a more unlikely housekeeper Nancy had never seen. She was dirty and slovenly in appearance and had an unpleasant way of shuffling her feet when she walked. (16)

The second applicant for the housekeeping job, Mary Mason, is described in the following manner: "As she swung open the massive oak door she beheld a tall, wiry, dark-complexioned girl who was obviously the one sent from the agency. She had dark piercing eyes and stared at Nancy almost impudently" (18). Again, Bobbie Ann Mason succinctly describes the significance of this characterization:

> Appearances are never deceptive in Nancy's Ivory-pure life. Good and evil are strictly white and black terms. Criminals are dark-hued and poor. . . . Piercing dark eyes are the most common characteristic of Nancy's foes. Their greedy eyes are piercing because they are disrespectful, gazing threat-

eningly beyond their station, perhaps seeing through the façades of the gentry whose power they crave. (68–69)

Readers of the series come to recognize that Mary's "dusky" complexion, "piercing eyes," and impudent manner clearly mark her as a criminal in the world of Nancy Drew.

Similarly, in "Nancy Drew and the Myth of White Supremacy,"[10] Donnarae MacCann delineates the white supremacist consensus concerning the natural inferiority of African Americans which she then contextualizes to the overtly racist depiction of the black caretaker in *The Secret of the Old Clock* (1930), the original volume of the Nancy Drew series. She writes:

> The author presents him as a drunkard, a liar, a person who has constant run-ins with the police, an unreliable employee, and a fool. As you watch the details of the character emerge in just a few pages of text, you feel as if you have been transported to a black-face minstrel show and are watching a skit in which the actors blackened their faces and drew huge white mouths as a way to ridicule the African American. (132)

Moreover, other people of color are reduced to similar racist representations throughout the original series. For example, revisiting *The Clue of the Leaning Chimney* (1949)—one of my perennial favorites, and one of the few which prominently featured Asian characters and culture—provides a compelling vision of the structure of American cultural values and social relations in the Nancy Drew worldview. The novel recounts Nancy's efforts to locate a mythical site of precious clay, free the imprisoned Chinese artisans, Eng Moy and Eng Lei, and bring wily dealers of fake Chinese porcelain to justice. When Nancy first visits Mr. Soong, the River Heights "retired Chinese importer" who plays a leading role in the mystery, she notes that his study "reflected the cosmopolitan tastes of a widely traveled Chinese gentleman" (10, 14). Furthermore, he is described as "a short gentle-faced Chinese with spectacles and a tiny goatee. He wore a richly brocaded mandarin coat and beautifully embroidered Chinese slippers" (14–15). Readers know immediately from these descriptions that "cosmopolitan" Mr. Soong—coupled with his many valuable "Oriental" *objets d'art*—is a definite good guy in the class-conscious world of Nancy Drew.

In contrast, Mr. Soong's compatriots, the missing Engs, are pitiful, tragic figures. These Chinese artisans are kidnapped by evil mixed bloods and forced against their will to create fakes of priceless Chinese potteries.

Prevented from learning English and hidden away in an abandoned Civil War iron mine and smelter, they are completely at the mercy of their captors. The Engs' only modes of resistance are to hang the Chinese characters for "Help!" on the leaning chimney and to try and inscribe their names into the faked vases in the hopes that someone might recognize them. Surely, these pitiable creatures are deserving of Nancy Drew's help! Lucky for them Nancy Drew has learned from Mr. Soong how to "read" Chinese.

The most telling construction in *The Clue of the Leaning Chimney* is the characterization of its villains. Here, the bad guys are mixed-blood Chinese American brothers who take advantage of their biracial/bicultural status for evil ends. Again, the series' stock depictions of "others" clearly paint the men as criminals. For example, Ching, Mr. Soong's deceitful employee, is described as "a short, inscrutable-looking Chinese servant" who takes after his Chinese mother (14). David Carr (alias John Manning), Ching's brother and partner in crime, is described as "a man with black hair and dark skin. But the most striking thing about him was his eyes. They seemed to stare from his head like two small glittering black marbles" (182). The opposite of his brother, Carr "resemble[s] his [American] father" (130).

The depiction of biracialism here plays into fears of miscegenation prevalent at the time; likewise it precludes any positive space for biracial/bicultural people.[11] What does this say to Asians like me who are also culturally American? Ching and Carr "pass" as both Chinese and American; both also pass off fake Chinese art to gullible consumers. They violate set racial/cultural boundaries and therefore must be punished. In contrast, Nancy Drew crosses cultures—by learning Chinese—but only for the express reason of apprehending the criminals. Thus, her actions exemplify the only kind of cultural crossing sanctioned throughout the series: Nancy seeks out and then utilizes her knowledge of Chinese only to reinforce and maintain WASP hegemony. Any intimacy with non-WASP cultures then must complement Nancy's tireless efforts to defend the status quo and its beautiful accouterments.

The mystery ends with Nancy's daring escape and her return (with police reinforcements) to save the Engs and Mr. Soong from the clutches of Ching and Manning. Nancy receives a precious souvenir of her work on this mystery. The grateful Engs, unable to express their gratitude in English, create a commemorative vase that depicts Nancy as a cross between St. George and Joan of Arc, defending the meek Engs and Mr.

Soong from the villains: "Against a soft green background was pictured a slender, golden-haired girl in a suit of armor, pitting a lance at a scaly green dragon. Behind her stood a Chinese girl and two men in long Oriental robes" (209).

Thus, *The Clue of the Leaning Chimney* neatly delineates Nancy Drew's tireless efforts "to preserve the class lines . . . [and defend] beautiful objects, places, and treasures from violence": In short, to maintain the status quo (Mason 73). The lesson seems to be the following: The Carr/Manning brothers, suspect mixed bloods, try to confound systems of racial/cultural purity by taking advantage of their dual identities. They transgress set boundaries, pimping Chinese culture by selling copies of stolen authentic Chinese antiques to unsuspecting Americans. Like all the criminals in the Nancy Drew world, Ching and Carr threaten WASP societal conventions and therefore force Nancy's actions to defend the crumbling aristocracy as well as to maintain the market value of "Oriental" heirlooms in River Heights and its environs.

As I reread my old Nancy Drew books, I wonder where my mother situated herself, and how she dealt with the stereotypical depictions of non-whites as laughable and stupid, evil villains, or household help. Rather than evoking nostalgia, revisiting River Heights forced me to relive my own discomfort upon reading these passages as a young girl while simultaneously underscoring the complex negotiations I made as a reader in order to enter this world: with whom should I identify—the smart, fearless girl detective (whom I aspired to be) or the inscrutable Asian, the dark complexioned villainess, or comical "darkie" who *looked* like me? Given the realities of cultural imperialism and colonial mentality, legacies of my family and my culture, these "choices" were never really choices at all.

Reading Nancy Drew: Strategies and Questions by Women of Color

Bobbie Ann Mason writes that the Bobbsey Twins "were . . . the source of many of my ideas, prejudices, and expectations. They were like cookie cutters on my imagination" (33). Did reading Nancy Drew mysteries have the same "cookie cutter" effect for women of color in the United States? I believe so. In our aspirations for a feminist role model in the girl sleuth, we were also forced to take in the cultural baggage of white supremacy inherent in the series' depictions of American girlhood and its possibilities. This valorization of whiteness often led to the denigration or negation of self and whole communities of color.

For example, Pinay playwright and novelist Jessica Hagedorn describes how her reading of Nancy Drew, juxtaposed to more high-culture texts such as Balzac, is an integral part of what she sees as the "chaos" of colonialist Filipino culture:

> I was taught to look outside the indigenous culture for inspiration, taught that the label "Made in the USA" meant automatic superiority; in other words, like most colonized individuals, I was taught a negative image of myself. In school, classes were taught in English, Tagalog was taught as a foreign language . . . and the ways of the West were endlessly paraded and promoted. . . . My lopsided education in Anglo ways was sophisticated; by the age of nine or ten, *while enjoying the cheap thrills provided by adolescent Nancy Drew mysteries,* I was already reading Walt Whitman, Emily and Charlotte Brontë, Honoré de Balzac, Edgar Allen Poe, Charles Dickens, and Jane Austen. (174, emphasis added)

Similarly, Dinah Eng in "Befriending Nancy Drew across Cultural Boundaries" cites Nancy Drew as providing a model for compassion but, most importantly, assertiveness and questioning of authority—qualities she felt she lacked as an Asian American. Disturbingly, Eng describes how her desire to be white, to be Nancy Drew, created self-conflict and erasure of herself as Asian. Her remembrances illustrate how the Nancy Drew text functions as a site of colonization: how "absence" (not seeing her own image), coupled with the pervasive white hegemony of American culture in general, leads to psychological conflict and self-obliteration:

> When we don't see ourselves on television, in the newspaper or other media, it's as though we don't exist. As a child, I think that translated into the feeling that I wasn't really Asian. I could look in the mirror; I could see that my face was different from everybody else's, but inside I felt that I was white. I felt like I was Nancy Drew at times. . . . I had constant cultural conflicts to resolve. (141)

Unlike Eng, in "Fixing Nancy Drew: African American Strategies for Reading," Njeri Fuller notes that her process of identifying with Nancy Drew involved making "Nancy a black girl like me. . . . I began imagining that I was Nancy Drew. I would also make some of her friends black" (137). Fuller's positive "colorizing" of Nancy certainly indicates her own positive self-image as a girl of color; nevertheless her successful negotiation of Nancy Drew and racial identity should not diminish the fact that all girls of color need heroines with whom they can identify. Like Eng, Fuller objects to the erasure of people of color in the revised editions of the series. She writes: "The Nancy Drew books didn't destroy me. But I have to ask: when will there ever be books we can call classics in which I am represented in a wonderful way? And when will such books become as accessible in libraries and bookstores as are their mainstream white counterparts?" (139). In addition to highlighting the political implications of the absence of "color" in the revised Nancy Drew mysteries, her comments introduce salient questions concerning the marketing and availability of responsible, multicultural texts.

As Fuller noted, the Nancy Drew revisions have removed racial and ethnic stereotypes to the extent that no people of color exist within the series. Donnarae MacCann comments on this obliteration and also raises important questions concerning the messages and politics inherent in children's literature today, and how these texts affect children of color:

> What do children of color feel when they see themselves excluded from such an important cultural phenomenon as literature? What do they feel when they see their language and culture reduced to inferiority? What happens when the so-called mainstream white child sees black characters as incapable, insignificant, or unattractive? And what happens when young people who are white see racism receiving approval in children's literature? What kind of society is it that entertains one group of children at the expense of another? (134–35)

I contend that this process of "whiting out" both manifests and demonstrates the racist rhetoric of "The Nancy Drew Mystery Stories." Stratemeyer scholar Carol Billman, in *The Secret of the Stratemeyer Syndicate* (1986), unwittingly collaborates my stance through her analysis of the revision phenomenon:

> In the early years of the series, it has been well documented, Nancy Drew exhibited a distinct prejudice against ethnic and racial minorities—blacks, Jews, Italians, and Irish, most obviously. Now the egregious bigotry has disappeared, but fundamental beliefs about social propriety remain the same. The value system inherent in the Drew books is nicely summed up by one of the most prevalent images in the series: the great house now in decay and overgrown by unruly shrubs and weeds. It is part of Nancy's

role as detective to do the "landscaping" necessary to restore the fine old house to its former glory and its rightful owners. (114)[12]

Billman's diction here is chilling. Whether intended or not, the phrases "great house," "former glory," and "rightful owners" breezily invoke images of the "good old days" of the antebellum South and consequently offer a very telling commentary on how white supremacy clearly underscores the Nancy Drew mysteries' "fundamental beliefs about social propriety." As such, the Nancy Drew mystery itself must be read as a site of colonization: explicitly valorizing an all-American, all-WASP world, this beguiling text seeks to persuade readers (particularly readers like Eng, Fuller, and myself) to embrace "whiteness" and be subsumed within its lulling "normalcy."

Moreover, Billman contends that reading serial fiction gives children important skills and tools that they may then apply to reading other texts:

But readers do not simply abandon those books they once regarded so highly, taking with them only fond memories of their favorite heroes and heroines. They also carry over the confidence gained from stories about successful young discoverers and a literary template—a sense of how stories are constructed and proceed—that will be helpful later. Schooled in the elementary virtues of fiction and having fully discovered all the secrets of the series mysteries for themselves, they are ready, in both senses of the word, to explore what is beyond. (155)

Billman implies that reading serial fiction like Nancy Drew mysteries provides the reader with the helpful "literary templates" of racism and classism. When viewed within the larger economy of U.S. cultural imperialism in the Philippines and elsewhere (as well as within the internally colonized United States itself), these books relentlessly continue to mold expectations of how all "stories"—nationalist narratives and personal histories alike—"are constructed and proceed," and thus in actuality impede readers from exploring what is truly "beyond."

Voilà! Unmasking the Real Villain

In my analysis of female acculturation via Nancy Drew books from the Filipina American perspective, I hope to have demonstrated the importance of recognizing the hegemonic forces embedded not only within popular culture but also in current modes of critical analysis. By this I mean exploring how cultural capital and ideology circulate in order to discern the roots of their power, their modes of persuasion, and their desired effects upon intended subjects. Thus, Euro-American feminist theorists, rather than making the obligatory references acknowledging "differences" among women, need to radicalize feminist praxis: to utilize a conscious feminist analytical process which can recognize and engage with the reality of white dominance as pervasive in all economic, political, social, and cultural contexts. Such a stance is a necessary corrective to naive and dangerous visions of sisterhood which can only reinscribe, in this case, American imperialism.

In her poem "To Live in the Borderlands . . . ," Gloria Anzaldúa uses the metaphor of white bread to describe the process of assimilation and deracination:

> the mill with the razor white teeth wants to shred off
> your olive-red skin, crush out the kernel, your heart
> pound you pinch you roll you out
> smelling like white bread but dead. (195)

This pervasive "whitening" is enforced by the media, the educational system, libraries, our families, and Filipino culture itself. Recognizing and resisting the hegemonic forces of assimilation and deracination can entail the creation of more positive images of people of color in children's literature; more urgently, we need to develop strategies of cultural resistance that will enable Pinays (as well as other girls of color) to resist the debilitating colonial mentality that characterizes Filipino American culture.

Sometimes as I speed along winding, tree-shaded country lanes in my own blue roadster, that ten-year-old in me who imagined herself as a famous girl detective reappears. I can easily recall the sense of excitement that fueled my love of Nancy Drew mysteries: the danger, anticipation, and assurance of that inevitable happy ending, complete with the requisite blurb describing the next mystery to be solved. However, writing this piece—that I've nicknamed *The Case of Pinay Acculturation*—I realized that Nancy trained me to look for the wrong kind of criminal. Rather than the stock beady-eyed, "swarthy" thugs of the past, the true villain is Nancy herself.

NOTES

1. In the "Proclamation of December 21, 1898," President McKinley used the term "benevolent assimilation" to characterize American colonial policy in the Philippines:

Finally, it should be the earnest and paramount aim of the military administration to win the confidence, respect and affection of the inhabitants of the Philippines by assuring them in every possible way that full measure of individual rights and liberties which is the heritage of a free people, and by proving to them that the mission of the United States is one of benevolent assimilation, substituting the mild sway of justice and right for arbitrary rule. (Epigraph to *Benevolent Assimilation*)

See Stuart Miller's *Benevolent Assimilation* for a cogent history of the Philippine-American War (1898–1901) and its aftermath.

2. Tagalog (Pilipino) word for "Filipina."

3. Glenn May in *Social Engineering in the Philippines* defines "social engineering" as "an effort to mold, and often to restructure, a society" (1).

4. See Glenn May's and Bonifacio Salamanca's works for curiously unpoliticized accounts of the American educational system in the Philippines.

5. Tagalog term denoting respect as in "older brother."

6. See Chan, Espiritu, and Takaki for cogent histories of Filipinos in the United States. The film *A Dollar a Day, Ten Cents a Dance* is a poignant documentary of the experiences of Filipino farmworkers during this period.

7. David Joel Steinberg in *The Philippines, A Singular and Plural Place* claims that burgeoning Filipino nationalism prompted the people's rejection of Japanese claims to be "fellow liberating Asians" who came to "emancipate the Filipinos, drive out the wicked white rulers and establish a true bond with the Filipinos" (102). Filipino writer and activist E. San Juan, Jr., views this situation very differently. In "The Predicament of Filipinos in the United States: 'Where Are You From? When Are You Going Back?' " he contends that the Filipino guerrilla war against the Japanese invaders is yet another aspect of American imperialism and colonial mentality:

The much-touted U.S. legacy of schools, roads, public health programs, artesian wells, "democratic" politicians, and "the most gregariously informal backslapping imperialist rulers known to history" serves to explain, for Stanley [Karnow], why Filipinos cherish a "deferential friendship" for Americans. Does this then explain why Fred Cordova, in his pictorial essay *Filipinos: Forgotten Asian Americans* boasts that "an estimated one million innocent Filipino men, women and children died while defending Americanism during World War II from 1941 to 1945"? Indeed isn't the appropriate question: Are so many Filipinos really so screwed up that they would make such a sacrifice? Think of it: one million natives defending the cause of [the] Lone Ranger and Charlie Chan. One million dark-skinned natives sacrificing their lives for Americanism. (214)

8. See Carol Billman's *The Secret of the Stratemeyer Syndicate* for a detailed history and analysis of children's series fiction in the United States. I find it ironic that Edward Stratemeyer's first best seller was the volume *Under Dewey at Manila* (1898), the first of the "Old Glory Series." Billman glibly notes: "[T]here was the lucky coincidence of Dewey's attack and Stratemeyer's war novel for boys" (18).

9. See Dyer and Romalov's *Rediscovering Nancy Drew* and Billman's *The Secret of the Stratemeyer Syndicate* for comprehensive readings of how Nancy Drew mysteries were revised beginning in 1950 in order to eliminate ethnic and racial stereotyping. My mother read the original mysteries; I read both original and revised versions.

10. MacCann's study purports to describe the American racial climate (social/ political setting) up to the publication of the first Nancy Drew mystery in 1930; unfortunately her work is limited to an analysis of black/white relations. She does not include any references to the virulent anti-Asian violence of this same period, nor does she describe parallel Latino and Native American struggles.

11. See the film *Slaying the Dragon* for an analysis of how fears of Asian/ American unions were manifested through popular films of the period.

12. Billman also notes that the revisions themselves were motivated not only by the civil rights movement, but by marketing: Modernizing the Nancy Drew plots, descriptions, and characters invigorated the mysteries' "up-to-date" outlook—an essential component to their enduring popularity (146).

WORKS CITED

Aguilar, Delia D. "Gender, Nation, Colonialism: Lessons from the Philippines." [Online]. Available WWW.maxwell.syr.edu. Directory: Centennial/texts File: dda_95a.html.

Anzaldúa, Gloria. *Borderlands/La Frontera: The New Mestiza*. San Francisco: Spinsters/Aunt Lute, 1987.

Billman, Carol. *The Secret of the Stratemeyer Syndicate: Nancy Drew, the Hardy Boys, and the Million Dollar Fiction Factory*. New York: Ungar, 1986.

Bulosan, Carlos. *America Is in the Heart*. 1943. Seattle: U of Washington P, 1993.

Chan, Sucheng. *Asian Americans: An Interpretive History*. Boston: Twayne, 1991.

A Dollar a Day, Ten Cents a Dance: An Historic Portrait of Filipino Farmworkers in America. Prod. Geoffrey Dunn and Mark Schwartz. Videocassette. National Asian American Telecommunications Association/Cross Current Media, 1984.

Dyer, Carolyn Stewart, and Nancy Tillman Romalov, eds. *Rediscovering Nancy Drew*. Iowa City: U of Iowa P, 1995.

Eng, Dinah. "Befriending Nancy Drew across Cultural Boundaries." Dyer and Romalov 140–42.

Espiritu, Yen Le. "Filipino Settlements in the United States." *Filipino American Lives*. Philadelphia: Temple UP, 1995. 1–36.

Fuller, Njeri. "Fixing Nancy Drew: African American Strategies for Reading." Dyer and Romalov 136–39.

Hagedorn, Jessica. "The Exile Within/The Question of Identity." With an interview by Karin Aguilar-San Juan. *The State of Asian America: Activism and Resistance in the 1990's*. Ed. Karin Aguilar-San Juan. Boston: South End P, 1994. 173–82.

Heilbrun, Carolyn. "Nancy Drew: A Moment in Feminist History." Dyer and Romalov 11–22.

Keene, Carolyn. *The Clue of the Leaning Chimney*. New York: Grosset and Dunlap, 1949.

——. *The Mystery at Lilac Inn*. New York: Grosset and Dunlap, 1930.

MacCann, Donnarae. "Nancy Drew and the Myth of White Supremacy." Dyer and Romalov 129–35.

Mason, Bobbie Ann. *The Girl Sleuth: On the Trail of Nancy Drew, Judy Bolton and Cherry Ames*. Athens: U of Georgia P, 1995.

May, Glenn Anthony. *Social Engineering in the Philippines: The Aims, Execution, and Impact of Colonial Policy, 1900–1913*. Contributions to Comparative Colonial Studies, Number 2. Westport: Greenwood, 1980.

Salamanca, Bonifacio. *The Filipino Reaction to American Rule 1910–1913*. Hamden: Shoe String P, 1968.

San Juan, E., Jr. "The Predicament of Filipinos in the United States: 'Where Are You From? When Are You Going Back?' " *The State of Asian America: Activism and Resistance in the 1990's*. Ed. Karin Aguilar-San Juan. Boston: South End P, 1994. 210–18.

Slaying the Dragon. Prod. Pacific Productions, in association with Asian Women United and KQED. Videocassette. National Asian American Telecommunications Association/Cross Current Media, 1987.

Steinberg, David Joel. *The Philippines: A Singular and Plural Place*. Third edition. Boulder: Westview, 1994.

Takaki, Ronald. *Strangers from a Different Shore: A History of Asian Americans*. New York: Penguin Books, 1989.

11

"No Place for a Girl Dick"

*Mabel Maney and the Queering
of Girls' Detective Fiction*

Julia D. Gardner

One of the most popular heroines of girls' series fiction, Nancy Drew, has been held up as a role model to girls since her inception in 1930. The series' longevity invites the assumption that Nancy has universal appeal for readers, that all girls can and do identify with the heroine. Closer analysis, however, reveals that is not necessarily the main character who appeals to readers, but the ideology represented in the series. Non-white characters are conspicuously absent, and Nancy's bourgeois existence continues unquestioned. Even less attention is paid in such books to representing sexuality. While girls' series fiction may not seem like an obvious source of sexual information for young readers, such novels do contribute to the cultural discourse of girls' gender and sexual identities, even in their attempts to suppress such issues. With few exceptions, girls' fiction tends to reproduce a heterosexual presumption about its heroines' identities and desires, refusing to acknowledge possibilities for same-sex eroticism.[1] Given the increase in media coverage of teen lesbians, from the November 1996 cover of *Seventeen* proclaiming "I Can't Tell Anyone I'm Gay" to an HBO special featuring a lesbian couple attending their high school prom, such "compulsory heterosexuality" within girls' books appears out of step with contemporary girls' culture. One may wonder if, or how, girl's fiction has changed since Nancy Drew first donned her driving gloves and sped her roadster to the site of a mystery.

A humorous but critical evaluation of mainstream girls' fiction can be found in Mabel Maney's "Nancy Clue" series of novels, which spoofs juvenile series from Nancy Drew and Hardy Boys mysteries to the Cherry Ames nursing stories for girls. Designed for adults, Maney's revision of these "classics" in popular girls' fiction deconstructs, rewrites, and subverts the hegemonic girls' culture as reproduced in the original books. While not part of juvenile fiction, Maney's work depends on readers' familiarity with girls' fiction of the past, and offers a campy critique of problematic representations of sexuality, race, and class consciousness found in girls' popular series. To date, Maney has published three novels in her series: *The Case of the Not-So-Nice Nurse* (1993), *The Case of the Good-for-Nothing Girlfriend* (1994), and *The Ghost in the Closet* (1995). Although the books assume a certain degree of familiarity with the original girls' series, Maney's works are not merely an exercise in fifties nostalgia. Rather, they offer a history that might have been, had lesbian characters inhabited the worlds of girls' fiction. Maney situates her novels in the year 1959, the same year Grosset and Dunlap published the first two titles of the revised thirty-four Nancy Drew novels, changing Nancy Drew from self-reliant and independent to the more passive model of fifties femininity.[2] Thus, Mabel Maney situates herself within an already established tradition of rewriting the Nancy Drew stories; her revisions, however, fashion Nancy and another prominent girls' fiction heroine, Cherry Ames, into representatives of 1990s queer sensibilities which include the racial and sexual identities erased from the Nancy Drew series. Ultimately, her novels imagine how girls who read between the lines of mainstream girls' fiction might tell their stories.

Sex and Gender for the Junior Miss

Reading between the lines of Nancy Drew and Cherry Ames novels reveals the conflicting standards of girls' behavior represented by these characters; they are expected to be both conventionally "feminine" yet unconventionally adventurous, consistently participating in dangerous, physical adventures. Additionally, the heroine must be physically attractive and desirable, but heterosexual in behavior, if not asexual. Comparing the two series brings forth the different approaches used to represent heroines of the 1930s and 1950s. Nancy emerges as more independent both financially and professionally, while Cherry is frequently constrained economically.

She is often shown as spending her last few cents on a present for a friend, on cabfare, or other small expenses. She also works in a more "feminized" profession, nursing, while Nancy's occupation as detective is a role more typically held by men. The Cherry Ames series does allow its heroine unusual freedom in travel, with Cherry taking her turn as student nurse, army nurse, cruise nurse, boarding school nurse, and even department store nurse. While pursuing her nursing profession, Cherry travels the country, moving from urban to rural environments, from land to sea, exploring more of the world than many of her readers could hope to do themselves.

Yet a dual message emerges from both the Nancy Drew and Cherry Ames novels. For all the freedom accorded these heroines, the characters must also concede to social norms regulating gender and sexual behavior for young women. Nancy is exceptional among teenagers in her extensive travels and exposure to danger, but she never compromises her position as a proper middle-class girl. Deidre Johnson argues that Nancy's autonomy can be traced to her adherence to social codes of class and gender, noting that "Nancy is well mannered, well dressed (usually in skirts or 'frocks'), and well versed in social graces. . . . Nancy is thus able to adopt many characteristics associated with male protagonists without seeming masculine" (151). Bobbie Ann Mason identifies the inconsistency in Nancy Drew by writing that "Nancy's daring exploits release readers from the abyss of sorority teas and sewing bees while at the same time congratulating that tea-party and sewing-basket world" (60). As both critics point out, Nancy's participation in more "feminine," domestic activities allows her to operate in the "masculine," public world of detective work and adventure. Similarly, while Cherry Ames may be unusual in turning down the marriage proposals she receives from young male doctors, her attractive, "young and gay" appearance helps maintain her position within socially acceptable female gender behavior; Cherry may remain single, but she is no old maid. These heroines present girls with images of capable young women, but this message of empowerment is subtly undercut by the novels' insistence on adherence to traditionally "feminine" manners and appearances.

The revised editions of Nancy Drew and the later Cherry Ames novels become even more blatant in their containment of the characters to 1950s-era gender roles. Several critics reference the 1959 second edition of the Nancy Drew series as the point at which not only gender behavior was modified, but so was other content, such as racist language or representation. While the revisions were motivated by a desire to "correct" earlier cultural stereotypes and make the novels reflect the current social standards, such "improvement" is not without problems. As Diana Beeson and Bonnie Brennen write in "Translating Nancy Drew from Print to Film":

> The simplified stories exclude many of the cultural signposts and messages relevant to the 1930s. Nancy's independent character is softened and in these newer texts she relies much more heavily upon others for help and guidance. The post-1959 editions encode very different messages which reflect the mores, expectations, and experiences of postwar American society. (194)

The later books rewrite Nancy as the patriarchal ideal of 1950s white womanhood. While the second editions may not have engaged in as much explicit racism as did the first, they seem to have instead become more sexist, having Nancy rely more on male assistance. Johnson notes the irony of such revision, writing that "as women have gained freedom and independence, Nancy has gradually lost hers" (152). Maney rewrites these later versions, "restoring" Nancy to her earlier independence, as well as adding some new twists for the character.

Cherry Ames undergoes a similar transformation over the decades, changing from a patriotic, adventure-seeking nurse during the 1940s to a more passive, complacent assistant to male physicians in the 1950s. For instance, in *Cherry Ames, Senior Nurse* (1944), Cherry graduates from nursing school and decides to enter the armed forces as a nurse, illustrating the active roles women filled during prewar and war years. In *Senior Nurse*, Cherry and another nurse help trap a criminal who has stolen medicine vital to the war effort. In catching the thief, the two women succeed where male doctors have failed. Cherry thrives in her female-dominated milieu of the nursing school, demonstrating that women can succeed in the public, working world.[3]

Yet by the 1950s stories, Cherry's travels remain contained within strictly defined gender norms. She may travel, but her position as subordinate to the physician in charge remains clear. In *Cherry Ames, Boarding School Nurse* (1955), Cherry relies more heavily on a male doctor's advice and approval. For example, at one point Cherry has recently met a handsome young doctor, Alan Wilcox, who now examines her patient: "Cherry watched anxiously as Dr. Alan very gently examined the splint. She hoped that he approved of what she had done, for she wanted to

merit this young man's respect" (Wells 38). Compare this attitude of
seeking male approval to her reaction to the young doctor in *Senior Nurse*,
where "that bold male walk of his infuriated Cherry. He had the darndest
air of being someone special, she thought" (Wells 15). In Maney's 1990s
reincarnation of Cherry, the young nurse pays little heed to male attention. Playing on Cherry's desire to try all the career options available to
her as a nurse, Maney exposes the limitations imposed on Cherry in the
original series and by society, giving her a career history as dude ranch
nurse and shoe store nurse. As she drives past the Iowa Institute for the
Feeble-Minded, Cherry wonders "if someday she, too, could be a Feeble-
Minded Nurse" (*Good-for-Nothing* 117). Maney's Cherry remains earnest
but ultimately abandons the passivity that marks Helen Wells' version of
the character. The original Cherry Ames was constrained by dueling
agendas; she was to be both a progressive role model to girls as a successful career woman, but was also subject to social norms that did not allow
a woman to be *too* independent. In refashioning Cherry, Maney draws on
Cherry's refusal of heterosexual romance, a quality also noted by Bobbie
Ann Mason, who writes that Cherry seems "almost above romance,
though it occurs regularly, and she is without commitment" (110). Maney
emphasizes the active, capable side of Cherry demonstrated in the earlier,
1940s Wells novels, while allowing her to indulge in romance not with a
supervising doctor, but with another woman. Cherry not only becomes
more professionally active in the Maney series, but she also becomes
sexually active.

One of the most important assumptions challenged in the Nancy Clue
series is that of the sexually ignorant or implicitly heterosexual teen
heroine. Not only does Cherry Aimless discover her own desires, but the
novels also feature the butch-femme couple, Midge Fontaine and Velma
Pierce, who spend all their spare moments away from adventure either in
bed or plotting ways to arrange trysts. Maney also pairs two characters
from the original Nancy Drew series as lovers; Nancy's friends George
Fayne and Bess Marvin become George Fey and her girlfriend, Bess
Marvel. Maney's creation of these lesbian pairings has a strong basis in
the original books. George is repeatedly described as "athletic" and has
the shortest hair of any of the main characters; Maney elaborates on these
signifiers to create George as the butch sweetheart of Bess.

Just as the Nancy Drew series contains characters and events that
Maney has reworked to queer the stories, the Cherry Ames books also
contain information that lays the foundation for Maney's interpretation

of Cherry as a lesbian. Cherry always privileges her career over marriage, choosing to remain in the more exclusively female environment of nursing rather than be removed to the domestic by becoming a wife. She operates from a base apartment in New York that she shares with several close female friends.[4] Except for the intrusion of the doctors with whom she works, Cherry Ames lives in a primarily female world, as does Nancy Drew. Maney expands on this homosocial world, providing representation for lesbian readers by creating an explicitly homoerotic environment for the characters.

Maney's expansion of the homosociality common in girls' fiction to imagine the homoerotic possibilities of an all-female environment represents a common reading strategy for queer girls, as suggested by Rosemary Auchmuty's study, A World of Girls (1992). Auchmuty explores the changing social attitudes toward gender and sexuality found in girls' boarding school stories published in the first half of the twentieth century. She argues that "during the period in which the girl's school story flourished, lesbianism was progressively redefined," but that eventually "a new equation sank into the public mind: close friendships between women equaled lesbianism equaled sexual perversion" (178). Thus, while school stories were popular in the twenties and thirties, public mores dictated the extinction of the school story genre as sexual identities became increasingly codified. Auchmuty notes the resurgence of schoolgirl stories beginning in the 1980s, which she reads as "testament . . . to the enduring appeal of these novels for girls and women who want an alternative vision to the patriarchal world we live in" (180). Maney's reworking of popular American girls' stories can be seen as part of this tradition noticed by Auchmuty; the Nancy Clue series is particularly likely to appeal to women who read the original Nancy Drew or Cherry Ames books. Nancy Drew and Cherry Ames function in a female-dominated environment, demonstrating the same initiative and "pluckiness" of the characters discussed by Auchmuty. Maney's novels build on qualities already present in the original novels and rewrite the books to make explicit the lesbian possibilities found implicitly in girls' fiction.

The Nancy Clue series eliminates the need for contemporary readers to imagine Nancy or Cherry as lesbians, putting into print what some had already practiced in their own reading. Consumers of girls' fiction in more closeted times report finding ways of interpreting girls' novels "against the grain" or refashioning the characters in ways that would allow more satisfactory identification. For instance, in offering her personal experience as a young reader, Auchmuty tells us that "reading them [girls' serial novels] offered me as a young woman a temporary escape and refuge from the pressures of that profoundly heterosexual society I lived in" (205). The Nancy Clue series directly addresses this desire of the young lesbian reader for a non-heterosexual society by providing a similar context to juvenile fiction, yet offering a queered content.

Assumed heterosexual desire vanishes in Maney's work, replaced by lesbian liaisons. Providing this kind of lesbian visibility, particularly when the characters are derived from popular fiction, challenges the implicit heterosexuality endorsed by much of girl's fiction and offers an alternate vision. For teen girls who identify as lesbian, the presence of lesbian characters can be particularly important in dealing with the sense of isolation often resulting from the lack of gay role models, fictional or otherwise. Researching the experience of lesbian and gay teens in school, Andi O'Conor observes that "gay and lesbian teens are often isolated from gay, lesbian, and bisexual adults . . . [and] often feel they have no place to go, that there is no room in the world for them to exist" (99–100). A similar feeling of isolation can be found in an interview for that arbiter of teen taste, *Seventeen*, where one girl explains the difficulties of being an out lesbian as a teenager: "You can feel like you're the only gay person on the entire planet" (Van Gelder, "It's Who I Am" 143). In contrast to this sense of invisibility, Maney's series presents a world in which all the main characters are lesbians. Just as girls of the 1990s are becoming more open about their same-sex relationships, so do Maney's characters assert their desires.

Unlike their predecessors, the Nancy Clue books call attention to the erotic potential of the ostensibly desexualized, homosocial worlds inhabited by the original characters and refuse to explain relationships between women as simply "friends." The first book in the Maney series, *The Case of the Not-So-Nice Nurse*, initiates Cherry into the possibilities of same-sex relationships. After inquiring and learning that Cherry is single, Midge assures her "You'll meet someone. . . . I hooked up with a couple of losers before I met Velma" (64). The possibility that Cherry will ever be interested in men is never an option in the conversation, even to Cherry, who realizes "try as she might, [she] didn't find the doctors and interns at the hospital very interesting" (64). Rather than repeating heterosexist assurances that Cherry will eventually meet Mr. Right, the Nancy Clue novels place Cherry in an exclusively lesbian environment. The creation of a lesbian world for the characters resists the patriarchal, heterosexual world of the original novels.

In addition to "bringing out" Cherry as a lesbian heroine, the novels instruct the reader in fifties lesbian culture, particularly sexual identities such as butch and femme. One mystery requires Cherry to radically alter her girlish appearance, a problem Midge solves by transforming Cherry from femme to baby butch. After buying Cherry men's clothing, instructing her in how to walk, roll her pants cuffs, and use Butch Wax, Midge finally decrees that Cherry's purse must go: "No self-respecting butch would ever be seen with a purse" she explains (*Not-so-Nice* 83). Once again, Cherry Aimless functions as the ingenue initiate into lesbian life, complaining, " 'But where will I keep my lipstick?' Cherry gasped. 'And who's this Butch person you're always talking about?' " (*Not-so-Nice* 83). Readers learn about sexual styles available to lesbians, and the novels also historicize lesbian culture, telling a story of existence frequently overlooked by mainstream fiction. Girls learn about the gender and sexual roles expected of them while reading mainstream girls' fiction, and the behavior presented in such books promotes heterosexuality as desirable. Maney's books, in contrast, take on the role of instructing their readers in the sensibilities of lesbian culture. When considered in relation to the profound isolation experienced by many young lesbians, as discussed previously, fiction that addresses lesbian history takes on added importance. In discussing the significance of lesbian history, particularly the history of butch and femme styles, Joan Nestle argues that "it is hard to re-create . . . what Lesbian sexual play meant in the 1950s, but I think it is essential for Lesbian-feminists to understand, without shame, this part of their erotic heritage" (103). The Maney novels deal with history in a humorous style, but also belatedly fulfill the desire of adults who longed for such information about lesbian culture and/or history, or wished to inhabit such a world as young readers.

The Nancy Clue books depart from the kinds of gender and sexual knowledge girls traditionally learn from fiction and open up an array of potential identities. Providing a range of possibilities again answers desires adults may have had as children for books which addressed non-normative impulses. The connections between reading and a girl's ability to imagine different identities for herself are significant. In her study of girls' reading habits, *Private Practices* (1994), Meredith Rogers Cherland explains that fiction provides ". . . girls with access to *textual* constructions of gender and these constructions were also positioning the girls to grow into certain kinds of women" (96). While Cherland is more concerned with the formation of gender identity than sexual identity, her remarks on reading and gender also apply to the connection between reading and sexuality. Readers of the Maney novels do not have to negotiate a straight, male-dominated culture; instead they are allowed to explore other sexual and gender systems. Perhaps the series' greatest critique of gender norms can be found in Uncle Nelly's explanation to the Hardly Boys of his sister's transgender identity as detective Fennel Hardly. Citing "prejudice against girls" and misconceptions that "[girls] weren't as smart as boys, weren't logical or strong," Uncle Nelly concludes that Fanny/Fennel realized there was "no place in that world for a girl dick" and instead passed as a man (*Ghost* 118). The realm of gender possibility in the Maney series includes transgender practices, addressing an issue which has scant representation even in gay and lesbian fiction.

Detecting Race

The Maney series also addresses a problem that persists in the newer Nancy Drews: the absence of people of color as main characters. In "Fixing Nancy Drew: African American Strategies for Reading," Njeri Fuller explains that, as a child, she ignored the character descriptions and was busy "making Nancy a black girl like me.... George seemed the closest in description to African American friends I might have"(137). Much as Maney has re-imagined the characters to reflect a desire for heroines who represent a marginalized sexual identity, Fuller recounts her attempts to imagine Nancy and the other characters as representing racial minorities. Fuller expresses disappointment in the 1990s Nancy Drew books, writing "I expected that she [Nancy] was going to be more in line with what I imagined a nineties woman would be. But I was disappointed to find the same formulas. There are no African Americans, there are no Asians, no Latinos" (138). Fuller might appreciate the Nancy Clue series more than the "straight" series. Readers of Nancy Clue do not have to imagine one of the characters as black; Maney provides Officer Jackie Jones, who emerges not only as Cherry's one true love, but also upstages Nancy as a detective and, in the course of the series, becomes "the first black female detective in the SFPD" (*Not-so-Nice* 159).

Jackie's first appearance in the series establishes her as sympathetic and attractive without fetishizing her racial difference. A scene where Midge and Cherry are awakened from their nap in Cherry's car by a policeman knocking at the window demonstrates Maney's approach to the issue of race: "the police officer leaned down and looked into the car. Midge sat up when she saw the face of a *girl*—a handsome girl with warm brown skin and dancing black eyes" (*Not-so-Nice* 86). Jackie goes through a series of identifications based first on her occupation, a "police officer," then on her gender, a "girl," and finally her race, "brown skin," illustrating the multiple identities she, and other women of color, continually negotiate. Significantly, Midge takes notice of Jackie's gender more than her race. Throughout the series, gender and sexual identities prove the main foundations of solidarity among characters. Yet racial difference and the problems faced by a non-white person are noted in each of the novels. When Jackie explains the difficulty she had traveling from San Francisco to River Depths, for example, she notes "I imagine that out here the color of my skin counts more than the color of my [police] badge" (*Good-for-Nothing* 139). Her comments provide contrast to the cross-country car trip recently completed by her white friends, Cherry, Nancy, Midge, and Velma, who never had to consider race as a factor in their travels or lodging.

The Maney series further critiques the racial exclusivity of girls' series by directly confronting racial prejudice. In one example, Jackie is mistaken as a maid by one of the society matrons who visits Nancy: "Oh good, you've hired more help. . . . and goodness dear, put on an apron. We have guests arriving soon" (*Good-for-Nothing* 273). Jackie is even arrested in one novel, with the clear suggestion that her race prompted the arrest. Jackie is harassed while being led to a cell, "the prisoners jeered at the girl, calling out names that made even a streetwise officer like Jackie Jones cringe," and the arresting policeman sneers at her "You know the chief won't be at all happy to find the likes of you in his town" (*Ghost* 139). Although Jackie always triumphs over the bigoted characters she encounters, the novels make their point about the often simplistic ways girls' fiction attempts to engage with racial difference. Race emerges as a constant component of the Nancy Clue stories, but never devolves into tokenism.

Indeed, rather than function as a secondary character, Jackie takes on increasing prominence as the series continues. Maney consistently portrays Jackie as attractive, and Cherry blushes with desire "after she got a good look at Jackie, who had recently stepped out of a refreshing bath.

Her jet-black hair was slicked close to her head, and she was clad in a pair of old, soft-looking dungaree trousers and a snug white tee-shirt that showed off her bulging biceps to their best advantage" (*Ghost* 35). The attraction between Cherry and Jackie becomes more apparent when Cherry must describe Jackie during a party game. After describing Jackie as having "warm, brown skin, the color of strong coffee with just a hint of cream," the smitten nurse becomes flushed with desire: "was it [Cherry's] imagination, or had the summer night suddenly turned much warmer?" (*Ghost* 94). Racial difference is noted in descriptions of Jackie, but race does not determine Cherry's affection. Rather, personality is emphasized, as seen in the conclusion of the series. After being cheated on by Nancy, Cherry eventually acknowledges her love for Jackie, and "kisse[s] Jackie with a fervor and sincerity of purpose she had never known before" (*Ghost* 224). Shifting Cherry's attraction from Nancy to Jackie disrupts the strategies employed in the original Nancy Drew books that encouraged the reader to desire Nancy, and the predominantly white world she occupies.

Readers of Nancy Clue are not forced to identify solely with the white, femme Nancy. Instead, alternatives are provided, with Jackie displacing Nancy, who ceases to be the model daughter, suffers from alcoholism, and displays jealousy of Jackie on a number of occasions. In the course of one mystery, for example, the Hardly boys reveal their ownership of a secret reel-to-reel recorder. Jackie remarks to Cherry, " 'We have one very much like this at detective headquarters.... You could call and leave me a message any time you like.' Nancy pouted. All she had was a private line to the pink princess telephone in her bedroom" (*Ghost* 111). Most revealing is Nancy's reaction when she recognizes her competition with Jackie for Cherry: " 'I've lost my one and only true love,' she sobbed, 'which has *never* happened to *me* before!' " (*Ghost* 61). As Nancy Clue, Nancy appears in a less flattering light than allowed by the Nancy Drew series. De-throning Nancy from her reign as the only desirable character is an important move, signaling a greater range of options for reader identification. The presence of Jackie marks an effort to amend the attitudes toward race found in girls' literature of previous decades, and also provides a commentary on the ways such exclusion prompted readers like Fuller to "fix" Nancy Drew. Informed by 1990s racial politics, Maney's books refashion girls' fiction into a more inclusive setting.

Such inclusion is important not only for its representation of racial difference, but for its simultaneous portrayal of racial *and* sexual differences within the same character. Jackie is not identified solely on the basis of her race, or her sexuality. Multiple identities are kept in play, reinforcing the shift away from simplistic representations found in mainstream girls' series. While this more sophisticated handling of racial and sexual identity occurs within a series aimed at adults rather than girls, Maney's use of familiar girls' series heroines and conventions points out the need for such representation in books available to girls.

Camp Critique

Throughout the novels, Maney uses camp as a means to address the racial and sexual oppression present in the original Nancy Drew and Cherry Ames series. Maney effectively utilizes campy humor to mock dominant culture's attempt to explain away lesbian desire when Cherry recalls her mother's advice: "when a girl likes an older girl, it isn't a crush in the romantic sense, but rather it's that she admires the way the older girl carries herself: her poise, charm, and attractive, modern way of dress" (*Ghost* 34). Such humorous juxtaposition of homophobic "explanation" of same-sex attraction with Cherry's dilemma over which girl to date highlights social erasure of lesbian culture, while asserting the existence of the marginalized group. In her classic essay, "Toward a Butch-Femme Aesthetic," Sue-Ellen Case explains that "Camp both articulates the lives of homosexuals through the obtuse tone of irony and inscribes their oppression with the same device. Likewise, it eradicates the ruling powers of heterosexist realist modes" (298). Maney's novels make more concrete the aspects of camp theorized by Case. In returning to girls' popular fiction of past decades, Maney succeeds in providing a queer revision of these works while calling attention to such fiction's explicit and implicit reproduction of sexual oppression.

Camp can also be seen in Maney's portrayal of less humorous aspects of lesbian life in the fifties. For instance, after a fight with then-girlfriend Nancy Clue, Cherry takes off for the local gay bar. Velma, Midge, and Jackie attempt to locate both Cherry and the nefarious chief of police, Chief Chumley. While searching for the chief, the girls follow a police car to a bar. When the bar turns out to be the same one Cherry was seeking, Velma worries their friend might be caught in a raid: "[Velma, Midge, and Jackie] leapt out of the car and raced toward the club just as a chorus line of tall girls in sparkly dresses and dramatic beehive hairdos danced out the door, smack into a half dozen burly cops. . . . A gorgeous blond girl outfitted in a slinky cocktail dress and a tiara snatched a billy club away from one cop and smacked him over the head with it. Then she kicked him in the shins with her red stilettos." (*Good-for-Nothing* 232) Maney rewrites history, creating a Stonewall-like encounter in 1959, and reversing the typical outcome of such raids in the fifties. Her rewrite empowers the queer characters, placing them in positions of power, control, and desirability. The representatives of dominant culture, indeed, of the Law, become the helpless group in this scenario. Sue-Ellen Case has written about "the camp success in ironizing and distancing the regime of realist terror mounted by heterosexist forces" (298). Maney's writing of this bar raid turns it into a humorous, campy incident, but her use of camp to rework the scene also calls attention to the history of police brutality and humiliation endured by patrons of gay bars.[5] Maney's book deals with the issue of violence against gays and lesbians in the same glib tone employed by children's fiction, but her self-consciously campy style calls attention to the seriousness of such history, while critiquing girls' fiction that continues to gloss over issues of difference. Young adult novels deal with more serious social issues, but girls' serial fiction rarely ventures into controversial territory. Issues of racism, for instance, are generally not dealt with overtly. Serial novels may attempt to pay lip service to multiculturalism by tossing in the occasional character of color, but juvenile series fiction historically shies away from directly confronting examples of social oppression. Certainly, few examples of gay history are to be found in girls' series.

Maney does not limit her revisions to historical events; the stereotypical nuclear family is radically rewritten as well. No example of the stereotypical nuclear family can be found in Maney's novels. Cherry's parents both have "complete and utter mental breakdowns" when their daughter's twin, Charley, informs them both their children are gay. Nancy shoots her father after suffering years of sexual abuse and later discovers her mother imprisoned in an insane asylum. Uncle Nelly reveals to the Hardly boys, Frank and Joe, that their father, Fennel P. Hardly, is actually his cross-dressing, transgender sister, Fannie Hardly. This revelation causes a personal crisis for Frank because "they had covered human reproduction in health class and something just didn't seem right. 'I can't possibly be Fennel's son!' Frank realized in true and utter anguish. '*I'm not really a Hardly boy!*' " (*Ghost* 125). Biological parents are either removed or killed; the only family group resembling the traditional construct of mother, father, and two children, the Hardly family, is revealed as consisting of two biologically female parents. Maney destroys any pretense of stereotypical family life in the novels, both pointing out the secrets often hidden by families and the ways in which gays and lesbians often form their own families, based on affinity rather than biology. As Frank comes to realize, "[I]t's not blood but fellowship between people that makes a *real* family" (*Ghost* 226). Maney critiques the ways the heterosexual paradigm continues to be invoked as a means of propping up the fantasy of the idealized nuclear family. Placing familiar characters in a queer environment calls attention to the ways juvenile fiction participates in the reproduction of dominant ideology. Rather than simply dismiss stereotypical representations like those offered by Nancy Drew or Cherry Ames, Maney turns such originals on their heads and underscores the inherent perversity of the novels, as well as skewering the middle-class ideals the original books promote. For those who read the original series as girls and have since rejected the image of femininity presented by Nancy or Cherry, Maney's characters validate such resistance to blindly accepting middle-class standards.

Class Lessons

The perils of an unquestioned bourgeoisie become clear in the Nancy Clue adventures. Often, members of the middle and upper classes function as enemies for Cherry Aimless and Nancy Clue. Mrs. Milton Meeks, the "meanest matron" in Nancy's hometown of River Depths, attacks the girls verbally throughout *The Case of the Good-for-Nothing Girlfriend*. She berates Nancy for attempting to free Hannah Gruel, the loyal housekeeper who has taken the rap for Nancy shooting her father:

> "How can you take *her* side after she murdered your poor, dear father? And you didn't even show up for the funeral," Mrs. Meeks sniffed. She glared at Nancy's sunny outfit. "And you're wearing pastels, and it's only been two weeks!" (*Good-for-Nothing* 187)

Nancy's failure to adhere to social codes triggers outrage among Mrs. Meeks and her ladies' club friends, representatives of the class-based gender norms Nancy and her friends refuse. Even Cherry's own mother, Doris Aimless, prize-winning baker of Apple Brown Betty, serves as an example that adhering to traditional standards of womanhood brings no satisfaction. Instead of being rewarded for performing her many household chores, Mrs. Aimless ends up living in the Pleasantville Sanitarium. Women who adhere to middle-class standards of behavior and ideology emerge as either evil or insipid.

Cherry's sexual identity as part of a butch-femme couple further removes her from middle-class markers, since butch-femme has historically been associated with working-class lesbians. Joan Nestle shares her personal confrontation with perceptions of butch-femme, writing: "I quickly got the message in my first Lesbian-feminist CR group that such topics as butch-femme relationships . . . were lower class." But she also states that "sexual style is a rich mixture of class, history, and personal integrity" (108). Pairing Cherry with a butch partner places Cherry and Jackie as part of a culture that refused to embrace mainstream values and lifestyles, and offers readers alternatives to the reproduction and acceptance of middle-class norms typically promoted in girls' fiction. Bobbie Ann Mason argues that much of Nancy Drew's allure stems from "the appeal of her high-class advantages" (49). Maney creates a darker subtext beneath Nancy's apparent privilege, making her seem less desirable and exposing the liabilities of maintaining her bourgeois privileges.

Maney's treatment of class ideology contrasts sharply with the values promoted in typical girls' series fiction of both the past and the present. The persistence of middle-class standing as desirable can be seen in series of the past, like Nancy Drew's world of teas and cotillions, as well as in a contemporary series like *Sweet Valley High*, which features teenage girls who live in an affluent California suburb. Although the Cherry Ames novels place Cherry in a slightly lower class position than Nancy Drew, Cherry's allegiance to middle-class values remains unquestioned. Her goal in *Cherry Ames, Mountaineer Nurse*, is essentially to gentrify the mountain folk she encounters, convincing them that vaccinations, good hygiene, and education are important and valuable. Her task is not easy since many of her patients inform her: "I don't hold with too much bathen. . . . Hit's apt to weaken a body" (Tatham 60). By persuading the patients that regular baths increase good health, Cherry eventually triumphs in cultivating middle-class desires in the mountain residents. Similarly, in *Boarding School Nurse*, Cherry succeeds in talking a girl out of eloping by appealing to her class sensibilities, pointing out "Even if Freddie were the young prince you take him for, don't you think elopement is a rather cheap way to do things? It would be hard on your parents, too. Here they just gave your older sister a beautiful wedding, while you sneak out of

262 Julia D. Gardner

school via a bed sheet" (101). The wayward girl agrees "It *is* cheap," and Cherry succeeds by pointing out that appearances must be maintained.

Maney's writing illustrates the connections between class and sexual identity. In the Nancy Clue series, Cherry's investment in certain standards of beauty and behavior receives different treatment. Her devotion to beauty emerges as not simply a desire to promote bourgeois values, but as constitutive of her identity as femme. Cherry's first encounter with Nancy illustrates this point. Sitting at a bar, Cherry "slyly checked her lipstick in her compact mirror. Suddenly, she desperately wanted to look her best!" (*Not-so-Nice* 108). Cherry's self-consciousness in this situation demonstrates to readers that women's emphasis on appearance is not always motivated by a desire to gain male attention. Cherry seeks to attract a woman, upsetting heterocentric assumptions that the well-groomed, middle-class woman directs her efforts toward snaring a man.

Maney also critiques the original books' desire to inculcate bourgeois values through the treatment of the teen character, Lauren, an aspiring young butch. Although the girl's table manners and personal dress appall Cherry, the nurse nonetheless attempts to "reform" Lauren. Lauren, however, patterns her behavior after Midge's and develops a crush on Velma. Cherry constantly misreads Lauren's behavior and desires, but Velma, amused by Lauren, tells Cherry, "I realized today that Lauren is turning into a miniature version of Midge! . . . with her scruffy clothes, tough attitude and bossy ways" (*Good-for-Nothing* 24). Lauren, ostensibly the teen who should be imbuing the lessons of womanhood as found in 1950s girls' fiction, here refuses such strict gender and sexual practices, and instead models herself after the prominent butch character. Such rejection of cultural norms can also be found in 1990s girls' reading practices. In her study of adolescent girls, Cherland notes that the girls she worked with "used their reading of fiction as a means of exploring new possibilities for female agency. They took the books that the culture produced for them and used them to try on, and analyze, forms of behavior that went *beyond* what was culturally approved for them. In short, they *resisted*" (189). Lauren functions as a fictional example of the resistant reader, not necessarily of books, but of culture in general. She rejects the socially sanctioned behaviors for her gender and patterns herself after a role model who successfully eschews both gender and sexual norms.

As Maney's 1990s characters remind us, girls' culture has long contained the possibility of lesbian desire, but only in more recent decades has such desire been acknowledged in girls' fiction. The Nancy Clue series engages with girls' culture and fiction of past and present, using popular series like Nancy Drew and Cherry Ames to provide a campy send-up of girls' novels from the 1930s through the 1950s. Normative gender and sexual behaviors are questioned and ironized throughout Maney's work, providing a counterpoint to the popular series fiction typically available to girls. While humorous, Maney's novels nonetheless critique mainstream girls' books by calling attention to the ways such works elide same-sex desire, erase racial difference, and reproduce middle-class ideology as desirable and necessary. Resisting heterocentric representations of heroines and providing information about lesbian history addresses the need for such material to be more available to all readers, both adults and youth. Although aimed primarily at adult readers, the Maney series makes explicit the queer reading strategies employed by young women who refuse the heteronormativity found in much of girls' popular fiction. As girls' culture grows more inclusive, providing more representation and acceptance of lesbian youth, the isolation recalled by adult readers of Nancy Clue and currently experienced by many teen lesbians need not be perpetuated. Already, girls increasingly claim a lesbian identity at younger ages, and Maney's world in which two icons of girls' detective fiction, Cherry Aimless and Nancy Clue, can exist as a lesbian couple may not be so imaginary anymore.

NOTES

1. Although underrepresented, lesbian youth do appear in young adult fiction. Earlier representations include Sandra Scoppettone's 1978 novel, *Happy Endings Are All Alike*, which, while sympathetic to the young lesbian protagonists, nonetheless portrays them as suffering tremendously when their relationship becomes known, with one girl violently beaten and raped. A different perspective is provided in Nancy Garden's young adult novel, *Annie on My Mind*, which explores the difficulties of coming out and being outed while in high school. Garden conveys the emotional turmoil of the protagonist and her lover, but without the sense of violence and despair found in Scoppettone's book. *Crush*, by Jane Futcher, follows many conventions of the girls' boarding school storyline, with the exception of its young lesbian protagonist, and has been through three editions since its first printing in 1981. In some instances, teenagers themselves have done the writing, as seen in the collection edited by Ann Heron, *Two Teenagers in Twenty: Writings by Gay and Lesbian Youth*.

2. For a more complete discussion of the changes made between the first and

second editions of the Nancy Drew series, see Diana Beeson and Bonnie Brennen's useful essay, "Translating Nancy Drew from Print to Film," or Deidre Johnson's book, *Edward Stratemeyer and the Stratemeyer Syndicate.*

3. Sally Parry provides a thorough analysis of the Cherry Ames series in relation to women's roles during the war years.

4. The apartment illustrates the intensely female environment inhabited by Cherry and provides a further detail that can be interpreted as supporting the possibility of a gay Cherry in *Boarding School Nurse*: "Cherry was delighted when one morning a fat letter arrived from No. 9, in New York's Greenwich Village, the Spencer Club's now-and-then headquarters. Gwen and Vivian wrote the letter together, reporting on what their fellow nurses were doing" (Wells 50). When read in light of Maney's revisions, Cherry's shared residence in Greenwich Village, historically home of a large gay population, takes on added significance.

5. For a graphic account of such brutality, see Leslie Feinberg's *Stone Butch Blues* or personal accounts in interviews, such as the one between Elly Bulkin and Doris Lunden ("An Old Dyke's Tale") in *The Persistent Desire.*

WORKS CITED

Auchmuty, Rosemary. *A World of Girls.* London: Women's P, 1992.

Beeson, Diana, and Bonnie Brennen. "Translating Nancy Drew from Print to Film." Dyer and Romalov 193–207.

Bulkin, Elly. "An Old Dyke's Tale." *The Persistent Desire.* Ed. Joan Nestle. Boston: Alyson, 1992. 110–23.

Case, Sue-Ellen. "Toward a Butch-Femme Aesthetic." *The Lesbian and Gay Studies Reader.* Ed. Henry Abelove et al. New York: Routledge, 1993. 294–306.

Cherland, Meredith Rogers. *Private Practices: Girls Reading Fiction and Constructing Identity.* Bristol: Taylor and Francis, 1994.

Dyer, Carolyn Stewart, and Nancy Tillman Romalov, eds. *Rediscovering Nancy Drew.* Iowa City: U of Iowa P, 1995.

Feinberg, Leslie. *Stone Butch Blues.* Ithaca: Firebrand, 1993.

Foucault, Michel. *The History of Sexuality.* Vol. 1. New York: Vintage, 1980.

Fuller, Njeri. "Fixing Nancy Drew: African American Strategies for Reading." *Rediscovering Nancy Drew.* Ed. Dyer and Romalov 136–39.

Futcher, Jane. *Crush.* 3rd ed. Boston: Alyson, 1995.

Garden, Nancy. *Annie on My Mind.* New York: Farrar, Straus & Giroux, 1982.

Heron, Ann, ed. *Two Teenagers in Twenty: Writings by Gay and Lesbian Youth.* Boston: Alyson, 1994.

Johnson, Deidre. *Edward Stratemeyer and the Stratemeyer Syndicate.* New York: Twayne, 1993.

Maney, Mabel. *The Case of the Good-for-Nothing Girlfriend.* San Francisco: Cleis, 1994.

———. *The Case of the Not-so-Nice Nurse.* San Francisco: Cleis, 1993.

———. *The Ghost in the Closet.* San Francisco: Cleis, 1995.

Mason, Bobbie Ann. *The Girl Sleuth.* Athens: U of Georgia P, 1995.

Nestle, Joan. *A Restricted Country.* Ithaca: Firebrand, 1987.

O'Conor, Andi. " "Who Gets Called Queer in School?" *The Gay Teen.* Ed. Gerald Unks. New York: Routledge, 1995. 95–101.

Parry, Sally. " 'You Are Needed, Desperately Needed!': Cherry Ames in World War II." Ed. Sherrie A. Inness. *Nancy Drew and Company: Culture, Gender and Girls' Series.* Bowling Green: Bowling Green State U Popular P, 1997. 129–44.

Scoppettone, Sandra. *Happy Endings Are All Alike.* New York: Harper and Row, 1978.

Tatham, Julie. *Cherry Ames, Mountaineer Nurse.* New York: Grosset and Dunlap: 1951.

Van Gelder, Sadie. "It's Who I Am." *Seventeen,* Nov. 1996: 142–49.

Wells, Helen. *Cherry Ames, Boarding School Nurse.* New York: Grosset and Dunlap, 1955.

———. *Cherry Ames, Senior Nurse.* New York: Grosset and Dunlap, 1944.

12

Can Anne Shirley Help
"Revive Ophelia"?

Listening to Girl Readers

Angela E. Hubler

An avalanche of recent scholarship demonstrates the damaging influences that intensify around the time of female adolescence. Carol Gilligan describes adolescence as the time when girls are most pressured to conform to the image of "the perfect girl," "whom everyone will promote and value and want to be with" (24). The development of this other-directed self entails the loss of voice, a reluctance to express one's needs and desires: " 'Cover up,' girls are told as they reach adolescence, daily, in innumerable ways. Cover your body, cover your feelings, cover your relationships, cover your knowing, cover your voice, and perhaps above all, cover desire" (Gilligan 22). As girls mature sexually, they begin to feel pressure to and perhaps want to enter into heterosexual relationships, demanding a new emphasis on beauty and modified behavior. Culturally, they are encouraged to curtail their own desire, psychic and physical, in favor of satisfying male desires.[1] That adolescence is a crisis point in female gender-role socialization is underlined by a 1991 study that found that girls' self-esteem begins to drop precipitously at about age eleven (*Shortchanging*).

Unfortunately, educational institutions often cooperate with this full-scale attack on girls' sense of selves. Myra and David Sadker describe the lack of attention girls receive in classrooms in comparison to boys and how little time is given to the history, lives, and achievements of girls and women. How might we help girls resist these socializing forces, seemingly unchecked in their ability to turn out, with cookie-cutter regularity, girls who are modern-day June Cleavers: dependent and conforming, passive and compliant, sensitive and warm? (Dellas and Gaier 400). (Of course, these last two attributes are positive, but when combined with the previous ones, they encourage self-sacrifice rather than health.)

Those of us who love literature will surely be quick to say "by encouraging girls' reading." However, which texts to offer girls in order to combat stereotypical images of women is debatable. Anne Hollander, for example, calls *Little Women* "a justly famous children's classic for a century . . . a pattern and a model, a mold for goals and aspirations" (qtd. in Murphy 564). Likewise, Sara Paretsky asserts the significance of competent, independent, and self-confident Nancy Drew as a role model who violates gender stereotypes (n.p.). Other readers and critics, though, challenge such assertions. Eugenia Kaledin sees *Little Women* not as encouraging artistic aspiration, but "the acceptance of the creed of womanly self-denial" (qtd. in Murphy 564). Jane, the university student interviewed by Catherine Ross about her series book reading, identifies Nancy Drew as the "perfect girl": "She can do anything. Nancy is perfect. She can act, she can sing, she can anything. She is absolutely sickening. I never did like her . . ." (220).

My own reading of classics for girls fails to clarify the issue. When I went back to books I loved as a girl, those I remembered as encouraging my own desires to rebel against a repressive version of femininity, I was shocked. My fond memories of Carol Ryrie Brink's *Caddie Woodlawn*, dominated by the exploits of the protagonist, did not include the conclusion to the novel in which her father folds her back into the cult of domesticity:

> It's a strange thing, but somehow we expect more of girls than of boys. It is the sisters and wives and mothers, you know, Caddie, who keep the world sweet and beautiful. What a rough world it would be if there were only men and boys in it, doing things in their rough way! A woman's task is to teach them gentleness and courtesy and love and kindness. (244)

Caddie is convinced, and the next morning:

> [S]he knew that she need not be afraid of growing up. It was not just sewing and weaving and wearing stays. It was something more thrilling than that. It was a responsibility, but, as Father spoke of it, it was a beautiful and precious one, and Caddie was ready to go and meet it. (246)

Anne Scott MacLeod argues that this conclusion, replicated in some version in Alcott's *Jack and Jill*, Susan Coolidge's (Sarah C. Woolsey's) *What Katy Did*, Kate Douglas Wiggin's *Rebecca of Sunnybrook Farm*, and L. M. Montgomery's *Anne of Green Gables*, represents the cultural reality of the nineteenth century: a physically and psychically unrestricted childhood followed by a "closing of the doors as the girl neared puberty" (99).

My forgetting of this ending is not unique. Many readers, upon going back to childhood favorites, are confronted by the gap between positive memories and discovery as adults of disturbing, even misogynistic, textual aspects they have forgotten. The authors of *What Katy Read: Feminist Re-Readings of "Classic" Stories for Girls* note this phenomenon:

> [O]ur views on thinking about those works from a more mature perspective had in some cases radically altered their meanings. . . . [W]e had completely failed to register Mary Lennox's exclusion from the inheritance of Misselthwaite Manor in *The Secret Garden*, so caught up were we in the sense of power and enabling fantasy that the central action of the story generated. (Foster and Simons ix)

The controversy over the ideological influence of key texts for girls suggests the need to test hypotheses about particular effects against the actual reports of adolescent female readers. However, very little reader-response criticism and few ethnographies of adolescent female readers exists. The pioneers in this field suggest that reading facilitates accommodation rather than resistance to traditional femininity. Given that much of the work done with girls' reading has been modeled on Janice Radway's *Reading the Romance*, a study of adult female romance readers, this is not surprising.[2] Predictably, romance typically depicts traditional gender dynamics. Linda K. Christian-Smith links romance reading to the maintenance of traditional gender roles: "romance texts offer adolescent female readers subject positions within femininity as future keepers of heart and hearth" ("Romancing" 77). In her book-length study of teen romance, which includes a chapter based on reader interviews, she argues that romance reading "both reinforces traditional gender ideologies and allows girls to reflect on these ideologies" (*Becoming* 98). She notes, for example, that the focus on beauty facilitates the belief that "pretty girls get nice boyfriends," a belief that "motivated [the readers'] wage work and consumption" (*Becoming* 114).

But how might girls' views of femininity be influenced by reading in genres other than romance? To begin to examine these issues, I interviewed forty-two girls. I talked with thirty-six girls in three groups of about twelve each, followed-up with individual interviews with ten of these girls, and interviewed six other girls individually only.[3] This essay is based primarily upon the interviews with individual girls, although their responses were very similar to those from the group discussions. The girls I talked with individually were predominantly white and middle class, although one-third were not part of this majority: one was Ghanaian, one Asian, one Nicaraguan from a low-income family, one Filipina living on an army base where her father was employed, and one was mixed race: her father was black and her mother white. Given the size of my sample, the girls' interpretations of texts cannot be taken as definitive nor comprehensive. However, given the very little research that includes the voices of adolescent girl readers, their comments complement and complicate existing research on children's literature and gender, most of which is based only upon the view of one reader, that is, the critic authoring the scholarship.[4]

The books discussed by the girls I interviewed were startlingly varied: Stephen King competed with L. M. Montgomery for status as favorite author. In addition to the writers and texts I discuss below, Sara Paretsky, Michael Crichton, John Grisham, Judy Blume, Roald Dahl, Laura Ingalls Wilder, Norma Klein, Mary Hahn's *The Doll in the Garden,* Harper Lee's *To Kill a Mockingbird,* and Ellen Raskin's *The Westing Game,* were all listed as favorites by more than one girl. This variety represents a common phenomenon—girls read both young adult and adult fiction simultaneously. For example, Amy had just finished reading *Rebecca of Sunnybrook Farm,* which she said she liked, but also identified Dean Koontz as one of her favorite writers.

Three of the girls listed *Caddie Woodlawn* as among their favorite books. Their comments about the novel confirmed my initial hypothesis, that one source of alternatives to the traditional vision of the "perfect girl" described by Gilligan, Christian-Smith, and others is girls' pleasure reading. Moreover, the strategies with which the girls interpreted *Caddie Woodlawn* were typical of the active reading strategies of girls throughout my sample. Despite the fact that "the Caddie Woodlawn Syndrome," as MacLeod describes the nineteenth-century phenomenon, is clearly a predecessor of the loss of voice and plummeting of self-esteem in adolescent girls in the twentieth century, the girls resisted the ideological effect of the novel's conclusion. Just as I had apparently done as a child, two of the girls simply ignored Caddie's transformation at the conclusion of the novel, even when I pressed them to recall it. Amy, age twelve, described Caddie as follows: "She is very independent. Her father doesn't approve of what she does very much but she still does what she believes in—what she likes." Christa, also twelve, said she liked this book "because of all the predicaments she [Caddie] gets into 'cause she's a tomboy and she doesn't like to be prim and proper like she was supposed to. 'Cause it was taking place in the olden days when women stayed in the house all the time. . . . [L]ike when they have company and all, she'll come in with pants under her dresses and her mom gets mad at her."

Despite this description, Christa astutely assessed what is, at least to me, the novel's contradictory message about proper female behavior. When asked whether the book encourages or discourages girls to be tomboys, she answered, "a little of both, probably mostly encouraging." Significantly, both girls discounted narrative closure in this novel, the point at which, as Rachel Blau DuPlessis argues, ideology exerts itself most forcefully (3). Christa and Amy's memories, or what can even be seen as their active constructions of *Caddie Woodlawn* (especially Christa's memory of Caddie's cross-dressing!), exemplify what I call "liberatory reading." Like Amy and Christa, girls in my sample commonly focused on aspects of texts that confirmed female behavior they found desirable while ignoring or forgetting aspects that undermined those behaviors. Liberatory reading helps account for the gap between childhood memories of a book and the substantially different analysis an adult critic might construct when returning to it.[5]

A third girl, Jody, did recall the conclusion of *Caddie Woodlawn* but resisted its ideological implications, including the binary notion of sex roles it implies. Jody felt that Caddie's behavior devalued women:

> Caddie should at least know that she's a woman. She thought that plowing was for men and cooking for women, and so she wanted to plow. Her father made her realize a woman's job was to do both. To be strong and gentle, to plow and cook. But then she gave up her wild ways. That bothered me.

Jody's critical rather than liberatory reading of this book—her conscious rejection rather than passing over of textual aspects that conflicted with her ideal of femininity—clearly reflected and perhaps contributed to her ongoing construction of identity, which entails a struggle against dichotomous notions of gender. She told me, for example:

I think I'm trying to be too much the opposite of what people are telling me to be because . . . if they tell me to not burp on the school bus then I would, simply because it's not fair. . . . I think I'd act totally the opposite of ladylike and stuff if I ever let my desires control me. But there's only so much I can do.

While Jody's identification with Caddie was frustrated by her conformity, Jody's description of *The True Confessions of Charlotte Doyle,* in which the main character leaves an upper-class English girls' school to become involved in a successful mutiny against a racist, sexist, elitist, and sadistic ship's captain, illustrates that identification is an important part of the reading experience for her, as for many of the girls I interviewed:

I really liked Charlotte Doyle a lot and the way she changed. . . . At first she was kind of prissy and wimpy and she was very jerky. She thought it was very cool to be a lady and she wanted to make her parents proud no matter [whether] what they wanted her to do was wrong or right or whatever. And then she really liked the captain of the ship a lot because he kind of represented all that her parents wanted her to do. . . . She was kind of naive and racist. But, at the end she changed into this very heroic person, like she woke up or something. It was actually almost too drastic of a change but I liked it a lot. . . . I thought she became more like a person I would be a friend to. And I could sympathize with her more when she changed. . . . It was kind of satisfying to me. . . . I kind of, she kind of realized it really wasn't that important to be a lady, just to be yourself.

Jody's active identification with fictional characters suggests that her reading allows her the opportunity to try out and vicariously experience alternatives to traditional gender roles. She, like others I interviewed, both constructed ideals based on the characters she connected to emotionally and modeled her behavior based on these ideals.

The three techniques of reading that my discussion of *Caddie Wood-lawn* has introduced, liberatory reading, critical reading, and identification, make it clear that girls are not passive recipients either of "positive" or "negative" images of women in literature. Rather, their reading strategies suggest they are actively engaged with the literature they read: they participate with the author in the construction of the text, at the same time that the text constructs them as readers. As reader-response theorists argue, the reader's subjectivity is not subsumed by the consciousness of the author, but the reader plays a role along with the author in the determination of meaning (Tompkins xiv). And, while these readers accept some aspects of traditional femininity, as we will find, they also resist sexism, both in their reading and as they translate what they read in terms of their everyday lives.

More than anything else, the girls' descriptions of their favorite female characters manifest their rejection of the stereotype of women as quiet, passive, dependent, compliant, weak, and timid, as well as their desires to be "different" from the social norm. Again, the process of identification is clearly involved. When asked to describe the kind of female characters they liked to read about, almost all answered "strong" and "independent," illustrating these characteristics with a wide variety of examples, ranging from Morgaine in *The Mists of Avalon*, to Rebecca of *Rebecca of Sunnybrook Farm*, to the main character in *Julie of the Wolves*. Ruth, a high school senior, described Polly, the main character in *A Ring of Endless Light*:

> She is independent. She thinks for herself. She's not part of a clique of friends who she blindly follows, and she, I guess she is sort of a loner, except she's very much a part of her family, but I think she's caring and she's very sensitive to people around.

Nancy Drew is another character seen as independent, relying not upon her friends or boyfriend, though she has both, but upon her own abilities and judgment. Sixteen-year-old Correy explained:

> I just liked Nancy because she didn't depend upon her boyfriend. She liked him, but he wasn't the center of her life. And I hate that. I hate books that are about a girl who goes to her boyfriend's basketball games and his football games and she waits for him to call her. I hate that. It drives me insane.

Another common favorite, *The Secret Garden*, illustrates the link for adolescent readers between independence and voice, the ability to express one's views and needs. Patricia, age thirteen, said she liked Mary, the main character "maybe because she was so outspoken, I guess, and she just stuck to what she believed. . . . She wouldn't let people push her around." Maria added: "Because in the beginning the girl is really mean and sour and people don't like her but I don't think she necessarily changes. I think she stays the same person but she opens up more to people, and so, for some reason it shows me that you don't have to be a nice, nice girl all the time to be liked by people. I don't know." For Maria, Mary's refusal to change contrasted with Jo's transformation in *Little Women*: "I like Jo, how they said she walked like a boy. . . . I just liked that because I always used to get in trouble in school because I wouldn't sit with legs like that. But I remember when I read it I kinda thought some of it was cheesy, [like] being good little girls for their father. . . . Even though I tried to be like that it still annoyed me." Maria's preference for *The Secret Garden*, like the other readers' descriptions of it, reveals her resistance to being "nice" and "good" when that requires a loss of self.

More than any other, Anne Shirley of the *Anne of Green Gables* series was identified as the female character the girls "particularly admired." One of the group discussions about this book revealed the way that the girls psychologically entered into Anne's struggles as well as the way in which their articulation of her struggles was focused on gender issues. One girl explained that because Marilla and Matthew expected Anne to be a boy, they made her feel unwanted and "gave her an attitude." Another offered as an example Anne's breaking of a slate over Gilbert's head (a scene that was a favorite of several in this group), and noted that as time goes on Anne "proves that girls can do just as well as boys." Yet another reader in this group asserted that Anne "gets heat because she's not a boy" which "creates competition." This reading is interesting in that while it is not inconsistent with the details of the text, it is decidedly an extrapolation from, rather than a retelling of, what is explicitly told to the reader. Moreover, the girls' own experiences as the disadvantaged gender obviously helped them in generating a theory of the psychological consequences of such a position.

In her interview, Correy said she liked Anne because

> Anne was just so different from everyone else. She was so colorful, and she never stopped. She was always making up little plays, and wanting to dress up. She was always different from everyone else. And she didn't think that was odd. She was always getting yelled at by her aunt, or whoever it was that she lived with, but she didn't care.

Like Jody and other readers, Correy's preference for characters was based on her ability to identify with their experiences. Correy's description of Anne as different, for example, resonated with Correy's own sense of herself as different because of her racial identity, reflected in her reading of books on "being mixed . . . those are really important to me, those books, because I don't know any like mixed students or kids that are willing to talk to me. See, all the black kids in my school kind of hate

me." Seventeen-year-old Heather said "Anne was cool and maybe that
did influence me growing up because she was not afraid of anything. She
spoke her mind, you know, and she was a really neat person."

Many of the characters that the girls described as strong and independent were those they saw as nonconformists—those who, in fact, changed
others. For example, Brigit says about Anne:

> [E]ven though all these bad things happen to her—she's always gettin'
> herself into trouble—she kept being the way she was. . . . They realized at
> the end, you know, how she had talked, how she really annoyed 'em at the
> beginning with all her big words . . . but they saw at the end that she hadn't
> really changed. They were the ones that had changed and had gotten used
> to her and I just thought that was neat that she would, you know, stay the
> same.

Mirroring their preference for the tomboy Caddie over Caddie the
young lady, readers valued Anne's youthful exuberance over her more
restrained maturity (which includes the transformation of her competition with Gilbert into romance). Again, as with *Caddie Woodlawn*, some
readers simply ignored the more traditional aspects of the text, while
others were critical of them. For example, echoing Gillian Thomas' explanation of the inferiority of the sequels to *Anne of Green Gables*, Julie felt
Montgomery "should have just left it [the novel] where it was because.
. . . I think [Anne] changed in the later ones. . . . She wasn't, I don't think,
as verbal. . . . I think she was more imaginative in the first one too. . . . I
think she kind of conforms."

Like Anne, Pollyanna was valued as a character who changes others.
Marlene described her as

> very stubborn. . . . [S]he's like one of those girls who's like Anne Frank. She
> doesn't like to, she likes to be treated like an individual. She likes to be
> outspoken. And her Aunt Polly is very rich and prim and proper, so you
> have to be at lunch, at dinner at this time like *Sound of Music*. She doesn't
> like that. And she kind of teaches her aunt to be a little bit more relaxed,
> almost. Her aunt gets to be liking her. . . . [S]he feels really bad that she
> broke her leg, and she can't walk. So she gets to be a little more understand-
> ing.

Clearly, one factor that appealed to these readers was a character's
ability to change adults, or even to effect some broader change, as in
another common favorite, *A Wrinkle in Time*, interpreted, like *The Hobbit*, as a book about "saving the world." Brigit described it as follows:

Meg . . . and this guy Calvin . . . they have to save the earth somehow. There
is this force that is trying to change everything so that everybody is the
same or something like that. And they don't know how to stop it and
finally she just loves it and that stops it because that conquers all I guess.

Thus, the girls' preference for books that show girls and women, or in
the case of *The Hobbit* a small pudgy creature, enacting change rather
than changing in order to conform confirms Jerry Griswold's analysis of
many of the books my readers liked: *The Secret Garden, Rebecca of Sunnybrook Farm, Pollyanna,* and *Little Women.* He argues that the "audacious kids," the "non-conformists," who are the protagonists of these
novels illustrate that there is an alternative to "a surrender to 'things as
they are,' ironic resignation, and 'level-headed realism.' In the world of
America's children's books, change for the better is still possible. Life
doesn't have to be taken as given. We are still free to make of it what we
will" (235–36, 234). While Griswold discusses only novels published from
1865 to 1914, many of the novels published after this date that the girls
favored also illustrate his point.[6]

While a reader's admiration for a character does not establish its
influence on her, the majority of these girls both identified with characters
they particularly liked and believed that their reading influenced them.
Ruth explained, "If I like the characters that means, sort of implies that I,
sort of, like to be like them." Marlene's discussion of Anne Frank's
influence upon her revealed the way she used her reading as a resource
in her effort to find her own voice and to resist conformity: "I'm kind of
one of those persons that I'm afraid. . . . I don't want my friends mad at
me. So I don't really like to speak out because I'm afraid . . . which is kind
of bad for me, because I need to stand out." In contrast to herself and to
Anne's sister Margot, Marlene described Anne as "strong" saying "I liked
her because she didn't need anybody, you know, she was very loud and
very rude and rowdy. . . . I'm kind of quiet, but you know, but this will
teach me to stand up, you know, for myself." Christa said that she felt
that she had been influenced by *Little Women* "because it talks about how
Amy was kind of selfish and how she was always kind of caring about
elegance and her looks. And I am kind of like that but not quite as bad.
And it helped me to realize that it's not always good."

The same function accomplished by the books discussed above—
offering hope that oppressive gender relations are not fixed, providing
examples of girls who rebel against gender stereotypes—are also, it seems,
accomplished for minority girls in terms of race. In addition to titles also

listed by white girls, several girls of color included among their favorites
books which focus on race: Efua listed *Black Boy*, *Black Like Me*, Barbara
Chase-Riboud's *The President's Daughter*, and Susan O'Donnell's historical novel *Pocahontas*. In addition to the "books about being mixed,"
Correy listed poetry by Langston Hughes, while Jane listed poetry by
Maya Angelou and Alice Walker. Disturbingly, however, only two white
girls listed minority writers other than Anne Frank as favorites: Patricia
listed Amy Tan's *The Kitchen God's Wife*, and Maria listed Maya Angelou
and Betty Greene. Only these two readers expressed an interest in understanding those different from themselves. Maria explained:

> I just always thought that Kansas wasn't where it was at or [where] any-
> thing [was] happening. So when I read books it kind of keeps me in touch
> with other people, 'cause I have always been around the exact same people
> all my life, like middle-class whites, suburban people, and only Christian
> people and I don't know, when I read these books, it sounds cheesy, but I
> met different people and it just brings me to an understanding of, I don't
> know, different customs. That is why I like Maya Angelou. Because I never,
> I don't know, I mean, because, I went to Catholic schools. There were
> never many black people there and at the high school it is not racist, but
> people will stay away from each other—segregated.

While the other white girls were aware of themselves as discriminated
against as a result of their gender, unlike Maria they did not show any
awareness of their racial identity and its accompanying privilege. Nor
were they able to develop their understanding of the relationship between
gender and race.

   While girls liked many books that they felt encouraged them to resist
conformity to stereotypes, they ruthlessly criticized others that failed them
in this respect. *The Scarlet Letter* was the target of two girls' invective,
both of whom had read it in high school English. Jane said,

> I hate Nathaniel Hawthorne's writing and I just thought it was the dumbest
> novel that was ever written. And I hated Hester. I hated Hester and she
> was like the weakest character that I ever read. She never asserted herself.
> She takes all the abuse from society.

Correy was concerned about the effect the novel would have on the boys
in her class:

> There were parts where the women seemed to be like seriously looked
> down upon, and that was like the emphasis of some themes that they were
> like that. And once she had committed her sin, she's wearing the letter on

her bosom, and she had to keep her head down when she was walking through the market place. The boys in that class are impressionable enough, and they are already pretty sexist. We really don't need more, and our teacher is so lax, he probably wouldn't even catch stuff like that. He's completely bored.

Amy also focused on depictions of traditional femininity in describing the kinds of books she disliked, including the Sweet Valley High series:

Authors seem to think that teenagers are kind of ditsy. I don't know why. ...It just seems to me that a lot of young adult books that I read from the library, a lot of them are just, they seem to think that, I mean, I've read a lot of books from the young adult section and I guess most of them when they talk about girls they're like in makeup clubs and stuff and I really don't think that a lot of people like me are interested in that kind of stuff. Christa once recommended *The Makeover Summer* and she's very different from me. And I did not like that very much and she did. It was just about the way they did their hair. Just the way, one of these girls goes jogging every morning and comes home and always takes a shower and does all this stuff.

Series books, although they were popular with many of the readers I talked to, were also recognized as depicting traditional femininity.[7] Delia, who named Fear Street series books as among her favorites, was unable to identify a female character she admired. Because she plans to become a doctor and enjoys sports, she could not identify with the female characters in the books she reads:

[W]hen I read books, it's just like typical kind of girls, you know, not really no character that stands out. They are all the same.... [I]t's the same old thing. I'm just thinking, they're not like me. I'm not like that. I don't really think they are role models.

The Sweet Valley High series also failed, for most, to provide characters that they could identify with, a failure that generated a critical reading even from most of those who had once liked them. Most of my interviewees had read at least one of these books, commonly when they were in late elementary school. When asked if she had read them, Correy responded:

Oh! I'm ashamed! No! It's a big lie!... Yeah. I read every single one of them. And they are all the same.... Jessica was the sunny little bitch and Elizabeth was the neat one. She was the smart one and she liked to read, and she was a lot more interesting than Jessica. I don't know why I read them. . . . I think that when you are in fifth grade I think you want to read about girls wearing makeup and . . . having boyfriends. Because that is all very interesting, and that's what you think you want at that point. I mean, they are not like well-written or anything.

Correy, now a *Ms.* reader who calls herself a feminist, was evidently not deeply influenced by the books, despite having read "like forty of them." For Ruth and Brigit the appeal of these books also lay in their description of unfamiliar experience, and like Correy, they had become critical of them. Marlene, a cheerleader, lacked their critical view:

I was young when I read that and I was like, that's so cool. They get to go out on dates and they get to drive. So, I was kind of like one of those girls who loved hearing about going out on dates and hearing about the guys, and they always seemed to have these big problems.

Fourteen-year-old Betsy, who described herself as "feminine," reported that she had read "a couple of" books from the series but did not like them. Like Heather and Jody, she criticized the depictions of the main characters:

They just seemed too fake. Everything was, I mean, beautiful blonde twins that go to this perfect place, and it was fake and unrealistic and all their problems seemed so stupid. I mean like, oh my gosh, mom and dad won't let me go to this rock concert so I've got to sneak out or whatever. And it's just like, not real life.

Despite Carlotta's report that she admired Jessica because "she was . . . serious and . . . she got good grades," Sweet Valley High and Fear Street series books fail to provide characters who might help girls struggle to be faithful to their own needs while not neglecting others. Unlike many of the books that girls described as containing characters they admired, many of which were given or recommended to them by mothers and grandmothers, series books are widely available. Thus, several girls said they read them when they didn't have anything better to read or like Ruth, "when they were really bored." Maria explained the popularity of series books in terms of her difficulty in choosing books at the library: "Well, it's just overwhelming to see all those books." It is easy, then, she explained, to simply grab a paperback, dominated by series books. Heather also described herself as "confused and overwhelmed" by the library. Clearly, some girls are eager to be guided to alternatives to series books, which they sometimes resort to out of desperation.

To provide such guidance, then, is not to impose a politically correct reading agenda on unsuspecting girls, but to address a need many girls articulate for themselves: all of the girls I interviewed were aware of sexism at some level, and many were consciously struggling with the issues of self and voice that Gilligan and others describe as common. In Ruth's words:

> I feel a duty to my friends. I try to be nice to people and I feel bad when I'm not. But, at the same time I don't want to be too nice, in a sort of "I have no opinion" sort of way. And that's always been a sort of conflict with me. To what extent can I be myself and yet still, and not intimidate others.

Like Ruth, who had read Gilligan's *In a Different Voice* and who saw women as having "more of a sense of responsibility" than men, and Margaret, who described women as more capable of expressing their emotions, it was clear that the girls favored change guided by female values. Efua contrasted women's position in the United States with women in Ghana:

> I think that women are respected much more in Ghana, and it's like . . . [a] matrilineal society, where everything is based off the woman, and you always will trace your relations back to a female ancestor. Everything is if you respect the queen mother, and if you respect your grandparents, and it's based off respect toward women.

As Betsy explained:

> [W]e don't see women up in the White House and it's still mainly male-dominated and I do think if we were ever up there we could make some changes . . . the kind of women who would be politically good. I'm not saying all women. I don't think it would be so money-dominated, that the president wouldn't have to be paid so much and that money is the focus of everything. Just because, I guess it's stereotyping, but females are usually more emotional and think about people's needs, I guess. And, um, the males, and I don't like to say this because it is stereotyping, it's putting them in a group, and not everyone is like that. But the males tend to be more logical and straight-forward.

Although Jane, who described herself as feminist, said that most of the characters she admired were male, she also said that if she were male "I would be more self-centered. . . . [T]here are less males that care about what goes on in the world as compared to . . . females." Maria, who also described herself as feminist, concurred:

I realize that all these men are fighting for what they say are rights for everyone, they just forget about women all the time, and it just makes me think, "Go away, boys. Go somewhere else," because I just have a feeling it would be better if it was just women sometimes, like we could sort things out a lot more, and stuff. When I say that to my mom she gets mad.

As evidenced by these reader responses, it is clear that at least some girls use their reading as one strategy in resisting the image of the "perfect girl," the girl who is "too nice" and has "no opinion." In order to understand the way that girls both resist and accommodate themselves to traditional gender-role socialization, listening to girls' own interpretations of texts is crucial. While no reader is fully capable of articulating the effect of her reading upon her, complementing critical readings with readers' responses like those above would give us a much more complex and accurate view of the way that reading functions as an agent of gender-role socialization.

Potentially, such a study of children's literature has a great deal to add to the study of female gender-role socialization, especially since the discipline of psychology has tended to focus on the way that women internalize rather than defy patriarchy.[8] This tendency, for example, emerges in women's studies textbooks describing the process of gender-role socialization.[9] Frequently absent is the recognition that more than one female gender role exists, and an examination of female agency in resisting traditional gender roles. Although most texts summarize the theoretical explanations of gender offered by psychoanalysis, behaviorism, social learning, and gender-schema theory, when they turn to a discussion of socializing agents, the approach reverts to a narrowly behavioristic or modeling approach. Textbooks typically present a series of research findings on gender-role socialization. Most, for example, summarize a study which found that by "white middle-class North American parents, female infants are viewed, as early as twenty-four hours after birth, as softer and more delicate than are their male counterparts" (Lips 128). Texts go on to show that girls are given different toys, get less attention in school, and are even communicated with differently by their parents than are boys. While the inequalities that this research points to are important, such material cumulatively suggests that no matter what we do, the majority of girls are doomed to become Stepford wives.

Most research that does examine agency focuses on accommodation rather than on resistance to traditional gender roles. For example, Virginia Sapiro, the author of *Women in American Society* says: "Children learn about themselves but they also learn to value themselves and, through generalization, people like themselves. As children learn about their gender, they begin to value it. Boys want to do 'boy' things, and girls want to do 'girl' things" (73). So, while girls are recognized as having agency, it is manifested only in their choice of traditional gender roles. Although the literature on socialization does correlate androgyny in children with parents who are "androgynous, loving, and egalitarian" (Basow 134), the role of reading, to my knowledge, has not been studied as facilitating an alternative to traditional femininity.

Despite the limited size of my sample, it is clear that girls are not blank slates that unthinkingly reproduce the ideological messages written upon them, as illustrated by their sophisticated readings of books like *Caddie Woodlawn* and those in the Sweet Valley High series. In fact, the books that the girls described as their favorites seemed to allow them the ability to consciously reflect upon the process of gender-role socialization as it impacts upon them. This awareness was clear, for example, in the girls' comments on the Sweet Valley High books, and in Christa's assertion that *Little Women* functioned as a corrective to her vanity, though that quality was fostered in a series book she had read, *The Makeover Summer*. Thus, at the same time that Christa and others maintained both positive and negative aspects of traditional femininity, the girls also actively resisted rigid gender roles in the books they chose to read, their interpretations of these texts, and in their identification with characters they described as outspoken, independent, caring, and different. The model of gender-role socialization that this suggests resembles one characterized by Kay Deaux and Brenda Major, in which "women and men make choices in their actions. In contrast to the deterministic models offered by both psychoanalysis and behaviorism, [this] framework presumes a repertoire of possibilities from which individual men and women choose different responses on varying occasions with varying degrees of self-consciousness" (91). In their work, and in recent "ethnographies of schooling," "instead of 'simply' being socialized (the image presented in much feminist literature), girls and boys are granted agency in constructing culture and resisting it as well as in adapting to dominant ideologies" (Thorne 112).

Many of the books that my interviewees described as their favorites, including those I too remembered as my favorites as a girl—*Little Women, Island of the Blue Dolphins, Julie of the Wolves, The Secret Garden, Anne of Green Gables*—facilitate this process by allowing girls to see and therefore participate in their socialization as gendered beings. The status of many classics for girls may, in fact, be based on their ability to foster this awareness of, and thus resistance to, repressive female gender roles.

NOTES

I am very grateful to the girls I interviewed for this essay.

1. Mary Ophir's *Reviving Ophelia: Saving the Selves of Adolescent Girls* provides numerous and disturbing examples of this.

2. In addition to Linda K. Christian-Smith's work on teen romance, Gemma Moss has written a very interesting article, "Girls Tell the Teen Romance: Four Reading Histories."

3. Initially, I interviewed five girls individually, all of whom I knew, in order to formulate questions. The group interviews took place during a day-long event for middle- and high-school girls held at my university. The girls were given a choice of nine or ten different sessions, so those that came to my session, titled "*The Makeover Summer* versus *The True Confessions of Charlotte Doyle*," presumably had an interest in reading. (A few girls, however, said they came to my session because they thought I was doing makeovers!) In these sessions, I took notes and conducted a paper survey. In addition to follow-up interviews with ten girls from the group discussions, I used the snowball technique, asking interviewees for names of friends who were heavy readers, especially in order to interview minority girls. My sample, then, is deliberately not random but self-selected, since I was only interested in interviewing avid readers.

4. A great deal of research on gender-role socialization and children's literature exists. Early research focused on demonstrating the existence of sex-role stereotyping, typically by counting male versus female characters or comparing the behaviors and traits typical of these characters. Other scholars have focused on providing alternatives to these stereotypes by compiling bibliographies. In addition, many studies of the effect of particular texts upon gender-role socialization, rather than a broad range of books, have been done. A good overview of this criticism is Ernst's "Gender Issues in Books for Children and Young Adults." She argues that an imbalance of male versus females characters, and stereotyping of female characters continues in children's literature. Her conclusion is both disturbing and unarguable. As I have suggested, however, I am interested in what girls say about the influence of literature upon them.

5. Elizabeth Ford discusses just such a gap in her memories in "How to Cocoon a Butterfly: Mother and Daughter in *A Girl of the Limberlost*."

6. I disagree, however, with Griswold's suggestion that the reason that the

female characters he discusses do not want to grow up is explained by their inability to violate the "oedipal taboo," an inability he also refers to in explanation of Jo's "identification with males" (89). Thus, rather than understanding Jo's behavior in terms of societal restrictions upon women, he understands it as linked to the Oedipal conflict. I am more convinced by his social than by his psychological arguments.

7. I was not satisfied with my ability to solicit an explanation for the popularity of the Fear Street series. One reader, for example, said she liked the books "because you get to read it [the book] real fast."

8. The authors of *Feminist Scholarship: Kindling in the Groves of Academe* note that "[w]orks by Juliet Mitchell, Dorothy Dinnerstein, and Nancy Chodorow all attempt in different ways to comprehend the process by which individuals incorporate the ideology of sexual hierarchy and learn to live by its dictates" (DuBois et al. 109).

9. It was in the process of teaching the topic of gender-role socialization in an introductory women's studies class that I became dissatisfied with the approach taken in most textbooks and embarked upon this research.

WORKS CITED

Basow, Susan. *Gender: Stereotypes and Roles.* Belmont: Brooks/Cole Publishing, 1992.

Brink, Carol Ryrie. *Caddie Woodlawn.* 1935. New York: Scholastic, n.d.

Christian-Smith, Linda K. "Romancing the Girl: Adolescent Romance Novels and the Construction of Femininity." *Becoming Feminine: The Politics of Popular Culture.* Ed. Leslie G. Roman, Linda K. Christian-Smith, and Elizabeth Ellsworth. London: Falmer, 1988. 76–101.

———. *Becoming a Woman through Romance.* New York: Routledge, 1990.

Deaux, Kay, and Brenda Major. "A Social-Psychological Model of Gender." Rhode 89–99.

Dellas, Marie, and Eugene Gaier. "The Self and Adolescent Identity in Women: Options and Implications." *Adolescence* 10 (1975): 399–407.

DuBois, Ellen, Gail Kelley, Elizabeth Kennedy, Carolyn Korsmeyer, and Lillian Robinson. *Feminist Scholarship: Kindling in the Groves of Academe.* Urbana: U of Illinois P, 1987.

DuPlessis, Rachel Blau. *Writing beyond the Ending: Narrative Strategies of Twentieth-Century Women Writers.* Bloomington: Indiana UP, 1985.

Ernst, Shirley B. "Gender Issues in Books for Children and Young Adults." *Battling Dragons: Issues and Controversy in Children's Literature.* Ed. Susan Lehr. Portsmouth: Heinemann, 1995.

Ford, Elizabeth. "How to Cocoon a Butterfly: Mother and Daughter in *A Girl of* the *Limberlost.*" *Children's Literature Association Quarterly* 18.4 (1993–94): 148–53.

Foster, Shirley, and Judy Simons. *What Katy Read: Feminist Re-Readings of "Classic" Stories for Girls.* Iowa City: U of Iowa P, 1995.

Gilligan, Carol. "Women's Psychological Development: Implications for Psychotherapy." *Women and Therapy* 11 (1991): 5–29.

Griswold, Jerry. *Audacious Kids: Coming of Age in America's Classic Children's Books.* New York: Oxford UP, 1992.

Lips, Hilary. "Gender-Role Socialization: Lessons in Femininity." *Women: A Feminist Perspective.* Ed. Jo Freeman. Mountain View: Mayfield Publishing, 1995. 128–48.

MacLeod, Anne Scott. "The *Caddie Woodlawn* Syndrome: American Girlhood in the Nineteenth Century." *A Century of Childhood 1820–1920.* Rochester: Margaret Woodbury Strong Museum, 1984. 97–117.

Moss, Gemma. "Girls Tell the Teen Romance: Four Reading Histories." *Reading Audiences: Young People and the Media.* Manchester: Manchester UP, 1993. 116–34.

Murphy, Ann. "The Borders of Ethical, Erotic, and Artistic Possibilities in *Little Women.*" *Signs* 15 (1990): 562–85.

Ophir, Mary. *Reviving Ophelia: Saving the Selves of Adolescent Girls.* New York: Ballantine Books, 1994.

Paretsky, Sara. Introduction. *The Secret of the Old Clock.* Carolyn Keene. 1930. Bedford: Applewood Books, 1991. No pagination.

Radway, Janice. *Reading the Romance.* Chapel Hill: U of North Carolina P, 1984.

Rhode, Deborah L., ed. *Theoretical Perspectives on Sexual Difference.* New Haven: Yale UP, 1990.

Ross, Catherine Sheldrick. " 'If They Read Nancy Drew, So What?': Series Book Readers Talk Back." *Library and Information Science Research* 17 (1993): 201–36.

Sadker, Myra, and David Sadker. *Failing at Fairness: How America's Schools Cheat Girls.* New York: Scribner's, 1994.

Sapiro, Virginia. *Women in American Society: An Introduction to Women's Studies.* Mountain View: Mayfield Publishing, 1994.

Shortchanging Girls, Shortchanging America: A Call to Action. Washington, DC: American Association of University Women, 1991.

Thomas, Gillian. "The Decline of Anne: Matron vs. Child." *Such a Simple Little Tale: Critical Responses to L. M. Montgomery's Anne of Green Gables.* Metuchen: Children's Literature Association and Scarecrow Press, 1992. 23–28.

Thorne, Barrie. "Children and Gender: Constructions of Gender." Rhode 100–13.

Tompkins, Jane. "An Introduction to Reader-Response Criticism." *Reader-Response Criticism: From Formalism to Post-Structuralism.* Ed. Jane Tompkins. Baltimore: Johns Hopkins UP, 1980. ix–xxvi.

13

Producing Girls

Rethinking the Study of Female Youth Culture

Mary Celeste Kearney

As one of the first contemporary studies of teenage girls' cultural practices, Simon Frith's *Sound Effects* helped solidify the popular and intellectual understanding of female youth leisure activities as operating in a privatized, domestic "bedroom culture" centered around heterosexual romance and the consumption of mainstream cultural commodities.[1] As he argued, "Girl culture . . . starts and finishes in the bedroom" (228). Frith's analysis of female youth culture importantly delineated aspects of girls' unique leisure activities, especially the amount of labor involved in girls' pursuits of Mr. Right. However, it did not involve an investigation into other productive practices undertaken by female adolescents, and therefore ultimately reproduced the dominant notion that girls are capable only of cultural consumption.

Though Frith's conceptualization of girls' "bedroom culture" was formulated over fifteen years ago, it is one that remains prevalent in our intellectual analysis and theorization of girls' culture. Unfortunately, youth scholars have yet to adequately document and analyze one of the most interesting transformations to have occurred in youth culture in the last two decades—the emergence of girls as cultural producers. In light of this increasing cultural productivity among female youth today, I am concerned with the effects the continued representation of girls as consumers may have on our understanding of contemporary female adolescent subjectivity. If scholars involved in the field of girls' studies desire to keep current with the state of female youth and their cultural practices, we must expand the focus of our analyses to include not only texts produced *for girls* by the adult-run mainstream culture industries, but also those cultural artifacts created *by girls*. This essay, therefore, attempts to move the study of contemporary female adolescents beyond the realm of their consumerist practices and toward an understanding of girls as active producers of culture. Thus, the title of this essay has a double meaning. "Producing Girls" is used first to draw attention to the processes by which female adolescent subjectivity is (re)produced ideologically (for example, through girls' interactions with cultural texts like teen magazines). Second, "Producing Girls" is used to describe one of the subject positions finally afforded to female youth in our society, that of *cultural producer*.

In my examination of the relationship between the construction of contemporary female adolescent subjectivity and girls' modes of cultural production, I take as my primary objects of study those cultural texts most often consumed and, increasingly, produced by female adolescents— teen magazines. In light of recent debates within cultural studies about the "politics of representation,"[2] I am particularly interested in analyzing the relationship between the depictions of female adolescence mass-produced by adults in teen magazines such as *Seventeen* and *Sassy* and those texts created by girls in the attempt to produce their own unadulterated culture.

In order to explore the recent emergence of acts of cultural production among female adolescents and how that transformation is being understood and represented by mainstream culture, I first analyze the contemporary depiction of girls in mass-produced teen magazines, as those representations provide one way of understanding the construction of contemporary modes of female adolescence and girls' culture. However, it is my belief that by studying the texts girls themselves produce, we can better understand female adolescents' practices of consumption, levels of critical engagement with cultural texts, and, finally, willingness to accept, resist, or subvert the dominant discourses and representational strategies of female adolescence. In my analysis of girl-produced zines, I specifically examine the ways in which female adolescents appropriate and reconfigure the discursive strategies of mass-produced teen magazines such as *Seventeen* and *Sassy* in order to resist or subvert the images and narratives of girlhood offered by mainstream culture.

Girls Just Want: Previous Studies of Female Youth Culture

In response to new theoretical perspectives formed in the late 1960s and 1970s which challenged the notion that all anyone needed to know about books, films, and music could be found in texts themselves, cultural scholars (especially in the fields of literature and the visual media) shifted their focus to consumers and the practices of consumption. There is no doubt this change in emphasis was a reaction to previous conceptualizations of consumers as passive victims of false consciousness caught up in the allegedly deceptive, alienating, and exploitative relations of commodity consumption and mass culture.[3] The British cultural studies movement of the 1970s was instrumental in connecting the practices of consumption with forms of political empowerment and resistance. By embracing and extending Antonio Gramsci's theories of ideology and hegemony, for example, British cultural scholars rethought practices of consumption in ways which validated the consumer as an active participant in cultural relations and politics.[4]

In their attempt to restore consumers to a state of active subjectivity and participation in social relations, however, cultural scholars have often over-privileged consumerism as a form of political resistance. As Angela McRobbie argues, commenting on this transformation in cultural studies, consumption is often "inflated" to the point that "each and every transaction or acquisition becomes a grand gesture of will, an act of opposition or an expression of identity" ("New Times" 32–33). Interestingly, the theorization of consumption during the 1980s began to mimic the promise made by late consumer capitalism: the practices of consumerism are indeed political actions, the purchase of commodities the best way to take a stand.

Characteristic of this period in cultural studies, many early analyses of female youth culture focused on girl consumers as active cultural participants. This emphasis was tied to feminist scholars' larger attempts to acknowledge and validate everyday activities, many of which were associated with the practices of consumption. Much feminist cultural criticism in the 1970s and 1980s sought to counter the popular understanding of female consumers as uncritical victims upon whom cultural texts worked their deceptive, alienating charms by formulating theories about the pleasures involved in consuming texts produced for, yet often considered oppressive to, women. This shift in feminist scholarship from theories of women's oppression by the cultural industries to examinations of the various negotiative processes involved in commodity consumption was instrumental in breaking down the opposition of feminism/femininity constructed by many earlier feminists.[5] In turn, by acknowledging an identification with, rather than an opposition to, women consumers, feminist scholars troubled the "us/them" dichotomy found in earlier studies of female consumerism.

In "Alice in the Consumer Wonderland," Erica Carter traces the academic connection between girls and consumption to earlier studies of youth and adolescence such as Paul Willis's *Learning to Labour*, which argues that girls function in youth cultures only as objects of consumption for males. As Carter notes, this understanding of female youth resulted in the perception of girls as "an absence, a silence, a lack which could perhaps only be filled in some separate world of autonomous female culture" (186).

In response to what was seen as a myopic, masculinist vision of youth culture, feminist scholars Angela McRobbie and Jenny Garber argued for a new approach that would open the field to issues of gender and examine female adolescents' active participation in culture. In their groundbreaking 1976 study, "Girls and Subcultures," McRobbie and Garber asserted that "[t]he important question may not be the absence or presence of girls in male subcultures, but the complementary ways in which young girls interact among themselves and with each other to form a distinctive culture of their own . . ." (219). Focusing specifically on girls' teenybopper culture, they demonstrated that female youth culture, unlike its male counterpart, is connected more to family, domesticity, and romance and, therefore, offers girls different possibilities for resisting social expectations.

Though McRobbie and Garber's analysis of girls' culture broke new ground and initiated the study of gender in relation to youth culture, as Carter argues, "the search for autonomous female cultural forms in the bedroom hideaways of teenage girls has been consistently dogged by nagging doubts as to the creative, productive and potentially subversive power of this mode of femininity" (187). Since traditionally girls have been presented with different options of cultural and social activity from boys, scholars wanting to analyze the specific nature of female youth culture "have had to plunge, head-on at times, in to the seething morass of capital flows, emerging with a proliferation of critiques of the commodities which pattern the fabric of girls' lives: advertising images, fashionable clothes, mass magazines, popular fiction" (188). Thus, in contrast to many male scholars of youth who demonstrated their distaste for mass culture by focusing predominantly on the subcultural practices of working-class male youth, feminist scholars have repeatedly placed their attention on girls' interactions with the commodities mass-produced by the mainstream culture industries.

Unfortunately, this focus on the consumerist practices of female adolescents has not only reproduced the dominant gender ideology that ties femininity and females to the practices of consumption, but, in doing so, has precluded analyses which explore girls' involvement in cultural production.[6] In turn, by not fully problematizing the *adult* production of the mainstream cultural texts girls consume, many scholars reproduce the popular understanding that adults are the only producers of culture and girls are capable only of consumption.

Recent transformations in female adolescent subjectivity and girls' culture (specifically the feminist youth movement, riot grrrl) are seriously challenging previous conceptualizations of girls and female youth cultures as only consumption-oriented. Because of the success of the feminist movement in decreasing discriminatory practices based on sex, as well as in empowering females of all ages, the number of girls completing high school and college education is greater than ever before, and there are more opportunities for girls who want to move outside the traditional female roles of wife and mother and the conventionally feminine spaces of the domicile and shopping center. In numbers now too big to ignore, female adolescents are increasingly involved in the production of films and videos, the recording of music, the publication of literature, and the manufacturing of clothing and fashion accessories.

My point here is not to privilege girls' productive activities as a somehow inherently more progressive, revolutionary, or unalienated practice than their practices of consumption. Indeed, more thought needs to be given to how these practices are highly interdependent. Rather, I want to move the focus of girls' studies toward the sphere of production so that we might better understand the multiple activities involved in contemporary female youth cultures and the various subjectivities and social relations afforded girls today. By analyzing the ways in which girls are understood as, as well as occupy the subject position of, cultural producers, I believe we can more fully understand their negotiative, resistant, and perhaps even oppositional cultural practices, practices that may be indicative of a feminist consciousness and praxis occurring at younger ages than previously imagined.

Sassy Girls: Transformations in the Mainstream Depiction of Female Adolescence

Arguing that teen magazines must be analyzed in relation to their unique participation in the construction of female adolescence, Angela Mc-Robbie's in-depth studies of British female youth and teen magazines— "*Jackie*: An Ideology of Adolescent Femininity," "*Jackie* Magazine: Romantic Individualism and the Teenage Girl," "Just Like a *Jackie* Story," "*Jackie* and *Just Seventeen*: Girls' Comics and Magazines in the 1980s"— set the stage for what has become known as "girls' studies." Following in McRobbie's footsteps, several British scholars have extended the study of teen magazines and girls' culture. For example, Valerie Walkerdine has analyzed girls' comics to study the effects of a romantic ideology on female youth; Elizabeth Frazer has interviewed groups of female adolescents to explore *Jackie* magazine's ideological effect on the acquisition of gender and sexual identity; and Janice Winship, known for her work on women's magazines, has examined teen magazines introduced in the 1980s like *Etcetera* and *Mizz* in relation to transformations in contemporary feminist politics. In turn, U.S. scholars like Kate Peirce have examined teen magazines like *Seventeen* and *'Teen* from sociological and historical perspectives to explore such magazines' effects on the formation of female adolescent subjectivity.

Though teen magazines are certainly not the only objects of exploration in the study of girls' culture, McRobbie and other youth scholars have argued that such magazines remain privileged objects of analysis in girls' studies because they are the only media specifically produced for female youth (McRobbie, "*Jackie* Magazine" 83; Peirce, "Socialization of Teenage Girls" 66). Although I do not deny the significance of magazines in the lives of teenage girls at large, I think it is important for us to reconsider the extent to which the study of such texts reproduces certain notions of female adolescence while, at the same time, precluding others. Because teen magazines rarely represent female youth as cultural producers, girls are consistently portrayed in these texts as capable only of consumption. McRobbie notes this in her essay "Just Like a *Jackie* Story," a harsh critique of what mainstream teen magazines "don't say, don't include, don't consider" about female adolescence (127). For example, she notes that, in spite of the overwhelming emphasis on popular music in such magazines, "girls are provided with no information about how to set up a band, nor are they encouraged to learn to play an instrument. Genius of the type represented by the pin-ups, is, it seems, something that one is born with and something that girls seem to be born without" (127–28). As she argues elsewhere, "The girls, by implication, are merely listeners" ("*Jackie* Magazine" 127).

With regard to representations of female adolescence in contemporary U.S. teen magazines such as *Seventeen* and *Sassy*, we can recognize that, in spite of the growing number of opportunities encouraging girls today to become active producers of culture, as well as magazines' increasing attention to female youth who seize such opportunities (especially media celebrities like Alicia Silverstone, Claire Danes, and Brandy Norwood), most girls' magazines continue to over-privilege the spheres of consumption and leisure in comparison to production and work. This is especially true of mass-produced girls' magazines such as *Seventeen*, *YM*, and '*Teen* where the focus of each issue is predominantly on the spheres of fashion and beauty and secondarily on entertainment and (mostly male) celebrities.

Certainly, there are a number of reasons why female youth are rarely depicted (or analyzed) as active producers of culture. First, the traditional characterization of adolescence as a time of "acting out"—a time of playful experimentation with different forms of subjectivity—significantly informs the representation of girls as non-producers in these texts. Moreover, since adolescence is a mode of subjectivity typically defined by its opposition to adulthood and the responsibilities adult identity usually entails, the mass production of youth culture has relied on this opposition (as well as its many connotations: work/play, responsibility/freedom, and other similar oppositions) in order to capitalize on a market of young people whose feelings of self-worth are often unstable and less related to parental or adult approval.

Second, the lengthy historical association of femininity and females with the practices of consumption and consumerism, an association which has served to further reinforce the notion of production as a masculine and male activity also informs the lack of girls' representations as cultural producers. Mainstream teen magazines such as *Seventeen* significantly participate in reproducing the traditional gendered ideologies of production and consumption, reinforcing the popular notion that fashion consumption and beauty routines are "natural" activities for females. Moreover, such texts' use of rhetoric about experimentation, freedom, play, and personal choice (conveniently appropriated from feminist discourse) displaces the reality that making oneself beautiful requires considerable labor, expense, and time.

Since their emergence in the 1940s, teen magazines such as *Seventeen* were specifically produced to garner for advertisers the attention (and buying power) of a specific group of female adolescent consumers. Though such magazines often attempted to tap into girls' individual needs and concerns by offering a variety of information on relationships, education, and world politics, the primary emphasis in such texts was on girls' consumption of goods in the quest for perfect beauty. In spite of over fifty years of considerable social and cultural transformation since their introduction, mainstream teen magazines' emphasis on consumption and beauty appears just as strong as ever; girls continue to be presented as consumers, rather than producers, of culture.

Analyzing issues of *Seventeen* magazine published between 1990 and 1996, I found very few representations of girls as cultural producers other than the occasional young female celebrity. (There are rarely more than two such celebrities highlighted in an issue.) Despite some effort to reveal the private lives of these media stars through biographical information and/or interviews, they are never portrayed working, and the reader is left with the implication that celebrities are born with talent and that there is no work involved in being a star. Carefully coifed and dressed in trendy fashions, featured celebrities more closely resemble the (passive) fashion/beauty models that typically populate such publications than working girls.

In spite of significant transformations in girls' physical assertiveness and confidence in the last two decades (especially in relation to their increasing participation in sports activities), mainstream magazines like *Seventeen* continue to depict "ordinary" (non-celebrity) girls—whether in advertisements or fashion/beauty layouts—as passive objects. Those represented are stationary, immobile human sculptures, their only movement (typically jumping up and down or swirling) forever frozen by the click of a camera shutter. Even when depicted out-of-doors in sports or adventure-like settings, girls are rarely shown as actively engaged. When female youth are depicted as physically exerting themselves, the context is almost always one of exercising, the emphasis invariably on improving one's bodily appearance (despite the recent increase in discourse about improving girls' self-esteem). Such a de-emphasis on girls' physical activity reproduces the traditional understanding of female bodily comportment as one of limited movement and passive engagement.[7]

Further analysis also confirms *Seventeen*'s lack of interest in representing female youth as socially and culturally productive. For example, despite the magazine's earlier focus on girls' education in preparation for careers, contemporary *Seventeen* allots very little space to career planning. The magazine has a semi-regular column entitled "College" which features information such as how to apply for scholarships. However, the jobs depicted in the pages of *Seventeen* demonstrate few opportunities for girls beyond traditionally feminine spheres and practices. The April 1991 issue, for example, features a story about fashion school (a good alternative for those girls not attractive enough to be fashion models), noting that innovative design ideas "could be the ticket to stardom" ("Students of Style" 173).

Of the few feature articles published recently by *Seventeen* about girls who labor, one was about a "working girl" prostitute and the other was about a high school volunteer (LeBlanc; Lahman). As these activities are directly related to the traditional feminine roles of sexual object and unpaid caretaker, *Seventeen* demonstrates little investment in those jobs that challenge the dominant ideologies of femininity. This limited investment is also noticeable in articles about female entrepreneurs and political activists, girls who are far less represented than those who occupy traditionally feminine roles. For example, *Seventeen*'s February 1995 issue which features DeDe Lahman's article on Emily Greble's volunteerism also contains an article on Melissa Poe who began Kids for a Clean Environment, an environmentalist youth group which coordinates a tree-planting outreach program (Scott). While Greble's story is allotted a full page, however, Poe's is subordinated as a quarter-page news bite and shares a page with readers' mail and other brief snippets about musical condoms and song trivia.

Though *Seventeen* does feature material written by some readers, it provides no connection between such cultural activity and that engaged in by media celebrities, the primary cultural producers to occupy its pages. Indeed, though *Seventeen* has several venues for such reader participation (readers' comments on previous issues as found in "Letters" and essays about personal problems), only the column "Voices" publishes readers' creative work and provides a place for their views on issues of concern to themselves and other girls. In turn, "Voices" opens a space for constructive debate of topical social or political issues like environmentalism. Unfortunately, other than the requests for reader responses that appear in problem/advice columns like "Relating," there is no encouragement for readers to participate in the production of *Seventeen* through the submission of their own work (including essays for "Voices").

Unlike *Seventeen*'s editorial staff which has traditionally relied on discourses of consumerism for the representation of female adolescence, the publishers and editors of the original *Sassy* magazine were determined to create a publication for intelligent, discerning readers which broke free of the boy-crazy, mall-rat clichés of girlhood typically found in other mainstream teen magazines. Introduced in February 1988 and modeled after the Australian girl magazine *Dolly*, *Sassy* ushered in a new era in U.S. teen magazine publication by injecting itself with an irreverent sense of humor, controversial topics, and a personal writing style that echoed the jargon of adolescents. Though fashion and beauty, the mainstays of mass-produced teen magazines, were not disregarded in *Sassy*, these areas were considerably subordinated by the original editorial staff to feature articles and regular columns dealing with teen problems such as sexuality, suicide, eating disorders, and AIDS.

By embracing a feminist ideology of empowerment which encouraged girls to think critically, the original *Sassy* boldly highlighted acts of cultural production on the part of its readers through reader-produced columns such as "It Happened to Me" and "Stuff You Wrote," as well as by foregrounding alternative, "Do It Yourself" (DIY) forms of cultural production such as those practiced among members of the feminist youth culture, riot grrrl. (Indeed, *Sassy* has been credited with spreading the riot grrrl message beyond its small group of original members. As Joanne Gottlieb and Gayle Wald argue, "*Sassy* has . . . attempted to popularize Riot Grrrl, without ridiculing or demeaning its significance. The magazine has featured band/celebrity interviews, record reviews and a monthly feature of zine addresses . . ." [265].)[8] Perhaps *Sassy*'s largest step towards recognizing and encouraging female youth as active producers of culture was its annual "Reader Produced Issue" (introduced in 1990) that allowed girls to take over creative control from editors and participate in different aspects of magazine production including photography, writing, and layout. A step beyond the annual feminist "Take Our Daughters to Work" campaign, the adults at *Sassy* actually handed over the means of cultural production to female adolescents.

Unfortunately, *Sassy* and its readers have had to pay for such bold acts of girl empowerment. For example, shortly after a boycott of the magazine was initiated in 1989 by the Moral Majority and several advertisers reneged on their contracts, *Sassy*'s second publisher, Matilda Publications, sold the magazine to Lang Communications ("Trying to Silence *Sassy*"). In addition, *Sassy*'s publisher, Helen Barr, resigned apparently because she felt *Sassy* had developed an aggressive editorial approach and penchant for controversial subjects (Rothenberg). In 1994, after consistently losing money, *Sassy* was sold once again, this time to the Petersen Publishing Company (which also publishes the teen magazines *'Teen* and *All About You*). With the magazine's popular editor, Jane Pratt, and her staff gone, Petersen redefined *Sassy*'s image and mission, eliminating its irreverent, feminist ideology in the hopes of better competing with the other "Big Four" teen magazines: *Seventeen*, *YM*, and *'Teen*.[9] As *Sassy*'s executive publisher, Jay Cole, noted after Petersen's acquisition:

> In the last year or so, *Sassy* became more of a fringe publication rather than a cutting-edge magazine. It missed a large part of the teen market and concentrated on a small number of teens that don't relate to the mainstream. In the last couple of years there was a darker side to *Sassy*, and I think they alienated part of their market. (qtd. in Carmody)

Unlike the original *Sassy* staff members who had downplayed the traditional discourses of teen magazines to focus on the more controversial concerns of female adolescents, Cole insisted that the new publication would be "forward in fashion, beauty and entertainment" (qtd. in Carmody).

In less than a year, the original *Sassy*'s subordination of fashion/beauty to feature articles and columns was fully reversed, and the conventional discourses of consumerism and leisure began to dominate its pages, an emphasis that was hammered home by the vast number of pages allotted to the advertisement of beauty and fashion products. In spite of *Sassy*'s interim editors' promise to create a "Your Page" to showcase readers' creative work, the magazine actually *reduced* the opportunities for girls to participate in the production of its text by eliminating regular columns such as "Stuff You Wrote" and "It Happened to Me," as well as the popular "Reader Produced Issue." In addition, "Read On," a column started by the original *Sassy* staff which featured literature of interest to female youth and "revelations from real girls" (e.g., Hillary Carlip's *Girl Power: Young Women Speak Out* and Barbara Findlen's anthology of girls' essays, *Listen Up: Voices from the Next Feminist Generation*), was eliminated as a regular column.

Interestingly, though columns such as "*Sassy* Wired" (about new computer/interactive technologies) that encouraged girls to participate actively in cultural production were introduced when Petersen acquired the magazine, such columns were eliminated when a new editorial staff took over in December 1995. In turn, in spite of the addition in April 1996 of a new column entitled "She's Way Sassy" that featured young female artists, activists, and (increasingly) business entrepreneurs, the magazine rarely published articles on career planning and training which might have encouraged girls to become active cultural producers. (Like its major competitor, *Seventeen*, Petersen's *Sassy* typically featured media celebrities as the primary type of female cultural producer.) And while the original *Sassy* devoted entire issues to college (as in the November 1994 issue), the new *Sassy* allotted considerably less space to girls' education. For example, although Petersen's original goal was to make the new *Sassy* appeal to older (15- to 24-year-old) readers and the regular column "Campus Scene" originally addressed college concerns such as dormitory life, loan debt, and internships, by the December 1995 issue, *Sassy* had begun to feature articles about life on "campuses" such as Beverly Hills High.

The radical transformation of *Sassy* magazine since 1995 did not happen without resistance from some of its original readers. After receiving many complaint letters in the first year of Petersen's publication, *Sassy*'s new editors finally published some of the readers' "hate mail" in their January 1996 issue. (A slew of readers' letters of praise and encouragement were published earlier in the September 1995 issue.) Readers' criticisms of the new *Sassy* ranged from "lameass," "boring," and "repetitive" to "*Sassy* should be renamed *YMII* or *Seventeen, The Sequel*," "Some of your articles make me want to yak," and "Did *YM* have you buy out *Sassy*, or are you merely doing the work of Satan?" ("Pushing the Envelope"). In addition, many of the letters begged for Jane Pratt to be reinstated as editor. In response, the new editorial staff called the critical readers "writers of . . . paeans to pissiness" and suggested that they "Get Over It! Get a Clue! Get a Life!" Arguing that the new "*Sassy* caters to eclectic tastes, not some exclusive girls club for the terminally hip," Petersen's editorial staff distanced themselves from those with complaints by relying

on the discourses traditionally associated with female adolescence: "[W]e
relate to . . . readers whose minds are not just bright, but open; who have
a sense of humor as well as a sense of style and who aren't too cool to
have fun" ("Pushing the Envelope"). Interestingly, the letter was un-
signed, as were all the editorials published by Petersen's *Sassy*.

Though the original *Sassy* seemed to affirm McRobbie's findings that
the editors and journalists working on contemporary teen magazines
"have asserted their commitment to gender-equality and to creating a
more confident femininity" ("*Jackie* and *Just Seventeen*" 186) and "attempt to integrate at least aspects of . . . political or feminist discourses
into their work ("More!" 183), the transformations occurring on the
editorial board and within the pages of Petersen's new *Sassy* attest to the
mainstream media's continued uneasiness with any troubling of traditional gender roles and modes of representation. Indeed, in the fall of
1996, Petersen abruptly stopped publication of *Sassy*, and now incorporates portions of it as "Sassy Slant" in the more popular, and less threatening, magazine *'Teen*. Recuperating *Sassy* from the hands of feminists
(both editors' and readers'), and thus containing its power of encouraging
girls to expand themselves beyond traditional modes of female adolescence, Petersen's plan to be "forward in fashion, beauty and entertainment" has led many girls to look elsewhere for media which more directly
engage their specific concerns, needs, and pleasures.

Representing Her Self: Girls as Cultural Producers

Any discussion of the representation of female adolescents in mainstream
culture should lead to questions about how girls interpret and negotiate
such constructions and, considering the increasing accessibility and
cheapness of media technologies today (especially photocopiers and computers), how girls represent *themselves* through culture. In an attempt to
theorize the various forms self-representation might take for adolescent
girls, psychologist Lyn Mikel Brown ponders the following questions:

> What would it mean for a girl—against the stories read, chanted, or
> murmured to her—to choose to tell the truth of her life aloud to another
> person at the very point when she is invited into the larger cultural story
> of womanhood . . . ? To whom would a girl speak and in what context? . . .
> [W]hat does she risk in the telling? (72)

As Brown suggests, for girls to speak about such things would mean their refusal to accept "the established story of a woman's life" (72). In light of the many texts produced by girls today which appropriate images, words, and discursive strategies from mainstream material such as teen girl magazines, I would argue that there is much evidence that female youth are also refusing the established stories of a *girl's* life. The increasing numbers of culturally productive female youth in our society indicate that more and more girls are successfully resisting the dominant ideologies of gendered and generational subjectivity by telling their *own* stories of female adolescence. The work of these girls, diverse as it may be, requires scholars of youth culture to re-examine the ways in which we discuss and represent female adolescents and their specific cultural experiences.

As youth are often barred from mainstream spheres of cultural production, it is important to note that much of this creative work is happening outside the typical channels via a DIY ethos apparent in the formation of independent recording studios and publication houses, as well as in the cyber spaces of the Internet and the World Wide Web. At the same time, however, it is important to note that much of this (sub)cultural activity on the part of today's youth is not entirely independent from the mainstream media and popular culture upon which it must rely not only for publicity and promotion, but also for source material, as George Lipsitz notes:

> Revolutionary politics and oppositional art have traditionally been rooted in a transcendent critique whereby activists and artists attempt to stand outside their society in order to change it.... Today's youth culture proceeds from a different premise. Instead of standing outside society, it tries to work through it, exploiting and exacerbating its contradictions to create unpredictable possibilities for the future. (25)

As the riot grrrl zine *Bikini Kill* #2 argues, today's female youth "must take over the means of production in order to create our own meanings." In recognizing that what is represented in the mass media has little to do with their lives and experiences, many female adolescents employ the practices of *detournement* (appropriating and reconfiguring mass-produced cultural artifacts into personalized and politicized creations) in the subversion and resistance of privileged notions of gender, generation, race, class, and sexuality. Such acts of cultural resistance are perhaps best demonstrated through an analysis of girls' zines, not-for-profit publications independently produced by female youth in the attempt to express alternative visions of female adolescence.[10]

Though contemporary zines are often traced back only as far as the punk fanzines of the late 1970s which were created in opposition to the mainstream music press, these self-produced publications have a history in a variety of underground, subcultural groups such as the popular science fiction press of the late 1930s and the beat poets of the 1950s.[11] Zine creators, empowered by the DIY ethos (which, according to Greil Marcus, has roots not in punk, but in the French leftist intellectuals of the 1950s and 1960s), often rely on illicit means of producing their zines (for example, scamming free copying services or postage) and typically violate copyright laws by refusing to adhere to standards of intellectual/artistic property and ownership. Since many zines are created on-the-job using office equipment and supplies, they are one of the cheapest means of producing independent forms of cultural expression. In order to avoid criminal prosecution and censorship, many zine producers do not reveal their real identity, use post office boxes instead of home addresses, switch the titles of their zines, and accept only cash, stamps, or traded zines as payment. In addition to appropriating the means of production from mainstream sources, independent zine producers employ "cut up" collage techniques to innovatively critique, ridicule, and oppose messages and images disseminated by the mass media. "When people mock and ask me why I love fanzines so much," one zine producer argues, "I just laugh knowingly and say, 'Have you considered the alternatives?' " (qtd. in Vale 4).

Viable substitutes for mainstream teen magazines such as *Seventeen*, independently produced girl zines not only establish a place where female youth can publicly express their most personal and political concerns, but also function as networking tools among female adolescents who otherwise may feel isolated in their homes, schools, or jobs. The circulation of zines, for example, has been instrumental in disseminating riot grrrl's "Revolution Girl-Style Now!" message to female adolescents interested in empowering themselves and others. (Though contemporary girl zines are often associated with riot grrrls, many zines produced by female adolescents are connected to other alternative youth cultures such as those formed by punks, gays, and skateboarders.)[12] Often criticized for being the creations of self-absorbed individualists (J. Peder Zane of the *New York Times* describes zines as "fueled by the same sloppy solipsism that is transforming America into a land of self-obsessed jabber-jaws" [4]), zines become a public forum not just for the girls who produce them, but for their readers and other zine makers whose letters, comments, essays, and cartoons they willingly (re)print.[13]

Since girl zines are often created to either resist or oppose representations of gender, sexuality, class, race, and age found in mainstream culture, many zine producers openly ridicule the dominant ideologies of female adolescence reproduced in mainstream girl magazines. For example, *Fat Girl*, a zine published by the Fat Girl Collective out of San Francisco, admonishes Petersen's new *Sassy* for reproducing a fat-phobic ideology of female beauty.[14] In an article entitled "*Sassy* Sells Out," one of *Fat Girl*'s contributors writes:

> Remember how in *FG* #2, we sing the praises of a glossy teen-mag that makes good with their "10 reasons not to diet list" and a binder that said "If they call you a fat pig, say thanks"? Well, you can forget all that. They sold ownership, and it shows. Their April [1995] issue features such heartwarming material as "The truth about fat" (Uh, right, and take one guess as to what that is), and a precious photo of a repulsed girl cowering near her salad at the sight of another girl (literally donning pig ears and a snout!) devouring a hamburger & fries. Junior *Cosmo*.[15]

Other zine makers use a different approach in their critique of mainstream representations of femininity. For example, rather than using words to disparage popular female fashion accessories, the creators of *Ms. America* #2 merely reprint a pictorial advertisement for five-inch heeled shoes and boots, thus appropriating the ad's images in their own critique and subversion. This approach is also used by the producer of *Groove Kitchen* whose eighth issue includes columns such as "Ripped Off" and "The Groove Box" which contain snippets of articles and graphs cut out of mass-produced magazines. Juxtaposing subjects such as sperm counts, statistics on refugees, and the results of a survey on the impact of feminism, "Ripped Off" provocatively calls into question the type and relevancy of "information" relayed to girls in mainstream magazines.

In addition to critiquing teen magazines' reproduction of traditional modes of female adolescence, girl zines often focus on taboo subjects such as domestic rape, adolescent homosexuality, and witchcraft and disseminate information on topics such as self-defense, masturbation, and contraception that is not made available in most mainstream publications mass-produced for teen girls. For example, an issue of *Thorn* reprints a reader's letter which imparts helpful hints on feminine sexual hygiene: "Remember to wipe from front to back—to keep any bacteria away from vagina & stay away from petroleum jelly—during intercourse—hard to wash away & bacteria likes to hang out in it—Avoid douching—it messes up our pH balance if uses [*sic*] too often." Another zine, *Girl Luv #1*, shares the following information on the global aspects of female adolescent labor: "Factories in third world countries are run by teenage girls who work 18 hour days—they are forced to work overtime, are sexually harassed, and constantly threatened—all to bring us Americans delightful GAP, JC Penney, and Eddie Bauer apparel. For every $20 shirt, they get 12 cents."

In turn, most girl zines contain quotations from well-known feminist activists and provide lists of texts considered important for the development of girls' critical consciousness, information noticeably absent from the "Big Four" teen magazines. For example, *Ms. America #2* publishes quotations from Angela Davis (on rape by U.S. soldiers in Vietnam) and a list of "Riot Grrrandmas" that includes Harriet Tubman and Anne Sexton. Similarly, *Housewife Turned Assassin #3* contains a list of "music that keeps us from going nutty," as well as the column "Books We Dig" with the explanation: "all these books touched us in so many ways; helped us see things in a new light & taught us to appreciate different people's circumstances. Hope they do the same for you."

While independent zine producers often pride themselves on their ability to create zines that bear no resemblance to mainstream publications (that is, no page numbers, no tables of contents, no glossy color photo spreads, no paid advertisements), many girl zine makers include typical teen magazine features in their zines such as letters to the editor, quizzes, and product reviews while, at the same time, employing the discursive and representational styles of such magazines to mockingly disparage those texts and the ideologies privileged in them. For example, girl zines often debunk the ideology of feminine imperfection and ridicule the patronizing morality apparent in teen magazines by creating parodic "problem pages" where outlandish situations of teen angst are handled by humorously named "agony aunts" who respond to readers' requests for advice. *Canadian Penny*'s advice giver, for instance, is a high school male called "Thrasher" who repeatedly directs readers' bizarre beauty questions ("how to keep lipstick on for longer than five minutes") to lead singer of The Cure, Robert Smith, who uses large amounts of eye makeup and lipstick as part of his androgynous stage persona. In another stab at the inane subject matter of teen magazines' problem pages, "Oola" from *Girlie Jones* offers this advice to an older girl who wants to participate in Halloween activities: "First, ask yourself this: 'Am I under 5 feet tall?' . . . If you cannot pass for twelve or under, try renting a neighbor child and strike up a deal with them to split the loot." Other girl zines, following the lead of mainstream magazines, publish real letters from their readers, yet offer blunt advice meant to build girls' self-confidence and embolden them to act assertively. For example, "Dr. Love" of *Groove Kitchen* writes to one reader: "By kissing another guy when you really wanted your ex, YOU DONE FUCKED UP. Sorry, but it looks like your ex has a good reason to not take you back, I wouldn't. Stop playing games girlfriend."

The Spring 1994 issue of *Ben is Dead* is an exemplar of girl zines' *detournement* of the codes and discourses of female adolescence reproduced by mainstream teen magazines.[16] After failing to win *Sassy*'s "Reader Produced Issue" contest, the editor of *Ben is Dead* decided to put out a "Very Essential Super Extra-Special *Sassy* Issue" that would critique and ridicule all mass-produced teen magazines. Using *Sassy*'s specific layout and writing style, *Ben is Dead*'s parody begins with the front cover. Featuring a large full-color photograph of Chelsea Clinton (as "the Sassiest Chick in the U.S.A."), the cover boldly asserts that it will *not* feature Evan Dando, Juliana Hatfield, and Kim Gordon, media celebrities who are typically spotlighted by teen magazines. In addition, *Ben is Dead*'s cover asserts that this issue does not feature information "on how you too can be alternative, cute, happy, healthy . . . and, of course, unique in the '90s."

Reworking traditional *Sassy* features such as "Read On," "It Happened to Me," and "What Now," the special "*Sassy*" issue of *Ben is Dead* lampoons teen magazines' attempts to connect with and speak for real girls. Like many other girl zines, it contains a send-up of *Sassy*'s "letters to the editor" page, "Hello! Anybody Home?", which contains letters from readers as well as a few tongue-in-cheek responses from the editors, Darby and Kerin: "We're gonna DIY your face if we get another letter like this from you—and that is a threat. We're Sassy, huh? HUH!" While *Sassy*'s "It Happened to Me" regularly features the depressing realities of adolescent life, *Ben is Dead*'s version is subtitled "The Night I Ran Out of Lipstick on the Ventura Freeway . . . !" (Niccoli). Other parodies of typical *Sassy* fare include articles on beauty like "I, Brow: Celebrating the Pluck" (Jones), as well as features such as "It Had to Happen . . . Grunge Prostitutes" (Jordan) and "Are You Still on Drugs and Don't Even Know It?" (a parody of a typical teen magazine quiz) (Iannone).

While it is clear that the creators of *Ben is Dead* find *Sassy* to be better than the "whorably insipid, complacent teen magazines like *Mademoiselle, Teen, Seventeen,* and *Young Miss* [*YM*]" (Darby "What Does 'Sassy' Mean to You?" 12), their parody of *Sassy* provides readers with more distance (and considerably more ammunition) to critically assess the dominant discourses and strategies of mass-produced teen magazines, a point which is hammered home in Amanda Burr's contribution to the issue, "Competition? What Competition?" As Burr notes in the introduction to her critique of other teen magazines:

> After *Sassy* was launched with the mission of ignoring the traditional formula for women's magazines, the other magazines looked so outdated that they had to make some superficial changes. Like, they tried to be more on top of entertainment and loosen up their tone. But they read like cheap knock-offs and have no souls. *Sassy*'s purpose really is to inspire girls to be opinionated and informed and rebellious and funny, while other magazines don't have a clue. They just want to sell sell sell. (41)

Clearly inspired by both *Sassy*'s rebellious spirit ("it all started with a simple admiration for the thing") and the DIY ethos of the underground press, *Ben is Dead*'s main editor, Darby, like many other girl zine producers, encourages her readers to move beyond the mainstream magazines that Burr dismisses in her article. Thus, in addition to parodying the discursive and representational strategies found in magazines such as *Seventeen* and *YM*, *Ben is Dead*'s special "*Sassy*" issue provides readers with an extensive list of girl zines (Darby "Zines"), as well as an article on how to create electronic zines (Swenson). As Darby notes in the introduction to her list of girl zines:

> What [the media] continually lack the insight to mention is the number of zines that are produced by women and how women's participation in the zine world has contributed immensely to the rise of the format. Women continue to bring diversity, creativity, emotion, and energy to zines. They are fresh and deep and inspiring (can you handle that?). They have helped move zines out of the music-only format to encompass a greater variety of topics and issues.... Girl zinesters are truly showing their force ("Zines" 43).

The intelligent, critical, and humorous tone of *Ben is Dead* and other numerous girl zines that have emerged out of the punk, queercore, and riot grrrl movements of the late 1980s and early 1990s supports Vale's assertion that "the zine movement has arisen everywhere like hydra of discontent. . . . This is a movement without leaders or spokespersons, and there are no rigidifying standards dictating what may or may not be presented" (Vale 5). Unlike the advertiser-driven teen magazines that promote not a variety of subject positions, only a variety of *consumer* positions, girl zines explode the myth of a single form of female adolescent subjectivity (as well as a homogenous girls' culture) by creating *a* story, rather than *the* story, of a girl's life.

Those Who Can Do, and Those Who Can't . . . ?

With the expansion of personal computers and on-line technology into most offices and many homes during the early 1990s came new ways for female adolescents to express themselves and reach a wide audience. One of the newest forms of girls' independent cultural production is the electronic zine ("e-zine") published via the Internet and the World Wide Web. *Geek Girl*, *Nrrrd Grrrl*, and *Girls Can Do Anything* are just some of the Web e-zines created by female youth.

In spite of the "whiz bang" appeal of new electronic media, as many paper zine makers have argued, there are considerable problems associated with e-zines. Not only is paper more readily accessible and portable than a modem or computer, but, as Stephen Schwartz notes, "[Paper zines] don't crash, and nobody can pull the plug on them" (159). In other words, there are far more opportunities for e-zines and their creators to be monitored and censored by unwanted parties. In comparison, paper zine makers have much greater control over the distribution of their products and the types of individuals reading them. In addition, compared to the multiple issues of most paper zines, e-zines are often created as one-time ventures, the expenditure of large amounts of time limiting future editions. Thus, though Vale notes that "arguably every person's web site is a zine," many e-zines appear to be little more than a personal home page ("From the Editor" 5).

More significantly, however, not everyone has access to or can afford the training, software, and equipment (personal computer, modem, scanner) required to produce an e-zine. Vale makes this point clear in her introduction to *Zines!* "The Internet has been hailed as the communications innovation of the glorious future. . . . While . . . there are plenty of optimistic projections about how e-zines will replace paper zines, never-theless, access to computers and scanners is still for the privileged few, and part of the appeal of a zine is its power to grant a voice to the most underprivileged in society, including citizens of high school age who have few resources." ("From the Editor" 5)

Certainly there is little argument that the decreasing expense of per-sonal computers, video cameras, and photocopiers—along with changes in social relations and education initiated by the feminist and other civil rights movements—have provided girls with more opportunities to give voice to their subjective and personal experiences. Yet, Vale's and Schwartz's criticisms of the new electronic media's potential for cultural resistance and rebellion offer provocative analyses of the class politics involved in recent forms of cultural activity. It is important, therefore, for us to problematize which girls are given access to and training in the means of cultural production (that is, which girls are allowed to partici-pate in the "politics of representation") and which girls have little oppor-tunity to resist or challenge the representations made of them by the media. For every girl zine maker who feels empowered to come to voice and articulate her personal experiences on the pages of a zine, there are hundreds of girls who feel incapable of finding any positive meaning in their lives and are unable to speak, much less write, about their particular position as female adolescents. For every girl zine maker who finds a safe, secure, nurturing, and creative place with other like-minded girls who trade and share their zines, there are hundreds of female youth who feel unsupported and community-less. For every girl zine maker who boldly expresses her own particular view of female adolescence through the clever *detournement* of the discourses and images created for her in mainstream teen magazines, there are hundreds of girls whom the mass media degrades through stereotypical representations like the African-American "welfare queen" or the "gang-banging home girl."

It is important to remember, therefore, that many girls' opportunities for self-authorization (which might counter such offensive stereotypes) are limited not just by their gender and generational position, but also by their class, race, ethnicity, and sexuality. Though there are some signs that working-class, non-white, and homosexual adolescents are gaining more access to the means of cultural production and, thus, more agency in representing themselves, their numbers do not compare with those of white, middle-class youth who have considerably more time, money, education, and support to pursue such activities. Thus, while the increasing amount of cultural production on the part of female adolescents is surely one of the distinguishing characteristics of contemporary girls' culture, and though we, as cultural scholars, might celebrate this phenomenon as indicative of social progress, we must be ever mindful of what and for whom we speak. For, as I demonstrated in relation to earlier analyses of girls' "bedroom culture," our representation of female youth significantly inflects the popular understanding of female adolescence. We, too, contribute to the established story of a girl's life.

NOTES

1. Frith's analysis of girls' "bedroom culture" first appeared in his 1978 *The Sociology of Rock*, an academic study reformulated for a more general audience in 1981 as *Sound Effects: Youth, Leisure, and the Politics of Rock 'n' Roll*. Though other scholars such as Angela McRobbie and Jenny Garber were researching girls' culture at the same time (see "Girls and Subcultures"), Frith was the first scholar whose analysis of girls' cultural practices as distinct from boys' was disseminated to a mass (not solely academic) audience. In contrast, McRobbie's work, though overwhelmingly significant, was published in smaller quantities by academic presses, and the collection of her writings, *Feminism and Female Youth Culture*, was not published until 1991.

2. See Stuart Hall, "New Ethnicities."

3. See Theodor Adorno and Max Horkheimer's *Dialectic of Enlightenment*.

4. Gramsci's *Selections form the Prison Notebooks* was extremely influential for cultural scholars working during this period.

5. For example, see Betty Friedan's *The Feminist Mystique*.

6. The most notable exception to this early conflation of girl culture and consumption is McRobbie's essay, "Second-Hand Dresses and the Role of the Ragmarket."

7. See Iris Young's "Throwing Like a Girl."

8. In comparison to *Sassy*'s support of riot grrrl, *Seventeen* has published only one article on this community. Not surprisingly, this article appeared two years after the emergence of riot and focused on its (allegedly) imminent death (Malkin 81).

9. In addition to *Sassy*, the "Big Four" teen magazines include *Seventeen* (which premiered in 1944 and has the largest circulation of all U.S. girl magazines), *YM: Young and Modern* (introduced in 1940 and formerly titled *Calling All Girls*, *Polly Pigtails*, and, most recently, *Young Miss*), and *'Teen* (introduced in 1957).

10. It is important to differentiate between the various texts published for

teenage girls: *mass-produced, mainstream teen magazines* such as *Sassy, Seventeen, YM,* and *'Teen* which cater to corporate advertisers; *mass-produced "alternative" niche magazines* like *Wig* and *Foxy,* which appeal to specific non-mainstream markets such as skateboarders yet still cater to corporate advertisers; and *independently produced girl zines,* which contain no paid advertising—though often willingly promote other independent products—and rarely have a consistent subscriber readership. Although it is often difficult to discern the age of zine makers, many girl zines are not produced by female adolescents per se, but by young women who have appropriated the term "girl" as a marker of their youthful rebelliousness.

11. See Frederic Wertham's *The World of Fanzines* and Stephen Schwartz's "History of Zines."

12. See Mark Fenster's "Queer Punk Fanzines," which relates girl zines to the riot grrrl and queercore movements.

13. *Seventeen*'s only article on zines focuses on the power of these texts to make a girl "cool" rather than on their ability to empower self-expression and bonds with others (Kennedy).

14. Though *Fat Girl* is produced by adult women who put "Not Sold to Minors" on their zine covers (to discourage the accusation of kiddy porn), I include it as a girl zine because: the members of this collective identify strongly with the label "girl"; *Fat Girl* often critiques mainstream cultural texts directed towards female youth; and it is read by many female adolescents.

15. The actual title of the first article mentioned is "Thirteen Reasons Not to Diet" (Ingall). In addition, the picture *Fat Girl* describes appeared in *Sassy*'s May 1995 issue (Lewellen). Interestingly, the title of the second article has been modified to suit *Fat Girl*'s purpose here; the real title of the article is "The Lowdown on Low-Fat Snacks" (Lark).

16. Although *Ben is Dead* is easily categorized as a niche magazine (rather than a girl zine) because of its support by alternative companies (especially independent record labels) and readers involved in alternative scenes, I include it here because its Spring 1994 issue significantly connects with other girl zines, primarily in its rhetorical and representational style, but also in its critique of mainstream teen magazines and its support of other independent girl-produced texts.

WORKS CITED

Adorno, Theodor, and Max Horkheimer. *Dialectic of Enlightenment.* Trans. John
    Cumming. New York: Continuum, 1993.
Bikini Kill [zine].
Brown, Lyn Mikel. "Telling a Girl's Life: Self-Authorization as a Form of Resis-

tance." *Women, Girls, and Psychotherapy: Reframing Resistance.* Ed. Carol Gilligan, Annie G. Rogers, and Deborah L. Tolman. New York: Harrington Park, 1991. 71–86.

Burr, Amanda. "Competition? What Competition?" *Ben is Dead* 23 (Spring 1994): 41.

Canadian Penny [zine].

Carlip, Hillary. *Girl Power: Young Women Speak Out.* New York: Warner, 1995.

Carmody, Deirdre. "Petersen Will Restart *Sassy* with Push for Older Readers." *New York Times* 8 Dec. 1994: D19.

Carter, Erica. "Alice in the Consumer Wonderland: West German Case Studies in Gender and Consumer Culture." *Gender and Generation.* Ed. Angela McRobbie and Mica Nava. London: Macmillan, 1984. 185–214.

Darby. "What Does 'Sassy' Mean to You?" *Ben is Dead* 23 (Spring 1994): 12.

———. "Zines: Girl Powered!" *Ben is Dead* 23 (Spring 1994): 43–44.

Darby, and Kerin. "Hello! Anybody Home?" *Ben is Dead* 23 (Spring 1994): 8.

Fat Girl [zine].

Fenster, Mark. "Queer Punk Fanzines: Identity, Community, and the Articulation of Homosexuality and Hardcore." *Journal of Communication Inquiry* 17.1 (1993): 73–94.

Findlen, Barbara, ed. *Listen Up: Voices from the Next Feminist Generation.* Seattle: Seal P, 1995.

Frazer, Elizabeth. "Teenage Girls Reading *Jackie.*" *Media, Culture and Society* 9 (1987): 407–25.

Friedan, Betty. *The Feminist Mystique.* New York: Norton, 1963.

Frith, Simon. *The Sociology of Rock.* London: Constable, 1978.

———. *Sound Effects: Youth, Leisure, and the Politics of Rock 'n' Roll.* New York: Pantheon, 1981.

Frith, Simon, and Angela McRobbie. "Rock and Sexuality." *Screen Education* 29 (1978–79): 3–19.

Geek Girl [e-zine].

Girlie Jones [zine].

Girl Luv [zine].

Girls Can Do Anything [e-zine].

Gottlieb, Joanne, and Gayle Wald. "Smells Like Teen Spirit: Riot Grrrls, Revolution and Women in Independent Rock." *Microphone Fiends: Youth, Music, and Youth Culture.* Ed. Andrew Ross and Tricia Rose. New York: Routledge, 1994. 250–74.

Gramsci, Antonio. *Selections from the Prison Notebooks.* Ed. Quintin Hoare and Geoffrey Nowell Smith. London: Lawrence and Wishart, 1971.

Groove Kitchen [zine].

Hall, Stuart. "New Ethnicities." *Stuart Hall: Critical Dialogues in Cultural Studies.* Ed. David Morley and Kuan-Hsing Chen. London: Routledge, 1996. 441–49.

Housewife Turned Assassin [zine].

Iannone, Paul. "Are You Still on Drugs and Don't Even Know It?" *Ben is Dead* 23 (Spring 1994): 28–29.

Ingall, Margie. "Thirteen Reasons Not to Diet." *Sassy* Aug. 1994: 78–79.

Jones, Jessy. "I, Brow: Celebrating the Pluck." *Ben is Dead* 23 (Spring 1994): 23.

Jordan, Amiee. "It Had to Happen . . . Grunge Prostitutes." *Ben is Dead* 23 (Spring 1994): 89–90.

Kennedy, Pagan. "Behind the Zines." *Seventeen* Mar. 1995: 142+.

Lahman, DeDe. "Making It Happen." *Seventeen* Feb. 1995: 62.

Lark, Edie. "The Lowdown on Low-Fat Snacks." *Sassy* Apr. 1995: 12.

LeBlanc, Adrian Nicole. "I'm a Shadow." *Seventeen* Mar. 1993: 212–18.

Lewellen, Judie. "Eating Out: The Big, Fat Truth." *Sassy* May 1995: 14.

Lipsitz, George. "We Know What Time It Is: Race, Class and Youth Culture in the Nineties." *Microphone Fiends: Youth Music and Youth Culture.* Ed. Andrew Ross and Tricia Rose. New York: Routledge, 1994. 17–28.

Malkin, Nina. "It's a Grrrl Thing." *Seventeen* May 1993: 80–82.

Marcus, Greil. *Lipstick Traces: A Secret History of the Twentieth Century.* Cambridge: Harvard UP, 1989.

McRobbie, Angela. "*Jackie*: An Ideology of Adolescent Femininity." Birmingham: CCCS Stenciled Paper, 1978.

———. "*Jackie* and *Just Seventeen*: Girls' Comics and Magazines in the 1980s." *Feminism and Female Youth Culture.* Boston: Unwin Hyman, 1991. 135–88.

———. "*Jackie* Magazine: Romantic Individualism and the Teenage Girl." *Feminism and Female Youth Culture.* Boston: Unwin Hyman, 1991. 81–134.

———. "Just Like a *Jackie* Story." *Feminism for Girls: An Adventure Story.* Ed. Angela McRobbie and Trisha McCabe. London: Routledge and Kegan Paul, 1981. 113–28.

———. "*More!*: New Sexualities in Girls' and Women's Magazines." *Cultural Studies and Communications.* Ed. James Curran, David Morley, and Valerie Walkerdine. London: Arnold, 1996. 172–94.

———. "New Times in Cultural Studies." *Postmodernism and Popular Culture.* London: Routledge, 1994. 24–43.

———. "Second-Hand Dresses and the Role of the Ragmarket." *Zoot Suits and Second-Hand Dresses: An Anthology of Fashion and Music.* Ed. Angela McRobbie. Boston: Unwin Hyman, 1988. 23–49.

McRobbie, Angela, and Jenny Garber. "Girls and Subcultures." *Resistance through Rituals: Youth Subcultures in Post-War Britain.* Ed. Stuart Hall and Tony Jefferson. London: HarperCollins, 1976. 208–22.

Ms. America [zine].

Niccoli, Casey. "The Night I Ran Out of Lipstick on the Ventura Freeway . . . !" *Ben is Dead* 23 (Spring 1994): 51.

Nrrrd Grrrl [e-zine].

Peirce, Kate. "A Feminist Theoretical Perspective on the Socialization of Teenage
Girls through *Seventeen* Magazine." *Sex Roles* 23.9–10 (1990): 491–500.
———. "Socialization of Teenage Girls through Teen-Magazine Fiction: The
Making of a New Woman or an Old Lady?" *Sex Roles* 29.1–2 (1993): 59–68.
"Pushing the Envelope." *Sassy* Jan. 1996: 7.
Rothenberg, Randall. "Resignation and Boycott at *Sassy*." *New York Times* 3 Nov.
1988: 45.
Schwartz, Stephen. "History of Zines." *Zines!* Ed. V. Vale. Vol. I. San Francisco:
V/Search, 1996. 155–59.
Scott, Cintra. "Poe vs. Pollution." *Seventeen* Feb. 1995: 50.
"Students of Style." *Seventeen* Apr. 1991: 172–75.
Swenson, Eric. "DIY Hypermedia Publishing: A Primer." *Ben is Dead* 23 (Spring
1994): 103–6.
Thorn [zine].
"Trying to Silence *Sassy*." *Time* 9 Sept. 1988: 45.
Vale, V. "From the Editor." *Zines!* Ed. V. Vale. Vol. I. San Francisco: V/Search,
1996. 4–5.
Walkerdine, Valerie. "Some Day My Prince Will Come: Young Girls and the
Preparation for Adolescent Sexuality." *Gender and Generation*. Ed. Angela
McRobbie and Mica Nava. London: Macmillan, 1984. 162–84.
Wertham, Frederic. *The World of Fanzines: A Special Form of Communication*.
Carbondale: Southern Illinois UP, 1973.
Willis, Paul. *Learning to Labour: How Working Class Kids Get Working Class Jobs*.
London: Saxon House, 1977.
Winship, Janice. " 'A Girl Needs to Get Street-Wise': Magazines for the 1980s."
Feminist Review 21 (1985): 25–46.
Young, Iris. "Throwing Like a Girl: A Phenomenology of Feminine Body Com-
portment, Motility, and Spatiality." *Throwing Like a Girl and Other Essays on
Feminist Philosophy and Social Theory*. Bloomington: Indiana UP, 1990. 141–59.
Zane, J. Peder. "Now, the Magazines of 'Me.' " *New York Times* 14 May 1995: 4.

Contributors

Melinda L. de Jesús is an Assistant Professor of Asian American Studies at San Francisco State University. She writes on Third World feminist literature and theory, Asian American literature and culture, and feminist theory. Her dissertation is currently under consideration with a number of university presses.

Rachel Devlin is a doctoral candidate in history at Yale University. She works on the cultural history of gender, sexuality, and the family. At present, she is completing her dissertation, " 'Their Father's Daughters': Female Adolescence and the Problem of Sexual Authority in America, 1945–1965."

Miriam Formanek-Brunell is an Associate Professor of History and Director of Women's Studies at the University of Missouri, Kansas City. She is the author of *Made to Play House: Dolls and the Commercialization of American Culture, 1830–1930* (Yale University Press, 1993) and is the editor of *The Story of My Life, An Autobiography by Rose O'Neill* (University of Missouri Press, 1997). Formanek-Brunell is currently researching and writing a book on the history of babysitters in modern America.

Julia D. Gardner received her Ph.D. in English from the University of California, Riverside. Her research interests include Victorian novels and melodrama, sensationalism, and lesbian-feminist studies. She has an article on same-sex desire in Charlotte Brontë's *Shirley* forthcoming in *Victorian Literature and Culture*.

Angela E. Hubler is Assistant Professor of English and Women's Studies at Kansas State University. Her research interests include the literature of girlhood, American literary modernism, and the autobiographies of

radical American women. Her essay on the American writer Josephine
Herbst appears in *Papers on Language and Literature*. She has also
published essays in *The Oxford Companion to Women's Writing in the
United States* and in *Children's Literature*.

Sherrie A. Inness is Assistant Professor of English at Miami University.
Her research interests include nineteenth- and twentieth-century
American literature, children's literature, girls' culture, popular culture,
and gender studies. She has published articles on these topics in a
number of journals, including *American Literary Realism, Journal of
American Culture, Journal of Popular Culture, NWSA Journal*, and
Women's Studies. Inness is also the author of *Intimate Communities:
Representation and Social Transformation in Women's College Fiction,
1895–1910* (Bowling Green, 1995) and *The Lesbian Menace: Ideology,
Identity, and the Representation of Lesbian Life* (University of Massa-
chusetts Press, 1997), as well as the editor of *Nancy Drew and Company:
Culture, Gender, and Girls' Series* (Bowling Green, 1997) and the co-
editor (with Diana Royer) of *Breaking Boundaries: New Perspectives on
Regional Writing* (University of Iowa Press, 1997).

Mary Celeste Kearney is a Ph.D. candidate in the Film, Literature, and
Culture Program of the Division of Critical Studies at the University
of Southern California's School of Cinema-Television. She is writing
her dissertation on the relationship of contemporary female youth cultures, feminist politics, and the popular media. She has published several articles on the riot grrrl movement, the most recent of which,
"The Missing Links: Riot Grrrl—Feminism—Lesbian Culture," appears in *Sexing the Groove*, an anthology on gender and music forthcoming from Routledge Press.

Rhona Justice-Malloy is Assistant Professor of Theatre at Central Michigan
University. She has published articles on women and hysteria, gothic
and post-gothic theatres, and futurist painters. As a member of the European Institute of Theatre Research and the International Federation
for Theatre Research, Dr. Justice-Malloy has delivered several papers in
Greece and Italy. Justice-Malloy is a professional actress who serves as
associate producer, resident director, and Equity guest artist at High-
lands Playhouse, a professional summer theatre in North Carolina.

Mary C. McComb is in the American Studies doctoral program at George
Washington University. Her research interests include nineteenth- and

twentieth-century women's history, popular culture, social history, feminist theory, cultural theory, and gender studies.

Vicki L. Ruiz is Professor of History and Chicana/Chicano studies at Arizona State University where she also serves as Chair of the Department of Chicana/Chicano Studies. Her publications include *From Out of the Shadows: A History of Mexican Women in the United States, 1900–1995* (Oxford, 1997); *Cannery Women, Cannery Lives* (New Mexico, 1987); *Unequal Sisters: A Multicultural Reader in U.S. Women's History* co-edited with Ellen DuBois (Routledge, 1990, second edition 1994); *Western Women, Their Land, Their Lives* co-edited with Lillian Schlissel and Janice Monk (New Mexico, 1988); and *Women on the U.S.-Mexico Border* co-edited with Susan Tiano (Allen and Unwin, 1987). She formerly held an endowed chair at The Claremont Graduate School.

Jennifer Scanlon is an Associate Professor and the Director of Women's Studies at SUNY Plattsburgh. Her research interests include the relationship between gender and consumer culture and feminist pedagogy. She is the author of *Inarticulate Longings: The Ladies' Home Journal, Gender, and the Promises of Consumer Culture* (Routledge, 1995), co-author of *American Women Historians, 1700s–1990s: A Biographical Dictionary* (Greenwood Press, 1996), and editor of *Significant Contemporary American Feminists* (Greenwood Press, forthcoming). She has also written articles for *Radical History Review, Women's Studies International Forum, NWSA Journal, Feminist Teacher,* and other journals.

Kelly Schrum is a doctoral candidate in history at Johns Hopkins University with emphases in twentieth-century United States social and cultural history, consumer culture, youth culture, and gender. She is currently writing her dissertation, "Some Wore Bobby Sox: The Development of Teenage Girls' Culture in the United States, 1930–1960."

Laureen Tedesco is a doctoral candidate in English at Texas A&M University, studying children's literature with Lynne Vallone. Tedesco's scholarship focuses on turn-of-the-century girls' fiction, girls' series fiction, and evangelical children's literature. Her dissertation, currently in progress, is entitled, "The Shape of Girlhood: Girl Scouts, Girl Guides, and Girls' Fiction, 1880–1920."

Index